GEOPOLITICAL DISRUPTION IN SHIPPING

This book examines how the shipping industry is responding to the commercial challenges caused by geopolitical risk.

Geopolitical volatility in the modern world is generating physical and economic obstacles that are disrupting shipping activities and causing disputes that raise fundamental questions of commercial law. Studying this phenomenon by exploring common themes among varied dimensions of business disruption, the book first surveys physical disruption to shipping activities across the categories of war, unrest and piracy. It then turns to the purely economic disruption caused by sanctions and alternative forms of statecraft deployed in' 'trade wars'. The book examines each of these categories by highlighting geopolitical and regulatory context, assessing industry adaptations, and analysing cross-jurisdictional case law to gather insight into the contractual rights and responsibilities impacted by these scenarios.

Assessing solutions – including the development of bespoke contract clauses and the application of broader principles of illegality, impossibility, frustration, and force majeure – the book demonstrates that this rapidly evolving area of international commercial law demands a readiness to borrow analytical approaches across categories of business disruption.

With industry participants, courts, arbitrators and scholars in mind, the book provides a contemporary perspective on the geopolitical challenges affecting shipping through a distinctive commercial law lens.

The Future of Shipping Law: Volume 1

The Future of Shipping Law

Stimulating, forward-looking books on the commercial, technological, humanitarian, societal and environmental challenges of shipping law. This series offers a venue for publishing imaginative books on the theoretical and practical aspects of shipping law, and current and future challenges of the 21st century and beyond. It understands shipping law in its wider context covering all aspects of shipping, including the movement of goods or persons around the world – whether by sea, land, air or multimodal – and including freight forwarding and logistics. The series publishes works on the commercial aspects of shipping in light of developments such as digitalisation; artificial intelligence and automation; the agenda of environmental protection; green financing; climate goals; and the UN Sustainable Development Goals. Books in the series step beyond business as usual and embrace creative approaches to current and emerging issues or disrupters in shipping law. The series promotes research investigating the interrelationship between shipping law and topical issues of our time, including the environment; economics; political and human rights issues; health issues; the transport supply chain and logistics; and employment law and conditions.

Geopolitical Disruption in Shipping

Sanctions, War, and Force Majeure

Richard L Kilpatrick, Jr

•HART•

OXFORD • LONDON • NEW YORK • NEW DELHI • SYDNEY

HART PUBLISHING

Bloomsbury Publishing Plc

Kemp House, Chawley Park, Cumnor Hill, Oxford, OX2 9PH, UK

1385 Broadway, New York, NY 10018, USA

Bloomsbury Publishing Ireland Limited, 29 Earlsfort Terrace, Dublin 2, D02 AY28, Ireland

HART PUBLISHING, the Hart/Stag logo, BLOOMSBURY and the Diana logo are trademarks of Bloomsbury Publishing Plc

First published in Great Britain 2026

A catalogue record for this book is available from the British Library.

A catalogue record for this book is available from the Library of Congress.

Library of Congress Control Number: 2026934448

ISBN: HB: 978-1-50998-321-6
ePDF: 978-1-50998-319-3
ePub: 978-1-50998-320-9

Typeset by Compuscript Ltd, Shannon
Printed and bound in Great Britain

For product safety related questions contact productsafety@bloomsbury.com

To find out more about our authors and books visit www.hartpublishing.co.uk. Here you will find extracts, author information, details of forthcoming events and the option to sign up for our newsletters.

ACKNOWLEDGEMENTS

I would like to express my gratitude to everyone at Hart Publishing for believing in this project and working diligently to bring it to press as the first book in its series on the Future of Shipping Law. There are also three institutions I would like to thank for their support throughout the writing process. First, thanks to Kadir Has University Faculty of Law in Istanbul, where I spent the spring of 2024 as a Visiting Researcher drafting and discussing the proposal for this book. Second, I would also like to thank the University of Arkansas at Little Rock, William H Bowen School of Law, which has graciously hosted me as a Visiting Professor during academic years 2024–2026 as I have written this book and taught courses in contracts, commercial law, and maritime law. I am also especially grateful for a research grant the School of Law provided, which financed travel and resources supporting this project. Finally, I would like to thank the National University of Singapore, Faculty of Law, Centre for Maritime Law, where I have been blessed to work alongside some of the world's leading maritime law scholars at intervals throughout much of the last decade, including as an Academic Fellow and Visiting Scholar during the summer of 2025. Friends and colleagues at these and other institutions around the world have been integral to making this book possible. Thanks to all of you for your encouragement, advice, and feedback along the way.

CONTENTS

ABBREVIATIONS

AIS	Automatic Identification System
AWRP	Additional War Risk Premium
BIMCO	Baltic and International Maritime Council
CA	Court of Appeal
COGSA	Carriage of Goods by Sea Act (US)
DEA	Drug Enforcement Agency (US)
EU	European Union
FC&S	Free of Capture and Seizure
FDA	Food and Drug Administration (US)
G7	Group of Seven
GATT	General Agreement on Tariffs and Trade
HL	House of Lords
H&M	Hull and Machinery
IG	International Group (of P&I Clubs)
IMO	International Maritime Organization
INTERTANKO	International Association of Independent Tanker Owners
ISPS	International Ship and Port Facility Security
IWL	Institute Warranty Limits
JCPOA	Joint Comprehensive Plan of Action
LMAA	London Maritime Arbitrators Association
LOU	Letter of Undertaking
NAFTA	North American Free Trade Agreement
NATO	North Atlantic Treaty Organization
OFAC	Office of Foreign Assets Control (US Treasury)

P&I	Protection and Indemnity
PDVSA	Petróleos de Venezuela SA
SDN	Specially Designated National
SMA	Society of Maritime Arbitrators
STS	Ship-to-ship (transfer)
UAE	United Arab Emirates
UK	United Kingdom
UKSC	United Kingdom Supreme Court
UN	United Nations
UNCLOS	United Nations Convention on the Law of the Sea
US	United States
USTR	United States Trade Representative
USSC	United States Supreme Court
USSR	Union of Soviet Socialist Republics
WTO	World Trade Organization

TABLE OF CASES

TABLE OF UN AND IMO DOCUMENTS

UN Documents

IMO Documents

TABLE OF CLAUSES

1

Introduction

I. Overview

Maritime history is replete with imagery of merchant ships attacked, restrained, or threatened by external forces. War, piracy, civil unrest, and the full spectrum of category-defying conduct in between have long hampered maritime adventures, causing financial losses or the abandonment of commercial engagements altogether. Running parallel to these physical obstacles, and causing similar challenges, legal barriers such as boycotts, embargos, sanctions, and trade controls have been adopted by regulators seeking to parlay restrictions on the performance of shipping activities into an avenue for realising geostrategic aims. Irrespective of the political objectives they aim to promote, collectively, these physical and regulatory impediments have obstructed contract performance, generated security and compliance burdens, and produced risks and costs distributed among the various private actors that touch maritime transactions, including shipowners, charterers, cargo interests, and insurers. These scenarios have spurred many contract disputes, often requiring judicial and arbitral intervention to weigh intricate arguments that rattle and flex the fundamental principles of commercial law. This increasingly prevalent phenomenon – geopolitical disruption in shipping – is the inspiration for this book.

Although the commercial consequences of geopolitical turmoil have materialised over centuries, the present moment offers a vibrant illustration of the scope of these challenges. At the time of this book's publication, as the twenty-first century moves into its second quarter, physical risks affecting shipping are raging across maritime zones of navigational significance. A seminal moment of the contemporary era occurred in February 2022 when Russia commenced a full-scale invasion of neighbouring Ukraine. Russia immediately established a blockade of maritime traffic along Ukraine's Black Sea coasts, which trapped dozens of commercial vessels in the warzone.[1] As the fighting unfolded, ships were hit by missiles or damaged by mines, resulting in death and injury to civilian seafarers and extensive property damage.[2] The International Maritime

[1] See R Meade and B Diakun, 'Over 300 Vessels and at Least 1,000 Seafarers are Stuck in Ukraine' *Lloyd's List* (24 March 2022).

[2] See D Bush, 'Ships Hit by Missiles as Ukraine Forces Defend Odessa and Mariupol' *Lloyd's List* (25 February 2022).

Organization (IMO) issued advisories warning of floating mines drifting across the Black Sea.[3] The Lloyd's Market Association Joint War Committee also updated its 'listed areas' to include the Russian and Ukrainian coasts and a large swath of the Black Sea and Sea of Azov, signalling that war risk insurers would be justified in assessing an additional premium for vessels trading in these waters.[4] Regional vessel traffic reduced to a trickle, which sparked humanitarian concerns far from the warzone.[5] During peacetime, Ukraine had produced and exported a significant proportion of the global food supply in wheat, corn, and other grains. To reduce supply chain pressures and prevent famine in vulnerable economies dependent on these sources, during the summer of 2022 UN and Turkish officials brokered a diplomatic compromise under which Russia and Ukraine agreed to allow the safe passage of grain-carrying commercial ships in convoys through a mine-swept channel in the Black Sea to the Bosphorus Strait. This Black Sea Grain Initiative functioned for a full calendar year, with hundreds of commercial voyages successfully exporting tens of millions of tons of grain.[6] But as the war protracted, the agreement lapsed. In the summer of 2023, Russia again began bombing Ukraine's ports and grain export facilities.[7] Despite the risk and reality of further attacks, commercial actors continued facilitating trade with Ukraine.[8] Rather than moving through the humanitarian corridor that had been established under the UN grain deal, merchant ships diverted from the direct customary route to export either through the Danube River or by hugging the Black Sea coastlines of North Atlantic Treaty Organization (NATO) members Romania, Bulgaria, and Türkiye.[9] These efforts were aided by a public-private partnership between the Ukrainian government and commercial insurers to provide a subsidised source of war risk insurance.[10] Remarkably, Ukrainian grain exports bounced back nearly to pre-war levels, even as occasional attacks on ships and port infrastructure continued.[11]

[3] International Maritime Organization (IMO), Circular Letter No 4573 – Maritime Security Threat Posed by Free Floating Sea Mines in the Black Sea Region (24 May 2022).

[4] Joint War Committee, Circular JWLA-030 – Hull War, Piracy, Terrorism and Related Perils (4 April 2022).

[5] A Zagorodnyuk, 'Putin's Black Sea Blockade Leaves Millions Facing Global Famine' *Atlantic Council* (13 June 2022).

[6] United Nations, 'One Year of the Black Sea Initiative: Key Facts and Figures' (10 July 2023).

[7] International Maritime Organization (IMO), Resolution A.1183(33) – The Impact of the Russian Armed Invasion of Ukraine on International Shipping (4 December 2023).

[8] N Berman, M Ferragamo, and S Baumgartner, 'How Ukraine Overcame Russia's Grain Blockade' *Council on Foreign Relations* (22 August 2023).

[9] B Diakun, 'Reward Outweighs Risk for Owners Trading into Ukraine's Danube River Ports' *Lloyd's List* (3 November 2023); G Miller and B Diakun, 'Ukrainian Grain Exports Rebound as Ship Arrivals Near Pre-War Levels' *Lloyd's List* (26 April 2024).

[10] F Churchill, 'Marsh McLennan Launces Ukraine Black Sea Port Facility' *Insurance Day* (15 November 2023).

[11] B Diakun, 'Black Sea Risk Unchanged Despite Back-to-Back Incidents' *Lloyd's List* (23 September 2024). Ukraine also attacked or seized commercial ships engaged in activities to support Russia's war effort. 'Ukraine Strikes Cargoship it Claims was Laden with Iranian Weapons' *Lloyd's List* (15 August 2025).

Maritime security challenges intensified further after Hamas attacked Israel on 7 October 2023. Despite the immense scale of the Hamas attack and the heavy and controversial Israeli military response in Gaza, initially this caused only modest disruption to commercial vessel traffic in the region.[12] But militant activity soon spread across the region with fighting between the Israeli military and state and non-state actors based in Iran, Lebanon, and Yemen. Just weeks after the outbreak of hostilities, Houthi rebels controlling large portions of Yemeni territory – and claiming to act as the Yemeni military – began orchestrating an audacious spate of attacks on merchant ships attempting to navigate the Bab al-Mandab Strait at the southern entrance to the Red Sea. As commercial vessels moved through these waters under the customary route to gain access to the Suez Canal, the Houthis hijacked vessels, killed and kidnapped civilian seafarers, and executed many missile and drone strikes intentionally seeking to damage vessels and cargo.[13] The Houthi attacks mobilised a coalition of multinational military forces to intervene in efforts to safeguard freedom of navigation by performing airstrikes on Houthi targets inside Yemen.[14] This Red Sea crisis sent war risk insurance costs soaring, and substantially reduced insurance market access for vessels with any Israeli, US, or UK links, as Houthi leaders claimed to be enforcing a selective 'naval blockade' based on the perceived affiliations or trading histories of passing vessels (although in practice the attacks appeared largely indiscriminate).[15] The Houthi threat also caused many vessel operators to avoid the Suez Canal altogether, forcing re-routing around the Cape of Good Hope, which substantially increased transport costs. The fighting then spiralled into direct confrontation between Israel and Iran, with long-range missiles fired in both directions. In the summer of 2025, the US joined the fight by bombing Iran's nuclear enrichment sites.[16] Iran threatened a retaliatory closure of the Strait of Hormuz, placing the shipping industry on notice of the prospect of more violence against merchant vessels in another vital navigational chokepoint.[17]

With the Red Sea chaos requiring the immediate attention of coalition military forces in the region, this opened the door for opportunistic pirates in the Gulf of Aden to resume attacks on commercial vessels, as they had done routinely a decade prior.[18] Shortly after the Houthis began their attacks, in December 2023,

[12] J Saul and A Rabinovitch, 'Israel's Ports Feel Strain as Shipping Traffic Slows After Attacks' *Reuters* (10 October 2023).

[13] 'Reported Houthi Attacks in the Red Sea and Gulf of Aden: Maps and List of Attacks' *Lloyd's List* (8 September 2025).

[14] R Pedrozo, 'Protecting the Free Flow of Commerce from Houthi Attacks off the Arabian Peninsula' (2024) 103 *International Law Studies* 49.

[15] D Osler, 'Red Sea Transits Now "Impossible" for Ships with US, UK or Israel Ties, Say Underwriters' *Lloyd's List* (5 September 2024).

[16] DJ Trump, Remarks: Donald Trump Addresses the Nation After Iran Air Strikes (21 June 2025).

[17] L Nightingale, 'Hormuz Disruption Could Unplug Gulf Ports from Global Trade' *Lloyd's List* (24 June 2025).

[18] S Marks, 'Houthi Threat Triggers Surge in Pirate Attacks Off Somalia Coast' *Insurance Journal* (5 July 2024).

Somali pirates successfully hijacked a commercial bulk carrier for the first time in more than 10 years.[19] India's navy responded by capturing the pirates and freeing the vessel and its crew without loss of life, but subsequently several other vessels were attacked or threatened.[20] Intensifying the likelihood of pirate attacks, the many merchant ships that had diverted around the Cape of Good Hope to avoid Houthi attacks were forced to navigate through the waters directly east of the coast of Somalia, which was previously a hot spot for pirate seizures.[21] The Cape of Good Hope diversions also demanded navigation off the west coast of Africa where pirates based in the Gulf of Guinea raised the spectre of an additional threat.[22] These emerging risks renewed industry discussions on the need to implement best management practices to avoid attacks, including by navigating at higher speeds, carrying security guards, and adopting contract clauses to address the consequences of these additional and costly deterrence measures.[23] Resurgent Somali piracy risk also revived industry interest in supplemental kidnapping and ransom insurance designed to facilitate payments to pirates to secure the release of seafarers held hostage.[24] As these conventional piracy risks compounded, politically motivated hijackings – including those performed by the Houthis – were sometimes framed as 'piratical' acts, raising questions over the meaning of piracy in public and commercial law and its interplay with other forms of war risks.[25]

Parallel to these physical obstacles affecting shipping, regulatory authorities continued to build intricate regimes of economic sanctions with particular focus on regulating commercial maritime activities. Sanctioning authorities had refined restrictive trade measures during the 2010s with the aim of extracting policy concessions from North Korea, Iran, Syria, and Venezuela. But the war in Ukraine quickly refocused attention on Russia – one of the largest and most globally integrated economies in the world. Many nations reacted to the war in Ukraine not only with political condemnation but also restrictions on Russia-connected transactions going well beyond the measures imposed following Russia's 2014 annexation of Ukrainian Crimea. These sanctions increased incrementally over time, with an inflection point in a December 2022 agreement by the G7, EU, and other partner nations to cap exported Russian oil

[19] R Meade, 'Somali Piracy Is Back and a Show of Force from India May Not Be Enough to Stop It' *Lloyd's List* (25 March 2024).

[20] J Minchin, 'IMB Report Shows Somali Piracy Spike' *Lloyd's List* (12 April 2024).

[21] B Diakun, 'Piracy Exposure Increases in Somali Basin Because of Red Sea Diversions' *Lloyd's List* (28 November 2024).

[22] R Wright, 'Pirates Targeting Ships Diverted from Red Sea, Warns UN Shipping Chief' *Financial Times* (21 February 2024).

[23] J Minchin, 'Industry Updates Security Best Practice After "Unprecedented" Rise in Attacks' *Lloyd's List* (4 April 2025).

[24] D Osler, 'Somalia Piracy Resurgence Makes Kidnap & Ransom Cover Necessary' *Lloyd's List* (13 March 2024).

[25] See ch 4.

at an artificial price.[26] This experimental price cap regime was implemented by regulating 'maritime service providers' through onerous compliance mandates involving counterparty screenings, compulsory price attestation exchanges, and demands to monitor deception from nefarious actors seeking to circumvent these rules.[27] The sanctions were then enforced under the threat of civil penalties, blacklisting, and criminal prosecution against private sector actors. A knock-on effect of these layering maritime sanctions was the emergence of a hundreds-strong 'dark fleet' of aging sanctions-busting oil tankers with operators performing prohibited transactions through evasive techniques such as switching off vessel tracking transponders, engaging in unauthorised ship-to-ship cargo transfers at sea, and distributing fraudulent documentation of beneficial ownership, flag registration, safety certification, and proof of insurance cover.[28] In efforts to avoid becoming entangled with the liability consequences of these activities, commercial actors increasingly relied upon third party vendors to navigate compliance, including through sophisticated surveillance systems and pre-contracting counterparty and cargo origin and pricing investigations. They also adopted a variety of 'sanctions clauses' designed to allocate responsibility arising out of enforcement risk.[29]

National authorities reacted to these and other geopolitical controversies with boycotts, export controls, tariffs, and other trade barriers, along with the targeted provision of military, logistical, and humanitarian assistance. The war in Ukraine spawned massive economic investment in lethal military aid shipped from NATO member states to Ukraine, and spurred export control efforts to prevent the movement of 'dual use' goods to Russia.[30] Enacting trade repercussions for Israel's military tactics in Gaza, some countries imposed economic boycotts and restrictions on Israeli goods and even limited port access to Israel-connected ships.[31] In tandem, a long-simmering trade war between the US and China suddenly ignited with the US imposing heavy tariffs on Chinese goods and proposing a 'service fee' initiative targeting China-connected ships – measures that

[26] The G7 includes Canada, France, Germany, Italy, Japan, the United Kingdom, and the United States. See European Commission, Press Release: 'G7 Agrees Oil Price Cap: Reducing Russia's Revenues, While Keeping Global Energy Markets Stable' (2 December 2022).

[27] Office of Foreign Assets Control (OFAC), Guidance on Implementation of the Price Cap Policy for Crude Oil and Petroleum Products of Russian Federation Origin (Revised) (20 December 2023).

[28] In December 2023, the IMO General Assembly adopted a Resolution urging Member States to combat the illicit activity of dark fleet operators intentionally violating sanctions. International Maritime Organization (IMO), Resolution A.1192(33): Urging Member States and All Relevant Stakeholders to Promote Actions to Prevent Illegal Operations in the Maritime Sector by the 'Dark Fleet' or 'Shadow Fleet' (6 December 2023).

[29] See ch 5.

[30] J Masters and W Merrow, 'Here's How Much Aid the United States Has Sent Ukraine' *Council on Foreign Relations* (15 July 2025).

[31] E Goksedef and J Minchin, 'Türkiye to Refuse Entry to Israeli-linked Vessels' *Lloyd's List* (22 August 2025).

were rationalised under a multi-faceted policy basis, including the vague notion of enhancing 'national security'.[32] China responded with its own tariffs and threatened to more forcefully control the flow of its coveted rare earth minerals needed for high tech manufacturing.[33] These trade wars not only affected US–China relations but also destabilised the broader international trading system. In the spring of 2025, the US announced its intentions to impose widespread 'reciprocal tariffs' on countries around the world, including traditional allies in North America and Europe.[34] The US then began adopting a more assertive approach in the Western Hemisphere by attacking Venezuela, arresting its president, and establishing a 'quarantine' on its oil exports, while simultaneously alarming Colombia, Cuba, Panama, and even NATO members Canada and Denmark (Greenland) with territorial ambitions backed by economic and military threats. This provocative policy stance triggered retaliatory measures, including reactionary tariffs, travel and trade boycotts, and export controls, jeopardising free trade values in a 'deglobalisation' era already reeling from nationalistic movements exacerbated by the isolating impact of the Covid-19 pandemic.[35] As with other barriers, these statecraft measures sparked commercial law challenges and resulted in further contractual efforts to allocate costs and risks flowing out of emerging forms of geopolitical volatility.[36]

Viewing the world through the lens of this snapshot in time, it is difficult to deny that the present moment feels tumultuous for the international trading community as a whole and for the shipping industry in particular.[37] But, reverting to the bigger picture, the complex challenges of the present moment are not new to shipping. The modern world mirrors themes of commercial disruption familiar to the private actors effectuating international trade in a global environment perpetually fraught with ever-evolving tensions. Throughout history, as reflected in earlier case law, commercial actors have been forced to adapt to geopolitical controversy and its impact on worldwide trading conditions. Reflecting these previous trends, today's resurgent risks are producing a new wave of analogous jurisprudence. Demonstrating a subtle shift in geopolitical tactics, however, these cases largely examine the commercial implications of sanctions and trade controls, but with regular reference to doctrinal principles and contract wordings developed and revised in response to earlier periods of physical and economic confrontation. Both time-tested solutions and novel innovations are being applied to address

[32] US Trade Representative, 'Section 301 Investigation: Report on China's Targeting of the Maritime, Logistics, and Shipbuilding Sectors for Dominance' (16 January 2025).

[33] H Farrel and A Newman, 'The Weaponized World Economy: Surviving the New Age of Economic Coercion' *Foreign Affairs* (19 August 2025).

[34] G Miller, 'How New Trump Tariffs on China, Mexico and Canada Could Impact Shipping' *Lloyd's List* (26 November 2024).

[35] See generally E Braw, *Goodbye Globalization: The Return of a Divided World* (Yale University Press, 2024).

[36] See ch 6.

[37] Providing quantitative evidence of this perception, a Lloyd's List industry survey conducted at the end of 2024 revealed that responding industry participants considered 'geopolitical risk' as 'the greatest risk to shipping businesses over the next two years'. See J Minchin, 'Geopolitical Risk Shipping's Biggest Worry, Lloyd's List Poll Reveals' *Lloyd's List* (13 December 2024).

the consequences of contemporary commercial problems, and trends are rapidly materialising. Reflecting on the history of the interplay between geopolitics and shipping, and aiming to make sense of its future, this book seeks to capture the present movement and contribute to the discourse around it.

II. Scope

Geopolitical disruption can affect commercial transactions in a variety of industries, including banking, finance, logistics, sales, and other sub-sectors associated with international trade. This book aims to keep a narrow focus on the commercial maritime dimensions of these challenges. To maintain this limited scope, the book primarily analyses case law flowing from three different forms of maritime contracts: charterparties, bills of lading, and policies of marine insurance.[38] In an attempt to expand the accessibility of this book beyond maritime law specialists, this section briefly introduces each of these three contractual scenarios.

A. Charterparties

At a basic level, a charterparty is a maritime species of contract that delineates the rights and obligations of shipowners and charterers through an agreement to employ a vessel for a particular voyage or designated duration.[39] The three major categories of charterparties used in the carriage of goods context include time charters, voyage charters, and bareboat charters. Time charters run for an agreed duration in which the shipowner maintains control over the vessel and employs the shipmaster and crew, while the charterer enjoys the right and responsibility to give employment orders for the vessel to fulfil commercial objectives. The mutual benefit of the contract is that the charterer may direct the vessel loading and discharge destinations without the need to attend to nautical or navigation matters, which the shipowner fulfils and is therefore compensated for this performance with recurring payments of hire running continuously throughout the charter period, unless the vessel goes off-hire in the event of contractually designated circumstances. In contrast, under a voyage charter, the ports of loading and discharge are typically stipulated at the time of the agreement and the shipowner remains in control of the vessel's navigation. Accordingly, the costs of the voyage are incorporated into a lump sum freight payment, with potential adjustments to incentivise expediate loading and unloading. Bareboat charters are a distinct third category that operate more like a vessel lease under which the charterer takes full control not only of

[38] This book occasionally references other forms of commercial agreements, including letters of credit, contracts for the sale of goods, and property or business interruption insurance policies.
[39] See H Bennet et al, *Carver on Charterparties* (2nd edn, Sweet & Maxwell, 2021) ch 1.

the vessel's commercial undertakings but also its navigation, maintenance, and credentialling (although these roles may be outsourced to third parties such as vessel management companies). Regardless of type, charterparties are generally left ungoverned by international conventions, which leaves their terms to be negotiated under freedom of contract principles subject to general contract law. International uniformity is nevertheless achieved by the use of standard forms that have developed over time in commercial practice to respond to industry demands. Organisations such as the Baltic and International Maritime Council (BIMCO) and the International Association of Independent Tanker Owners (INTERTANKO) lead the way in facilitating the use of standard contract forms and clauses. They also regularly draft, update, and circulate new clauses to solve emerging problems.

Due to longstanding commercial practice, charterparties usually contain mandatory arbitration clauses.[40] Arbitration awards enter into the public domain in two ways: either through public distribution of the awards or by reference in judicial appeals. A significant number of charterparty arbitrations are commenced annually under the auspices of the London Maritime Arbitrators Association (LMAA). The LMAA maintains confidentiality rules designed to protect the privacy interests of the parties, which (unfortunately for maritime law observers) also conceals from public view the facts, arguments, and reasoning of the awards.[41] The substance of confidential awards are sometimes relayed with identifying information redacted via shipping industry news outlets, such as the Lloyd's Maritime Law Newsletter. But since these awards are not made publicly available in full, they generally only enter into the public domain by way of challenges to the awards through the English courts. On review, English court judgments generally cite positions, reasoning, and sometimes also quote passages from the arbitral awards, but they are rarely attached in full. In addition to the LMAA, however, there are many maritime arbitration bodies around the world that operate with their own rules and perspectives on confidentiality. Among them is the New York-based Society of Maritime Arbitrators (SMA), which provides publicly available awards that are even indexed with popular legal databases such as LexisNexis. Although these and other publicly accessible arbitration awards are not intended to create authoritative precedent, they provide a rich window into the types of disputes that materialise in commercial shipping practice and display useful reasoning that may be relevant for the resolution of future disputes. Both publicly available SMA awards and English court judgments reviewing confidential arbitration awards are discussed throughout this book.

[40] Sometimes courts adjudicate charterparty issues on the merits in the first instance without initial arbitration. Several cases discussed in this book fall within that category.

[41] See C Ambrose, K Maxwell, and M Collett KC, *London Maritime Arbitration* (4th edn, Informa, 2017) ch 13.

B. Bills of Lading

While charterparties govern the rights and obligations between shipowners and charterers, contracts of carriage evidenced through the terms of bills of lading may serve as the basis for resolving disputes between carriers and cargo shippers.[42] The two forms of contracts may overlap in the sense that a bill of lading may be issued by a carrier to govern the relationship with the shipper even as the use of the vessel and the relationship between the shipowner and the charterer is simultaneously governed under the terms of the charterparty. But the two forms of contracts serve as independent instruments referenced to answer different types of liability questions. Bills of lading can be particularly important in the context of the liner market, in which vessels – often container ships in the modern era – perform scheduled voyages between major ports. Many different customers may book space on the vessels to move cargo, which may be packed inside intermodal containers facilitating efficient transshipment, warehousing, or onward transport via additional land-based modes such as road or rail. In general, when a liner carrier accepts cargo for shipment, it will issue a bill of lading that not only serves as a receipt and document of title to allow the collection of the cargo after completion of the voyage but also as evidence of the contract of carriage between the carrier and the shipper. Invariably, printed on the bills of lading, the carrier provides its standard contract terms. Unlike freely negotiated charterparty contracts, bills of lading are regulated by both international conventions and domestic law. International harmony is achieved through the widespread adoption of the International Convention for the Unification of Certain Rules of Law relating to Bills of Lading (The Hague Rules) and its domestic implementation, such as the US Carriage of Goods by Sea Act (COGSA).[43] Some nations, including the UK, have agreed to the Hague-Visby amendments, leading to marginal variation even between leading maritime jurisdictions. These mandatory rules substantially influence bill of lading disputes, not only because they inform the drafting of the contract terms, but also because they articulate carrier duties and liability exceptions by statutory force.

C. Marine Insurance Policies

Marine insurance policies are a third type of contract discussed frequently in this book. For historical reasons, marine insurance cover is fragmented into sub-categories. For more than 200 years, coverage in the London market and

[42] See generally SD Girvin, *Carriage of Goods by Sea* (3rd edn, OUP, 2022).

[43] International Convention for the Unification of Certain Rules of Law relating to Bills of Lading (Hague Rules) (adopted 25 August 1924, entered into force 2 June 1931) 120 LNTS 155; 46 USC § 30701.

beyond was described through the language of the 'SG' policy, which referenced an expansive list of covered perils, including those that would be considered both marine and war risks today.[44] Eventually, however, recognising the distinct risk profile of war perils, as early as the eighteenth century, London-based insurers began separating marine and war risks through a Free of Capture and Seizure (FC&S) Clause.[45] Under its terms, certain war risks were excluded from the main policy, but could be added back through the payment of an additional premium. By the end of the nineteenth century, the FC&S Clause became a market standard that was formally recognised by a resolution in the Lloyd's market.[46] American insurers followed the same conventions at that time, largely aiming to align with English law and practice.[47] In addition to these developments, the advent of other forms of marine insurance, especially through protection and indemnity clubs (P&I clubs), created further cover fragmentation.[48] By the twentieth century, standard clauses developed by the Institute of London Underwriters were attached to the SG form in attempts to clarify and harmonise the scope of cover.[49] A similar framework was established in the American market with only minor variations in wordings.[50] The language, however, evolved over time – often informed by geopolitical events, particularly the two World Wars. Reforms in the London market during the 1980s eventually replaced the SG form with a new Lloyd's MAR form to be accompanied by separate hull or cargo clauses. The division between marine and war risk insurance remained throughout, with specialist war risk insurers or war risk mutual associations providing cover for these unique perils in the modern era. Many of the cases discussed in this book address the liability allocation between these various insurers.

III. Recurring Principles

Whether arising in the context of a charterparty, bill of lading, or policy of marine insurance, when shipping activities are disrupted by physical or economic interference this may generate similar types of contract disputes. As courts and arbitrators consider the contractual rights and obligations flowing out of these scenarios, parties have regularly rooted their arguments in doctrinal principles along with express contract clauses, revealing patterns and themes in the case

[44] The name 'SG' is believed to stand for 'ship and goods'.

[45] See ch 2.

[46] See M Davey, J Davey, and O Caplin, *Miller's Marine War Risks* (4th edn, Informa 2020) § 1.16.

[47] See LJ Buglass, *Marine Insurance and General Average in the United States* (3rd edn, Cornell Maritime Press, 1991) ch 3.

[48] See S Hazelwood and D Semark, *P&I Clubs: Law and Practice* (4th edn, Informa, 2010).

[49] See J Gilman et al, *Arnould Law of Marine Insurance and General Average* (20th edn, Sweet & Maxwell, 2021) ch 2.

[50] See Buglass (n 47) ch 3.

law. For background, this section highlights key doctrines and clauses that appear frequently in this book.

A. Frustration

The doctrine of frustration of purpose represents the notion that certain unforeseen external events that obstruct contractual performance may change assumptions or expectations so fundamentally that the parties are fully released from their obligations, ending the contract entirely. The doctrine has been refined over time, with characterisations in English law examining whether changes in circumstances, without the fault of either party, render the contract performance to be 'radically different' from the parties' intentions.[51] American courts have referenced the frustration doctrine using similar standards, although in the modern era the frustration principle has often been discussed synonymously with other avoidance frameworks (discussed below).[52] Given its 'radical' nature, frustration is applied reluctantly – as a last resort – to ensure that it is not used to escape the consequences of bad bargains. At the same time, it may be used to prevent the inequitable results of insisting on literal performance of the contract when genuine circumstantial barriers arise.

B. Impracticability

In American law, the doctrine of frustration has sometimes been recast through the lens of impracticability.[53] The impracticability doctrine shares attributes with frustration in that it is used to justify the avoidance of contractual obligations when performance no longer aligns with the fundamental expectations of the parties. The doctrine is explicitly referenced in both the American Law Institute Restatement (Second) of Contracts and the Uniform Commercial Code (UCC), with each using similar language to define the doctrine's application to situations in which a contingency occurs contrary to the 'basic assumption on which the contract was made'.[54] When applying the impracticability doctrine, courts generally look for several factors, including whether the non-occurrence of the disruptive contingency was an assumption underpinning the parties agreement and whether it resulted without the fault of either party.[55] Like frustration, the

[51] See H Beale (ed), *Chitty on Contracts* (35th edn, Sweet & Maxwell 2023) § 27-012. A 'multi-factorial approach' is the more recent test of frustration under English Law: ibid § 27-019.

[52] AE Farnsworth, *Contracts* (4th edn Aspen Publishers 2004) § 9.8.

[53] ibid §9.7.

[54] See Uniform Commercial Code § 2-615(a); Official Comment 3 of this UCC provision distinguishes impracticability from frustration in efforts 'to call attention to the commercial character of the criterion'. See also Restatement (Second) of Contracts (1981) § 261.

[55] Farnsworth (n 51) § 9.6.

doctrine is subject to a high burden of proof, as it is recognised that although increased costs or burdens alone may make performance 'impractical' from a business perspective, this does not necessarily equate to meeting the 'impracticable' threshold.[56]

C. Illegality

The doctrine of illegality of performance is narrower than both frustration and impracticability. It may be referenced to support contract avoidance only if performance would run afoul of statutory law or otherwise violate public policy.[57] The doctrine may resonate in several scenarios. For instance, it may apply if the law changes to impose a barrier while performance is pending. If the contract is deemed to be statutorily unlawful, the contract would be unenforceable, which, despite its narrow scope, makes the doctrine a particularly potent avoidance defence.[58] Critically, however, statutory illegality may be a temporary condition as it can be removed by a subsequent shift in the law or through a licence or permit. For this reason, it does not necessarily discharge performance in the same way as frustration or impracticability. Illegality based on public policy principles is more flexible, as it may require an assessment of competing policy interests before determining whether an agreement should be enforced. This flexibility, of course, causes uncertain application.[59] An additional difficulty surrounding the application of illegality principles in the context of international commercial agreements is the question of what sources of law may be used to judge the alleged unlawfulness. English courts have expressed the position that foreign illegality cannot be used to justify contract avoidance, while at least some American courts have been more amenable to the argument.[60]

D. Impossibility

Traditionally, the doctrine of impossibility has been referenced to allow avoidance only in cases involving changes in circumstances that prevent the physical ability to perform the obligation contemplated by the parties. In assessing such arguments, some American courts have recognised a difference between 'objective' impossibility that considers whether any party could reasonably perform the obligation, as opposed to a 'subjective' analysis that weighs the performing

[56] See E Peel, *Frustration and Force Majeure* (4th edn, Sweet & Maxwell 2022) § 6-003.
[57] ibid § 8-001.
[58] See JM Perillo, *Contracts* (7th edn, West 2014) § 22.
[59] One American law treatise has described public policy reasoning as an 'unruly horse': ibid § 22.11.
[60] Peel (n 56) § 8-074; Perillo (n 58) § 13.5.

party's unique circumstances.[61] More recently, both American and English courts have rejected these distinctions or simply assessed impossibility through the lens of other parallel doctrines, including frustration.[62] Although its application is notoriously narrow, counterintuitively, impossibility may at times have a broader application than some other avoidance doctrines, including illegality. For instance, impossibility may potentially resonate in situations where performance is obstructed because a third party expected to facilitate the transaction refuses to do so by complying with foreign law or by 'over-complying' with statutory law in a governing jurisdiction.[63] Such facts may theoretically activate the impossibility doctrine even if the illegality doctrine remains dormant. Like other avoidance principles, the standard of proof implicit in the impossibility doctrine remains high.

E. Clauses

In conjunction with doctrinal reasoning, courts and arbitrators regularly resolve commercial disputes flowing from geopolitical disruption by referencing explicit contract clauses. Among them are *force majeure* clauses that explicitly contemplate performance disruption by enumerating classes and categories of external events – or 'superior forces' – that trigger contractual rights and responsibilities. These provisions typically encompass many of the topics addressed in this study, including war, economic interference, and other related categories falling within their orbit, which, depending on the precise language of the clause, may provide an explicit basis to justify a solution in lieu of doctrinal reasoning. But maritime contracts also frequently utilise other standard provisions addressing contingencies and outcomes relevant to performance obstacles arising out of intervening forces. Classic examples in the charterparty context include safe port warranties that confer duties on the contracting parties to ensure the vessel is protected from entering hazardous waters, trading limit clauses that expressly permit or exclude zones of navigation, and off hire and demurrage provisions that apportion liability for performance delays. Moreover, terms referencing 'restraint of princes' or 'act of war' may offer exception to the shipowner in the context of a charterparty or release the carrier of liability in the context of a bill of lading. Likewise, standard insurance clauses may articulate explicit grounds to cancel cover, deny claims, prohibit unlawful trades, or shift burdens onto other insurers underwriting risks for the same adventure. In all of these contexts, bespoke contract clauses may attempt to more directly address disruption scenarios, particularly in the modern era, as shipping industry actors seek out options that are increasingly tailored and responsive to contemporary risk.

[61] See JE Murray, *Murray on Contracts* (Lexis Nexis 2011) § 113.
[62] See Peel (n 56) § 3-003–3-004.
[63] This line of reasoning may be particularly relevant in the sanctions context discussed in ch 5.

IV. Approach

The structure of this book is simple. Following this introductory chapter, each substantive chapter contains a background section providing a basic sketch of the relevant geopolitical, regulatory, and industry context for the form of disruption under scrutiny. These sections are then followed by a detailed analysis of illustrative chartering, carriage, and insurance cases sub-divided with descriptive sub-headings. Each chapter then concludes with a reflections section that examines the analytical frameworks used to resolve the cases. All of the five substantive chapters aim to strike a stylistic balance by standing alone for independent reference, while also seeking to avoid repetition. The last chapter provides some conclusory observations. The heart of the book is its carefully selected collection of cases. The coverage aims to highlight leading (or simply interesting) court judgments and arbitration awards for the purpose of providing illustrations of the way geopolitical disruption affects the performance of maritime contracts. The book does not aim to serve as a treatise or an entirely comprehensive statement of the law. Instead, it seeks to analyse the methods by which courts and arbitrators address the commercial consequences of these barriers. Relying predominantly on cases from the US and the UK, and occasionally other English-speaking jurisdictions such as Singapore, the book endeavours to tell their fascinating stories in accessible form.

Many of the war-related cases are decades old while some of the sanctions-related decisions were issued within just a few months leading up to publication. This is not only an editorial choice but also a reflection of shifting geopolitical strategies away from the total wars of the past and into an era of statecraft by other means. Recognising that other authors have covered many of the earlier cases in erudite detail, many of the war and conflict-related cases have been shelved to make room for contemporary or under-explored scenarios, particularly those examining economic disruption.[64] Wherever possible, the book highlights relatively recent cases, although seminal earlier cases are discussed to provide historical context. Other cases – admittedly there are many – remain in the archives for future study.[65] Although the book reveals an Anglo-American jurisdictional inclination, it also seeks to provide a holistic picture that is as geographically broad as possible to illustrate the genuinely global nature of the topic. The cases untangle commercial disputes arising out of events in Algeria, Chile, China, Cuba, Iraq, Italy, Nicaragua, Spain, Somalia, Vietnam, and many other countries spanning across the globe.

[64] See eg Davey, Davey, and Caplin (n 46); K Michel, *War, Terror and Carriage by Sea* (Informa, 2004); R Merkin, *Marine Insurance: A Legal History* (Edward Elgar Publishing, 2021).

[65] Following the approach used in American legal discourse, throughout this book reference is made to 'the court' rather than the particular judge or arbitrator deciding each case (for instance, the text might read: 'the court held …' or 'the arbitral panel reasoned …'). The first footnote for each principal case acknowledges the author(s) of the main judgments and awards. Dissenting judges and arbitrators are also named in the footnotes when discussed in the text.

They feature disruption caused by Japanese air raids, German U boats, Libyan embargos, Nigerian boycotts, American privateers, Eritrean guerrillas, Bolivian separatists, Indonesian extortionists, Venezuelan insurrectionists, Russian oligarchs, and a whole lot more. In truth, the more than 100 cases discussed in detail in this book scratch only the surface. Each substantive chapter could easily serve as the basis for a series of full-length books. This study instead targets a more modest goal: to reveal in one concise volume the contractual implications of geopolitical undercurrents flowing beneath the modern trading world.

2

War

I. Introduction

Among the geopolitical events carrying the potential to disrupt maritime commerce, war is the quintessential form. Throughout the history of shipping, the prospect of sudden obstruction by kinetic conflict was understood to be – alongside wind and waves – an inherent risk of trading by sea. As nation states emerged as the principal arbiters of political power, these war risks were characterised by sporadic periods of turbulence between governments seeking to project dominance through sea-powered expansionism, trade route hegemony, and naval supremacy administered by blockades and opportunistic prize seizures.[1] By the nineteenth century, as international interconnectivity was propelled forward by the development of steel-hulled and steam-powered ships, the economic consequences of political interference reverberated further than in previous generations. Industrialisation and globalisation created paradoxical impacts by prompting strategic and competitive colonialism between major powers to satisfy a growing appetite for natural resources to fuel domestic production, while simultaneously cultivating the conditions for mutually beneficial trade, which incentivised peaceful relations and established a self-interested check against political confrontation. With national economies fused together by trade, governments continued to manoeuvre for power and influence, but with the spectre of war threatening to upend economic objectives with a greater disruptive force than the more insular eras of the past.

Within the shipping industry, these evolving perceptions of war risks produced contractual adaptations. In the insurance context, war and marine perils were historically covered under the same policy written on the SG form or its equivalent.[2] Following the trade disruption caused by the Napoleonic Wars, the American Civil War, and other major conflicts of the nineteenth century, as geopolitical risks again mounted at the turn of the century with the first Sino-Japanese War, the Spanish-American War, and the 'war scare' of the Fashoda Incident between Britain and France in East Africa, this affirmed a trending industry consensus that war risks had become uniquely disruptive.[3] In 1898, by Lloyd's resolution, a Free

[1] See J Stavridis, *Sea Power: The History and Geopolitics of the World's Oceans* (Penguin, 2017).
[2] See M Davey, J Davey, and O Caplin, *Miller's Marine War Risks* (4th edn, Informa, 2020) § 1.8.
[3] ibid § 1.15.

of Capture and Seizure (FC&S) Clause was required to be included in all hull policies issued in the London market.[4] This clause, which was a modified version of those already in voluntary circulation, had the effect of placing the wartime perils 'capture, seizure and detention' – along with the more nebulous categories 'hostilities' and 'warlike operations' – beyond the standard marine insurance cover.[5] This excluded cover could then be reinstated by paying a separate war risk premium to delete the FC&S clause or to procure a parallel war risk policy which would 'dovetail' with the marine policy to close any gaps.[6] The growing American marine insurance market adopted the same practice using nearly identical language.[7]

The First World War swiftly followed in a conflict of unprecedented scale between the Allied and Central Powers during 1914–1918.[8] Throughout the war, thousands of merchant ships were deployed under American and British requisition orders to run supplies and passengers across the Atlantic Ocean and English Channel. These and other merchant vessels were routinely met with hostile attacks by German warships and torpedo-wielding U-boats operating under a policy of 'unrestricted' warfare against both military and civilian targets.[9] The new and more damaging weaponry deployed during this era created such extreme risks to merchant ships that commercial war risk insurers became unwilling or unable to underwrite the voyages. The American and British governments responded by assuming responsibility for war risk cover through state-issued war risk policies or by wartime charterparties incorporating the division between war and marine risks by referencing the FC&S language.[10] Under either wartime arrangement, merchant shipowners remained responsible for obtaining standard marine insurance to cover the traditional marine perils. As a consequence, wartime casualties led to many contract disputes centred on whether the loss was caused by a marine peril falling within the standard marine insurance cover or a war peril subject to the government-provided war risk arrangement.[11]

The interwar years spawned a flurry of international collaboration and diplomacy in efforts to prevent another major conflict, including through the

[4] This version of the FC&S Clause read: 'Warranted nevertheless free of capture, seizure and detention, and of the consequences thereof, or any attempt thereat, piracy excepted, and also from all consequences of hostilities or warlike operations, whether before or after the declaration of war.' ibid § 1.16.

[5] See R Merkin, *Marine Insurance: A Legal History* (Edward Elgar, 2021) § 7-039.

[6] See J Gilman et al, *Arnould: Law of Marine Insurance and Average* (20th edn, Sweet & Maxwell, 2020) § 24-02.

[7] See WD Winter, *Marine Insurance: Its Principles and Practice* (McGraw-Hill, 1919) 268.

[8] The Allied Powers included Britain, France, the United States, and Russia. The Central Powers included Austria-Hungary, Germany, and the Ottoman Empire.

[9] The First World War was also characterised by new naval warfare techniques, including floating mines, mounted machine guns, and carrier-based aircraft. See generally AF Krepinevich Jr, *The Origins of Victory: How Disruptive Military Innovations Determines the Fates of Great Powers* (Yale University Press, 2023) 30.

[10] See FD Rose, *Marine Insurance: Law and Practice* (2nd edn, Informa, 2012) § 17.7.

[11] The British FC&S Clause was subject to minor updates during and after the First World War. Davey, Davey, and Caplin (n 2) § 1.18.

establishment of the League of Nations. These multilateral initiatives also affected commercial law. Among the diplomatic achievements of the interwar years was the Hague Rules – an international convention governing bills of lading.[12] Even prior to the war, regulators around the world had aimed to limit liner carriers from unreasonably exculpating themselves from liability under contracts of carriage. By 1924, a group of leading maritime nations agreed to harmonise such liability allocation by treaty. The final language of the Hague Rules was naturally informed by the experience of the recent war. For instance, although its provisions prohibited carriers from reducing liability below mandatory thresholds, the rules also protected carriers from exposure to perils outside their control, including damage caused by 'act of war' and 'arrest or restraint of princes, rulers, or people'.[13] Although charterparties were not covered under the Hague Rules, shipowners and charterers also allocated war risks through contract forms containing mutually excepting war cancellation clauses, and through contract language incorporating the Hague Rules (or equivalent domestic implementing legislation) by way of a clause paramount.[14]

Despite sustained efforts to preserve the peace, by the end of the 1930s an even more geographically expansive crisis emerged as imperial Japan, fascist Italy, and re-armed Nazi Germany pursued territorial conquests across the world. As Britain and later the US intervened on the European front, Germany unleased its revamped U-boat fleet to again terrorise merchant ships in the Atlantic Ocean. Following its surprise bombing of the US naval base at Pearl Harbor, and extensive territorial conquests throughout Southeast Asia, Japan also deployed its submarines alongside carrier-supported air forces to attack both military and commercial ships in the Pacific. Thousands of vessels and vast amounts of cargo were lost on both fronts, and many commercial transactions were left unfulfilled. But despite this tremendous disruption, commerce continued flowing as the industrial military apparatus necessary to execute the war relied substantially on merchant shipping. As in the First World War, governments were often the patrons of the transactions through vessel requisitioning arrangements or by procurement agreements with private firms to fulfil military support objectives. Following the practices that had been established in the previous war, the American and British governments provided war risk insurance when private insurance was not obtainable. This led to another round of post-war insurance litigation analysing the fact-intensive line between marine and war perils.[15]

[12] See ch 1.

[13] See Hauge Rules, Art 4. Demonstrating the impact of the war on the drafting process, the previously adopted US Harter Act, which served as a model for the Hague Rules, did not include 'act of war' or 'restraint of princes' in its list of carrier defences. See 46 USC § 30706.

[14] See Y Baatz, 'Clauses Paramount' in B Soyer and A Tettenborn (eds), *Charterparties: Law, Practice and Emerging Legal Issues* (Informa, 2018) ch 13.

[15] See Gilman et al (n 6) § 24-05. See 'Overall War-Marine Risk Settlement Agreement', 1945 AMC 1014 (1945).

The US decision to end the war in the Pacific by detonating nuclear weapons over the Japanese cities of Hiroshima and Nagasaki in 1945 was a turning point in world history. The shocking aftermath generated much philosophical introspection and strategic recalibration. It also spurred contractual innovations. After the Soviet Union developed and tested its own nuclear weapons in 1949 and Western powers mobilised to form the NATO mutual defence alliance, the shipping industry responded with updated contract wordings. Conscious of the new and extreme risks of a major war between nuclear-armed militaries, war risk insurers began incorporating new clauses in policies that would automatically terminate cover in the event of the detonation of a nuclear weapon or the outbreak of war between any of four major powers: Britain, France, the US, and the USSR. When a large-scale war did in fact break out on the Korean Peninsula in 1950 as the Soviet-aligned North invaded the US-backed South, forces organised under the banner of a UN coalition intervened. The newly formed People's Republic of China joined the fight on the side of the North, which underlined stark ideological fault lines between a US-led Western capitalist democracy coalition and a Soviet-led communist bloc. Following the 1953 armistice, war risk insurers added the People's Republic of China to the automatic termination clause, bringing its total to five powers.[16] Charterparties, likewise, continued addressing war risks, largely 'mirroring' marine insurance provisions and articulating explicit grounds for cancellation in the event of major wars.[17]

The Korean War left an important legacy in military and geopolitical strategy that has shaped conflicts ever since. Despite the availability of nuclear weapons at the time, neither the US nor the Soviet Union chose to use them. In addition, recognising the intolerable risks of escalation, both sides were careful to avoid direct confrontation as US forces fought for the South under the UN flag while the USSR abstained from direct fighting and instead contributed by providing arms, logistical support, and political backing to the North. These decisions established norms and behaviours that continued for decades as the ideologically incompatible superpowers (and their respective allies) engaged in a Cold War that lasted until the 1990s. Despite the admirable mutual restraint, the Cold War was a precarious age involving the development and proliferation of even more powerful thermonuclear weapons and many violent proxy conflicts spanning across the globe.[18] These recurring hot wars revealed the willingness of the US and Soviet Union to participate in relatively large-scale conventional conflicts without resorting to the direct confrontation that might risk the use of weapons of mass destruction. The smaller conflicts of the Cold War era, of course, carried serious humanitarian and political consequences throughout the world, but in general they had a far more contained

[16] For more history on this clause, see RL Kilpatrick Jr, 'Revisiting the Five Powers War Risk Exclusion' (2024) 73 *International & Comparative Law Quarterly* 551.

[17] See T Young et al, *Voyage Charters* (5th edn, Informa, 2022) § 26.2.

[18] The UK, France, China, and India also obtained nuclear weapons capability during this period.

impact on maritime trade than the total wars of the first half of the twentieth century.[19]

One particularly violent exception during this phase of history was the major war between Iran and Iraq fought between 1980 and 1988. Although the war generally lacked the ideological character of other conflicts during the Cold War, in part due to its geographically significant location in an oil rich region, it had substantial impacts on the shipping industry, as numerous oil-carrying tankers suffered casualty in the Persian Gulf. Both Iran and Iraq sought to prevent one another from generating oil export revenue, leading each side to attack merchant ships during a 'Tanker War' episode that escalated to be the most serious threat to commercial shipping since the end of the Second World War.[20] Particularly hard hit by the conflict were Kuwaiti tankers that were repeatedly targeted by Iranian missiles and mines, which led the US to intervene by re-flagging the tankers and escorting them in convoy. War risk insurers reacted to this turmoil by designating high-risk Persian Gulf areas as subject to an additional war risk premium.[21] This Iran–Iraq conflict also resonated in the background as the London marine insurance market completed the task of retiring the SG form to make way for the new MAR form. Under the reforms completed in 1983, war risk in the London market was no longer separated from the main marine policy through the FC&S clause. Instead, both marine and war risks were described by an enumerated perils method using redrafted wordings.[22]

The Iran–Iraq conflict was followed by the rapid dissolution of the Soviet Union and a rather sudden end to the Cold War, which boosted hopes for a new era of peace. But significant regional conflicts continued to transpire during the final years of the century, including the First Gulf War after Iraq invaded Kuwait, and civil wars and conflicts in Haiti, Rwanda, Somalia, and the former Yugoslavia. The international community reacted to these wars through diplomacy, economic sanctions, and multilateral coalitions deploying relatively small forces using new and more precise targeted weaponry – an approach that diverged from the chaotic ideology fuelled proxy fighting of the Cold War. A new form of war risk emerged with major terrorist attacks on Western democracies during the early 2000s, which were swiftly followed by significant cross-border counterterrorism interventions – notably the US-led invasions into Afghanistan and Iraq – which shook the global

[19] Several of these Cold War era conflicts are examined in ch 3.

[20] See generally LA Zatarain, *America's First Clash with Iran: The Tanker War, 1987–88* (Casemate, 2010).

[21] This approach of requiring two war risk premiums developed following the Suez Canal blockages of the mid-twentieth century (discussed in ch 3). This process was later informed by the work of the Lloyd's Market Association Joint War Committee, which engages in risk analysis to determine whether zones should be listed as subject to an additional war risk premium. See Davey, Davey, and Caplin (n 2) ch 3; K Michel, *War, Terror and Carriage by Sea* (Informa, 2004) § 1.08.

[22] Under the new London clauses, marine risks described by the Institute Time Clauses, and the war risks described under the Institute War and Strike Clauses. Among the significant drafting changes was the replacement of the phrase 'hostilities and warlike operations', with 'war' and 'hostile act by or against a belligerent power'. Other principal differences are discussed in Gilman et al (n 6) § 24-11.

security landscape for a time. In contrast to the major wars and war scares of the twentieth century, however, these events had only limited effects on maritime commerce as a whole. Instead, continued global economic integration and a growing sense of multilateralism coalescing against common threats made for a persuasive case that the total war brand of commercial disruption was an outmoded risk that would fade into history.

Attitudes regarding the improbability of wars between major powers gradually began to shift with Russia's intermittent aggression toward former Soviet countries.[23] In 2008, Russia invaded Georgia, and in 2014 it annexed Ukrainian Crimea. Although both were contained regional conflicts that produced relatively subdued international reaction, retrospectively they were warning signs of a larger war on the horizon. When Russia commenced its full-scale war against Ukraine in February 2022, this was the largest ground force invasion on European soil since 1945. Ukraine fought to defend its borders through technology-fuelled tactics, substantially aided by financial support by a coalition of Western allies, including NATO, which even expanded its membership eastward to include Finland and Sweden. Russia meanwhile benefitted from diplomatic support from China, and weapons and soldiers from Iran and North Korea. In phases, the war in Ukraine resembled old world confrontation with blockades, mines, tanks, and trenches, while simultaneously revealing the capacity of cutting-edge tools such as aerial and sea drones. The war was also characterised by saber-rattling from a nuclear power, with Russia invoking bellicose Cold War rhetoric as violence raged along NATO's borders.[24] With Black Sea shipping substantially affected, and many commercial ships damaged or trapped in the warzone, the conflict re-shaped trade patterns, spurred commercial adaptations, and raised political and contractual questions echoing the total wars of the past.[25]

II. War in Commercial Maritime Disputes

A. Chartering and Carriage

i. War Cancellation

Courts and arbitrators have long grappled with the question of how to define 'war' when the term is embedded in commercial documents. Among the leading charterparty cases addressing the issue is *Kawasaki Kisen Kabushiki Kaisha v*

[23] See M Karlin, 'The Return of Total War: Understanding – and Preparing for – a New Era of Comprehensive Conflict' *Foreign Affairs* (22 October 2024).

[24] See G Allison, 'Putin's Doomsday Threat: How to Prevent a Repeat of the Cuban Missile Crisis in Ukraine' *Foreign Affairs* (5 April 2022).

[25] See eg American Institute of Marine Insurers, 'Background Explanation for AIMU's 5 Powers War Exclusion Clause' (31 January 2023).

Bantham Steamship Co Ltd.[26] The parties had agreed to a time charter for a period of 12 months, but performance of the contract was interrupted due to military conflict between China and Japan in 1937. The key question was whether the shipowner properly invoked a charterparty clause granting it the liberty to cancel the contract 'if war breaks out involving Japan'.[27] The shipowner argued that the military conflict justified invoking the clause in September 1937, while the charterer alleged this was wrongful termination. To support its position, the charterer had relied on correspondence with the British Foreign Office, which after being approached to weigh in on the matter, described the military and political situation as 'indeterminate and anomalous', falling short of a state of war.[28] Following arbitration, the umpire held in favour of the shipowner, finding that the conflict had spilled over into a war as used in the ordinary sense of the term. The umpire emphasised the geopolitical background preceding the cancellation during the summer and autumn of 1937: Japan had used aircraft to bomb multiple cities in North and East China; the Japanese navy had established a maritime blockade along the Chinese coastline; tens of thousands of soldiers had engaged in intense fighting leading to catastrophic losses on both sides; and political leaders acknowledged the immense scale of the hostilities, including the Chinese Prime Minister who had, in August 1937, publicly described the conflict as the 'undeclared Sino-Japanese War'.[29]

The charterer appealed the umpire's decision, but it was affirmed by the King's Bench.[30] The English Court of Appeal also agreed.[31] The court explained that the term 'war' in commercial documents should not be confined to 'technical meanings' relayed by 'various writers on international law'.[32] Instead, ascertaining 'the true construction of a private document' should involve weighing the 'general tenor and purpose of the document, in what may be called a common-sense way' that does not 'import into [the] contract some obscure and uncertain technicalities of international law rather than the common sense of business men'.[33] The court further clarified that the interpretation of the commercial term does not depend on whether the nations in the underlying conflict have declared a state of war against one another or whether external governments have formally recognised a state of war between them.[34] Instead, the inquiry must be addressed in a

[26] *Kawasaki Kisen Kabushiki Kaisha v Bantham Steamship Co Ltd* (1939) 63 Ll L Rep 155 (CA) (Sir Wilfrid Greene MR).

[27] ibid.

[28] ibid. However, the British Foreign Office also took the position that the term as used in a charterparty 'may simply be one of interpreting the relevant clause, and that the attitude of His Majesty's Government may not necessarily be conclusive on the question of whether a state of war exists'. ibid.

[29] ibid, 159.

[30] *Kawasaki Kisen Kabushiki Kaisha v Bantham Steamship Co Ltd* (1938) 60 Ll L Rep 70 (KB) (Branson J).

[31] *Kawasaki Kisen Kabushiki Kaisha v Bantham Steamship Co Ltd* (1939) 63 Ll L Rep 155.

[32] ibid, 163.

[33] ibid, 164.

[34] The court also rejected the argument that a judicial determination of war in the commercial sense of the term might embarrass or infringe on the rights of the executive role in government. ibid, 161–62.

holistic fashion considering the realities on the ground. Factors might include, for instance, the ferocity of the fighting, the scope of the human casualties and property damage, the involvement of soldiers on both sides, and statements by political leaders indicating the nature and motivations of the conflict. Using this framework, the court explained, diminished any need to provide a 'technical' definition of war, especially given that conceptions of war may change over time.[35] To illustrate this point, the court reasoned that in 'ancient days' the concept of war might have demanded a declaration of war, which was clearly no longer required. Presciently, the court wrote, 'the recent events in the world have introduced new methods … that writers on international law will dispute for many years to come'.[36]

Two decades later, an American court addressed a differently worded war cancellation clause in *Navios Corp v The Ulyssess II*.[37] The parties had agreed to time charters for three vessels, the *Ulysses II*, the *Elpis*, and the *Loida* under contracts containing the same clause, which provided: 'If war is declared against any present NATO countries … Owners or Charterers have a right to cancel this charter party upon completion of that particular voyage vessel is engaged upon'.[38] On 5 November 1956, the shipowner invoked the clause, alleging that the UK and France were 'engaged in' a war with Egypt following Egypt's nationalisation of the Suez Canal.[39] The charterer contested this view, arguing that that the clause could only be invoked 'in the event of a declaration of war "in the well-known sense of those words in international relations."'[40] Since war had not been formally declared against any of the countries listed, the charterer contended, the cancellation notice should be rendered invalid. The US District Court for the District of Maryland held for the shipowner. First, it found that the clause only permitted cancellation 'if there is a declaration of war against one or more of the named NATO countries'.[41] At the same time, the court determined that the words of the clause must also be read 'as they would be understood by business men engaged in the shipping business in the United States, in light of the purpose which the clause was intended to accomplish'.[42] The critical inquiry was whether the contingency 'if war is declared' had in fact occurred.[43] The court emphasised that there was not 'any real difference between the way the phrase would be interpreted by business men and the way it would be interpreted by most specialists in international law'.[44]

[35] ibid, 163.
[36] ibid, 163.
[37] *Navios Corp v The Ulyssess II*, 161 F Supp 932 (D Maryland 1958) (Thomsen CJ).
[38] ibid. The clause listed the NATO countries at the time as 'Belgium, Canada, Denmark, France, Iceland, Luxembourg, Netherlands, Norway, Portugal, United Kingdom, United States of America, Greece, Italy, and Turkey'.
[39] ibid, 933.
[40] ibid.
[41] ibid, 934.
[42] ibid.
[43] ibid, 940.
[44] ibid, 941.

The court also credited expert testimony of an international law professor who submitted that a 1 November speech by Egyptian President Nasser was a declaration of war. Supporting this view, the court weighed evidence of the constitutional structure of the Egyptian government confirming President Nasser was the head of state, recognised that his speech was distributed to the international press, and scrutinised the precise language of the speech itself. Although the word 'war' was only used one time during the speech, the court determined that President Nasser was speaking to 'comparatively simple people, using language which developed among nomadic tribes and nations, whose history has been very different from that of Britain and France'.[45] Thus, the word choice of 'aggression' and 'attack' were strategic linguistic choices 'better suited to his purpose of arousing the people to fight in a "total war."'[46] Although neither Britain or France 'disclaimed' in political statements 'any intention to make war on Egypt' and the 'war was terminated within a few days' after intervention by the UN, the court explained that '[t]he fact that war did not continue until other nations were drawn in or took formal action to show their neutrality does not prove that war had not been declared within the meaning of the war clause'.[47] Accordingly, the court held that '[w]ar was declared by Egypt against the United Kingdom and France, both in the ordinary sense of those words and in their technical sense in the field of international law'. The US Court of Appeals for the Fourth Circuit affirmed, aligning its decision with the 'reasons stated in the District Court's excellent opinion'.[48]

Determining whether a war cancellation provision has been invoked properly may also entail an assessment of whether hostilities are attributable to the particular nations listed in the clause. This was one of the central issues in the 1951 New York arbitration *Seven Seas Steamship Corp of New York v Prudential Steamship Corp of New York (The Simon Benson)*.[49] In that case, the parties had agreed to a one-year bareboat charter for the *Simon Benson* under a charterparty containing a clause that provided for the termination of the contract 'in case of war involving the United States'.[50] Shortly after the charterparty fixture in the summer of 1950, a major conflict began to unfold on the Korean Peninsula with substantial contributions from the US military under UN auspices.[51] The shipowner invoked the war cancellation clause to terminate the contract and demanded redelivery of the vessel.[52] But the charterer refused on grounds that the conflict in Korea

[45] ibid, 942.
[46] ibid.
[47] ibid, 943.
[48] *Navios Corp v The Ulysses II*, 260 F2d 959 (4th Cir 1958) (per curium: Sobeloff CJ, Soper J, and Haynsworth J).
[49] *Seven Seas Steamship Corp of New York v Prudential Steamship Corp of New York (The Simon Benson)*, 1951 AMC 585 (NY Arb 1951) (John W Crandall).
[50] ibid, 586.
[51] Although the charterparty was agreed on 14 June 1950, prior to the North's invasion of the South on 25 June 1950, the shipowner delivered the ship to the charterer after the fact on 7 July 1950. ibid, 587.
[52] ibid. The shipowner cancelled the charterparty on 16 August 1950.

was an 'episode' rather than a war.[53] In arbitration, two central questions were whether the fighting in Korea had risen to a level of a 'war', and, if so, whether the US was 'involved' in it.[54] Holding in favour of the shipowner, the sole arbitrator answered affirmatively to both questions. The arbitrator explained that immediately after the North's surprise invasion of the South across the 38th parallel dividing the Korean Peninsula on 25 June 1950, the newly formed UN Security Council issued a Resolution demanding the hostilities cease. When there was no response by the North Korean government, the Security Council resolved to send a large coalition of soldiers to support the South. US military officials were selected to lead this coalition, and, within months, tens of thousands of troops had been deployed to fight on behalf of the South. Meanwhile the North received its own support from many thousands of troops from the People's Republic of China. Although the UN coalition was technically a multinational force, most of the soldiers were American. In fact, by 1951, the US had sent nearly 90 per cent of the 160,000 coalition troops fighting in Korea. The arbitrator noted that the casualties to American soldiers during the Korean conflict were higher than many of the other wars previously fought in the nation's history, including the American Revolutionary War against Britain or the Spanish-American War. On the other hand, despite these factors, US President Truman had denied that the US was at war in Korea and instead branded the hostilities as a 'police action' against 'a bunch of bandits'.[55] Likewise, the US Congress never declared a war in Korea. Nonetheless, dismissing this relevance of these 'narrow and legalistic' political viewpoints, the arbitrator rejected the charterer's argument that the war cancellation clause was wrongfully invoked.[56] The arbitrator explained that '[t]he United States has been involved in the Korean War practically from its outset and the fact that it has been fighting as a member of the United Nations and not independently is clearly immaterial'.[57]

A panel of arbitrators reached the opposite conclusion on similar facts in the 1951 New York arbitration *Manning Brothers Inc of Delaware v Albatross Steamship Co Inc (The Yankee Fighter)*.[58] In that case, the parties had agreed to a short-term bareboat charter on 5 June 1950 for the purpose of carrying cargo predominately between the US and Europe. The charterparty contained a clause that allowed for termination 'in case of war involving the U.S.A.'.[59] After the conflict

[53] ibid.
[54] ibid.
[55] ibid, 601.
[56] ibid, 597.
[57] ibid, 593.
[58] The arbitration award was not published in full, but an excerpt is printed in the American Maritime Cases. See *Manning Brothers Inc of Delaware, Owners of Steamship Yankee Fighter v Albatross Steamship Co Inc*, 1951 AMC 579 (NY Arb 1951) (John F Fitzsimmons and Charles P Lambert) (Philip V Everett dissenting). Additional facts surrounding the case are relayed in the judgment of the US District Court for the Southern District of New York addressing preliminary matters. See *Albatross SS Co v Manning Bros Inc*, 95 F Supp 459 (SDNY 1951) (Weinfeld J).
[59] *Albatross SS Co v Manning Bros Inc*, 95 F Supp 459, 461 (SDNY 1951).

in Korea began to unfold and the US became a key contributor in the UN response, on 15 August 1950, the shipowner terminated the charterparty on grounds that 'war has been carried on in Korea since the latter part of June and has involved, and still involves, the U.S.A.'.[60] The charterer contested this view, pointing to statements by President Truman declaring that the actions in Korea were 'merely a "police action" pursuant to the provisions of the United Nations Charter'.[61] The panel majority held for the charterer. It reasoned that although the US had suffered 'many casualties' in the conflict, 'they can be said to have been suffered in a police action or in the suppression of banditing and uprisings without the classification of war'.[62] The panel majority emphasized that this finding was in part justified on the basis that the era of world wars was 'unlike any in past history'.[63] The subsequent emergence of the UN whose 'sole purpose in existence is the preservation of peace' meant that the efforts used to promote this purpose through a 'police force' could not be considered a war because it was 'not for offensive but for peaceful pursuit'.[64] Accordingly, the shipowner was not entitled to cancel the contract or repossess the vessel.

An assessment of state attribution for coalition action in the context of a war cancellation clause was also central in *CMA CGM SA v Beteilgung (The Northern Pioneer)*.[65] In that case, the issue was whether the charterer had properly invoked a clause contained in four time charters, which expressly allowed either the shipowner or the charterer to cancel the charterparties, 'in the event of the nation under whose flag the vessel sails becoming involved in a war'.[66] Each of the vessels under charter was German-flagged. In March 1999 NATO forces performed an aerial bombing operation in Kosovo during the conflict in the former Yugoslavia. As a NATO member, Germany, at least indirectly, participated in the military operation. Referencing these actions – albeit more than a month after the NATO operation in Kosovo began – the charterer invoked the war cancellation clause to terminate the charterparties. The shipowner challenged the cancellation in arbitration on grounds that the charterer had a 'commercial motive' for ending the contracts due to falling container line rates rather than any legitimate basis under the cancellation clause.[67] The arbitrator majority held for the shipowner on grounds that the events in Kosovo were not captured under the cancellation clause because the conflict in Kosovo was not a war and, in any event, Germany was not involved in it. The majority also found that notice of cancellation was

[60] ibid.

[61] ibid.

[62] *Manning Brothers Inc of Delaware, Owners of Steamship Yankee Fighter v Albatross Steamship Co Inc*, 1951 AMC 579 (NY Arb 1951).

[63] ibid.

[64] ibid. The 'Korea trouble', the majority noted, had not given rise to requisitioning of vessels, blockades, or major changes in war risk insurance rates.

[65] *CMA CGM SA v Beteilgung (The Northern Pioneer)* [2003] 1 Lloyd's Rep 212 (CA) (Lord Phillips of Worth Matravers MR).

[66] ibid, 214.

[67] ibid.

not relayed within a reasonable time after Germany's alleged involvement in the NATO operation. In deference to the arbitration panel, the English Commercial Court affirmed, as did the English Court of Appeal. While acknowledging that the 'nature of international conflict has changed over the years', the court emphasised that the arbitrator majority found '[a] businessman applying common-sense in the context [of the clause] would not regard the NATO operation in Kosovo as a war'.[68] Furthermore, the court highlighted that the arbitrator majority's finding that '[m]embers of NATO participating in a NATO operation are not "involved" in the operation as a nation'.[69] Despite these findings, the court acknowledged that the arbitrators were not unanimous, with one dissenting arbitrator noting that the majority, 'should have asked whether a businessman would have said that there was a war in Kosovo in March and April 1999, to which the answer would have been, "yes."'[70] Thus, in the view of the dissenting arbitrator, Germany had been 'involved' in the conflict in Kosovo.[71] Given the split nature of the arbitration award, the court found that this issue was 'at least open to serious doubt'.[72] But since the arbitrator majority found that the charterer was unreasonable in waiting more than a month after the NATO campaign began to invoke the clause, this 'rendered the question academic'.[73]

ii. Requisition and Restraint

Both American and English courts have held that vessel requisition by a sovereign government may excuse performance of a charterparty. Among the leading English cases addressing the issue is *Bank Line Ltd v Arthur Capel & Co.*[74] In the spring of 1915, a vessel called the *Quito*, which was under a one-year time charter, was in dry dock in England preparing to enter service when the British government requisitioned it for use in the First World War, preventing the immediate performance of the time charter. However, shortly after the requisition, the shipowner received an offer from a third party to purchase the vessel. The shipowner sought to be released from the requisition so that it could sell the vessel. The government agreed in exchange for the shipowner providing a different vessel (the *Mansuri*) for requisition. As agreed, the *Quito* was released from the requisition orders in September 1915. After the original charterer learned that the *Quito* had been released from requisition, it sought to enforce the charterparty. The shipowner refused on grounds that the charterparty had been terminated by frustration, and the charterer sued to collect damages. The

[68] ibid, 225.
[69] ibid.
[70] ibid.
[71] ibid.
[72] ibid, 226.
[73] ibid.
[74] *Bank Line Ltd v Arthur Capel & Co* [1919] AC 435 (HL) (Lord Finlay LC).

trial court rejected the claim and agreed with the shipowner that the contract had been frustrated by the requisition. The English Court of Appeal reversed, finding that the charterparty was still in existence during the requisition. But then the majority of the House of Lords reversed again on the grounds that the contract had come to an end once the *Quito* was requisitioned. It reasoned that the charterparty was expected to run for 12 months from the time of delivery in May 1915, but due to the requisition, it was not free until the following September. According to the House of Lords, a charterparty running for 12 months but starting at a much later date than anticipated would have required the shipowner to enter into a contract that was fundamentally different than the one that was agreed, which meant 'the adventure contemplated by the charter is entirely frustrated'.[75]

The American case *Earn Line Steamship Co Ltd v Sutherland Steamship Co Ltd (The Claveresk)* produced a similar result.[76] There, the vessel was approaching the final year of a long-term time charter and performing a voyage carrying coal and ore from the US to Cuba when the British government notified the English shipowner that the *Claveresk* had been requisitioned for use in the First World War. Through its agent, the shipowner wrote to the charterer to express its position that the charterparty had been frustrated. The charterer disagreed and sued for damages alleging the shipowner was not excused on the basis of frustration or under a 'restraint of princes' clause since there was no physical force that prevented performance. The US District Court for the Southern District of New York held for the shipowner.[77] The court reasoned that it was likely that the requisition would last beyond the duration of the charter and – whether framed as frustration or restraint – the shipowner was excused from performance. The US Court of Appeals for the Second Circuit affirmed.[78] On the issue of restraint, the court found that 'apprehension of restraint' could be sufficient to dissolve a contractual obligation, but noted that this was ultimately 'a question of degree'.[79] The court found it was not necessary to use the restraint clause as the basis to excuse performance because the obligations of the charterparty had been 'forever dissolved' at the time of the requisition 'because the commercial adventure was then frustrated'.[80] The court reasoned that the requisition of the vessel removed the shipowner from control of the vessel, which 'swept away the foundation of contract, as thoroughly as might a fire or a shipwreck'.[81] Accordingly, the contract was 'killed' by the requisition and the charterer was

[75] ibid, 508.

[76] *Earn Line Steamship Co Ltd v Sutherland Steamship Co Ltd (The Claveresk)*, 264 F 276 (2nd Cir 1920) (Hough J).

[77] *Earn Line Steamship Co Ltd v Sutherland Steamship Co Ltd (The Claveresk)*, 254 F 126 (SDNY 1918) (L Hand J).

[78] *Earn Line Steamship Co Ltd v Sutherland Steamship Co Ltd (The Claveresk)*, 264 F 276 (1920).

[79] ibid, 281–82.

[80] ibid, 282.

[81] ibid, 283–84.

entitled to no damages, despite the fact that the shipowner continued earning hire by the substitute charter ordered by the British government.[82]

The impact of requisition on shipping contracts has also been addressed outside the context of the World Wars. In *Sedco Inc v SS Strathewee*, an American court examined the commercial consequences of the British requisition of a vessel for use during the Falklands War between the UK and Argentina in 1982.[83] The parties had agreed to move a cargo of oil drilling equipment from the UAE to the US on the *M/V Strathewee*. After the vessel departed Dubai, the British Government requisitioned the vessel under its war powers 'for service in connection with the Falkland Islands Emergency'.[84] Pursuant to the requisition order, the shipmaster was required to proceed to England and to discharge the cargo at a convenient port. The shipmaster arranged to stop in Malta where it unloaded 18 boxes of equipment for transshipment. A few days later, the *Strathewe* was authorised to re-load the cargo and proceed to the US. However, despite the fact that the manifest noted 18 boxes had been re-loaded, by mistake only 16 had been loaded. Two were left in Malta and were not recovered in time for the cargo owner's purposes. The cargo owner brought a claim against the carrier for the full amount of the cargo, which exceeded $182,000. The carrier raised the defence that its liability was subject to the $500 per package limitation in US COGSA § 4(5), or, alternatively, that the loss was excused as caused by a 'restraint of princes' under COGSA § 4(2)(g). The US District Court rejected these arguments and held that the cargo owner could recover the full amount from the carrier because its negligence in losing the packages in Malta was an 'unreasonable deviation'.[85] On appeal, the US Court of Appeals for the Second Circuit reversed in part. The court found that the carrier's post-discharge conduct in Malta, while negligent – and clearly in violation of the COGSA § 3(2) safe stowage obligation – did not amount to a deviation that would void its default statutory limitations of liability of $500 per package. However, the court agreed with the trial court that although the *Strathewe* had been requisitioned, this did not excuse its obligation to safely care for the cargo after it was unloaded in Malta. The court explained that the 'negligent handling of [the] cargo was an intervening event which broke the causal chain between the restraint of the *Strathewe* by the British government and the ultimate injury'.[86]

iii. Avoiding War

The threat of attack in wartime has often caused shipmasters to divert from the intended voyage, resulting in a variety of contract disputes. In *North German Lloyd v Guaranty Trust Co of New York (The Steamship Kronprinzessin Cecilie)*,

[82] ibid, 282.
[83] *Sedco Inc v SS Strathewee*, 800 F2d 27 (2nd Cir 1986) (Miner J).
[84] ibid, 29.
[85] *Sedco Inc v SS Strathewee*, 630 F Supp 120, 122 (SDNY 1986) (Owen J).
[86] *Sedco Inc v SS Strathewee*, 800 F2d 27, 33 (1986).

the vessel was scheduled to sail from the US to England to deliver 93 kegs of gold bullion and then proceed to Germany.[87] This was in the summer of 1914 leading up to the First World War. At the time of departure, the shipmaster had been warned of an imminent 'European crisis' flowing from the recent assassination of Archduke Francis Ferdinand in Sarajevo, the Austrian declaration of war on Serbia, and the diplomatic troubles brewing between other major European powers.[88] The *Kronprinzessin Cecilie* sailed from New York, but when the vessel was less than 1,000 miles from arriving in England, the shipmaster received a wireless message that 'war had broken out, involving Germany and Russia, France, and England'.[89] In fact, at the time the message was received there had not yet been a declaration of war between these countries (although war was declared a few days after). Nevertheless, in anticipation of the war risk the vessel would face on arrival in Europe, the shipmaster diverted from the voyage, returned to the US, and arranged for re-delivery of the gold to the cargo owner. The cargo owner brought suit against the shipowner on grounds that failure to deliver the gold was a breach of the contract of carriage which resulted in the cargo owner suffering substantial economic loss. The shipowner claimed the shipmaster's decision was justified under the circumstances and also referenced a clause in the bill of lading, which purported to relieve the shipowner of liability for loss 'occasioned by arrest and restraint of princes, rulers, or people'.[90]

The US District Court for the District of Massachusetts held for the shipowner on grounds that the shipmaster was aware of the evolving war risks taking place in Europe during the voyage, and that Germany 'was upon the very edge of war with Russia, France, and England'.[91] Once the shipmaster received the message that war had broken out, he acted with 'reasonable apprehension of imminent peril' by prudently deviating from the intended route and turning back to the US.[92] The US Court of Appeals for the First Circuit reversed.[93] It held that under the language of the bill of lading it was not enough for the shipmaster to have apprehension of capture or detention in order to excuse non-performance of the contract. Instead, the court reasoned, there must be an 'actual and operative restraint, and that no merely expected and contingent restraint affords sufficient excuse'.[94] But the US Supreme Court reversed again, finding that the shipmaster's decision to turn back due to war risks was entirely justified. The court explained that once the Austrian

[87] *North German Lloyd v Guaranty Trust Co of New York (The Steamship Kronprinzessin Cecilie)*, 37 S Ct 490 (USSC 1917) (Holmes J). The vessel also carried nearly 2,000 people of many nationalities.

[88] *North German Lloyd v Guaranty Trust Co of New York (The Steamship Kronprinzessin Cecilie)*, 228 F 946 (1916) (D Massachusetts) (Hale J).

[89] ibid, 948.

[90] ibid.

[91] ibid, 956.

[92] ibid, 963.

[93] *North German Lloyd v Guaranty Trust Co of New York (The Steamship Kronprinzessin Cecilie)*, 238 F 668 (1st Cir 1916) (Dodge J).

[94] ibid, 675.

government declared war on Serbia, 'the great danger of a general war was known to all'.[95] The outbreak of war in Europe, the court reasoned, not only gave rise to the risk of damage but also the risk of seizure by prize and detention of the passengers. The court found that it was immaterial that the shipmaster turned back just before the First World War formally broke out because he would have been obliged to do so once it did. The court explained, '[i]f he would have been required to turn back before delivering [the cargo], it hardly could change his liability that he prophetically and rightly had anticipated the absolute requirement by twenty-four hours'.[96] For this reason, the court found the shipmaster 'acted as a prudent man' by turning back after anticipating the outbreak of war.[97]

The threat of Japanese submarine attacks on merchant ships during the Second World War gave rise to analogous problems. In *Pope & Talbot Inc v Blanchard Lumber Co of Seattle*, a carrier had agreed to move a cargo of lumber from the US West Coast (St Helens, Oregon) to the US East Coast (Philadelphia, Pennsylvania) on board the *Absaroka*.[98] Just before the commencement of the voyage, on 7 December 1941, the Japanese attacked Pearl Harbor. Despite the US being drawn into the war, less than a week later the carrier issued a bill of lading and commenced the voyage, even as there was 'speculation' over Japan's intention to engage in 'submarine warfare' along the US Pacific coast.[99] As the *Absaroka* sailed south it was ordered by US Navy officials to come into San Francisco Bay due to 'a rumor of the presence of a submarine on the coast'.[100] The shipmaster complied, but the next day the *Absaroka* resumed the voyage. When it was five miles out from Los Angeles, it was hit by a Japanese torpedo, which tore a large hole in the side of the ship. The US Coast Guard arranged to tow the *Absaroka* to a beach off Los Angeles, and the ship would have sunk if it were not for the submerged cargo of lumber, which gave the vessel buoyancy. Some of the cargo was lost, and some of it was damaged. The vessel itself needed significant repairs. After a damage survey, a repair contract was negotiated. Seven weeks after the attack, while the vessel was waiting to be repaired, the carrier gave the cargo owner notice of abandonment of the voyage to Philadelphia, which the cargo owner challenged.

The US District Court for the Northern District of California held for the cargo owner on grounds that the carrier's decision was made on the basis of the repair delays, which it found was not a justifiable reason to cancel the contract given that the cargo owner was willing to accept delayed performance.[101] The US Court of Appeals for the Ninth Circuit reversed. First, it highlighted that the delay would be likely to last several months since the attack on Pearl Harbor and that

[95] *North German Lloyd v Guaranty Trust Co of New York (The Steamship Kronprinzessin Cecilie)*, 37 S Ct 490, 491 (1917).
[96] ibid, 492.
[97] ibid.
[98] *Pope & Talbot Inc v Blanchard Lumber Co of Seattle*, 159 F2d 134 (9th Cir 1947) (Denman J).
[99] ibid, 135.
[100] ibid.
[101] The district court's decision in this case is unpublished.

the German and Japanese submarine warfare taking place on both coasts would cause shipyards to be 'crowded beyond their capacity and that priorities would be given by the government to those vessels most needed for a two ocean war'.[102] This long delay, according to the court, was not within the contemplation of the parties when the bill of lading was issued. In addition, although the bill of lading required the carrier to perform 'with such reasonable dispatch as the general business of the carrier permits', the carrier had a simultaneous obligation to protect the cargo along with the 'bodies and lives of the crew'.[103] And critically, although Pearl Harbor had been attacked prior to the bill of lading being issued, 'there was then no certainty that Japanese submarines would operate on the American Pacific Coast, 7,000 miles from their nearest bases'.[104] The attack on the *Absaroka* was the first of such actions, and was therefore a 'new factor in the problem of the voyage's accomplishment'.[105] Moreover, given that even the surviving lumber had been wet with sea water and soaked with oil from the vessel's damaged fuel tanks, it was 'impracticable to proceed' on the voyage with the cargo in such a condition even after the vessel was repaired.[106] A dissenting judge agreed with the trial court, relaying the additional point that the carrier not only knew of the risks to Japanese attack following the recent events in Pearl Harbor, but also the risks of German attack once the vessel reached the Atlantic, which was 'infested with submarines'.[107] Thus, the dissent contended, the carrier was 'hardly in a position to abandon the voyage because, as it turned out, a like menace existed in the Pacific'.[108]

The Second World War generated other disputes involving the implications of diversion measures affecting the cargo, including *Lekas & Drivas Inc v Basil Goulandris*.[109] That case involved disruption to the voyage of the *SS Ioannis*, which was under contract to carry perishable cargo of tobacco, olive oil, and soft cheese loaded in the Turkey and Greece to the US by way of the Strait of Gibraltar and North Atlantic. Although the voyage was to be performed during the Second World War in the Fall of 1940, it was expected to take less than a month. But two days after the vessel docked at Piraeus, Italy attacked Greece. Greek authorities requisitioned the *Ioannis* for a short mission and then released it, but because transit through the Mediterranean had become impracticable due to the outbreak of war, the vessel was directed by the Greek government to proceed to its intended destination by way of the Suez Canal and around the Cape of Good Hope. After delays at Port Said, the *Ioannis* proceeded and moved in convoy through the Suez Canal under the instructions of the British Admiralty, but eventually the vessel

[102] ibid, 136.
[103] ibid, 137.
[104] ibid.
[105] ibid.
[106] ibid, 138.
[107] ibid, 139.
[108] ibid.
[109] *Lekas & Drivas Inc v Basil Goulandris*, 306 F2d 426 (2nd Cir 1962) (Friendly J).

experienced mechanical problems that required repairs once the vessel reached Aden at the south end of the Red Sea. These repairs lasted 35 days due to a backlog caused by the war. During the repairs, much of the cargo had to be offloaded and stored on lighter vessels because there were no warehouses in Aden. During that time, the cheese was covered with tarps, but by the time the cheese was loaded back on the vessel, it showed signs of spoilage. Nevertheless, the spoiling cheese and other cargo was loaded back on the vessel, which proceeded to the US, with further stops in South Africa for bunkers and in Barbados for repairs before finally arriving in the US in May 1941. Ultimately, the voyage took approximately six months. Due to the longer voyage and hot equatorial weather via the Suez-Cape route, the cheese was '[m]elted with a terrible stench, and worthless'.[110]

The cargo owner made a claim against the carrier under the US COGSA on grounds that the damage to the cheese was caused by improper stowage, which, it alleged, violated the carrier's obligations under § 3(2) of the statute.[111] The carrier argued that the cheese was properly stowed for the intended voyage via the Gibraltar and North Atlantic route where air temperatures would not have exceeded 65 degrees Fahrenheit, and that, in any event, the cargo loss was actually caused by the 'restraint of princes' excepted peril under COGSA § 4(2)(g). The District Court for the Southern District of New York held for the cargo owner, finding that the carrier did not establish that it acted with due care in storing the cheese.[112] But the US Court of Appeals for the Second Circuit reversed. It found that the carrier had demonstrated a 'double restraint' under COGSA § 4(2)(g) by the threat of attack if it proceeded through the Mediterranean route and the subsequent Greek order to proceed via the Suez Canal.[113] The court emphasised that the restraint, 'altered the voyage from a four week trip of 5,000 miles through the Mediterranean and North Atlantic, in cool November weather, to a trip of 13,000 miles and five months around Africa, with two crossings of the Equator'.[114] Since the outside temperature would repeatedly rise above 100 degrees Fahrenheit, the cheese would have been subject to conditions susceptible to spoilage unless refrigerated. Although the cargo owner could have potentially demonstrated a secondary cause of improper stowage on the lighter vessels in Aden or the inaction in mitigating the loss by selling it before spoilage, it did not carry its burden of proof under the statute.

iv. Contraband Control

The risks associated with contraband control in wartime have caused further commercial problems. In *Steamship Styria v James L Morgan*, the parties had

[110] ibid, 428.
[111] ibid, 432.
[112] *Lekas & Drivas Inc v Basil Goulandris*, 173 F Supp 140, 179 (SDNY 1959) (Ryan J).
[113] *Lekas & Drivas Inc v Basil Goulandris*, 306 F2d 426, 430 (2nd Cir 1962).
[114] ibid.

contracted to move a cargo of sulphur from Italy to the US, and in April of 1898 the *Styria* loaded the cargo in Trieste and Sicily, issuing bills of lading covering the intended voyage.[115] But just before the vessel departed, the shipmaster received information from the vessel's managing agents that the Spanish-American war had broken out. As a consequence, Spain issued a decree authorising its Royal Navy to capture enemy ships and to confiscate contraband of war, which included 'powder, sulphur, saltpeter, dynamite, and every kind of explosive'.[116] Because of the *Styria*'s location in the Mediterranean, the shipmaster was aware that the route past Gibraltar would take the vessel close to the Spanish coast where Spanish warships were rumoured to be looking for ships carrying contraband, including sulphur. To avoid the risk of capture, the shipmaster returned the sulphur to Sicily despite protests from the cargo owners. Multiple cargo interests brought claims against the shipowner, alleging breach of the contract of carriage and conversion of the cargo, which the shipowner defended on grounds the bill of lading expressly contemplated the possibility of war and granted the shipmaster the liberty to react with prudence in protecting the ship and the cargo.

The US District Court for the Southern District of New York held for the cargo interests, reasoning that the shipmaster's decision to discharge the sulphur in Sicily was 'too hasty and precipitate' because shortly after the contraband restrictions were announced, at the behest of the Italian government which relied upon sulphur exports out of Sicily, the Spanish government gave assurances to the trading community that sulphur was an exception.[117] The US Court of Appeals for the Second Circuit reversed on grounds that the likelihood of blockade or contraband control performed by Spanish authorities in the Strait of Gibraltar was a 'restraint of princes' under the express terms of the bill of lading.[118] The court emphasised that it made 'no logical difference' whether the restraint was performed just off Sicily or in the Strait of Gibraltar, and that, in any event, it would be unreasonable for the shipmaster to sail carrying restricted sulphur under these circumstances.[119] The US Supreme Court affirmed.[120] It also found that although there were Italian news reports that Spain and Italy had agreed to a sulphur exception to the contraband control, this reporting could not be relied upon since the Italians had a strong economic interest in continuing the export of sulphur and 'to give the impression that it could be done with security to the carrying vessels'.[121] Accordingly, since the shipmaster had a duty to care for the vessel and its cargo, the decision to land and store the cargo was entirely justified once it became contraband subject to Spanish seizure.

[115] *Steamship Styria v James L Morgan*, 186 US 1 (USSC 1902) (Shiras J).
[116] ibid, 3.
[117] *Steamship Styria v James L Morgan*, 93 F 474, 478 (SDNY 1899) (Brown J).
[118] *Steamship Styria v James L Morgan*, 101 F 728 (2nd Cir 1900) (Lacombe J).
[119] ibid, 731.
[120] *Steamship Styria v James L Morgan*, 186 US 1 (1902).
[121] ibid, 21.

Another important American contraband control case is *Amtorg Trading Corp v The Wildwood*.[122] There, a cargo owner made a claim against a carrier for failing to carry machinery, brass, steel, and copper from the US East Coast through the Panama Canal and across the Pacific to Vladivostok, Soviet Union. The vessel, the *Wildwood*, was loaded in February 1940 and the carrier issued bills of lading governing the carriage before commencing the voyage. When the *Wildwood* approached Hawaii, the parties mutually agreed to divert the vessel north to first stop at Petropavlovsk to avoid congestion at Vladivostok with plans to return later to Vladivostok to discharge the balance of the cargo. But several days later, the shipowner wrote to the cargo owner notifying it of the decision to return the *Wildwood* to the US West Coast after international newspaper articles reported that multiple neutral ships bound for Vladivostok had been interrupted by British forces as a means of contraband control to prevent war materials from being transshipped to Germany via the Soviet Union.[123] To contractually justify this decision, the shipowner referenced a clause in the bills of lading, which granted the shipmaster the liberty to divert from the intended voyage where 'in the judgment of the carrier or master' there is a likelihood of 'capture, seizure, detention, damage, delay or disadvantage to or loss of the ship or any part of her cargo, or to make it unsafe, imprudent, or unlawful for any reason to proceed on or continue the voyage'.[124] Taking the view that it would be dangerous to proceed to any Soviet port with a cargo of high value metals that could give grounds for seizure or delay by the British, the shipmaster diverted the voyage to Seattle.[125]

The cargo owner sued the carrier in the US District Court for the Western District of Washington, which, holding in its favour, reasoned that the parties had already contemplated war risks during both the initial booking and the diversion modification to Petropavlovsk.[126] According to the court, the carrier had a duty to deliver the cargo, 'unless there was a change in the "World War" conditions, which increased the hazard to the *Wildwood* to a degree which would have deterred a reasonably prudent sailor from proceeding'.[127] Since such a change in risks had not occurred, the court found the carrier could not discharge its obligations. The US Court of Appeals for the Ninth Circuit disagreed. First, it highlighted that the bill of lading clause at issue granted the shipmaster substantial discretion to react to the likelihood of war risks.[128] Then, the court emphasised that although the British had previously engaged in 'isolated' seizures, the contraband control by the British had intensified even during *Wildwood*'s voyage as evidenced by the seizure of some neutral copper-carrying vessels bound for Soviet ports in the Pacific. The court explained these recent seizures were made, 'for contraband detention, irrespective

[122] *Amtorg Trading Corp v The Wildwood*, 133 F2d 765 (9th Cir 1943) (Denman J).
[123] ibid, 766. This was before Germany declared war on the Soviet Union.
[124] ibid, 767.
[125] ibid.
[126] *Amtorg Trading Corp v The Wildwood*, 41 F Supp 956 (WD Washington 1941) (Neterer J).
[127] ibid, 966.
[128] *Amtorg Trading Corp v The Wildwood*, 133 F2d 765 (1943).

of the prior or present ownership of the cargo, or the nature of its consignees, merely because there was war material on board, which was going into Russia, and might, thereafter, as it was feared, be made available to Germany'.[129] According to the court, it was 'immaterial' whether the threats amounted to a technical blockade or merely contraband control because, 'in any case, the danger of seizure and indefinitely prolonged detention was the same'.[130] The British policy created a 'reasonable apprehension of real danger of the seizure of the Wildwood', which was a 'far greater war hazard' than that existing when the bills of lading were issued.[131] As a result, the carrier was justified under the terms of the bills of lading to turn back to the US.

v. Blocking and Trapping

Decades later, the Iran–Iraq War led to a series of cases addressing the charterparty consequences of vessels trapped in the Shatt-al-Arab – the commercially significant river at the confluence of the Euphrates and Tigres that divides the two countries and links access to the Persian Gulf. In September 1980, Iran abrogated the treaty that granted Iraq shared commercial access over the river, and Iraq responded by declaring its own sovereignty over the waterway. These territorial claims quickly tumbled into hostilities, which caused dozens of commercial ships to be trapped in the Shatt-al-Arab. Initially, international stakeholders, including the UN and the International Red Cross, discussed the prospect of a ceasefire to allow the release of merchant vessels trapped in the river, but these efforts were unsuccessful. As the war escalated, some vessels suffered physical damage and it became too dangerous for the vessels to leave the area. Several charterparty cases from the era addressed the commercial fallout from these events, including *Kodros Shipping Corp v Empresa Cubana di Fletes (The Evia)*.[132] While the *Evia* was under a time charter, in March 1980, the charterer gave orders to move cement and other building materials from Cuba to Basrah, Iraq, which is situated along the Shatt-al-Arab.[133] Due to congestion in the port, the *Evia* was not allowed to berth for several months and discharge was completed on 22 September. Due to the sudden outbreak of war, however, the *Evia* became trapped and most of the crew was evacuated. The shipowner sought to collect hire for the remainder of the contract period, but the charterer refused on grounds that the charterparty had become frustrated on 22 September. In arbitration, an umpire appointed by a split arbitration panel found that Basrah was a 'safe port' under the charterparty at the time the *Evia* was ordered there and that it did not become dangerous

[129] ibid, 769.
[130] ibid, 771.
[131] ibid.
[132] *Kodros Shipping Corp v Empresa Cubana di Fletes (The Evia)* [1982] 2 Lloyd's Rep 307 (HL) (Lord Diplock, Lord Elwyn-Jones, Lord Keith of Kinkel, Lord Roskill, Lord Brandon of Oakbrook).
[133] Basrah is approximately 70 miles upriver from the Persian Gulf.

until 22 September. However, the umpire found that the charterparty had been frustrated on 4 October when it became clear that the conflict was not going to resolve quickly.

The English Commercial Court reversed the umpire's decision, finding that when the charterer ordered the vessel to proceed to Basrah, this triggered the safe port warranty that applied throughout the time the vessel remained there, including when the port became unsafe due to the war. This, the court explained, precluded the charterer from relying on the doctrine of frustration to end the contract because the frustration was effectively 'self-induced'.[134] But the English Court of Appeal reversed again, holding this was an improper way to view the safe port warranty and that the outbreak of war along the Shatt-al-Arab was an 'abnormal or extraneous occurrence' that warranted the umpire's finding of frustration.[135] The House of Lords agreed.[136] It reasoned that the safe port exception for an 'abnormal occurrence' such as a sudden outbreak of war was a well-settled principle.[137] The decision emphasised that when a charterer makes a contractual promise that it is ordering a vessel to a safe port, this means that the ship is 'prospectively safe for the ship to get to, stay at, so far as necessary, and in due course, leave'.[138] However, when 'some unexpected and abnormal event' occurs to suddenly create unsafe conditions that did not previously exist when the vessel was ordered to the port, it would be improper to place liability on the charterer as this would 'make the charterer the insurer of such unexpected and abnormal risks' that should fall on the marine insurers.[139] Since Basrah was 'prospectively safe' at the time the port was nominated by the charterer, the unsafe condition that later arose did not breach the safe port warranty. As a consequence, the safe port warranty did not bar the umpire's finding that the contract had become frustrated due to the outbreak of war.[140]

vi. Physically Unsafe Ports

Several other English cases arising during the Iran–Iraq War addressed the implications for safe port provisions embedded in charterparties. Among them is *Motor Oil Hellas (Corinth) Refineries SA v Shipping Corp of India (The Kanchenjunga)*.[141] The parties had agreed to four consecutive voyage charters to move oil from export

[134] *Kodros Shipping Corp v Empresa Cubana di Fletes (The Evia)* [1981] 2 Lloyd's Rep 613, 621 (Comm) (Robert Goff J).
[135] *Kodros Shipping Corp v Empresa Cubana di Fletes (The Evia)* [1982] 1 Lloyd's Rep 334, 338 (CA) (Lord Denning MR and Sebag Shaw LJ) (Ackner LJ dissenting).
[136] *Kodros Shipping Corp v Empresa Cubana di Fletes (The Evia)* [1982] 2 Lloyd's Rep 307 (HL).
[137] ibid, 310.
[138] ibid, 315 (Lord Roskill).
[139] ibid.
[140] ibid, 319.
[141] *Motor Oil Hellas (Corinth) Refineries SA v Shipping Corp of India (The Kanchenjunga)* [1990] 1 Lloyd's Rep 391 (Lord Goff of Chieveley).

terminals in the Persian Gulf to a discretionary range of destinations on the oil tanker *Kanchenjunga*. The contract specifically excluded trading in Iran and Iraq, but allowed for trading at several Persian Gulf islands, including Kharg Island, Iran. The area had been a recent target of Iraqi air strikes on storage tanks, and vessels loading at the oil installations at Kharg Island had engaged in 'black-out' procedures intended to limit exposure to attack. Despite the obvious risks, in November of 1980, the charterer ordered the vessel to load a cargo of crude at Kharg Island. The vessel arrived in the vicinity and was awaiting a berth on 1 December when Iraqi aircraft began heavy bombing in the area. The shipmaster quickly pulled anchor and departed. The shipowner then requested the charterer to nominate an alternative port, but the charterer refused and instead requested the vessel return to Kharg Island despite the bombing that had just occurred. The shipowner requested that the shipmaster comply with the charterer's orders, but the shipmaster declined due to safety concerns. In arbitration, the shipowner claimed damages for the charterer's refusal to nominate an alternative port and the charterer claimed the shipowner was in breach for failing to follow its orders after issuing a notice of readiness to load at Kharg Island. The charterer argued the shipowner waived any right to treat Kharg Island as an unsafe port by agreeing to proceed there initially, whereas the shipowner claimed it was entitled to rely on a War Risk Clause, which granted it the discretion to reject orders to 'dangerous or prohibited' ports.[142]

The arbitral tribunal found that Kharg Island was a prospectively unsafe port even before the 1 December bombing and that the shipowner had not waived the right to reject the orders there. The English Commercial Court reversed, in part, on grounds that the shipowner had accepted the orders to load at Kharg Island when it issued a notice of readiness to load with a clear understanding of the risks, but it found that the shipowner was protected from liability under the war risk clause.[143] Both the English Court of Appeal and the House of Lords affirmed.[144] The House of Lords reasoned that when the shipowner agreed to proceed to the prospectively unsafe port, it had elected to waive the right to reject the nomination because the port had not become more dangerous after the 1 December bombing than it already was at the time of the original orders. Although the shipmaster was at liberty to refuse to go back to an unsafe port in Kharg Island, this 'did not excuse the owners from their breach of contract'.[145] At the same time, however, the shipowner's election to waive the right to reject the charterer's orders did not alter the application of the war risk clause to 'protect the owners from liability in damages'.[146] This was because the War Risk Clause explicitly referred to the

[142] *Motor Oil Hellas (Corinth) Refineries SA v Shipping Corp of India (The Kanchenjunga)* [1987] 2 Lloyd's Rep 509, 518 (Comm) (Hobhouse LJ).
[143] ibid.
[144] *Motor Oil Hellas (Corinth) Refineries SA v Shipping Corp of India (The Kanchenjunga)* [1989] 1 Lloyd's Rep 354 (Lloyd LJ) (CA); [1990] 1 Lloyd's Rep 391 (HL) (Lord Goff of Chieveley).
[145] *Motor Oil Hellas (Corinth) Refineries SA v Shipping Corp of India (The Kanchenjunga)* [1990] 1 Lloyd's Rep 391, 400.
[146] ibid, 401.

'discretion which the owners and master are entitled to exercise in a situation of danger', which, by implication, meant that 'in the exercise of that discretion [the shipowner] may decline to load or discharge at the relevant port' without incurring liability.[147]

Following Iraq's bombing of Iran's oil export facilities, the Iran–Iraq War spiralled into a Tanker War episode as Iran commenced attacking merchant vessels using terminals in Saudi Arabia and Kuwait – both of which were viewed as Iraqi allies. Many of the attacks were performed in a narrow channel considered an 'Advisory Zone' in the middle of the Persian Gulf. Among the vessels attacked was the *Chemical Venture*, which was the time-chartered vessel at issue in *Pearl Carriers Inc v Japan Line Ltd*.[148] In the spring of 1984, the *Chemical Venture* was ordered on a voyage to load gas oil at Mina Al Ahmadi, Kuwait. While en route in the Persian Gulf navigating along the coasts of Saudi Arabia, it was damaged by a missile fired from an Iranian jet, which injured crew members and seriously damaged the vessel. The shipowner brought a claim against the charterer alleging breach of a safe port warranty clause, which required the charterer to 'exercise due diligence to ensure that the vessel is only employed between and at safe ports'.[149] The charterer resisted liability on grounds that the risks of Iranian attack were unexpected and therefore did not fall within the scope of the safe port warranty, or, alternatively, that the shipowner effectively waived the right to pursue a claim under the safe port warranty when it agreed to the charterer's orders to load cargo in the Persian Gulf in the midst of a major war. The English Commercial Court held in favour of the shipowner. It found that the charterer failed to exercise the due diligence required under the safe port warranty when it nominated Kuwait as the loading port. The court supported this holding by referencing earlier attacks on other commercial vessels in the Persian Gulf during the war and also publicly available information leading up to the attacks, including a broadcast by a prominent Iranian politician on the country's national radio service warning that 'Iran cannot allow the export of oil by other countries if Iran's exports of oil have been prevented by Iraq'.[150] Due to these threats and the reality that several tankers had already been attacked by Iranian aircraft in the days leading up to the bombing of the *Chemical Venture*, the court found that the attack could not be viewed as 'an abnormal and unexpected event'.[151] Instead, the risk of an attack was 'a normal characteristic of the approach voyage of any tanker bound for Mina Al Ahmadi', especially given the risk of 'mistaken identity or carelessness on the part of a jet pilot' performing bombings on vessels in the region.[152] Since the voyage to Kuwait required passing through the narrow and unsafe Advisory Zone, this was enough

[147] ibid.
[148] *Pearl Carriers Inc v Japan Line Ltd (The Chemical Venture)* [1993] 1 Lloyd's Rep 508 (Comm) (Gatehouse J).
[149] ibid, 509.
[150] ibid, 511.
[151] ibid, 518.
[152] ibid.

to establish a causal link between the breach of the safe port warranty and the damage to the vessel.[153] Nevertheless, since the shipowner did not refuse or expressly state that Kuwait was an unsafe port prior to the attack (and even offered war risk bonuses to the crew to perform the voyage), the court found that the shipowner had waived its right to contend the charterer was in breach of the safe port warranty.

Explicit geographic trading authorisations and limitations have also been found relevant in identifying whether a shipowner can reject a charterer's orders into war zones. This scenario was central to the SMA arbitration *Imbar Maritima SA v Palm Shipping Inc.*[154] In 1985, the parties had entered into a three-year time charter for the tanker *Jerom*. The contract contained war clauses that provided the vessel 'shall not be required, without the consent of the Owner, which shall not be unreasonably withheld, to enter any port or zone which is involved in a state of war, warlike operations or hostilities'.[155] The contract further provided that it 'shall be unreasonable to withhold consent to any voyage, route, or port of loading or discharge if insurance … is then available commercially'.[156] In January 1987, the charterer sub-chartered the vessel for a voyage from the Persian Gulf port of Ras Tanura, Saudi Arabia, to New Zealand, but the shipowner refused consent to enter the Persian Gulf on grounds that it was too dangerous. The charterer was forced to cancel the sub-charter. It then made a claim in arbitration against the shipowner for damages, alleging the refusal to grant consent to trade in the Persian Gulf was a breach of the charterparty, especially given that the vessel had performed multiple Persian Gulf trades during the duration of the charter and that commercial war risk insurance was readily available. The shipowner countered that it had a 'humanitarian concern' for its crew, which justified the refusal to follow the charterer's orders on 'both contractual and circumstantial grounds' and that the previous Persian Gulf voyages had been performed in 1986 before the 'escalation of attacks on non-aligned shipping' began in earnest, with the proliferation of more sophisticated weaponry presenting 'unforeseeable extreme conditions and extraordinary occurrences'.[157] The SMA panel held for the charterer. It reasoned that measuring whether the permission is 'unreasonably withheld' was defined by the contract as contingent upon whether insurance could be procured.[158] Since it was 'well known in the industry that commercial insurance against [Persian Gulf] war risks throughout the tanker war was indeed available', the panel explained, it was unreasonable for the shipowner to reject the orders.[159] The panel was also unpersuaded by the

[153] ibid, 520.
[154] *Imbar Maritima SA v Palm Shipping Inc (M/T Jerom)*, SMA 2790 (NY Arb 1991) (Hans A Proeller, Manfred W Arnold, and Lloyd C Nelson).
[155] ibid.
[156] ibid, 3.
[157] ibid, 5.
[158] ibid.
[159] ibid, 6.

shipowner's argument that the escalation of the war amounted to an unforeseeable event that permitted a 'unilateral and fundamental change of a contract' that had been agreed in 1985.[160] The panel reasoned, '[a]t that time, the tanker war had been a sad fact of tanker life for some two or three years' in which many tanker owners had acted to limit Persian Gulf exposure through explicit contract clauses.[161] Since the shipowner in this case did not negotiate such terms, it was therefore bound to follow the charterer's employment orders.

Occurring in the final years and geographic periphery of the Iran–Iraq War, another safe port warranty question was at issue in *Abu Dhabi National Tanker Co v Product Star Shipping Ltd (The Product Star)*.[162] In that case, the parties had agreed to a six-month time charter of the tanker *Product Star*, which was delivered to the charterer at Fujairah, UAE, in April 1987. The charterparty contained two War Risk Clauses, including a provision that required the charterer to pay an additional war risk premium for trading in areas near the warzone, including certain UAE ports. A second War Risk Clause stated that if 'owing to' war risks, entry to a port of loading or discharge is 'considered by the Master or Owners in his or their discretion dangerous' then the charterer had the right to nominate a new port that was not dangerous.[163] The purpose of the charter, which was known to the shipowner at the time of contracting, was for the charterer to move petroleum products on a series of voyages from the UAE to Bangladesh. During the first three months of 1987, there had been some casualties to merchant ships in the Persian Gulf, some of which were attacked in the southern area of the Persian Gulf below Qatar. Attacks had been performed by Iraqi forces, as well as the Iranian Navy 'following stop-and-search operations in which they sought to identify ships hostile to their cause', including vessels with Kuwaiti or Saudi Arabian connections.[164] Apparently, no ships trading only to the UAE had been targeted. After four successful voyages between the UAE and Bangladesh, in September 1987, the charterer ordered the *Product Star* to load at Ruwais, UAE (on the northwest side of the UAE in the Persian Gulf). The shipowner wrote back via telex: 'due to the most recent development in waters adjacent to Ruwais … Owner and Master consider the entry there to be dangerous'.[165] It then requested the charterer to 'nominate another load port, which would not place the vessel in a dangerous situation'.[166] The charterer refused and repeated the instructions to proceed to Ruwais, which the shipowner rejected. The parties then claimed and cross-claimed for repudiation of the contract.

[160] ibid.
[161] ibid, 7.
[162] *Abu Dhabi National Tanker Co v Product Star Shipping Ltd (The Product Star)* [1993] 1 Lloyd's Rep 397 (CA) (Leggatt LJ).
[163] ibid, 400.
[164] ibid.
[165] ibid, 401.
[166] ibid.

The English Commercial Court held for the charterer.[167] The court explained that the clauses at issue required the shipowner to demonstrate both a subjective bona fide belief that going to Ruwais would be dangerous as well as an objective degree of danger that would cause a reasonable shipowner to believe the same. The court found this standard was not met. As for the subjective component of the inquiry, the shipowner's corporate directors had testified of the concern that the *Product Star* would strike a mine or be attacked by Iranians, but the court found the evidence provided to support this view was 'exaggerated, ill-informed or unconvincing'.[168] Addressing the objective side, the court found that although there had been a number of attacks on merchant ships in the region, it was unreasonable to find the area dangerous as there had not been any attacks on vessels trading only in the UAE. The English Court of Appeal agreed.[169] Rejecting the shipowner's argument that the charterparty's discretionary language was 'purely subjective', the court found the discretion, 'must not be exercised arbitrarily, capriciously or unreasonably'.[170] The court determined that the shipowner had not met this burden because the shipowner was aware of the intended trade pattern of the *Product Star* at the time of contracting when the region was already under threat by a spate of attacks on merchant ships. The fact that measuring the extent of the risks under the charterparty 'might be difficult to perceive, define or prove' simply revealed the task of invoking its terms.[171] The court also emphasised the shipowner's apparent failure in appraising the relevant risks before rejecting the charterer's orders, which included the refusal to consult the shipmaster for an opinion on the matter, the short notice before the rejection, and the fact that other vessels managed by same directors continued trading in the region without protest. The court found these facts called into question the shipowner's good faith and 'strongly suggest[ed] that their refusal was arbitrary'.[172] Further demonstrating the weak evidence provided by the shipowner, the court noted that one of the testifying directors for the shipowner was 'almost entirely ignorant of the previous history of hostilities in the Gulf and of the geography of the region', which showed that he had 'failed to acquaint himself with information about whether or not vessels trading to ports in the UAE were subject to attack'.[173] This failure to show a 'real and substantial increase in the risks' caused the shipowner's withdrawal of the vessel to 'wear a capricious air'.[174]

[167] *Abu Dhabi National Tanker Co v Product Star Shipping Ltd (The Product Star)* [1991] 2 Lloyd's Rep 468 (Comm) (Diamond J).

[168] ibid, 476.

[169] *Abu Dhabi National Tanker Co v Product Star Shipping Ltd (The Product Star)* [1993] 1 Lloyd's Rep 397.

[170] ibid, 404.

[171] ibid, 405.

[172] ibid.

[173] ibid.

[174] ibid.

B. Marine Insurance

i. Hostilities and Warlike Operations

During the two World Wars, the FC&S clause used in both the British and American marine insurance markets gave rise to many cases addressing whether losses should be placed within war risk cover or marine cover. These cases fall into two general categories: the first type addresses the question of whether a loss falls within the main marine insurance policy or whether the risk should be placed under an accompanying war risk policy; the second category addresses the same question of designating the risk as marine or war peril, but instead of directly applying the language of two insurance policies, the division is reflected in charterparty language assigning the merchant shipowner the obligation to cover marine perils while the government agrees to accept the war risks. Although the latter category technically involves charterparty interpretation, since the charterparties at issue rely on the FC&S language to delineate between war and marine peril, the analytical frameworks used in these two types of cases are largely analogous.[175] Among the leading English decisions addressing this issue in both scenarios during the First World War is *Britain Steamship Co Ltd v The King*.[176] In that case, the House of Lords addressed the separate incidents involving the *Matiana* and the *Petersham*.

In the *Matiana*, the vessel was carrying a cargo of cotton from Egypt to England while sailing in a convoy with the escort of British warships in the spring of 1918. As the convoy sailed west from Alexanderia, Egypt, and approached Sardinia, Italy – a Mediterranean area 'usually infested with submarines' – the escorting naval officers signalled to the merchant vessels in convoy to alter the course and 'zigzag' to avoid enemy attack.[177] While complying with the orders, in calm seas, the *Matiana* struck a reef and stranded. Eleven hours later, although the vessel was already lost due to the stranding, the *Matiana* was torpedoed by a German U-boat. The shipowner brought a claim against the vessel's war risk insurer, and, alternatively, against its marine insurer, which raised the question of whether the loss was caused by a marine or war peril. The trial court held that the stranding was caused by sailing in convoy, which it viewed as a 'warlike operation' placing the loss within the war risk cover under the FC&S clause.[178] The English Court of Appeal reversed on grounds that it was not the merchant ships sailing in convoy but rather the British warships escorting them that were engaged in a warlike operation, which meant the stranding should be categorised as a marine rather than a war peril.[179]

[175] There are many other English and American cases addressing similar issues during the two World Wars. The cases discussed here are merely illustrative.
[176] *Britain Steamship Co Ltd v The King* [1920] Lloyd's Rep 245 (HL) (Viscount Cave).
[177] ibid, 247.
[178] *Britain Steamship Co Ltd v The King* [1919] KB 632 (KB) (Bailhache J).
[179] *Britain Steamship Co Ltd v The King* [1919] KB 670 (CA) (Warrington LJ, Duke LJ, and Atkin LJ).

The majority of the House of Lords affirmed, finding that the *Matiana* was not engaged in a warlike operation by sailing in convoy.[180] Although the risk of stranding was increased by the protective measure of sailing in convoy to avoid German U-boats, the House of Lords found that the stranding remained a marine peril that occurred during peaceful operations. Moreover, it determined that the subsequent torpedo by the German U-boat was effectively immaterial to the causation inquiry since the vessel was already lost due to stranding before the attack.

As for the *Petersham*, the vessel had been requisitioned by the British government and was under time charter on a voyage carrying iron ore from Bilbao, Spain, to Glasgow, Scotland. Under the orders of the British Admiralty, the vessel was required to sail without lights as a security measure. As the vessel approached the north coast of Cornwall on 6 May 1918, the *Petersham* collided with a Spanish steamship, the *Serra*, which was moving in the opposite direction on a voyage from Swansea to Bilbao and was also navigating without lights. The collision sank the *Petersham*. The shipowner claimed the British government was liable for the loss under the terms of the charterparty, which, referencing the FC&S clause, designating the government as responsible for losses found to be 'a consequence of hostilities and warlike operations'.[181] Therefore, again, the resolution of the case hinged on a determination of causation. The trial court held that the collision was caused by a marine peril, not a warlike operation.[182] Both the English Court of Appeal and the House of Lords agreed.[183] The House of Lords emphasised that, irrespective of the fact the vessels were sailing without lights, the shipowner failed to demonstrate that there were any warlike operations occurring at the time that could be attributed as the cause of the collision. Since there was no enemy ship or even a friendly warship in the vicinity, it was determined that both vessels were proceeding in peaceful missions with the intent to avoid warlike operations rather than engage in them.

Shortly after the *Petersham* and *Matiana* decisions, the US Supreme Court issued an opinion addressing a comparable scenario in *Queen Insurance Co of America v Globe & Rutgers Fire Insurance Co.*[184] That case involved the Italian steamship *Napoli*, which was lost in a collision off the coast of southern France in July of 1918. The *Napoli* had departed New York for Genoa, Italy, carrying a cargo of 'contraband' and 'munitions of war' consigned to the Italian government.[185]

[180] The House of Lords was divided on this point. Lord Atkinson, Lord Sumner, and Lord Wrenbury held that the loss was a marine risk, while Viscount Cave and Lord Shaw expressed the contrary view that the loss fell within the scope of 'a consequence of a warlike operation'. In separate speeches, they emphasised that the warships escorting the convoy were engaged in warlike operations and the shipmaster of the *Matiana* had no choice but to comply with the orders of the naval officers who directed the vessels on navigation and course, which ultimately led to the stranding.

[181] *Britain Steamship Co Ltd v The King* (1920) Lloyd's List Rep 245, 246.

[182] *Britain Steamship Co Ltd v The King* [1919] 1 KB 575.

[183] *Britain Steamship Co Ltd v The King* (1920) Lloyd's List Rep 245.

[184] *Queen Insurance Co of America v Globe & Rutgers Fire Insurance Co*, 263 US 487 (USSC 1924) (Holmes J).

[185] ibid, 491.

At Gibraltar, the *Napoli* joined a convoy of allied warships, which was required and 'practically necessary' for security.[186] The convoy proceeded eastbound using screened lights. As the convoy approached Genoa, it suddenly came upon another westbound convoy. Without time or space for the shipmasters to manoeuvre, the *Napoli* collided with the westbound *Lamington*, which caused the *Napoli* to sink. The *Napoli* was insured under both a marine policy and a war risk policy. The two insurers commenced litigation to determine whether the loss was a marine or war peril, which again hinged on the interpretation of the FC&S language.[187] The US District Court for the Southern District of New York held the collision fell within the marine policy. First, the court recognised that due to the scale of the war, at least in a broad sense, 'the very act of sailing was a consequence of hostilities' and that 'almost every act of the warring countries, after the home-staying population was fed, clothed, and sheltered, was but a manifestation of war'.[188] However, seeking to follow the more narrow views expressed in the English cases addressing similar issues, it found that that collisions were normally considered marine perils (up to that time). The US Second Circuit Court of Appeals affirmed, reasoning that '[t]he peril must be due directly to some hostile action, if it be considered a warlike risk'.[189] The US Supreme Court affirmed, famously remarking that '[t]here are special reasons for keeping in harmony with the marine insurance laws of England, the great field of this business'.[190]

The House of Lords reconsidered the war versus marine causation issue again during the Second World War in *Yorkshire Dale Steamship Co v Minister of War Transport (The Coxwold)*.[191] The *Coxwold* had been requisitioned by the British government under a charterparty in which the government took on the war risks. On the night of the casualty, 7 May 1940, the *Coxwold* was transporting fuel between allied war bases in Greenock, Scotland, and Narvik, Norway. The *Coxwold* was sailing in convoy of four vessels in poor and rainy visibility when the British Admiralty ordered the convoy to divert to a different course and zigzag to avoid enemy submarines. During the manoeuvring, the *Coxwold* lost sight of the leading ship and encountered an unexpected tidal set, causing the *Coxwold* to drift even further off course and strand on rocks near the Isle of Skye, Scotland. The parties admitted that the *Coxwold* was engaged in a warlike operation at the time of the stranding. The question was whether the stranding was a 'consequence' of the warlike operation or whether it was caused by a marine risk.[192] At first

[186] ibid.
[187] ibid, 490.
[188] *Queen Insurance Co of America v Globe & Rutgers Fire Insurance Co*, 278 F 770, 781 (SDNY 1922) (Hough J).
[189] *Queen Insurance Co of America v Globe & Rutgers Fire Insurance Co*, 282 F 976, 979 (2nd Cir 1922) (Manton J).
[190] *Queen Insurance Co of America v Globe & Rutgers Fire Insurance Co*, 263 US 487, 493 (1924).
[191] *Yorkshire Dale Steamship Co v Minister of War Transport (The Coxwold)* (1942) 73 Lloyd's List Rep 2 (HL) (Lord Chancellor, Viscount Simon).
[192] ibid, 4.

instance, the arbitrator held that the stranding was a war risk because it was a direct consequence of the warlike operations performed by the convoy, which the King's Bench affirmed.[193] The English Court of Appeal reversed, by reinterpreting the arbitrator's findings to show the proximate cause of the stranding was actually the unexpected tidal set.[194] But the House of Lords reversed again, unanimously holding that the Court of Appeal misinterpreted the arbitrator's findings. It held instead that although the tidal set contributed to the loss, this marine peril must be viewed alongside the navigational orders by the convoy escorts to avoid enemy submarine attack, especially since the orders were for the vessels to continue in a diverted direction for an extended period of time. In the principal speech, the House of Lords explained that the central issue was whether the '"dominant" or "determining" cause of the disaster was warlike operations'.[195] Emphasising the fact that after the orders to divert the *Coxwold* was not properly instructed to revert back to the normal course, the House of Lords found the arbitrator was correct to determine the stranding was due to warlike operations.

The US Supreme Court also revisited the line between marine and war peril during the Second World War in *Standard Oil Co of New Jersey v United States*.[196] There, the government-requisitioned tanker *John Worthington* collided with the US minesweeper *YMS-12* in New York Harbor, which caused significant damage to the minesweeper. At the time of the collision, *YMS-12* was in the process of clearing the channel along with two other minesweepers. The US government assumed war risk liability for the *John Worthington* under a time charter referencing the FC&S clause, while the shipowner secured cover for the marine perils.[197] The US District Court for the Southern District of New York found that both vessels were at fault in failing to comply with navigation rules, but held the collision was ultimately caused by a war risk.[198] The court explained, '[m]ine sweeping conducted by a belligerent in the waters of the channels in the approaches to a great harbor of the belligerent is most certainly a warlike operation'.[199] As to the relevance of the negligence by both shipmasters, the court found this 'did not break the chain of causation so as to prevent the loss from being attributable to the warlike operation' or have the effect of 'converting a war risk into a sea risk'.[200] The US Court of Appeals for the Second Circuit reversed.[201] It first explained that for a loss to fall within the category of a war risk, 'not only must the vessel's mission be one of war, but the warlike character of its operation must be the dominant and

[193] *Yorkshire Dale Steamship Co v Minister of War Transport (The Coxwold)* (1941) 70 Ll L Rep 160 (KB) (Scott LJ).

[194] *Yorkshire Dale Steamship Co v Minister of War Transport (The Coxwold)* (1941) 70 Ll L Rep 236 (CA) (Caldecote LCJ).

[195] ibid, 6.

[196] *Standard Oil Co of New Jersey v United States*, 340 US 54 (USSC 1950) (Black J).

[197] ibid.

[198] *Standard Oil Co of New Jersey v United States*, 81 F Supp 183 (SDNY 1948) (Ryan J).

[199] ibid, 189.

[200] ibid, 191.

[201] *Standard Oil Co of New Jersey v United States*, 178 F2d 488 (2nd Cir 1949) (Clark J).

effective cause of the resulting catastrophe'.[202] The court emphasised that 'proximate cause of a loss must have been warlike in order to make the loss a war risk.'[203] It explained that war risk cover, 'extends only to perils due directly to some hostile action, military maneuver, or operational war danger, and does not include the aggravation or increase of a maritime risk because of war operations'.[204] Applying this proximate cause analysis, the court found that although the minesweeper was engaged in a warlike operation at the time of the collision, failure to comply with the rules of good seamanship, not the warlike operation, was the effective cause of the accident. The US Supreme Court affirmed.[205] Declining to follow English cases on the subject on grounds that they 'cannot easily be reconciled', the Supreme Court explained that 'our practice is no more than to accord respect to established doctrines of English maritime law.'[206] Rather than attempting to apply inconsistent standards as a matter of law, the Supreme Court determined that it was more appropriate to deploy 'proximate cause' as an 'adaptable and useful' tool for delineating between marine and war perils in marine insurance cases.[207] Two dissenting justices disagreed with this approach, however, reasoning that proximate cause is 'at best, an elusive concept'.[208]

ii. Sovereign Restraint

Causation questions impacting liability allocations between war and marine insurers have also arisen in the context of casualties linked to governmental orders to engage in or abstain from navigation. *Muller v Globe & Rutgers Fire Insurance Co of City of New York* is among them.[209] There, during the First World War, a cargo owner sued its war risk insurers to recover for the loss of its cotton during a voyage from Texas to Sweden on the Danish steamer *Canadia*, with planned transshipment to manufacturers in Austria. Although the claimant was a resident of the US, he was a citizen of Austria. In part due to mined waters on the 'usual peace route', the *Canadia*'s intended course was to move north of Scotland's coast, beyond the Orkney and Shetland Islands, to Kirkwall, where the vessel would be inspected by British authorities.[210] During this phase of the war, the British government had

[202] ibid, 490.
[203] ibid, 493.
[204] ibid. Noting updates to the British FC&S clause following the *Coxwold* decision, the Second Circuit wrote, '[i]t is no longer necessary to conform to the supposed British rule in order that the same language shall mean the same thing in both America and England.' ibid, 494.
[205] *Standard Oil Co of New Jersey v United States*, 340 US 54 (USSC 1950) (Black J).
[206] ibid, 59.
[207] ibid, 61.
[208] ibid, 64. Justices Frankfurter and Jackson dissented, reasoning that it was important to place the words of the FC&S clause 'in its historical setting', which included the fact that the words did not derive from US wartime charterparties, but rather 'evolved by English maritime insurers'. ibid, 65.
[209] *Muller v Globe & Rutgers Fire Insurance Co of City of New York*, 246 F 759 (2nd Cir 1917) (Hough J).
[210] ibid, 760.

not yet announced the intention to seize goods on neutral ships bound for neutral ports, even if the vessel was 'shown to be intended for transshipment to a country at war with Great Britan'.[211] Nevertheless, when the *Canadia* was 120 miles off the British coast, it was intercepted by a British cruiser, boarded by British naval officers, and, despite the shipmaster's objections to the contrary, ordered to immediately go to Kirkwall via an alternative route splitting between the Orkneys and Shetlands at night, even though the lighthouse on Fair Isle was extinguished due to wartime precautions. During the ill-advised diversion, the *Canadia* grounded at the base of a 300-foot cliff, rendering the vessel and its cargo totally lost. The cargo owner made claims against its war risk insurers, which denied cover on grounds that the cargo owner had allegedly not disclosed that he was 'a subject of Austria-Hungary, a country at war with Great Britain' and that, in any event, the loss was not due to war risks, but rather a peril of the sea.[212] The US District Court for the Southern District of New York rejected these defences, and the US Court of Appeals for the Second Circuit affirmed.[213] The court found that the cargo owner repeatedly informed the insurer's agent that he was Austrian, so the insurer was unable to avoid liability on the basis of an alleged non-disclosure of a risk-related fact. On the causation issue, the court emphasised that the British authorities had 'compelled' the *Canadia* to take a 'dangerous route'.[214] Consequently, the cause of the loss was the control of the British boarding party assumed on the vessel. To support this holding, the court stressed the geopolitical motives of the intervention, explaining 'the very purpose of compelling such navigation was to prevent aid and comfort reaching enemies of Great Britain; therefore the insured cotton was lost in the continuing process of detaining the ship that carried it'.[215] Analogising the scenario to show the absurdity of holding otherwise, the court wrote: 'A workman compelled to handle familiar tools with one eye blindfolded, and injured by his own blundering use of them, is in truth injured by the person who put compulsion upon him.'[216]

Among the leading American cargo cases arising during the Second World War is *Baker Castor Oil Co v Insurance Co of North America*.[217] In that case, three merchant vessels owned by a Brazilian governmental entity had been engaged to transport thousands of bags of castor beans from Brazil to New York. Accordingly, bills of lading were produced naming New York as the discharge port. The cargo owner obtained an open cargo policy covering the beans during transport, as well as a war risk policy providing cover for war risks. Due to German submarine activity off the US coasts, both the US government and the Brazilian government ordered the vessels carrying the castor beans to proceed to New Orleans instead of

[211] ibid.
[212] ibid, 761.
[213] The district court opinion was unpublished.
[214] ibid, 763.
[215] ibid.
[216] ibid.
[217] *Baker Castor Oil Co v Insurance Co of North America*, 157 F2d 3 (2nd Cir 1946) (Chase J).

New York. This diversion gave rise to additional railroad transport costs to move the beans from Louisiana to the ultimate consignee near New York. The cargo owner brought a claim against its war risk insurer seeking recovery for these costs on grounds the orders by the Brazilian and US authorities constituted a 'sovereign restraint' within the language of the insurance policy.[218] The US District Court for the Southern District of New York held for the insurer. The court reasoned that although the vessels were owned by a Brazilian governmental entity, they were performing the voyages 'for the purpose of carrying privately owned cargoes in foreign trade for a profit in competition with privately owned vessels'.[219] When the Brazilian government gave the orders to divert to New Orleans, these instructions were not an 'exercise of sovereign power', but rather actions consistent with the actions of a private shipowner 'which might be given by any cautious ship owner for the purpose of protecting his vessels'.[220] Moreover, since Brazil was a neutral in the war, any restraint it performed was not acting 'in prosecution of hostilities' under the war risk policy.[221] The court also held the orders could not be construed as a restraint by the US government because the vessel owners had previously entered into a 'ship warrants' agreement with the US government that gave the vessels certain privileges such as access to docking facilities subject to an agreement to abide by routing instructions, which the US War Shipping Administration had provided before the vessels left Brazil.[222] Construing the diversion to New Orleans as 'voluntary conduct' of the vessel owner, the court found the governmental orders could not be viewed as a restraint falling within the war risk cover.[223] The US Court of Appeals for the Second Circuit affirmed.[224] It agreed with the trial court's findings that the act by the US and Brazilian government did not constitute 'sovereign restraint' under the war risk policy because the Brazilian government had acted as a private shipowner and the US government exercised a right that was voluntarily granted to it by the vessel owners.[225] Acknowledging that there would have been cover in the event of 'impact' by German submarines – such as direct torpedo attack – the court further reasoned that although the 'prudent acts' of avoiding the submarines 'may have been motivated by the presence of the war risk insured against, they were not, within the legal concept of cause, the result of that peril'.[226]

The US Supreme Court's last word on war risk insurance during the Second World War is a factually unique case involving requisition by allied governments.[227]

[218] *Baker Castor Oil Co v Insurance Co of North America*, 60 F Supp 32, 35 (SDNY 1944) (Goddard J).
[219] ibid.
[220] ibid.
[221] ibid.
[222] ibid, 36.
[223] ibid.
[224] *Baker Castor Oil Co v Insurance Co of North America*, 157 F2d 3 (2nd Cir 1946) (Chase J).
[225] ibid, 4.
[226] ibid, 5.
[227] *Calmar SS Corp v Scott*, 345 US 427 (USSC 1953) (Frankfurter J).

In *Calmar SS Corp v Scott*, pursuant to a US government charter, the steamship *Portmar* was transporting fuel, ammunition, and other military supplies from California to the Philippines when the Japanese attacked Pearl Harbor. At the time of the attacks, the *Portmar* was approximately 600 miles from Hawaii. The shipmaster learned about the events on the vessel's radio and immediately turned south to Fiji, before the US navy instructed it to divert to Sydney, Australia. On arrival, the Australian government ordered the *Portmar* up the north coast to Brisbane and then to Darwin to discharge the cargo. Shortly thereafter, the US and Australian authorities ordered the *Portmar* to perform a dangerous expedition in a convoy carrying troops, equipment, and arms to Koepang, on the Island of Timor, approximately 500 miles northwest of Darwin. During the mission, the *Portmar* came under fire by Japanese aircraft in the Timor Sea and the convoy was forced to turn back to Darwin. A few days later, Japanese aircraft bombed the *Portmar* while at anchorage off Darwin, causing severe damage to the vessel and forcing the shipmaster to beach and then abandon it. The US Army later towed the damaged *Portmar* to Brisbane, performed patch-up repairs, and deployed it on three additional missions until it was destroyed by Japanese torpedo. Since the charterparty agreement was made prior to the US entrance into the Second World War, under the terms of the charterparty with the US government, the shipowner had secured both marine and war risk insurance for the *Portmar* (although the US government had agreed to pay for the war risk insurance). The marine policy was written on the SG form with the equivalent of an FC&S clause that excluded war risks from the main policy.[228] A war risk rider was also included to reinstate cover for those risks excluded by the FC&S clause. In addition, there was a separate 'free of British capture warranty', which excluded liability for capture, seizure, requisition, and the like, 'by or under the authority of the government of Great Britain or any of its dominions or allies, or by any forces acting in cooperation with or under the control of them'.[229] But this provision, too, had a 'saving clause' that limited the effect of the free of British capture warranty, such as in the event of losses caused by 'gunfire, torpedoes, bombs, mines or other implements of war'.[230]

Examining the interaction between these clauses, the US District Court for the Southern District of New York held the war risk insurers responsible for the loss.[231] The US Second Circuit Court of Appeals reversed on grounds that the policy was no longer in force when the vessel was damaged in Darwin.[232] Although the court described the policy language as a 'labyrinth of verbiage', it emphasised the wartime environment to contextualise the contract.[233] The court explained that starting in 1942, the US and Australian authorities had 'seized

[228] ibid, 430.
[229] ibid, 431.
[230] ibid.
[231] *Calmar SS Corp v Scott*, 103 F Supp 243 (SDNY 1951) (Ryan J).
[232] *Calmar SS Corp v Scott*, 197 F2d 795 (2nd Cir 1952) (L Hand J).
[233] ibid.

and held anything that would float'.[234] The court underscored that at the time '[i]t made no difference whether a vessel was owned or chartered by the U.S. or by anyone else; military considerations alone governed, commercial were disregarded'.[235] Holding that the orders by the US and Australian government altered the nature of the insured voyage, the court found the insurance policy ceased when the voyage effectively ended at the time the *Portmar* was ordered to Brisbane.[236] But the US Supreme Court reversed the Second Circuit.[237] First, the court emphasised that the language of the policies was indeed difficult to decipher, providing a colourful disclaimer that '[c]onstruing such conglomerate provisions requires a skill not unlike that called for in the decipherment of obscure palimpsest texts'.[238] Then, drawing on authority from both American and English cases, the court determined that the various clauses, riders, and exclusions demonstrated the insurer was liable for the claim. Of particular importance was the 'saving clause' that referenced the insurer's liability for loss caused by 'bombs' and 'other implements of war'.[239] Although the court acknowledged that the *Portmar*'s Koepang expedition was 'undoubtedly a venture inconsistent with the voyage specified in the *Portmar*'s insurance', since the saving clause preserved some of the cover in the event of requisition by the British or other allies, the underwriters had agreed to insure the relevant risk.[240]

Similar questions of sovereign compulsion arose regarding vessels trapped in the Shatt-al-Arab during the outbreak of the Iran–Iraq War. Among them was the *Bamburi*, a cement carrier, which was on a voyage from Mombasa, Kenya, to Khor al Zubair, Iraq, carrying cement consigned to the Iraqi government. The *Bamburi* arrived at the mouth of the Shatt-al-Arab in September 1980. It continued upriver with a pilot and discharged the cargo on 22 September 1980 – the day of Iraq's invasion of Iran. The *Bamburi*'s shipmaster received word from Iraqi authorities that merchant ships were prohibited from sailing until further notice. Less than three weeks later, all of the *Bamburi*'s crew and officers were evacuated. A skeleton crew returned to the vessel in late December of that year, where they surveyed the vessel and found it undamaged. Although there was no physical Iraqi interreference with the vessel, and no navigational obstructions in the waterway, Iraqi officials did not give express permission for the vessel to depart. The *Bamburi* carried a standard marine insurance policy on the SG form with the FC&S clause. It also carried war risk insurance containing the Institute War and Strikes Clauses. Referencing the inability to obtain permission to depart the Shatt-al-Arab, in the

[234] ibid, 798.
[235] ibid, 798–99.
[236] ibid, 801.
[237] *Calmar SS Corp v Scott*, 345 US 427 (USSC 1953) (Frankfurter J).
[238] ibid, 432.
[239] ibid, 434.
[240] ibid, 439. Justice Douglas and Chief Justice Vinson dissented to emphasise the alternate view that at some point before the *Portmar* reached Darwin, 'the purposes of the venture, commercially speaking, had ended'. ibid, 445.

autumn of 1981 the shipowner filed a notice of abandonment with its insurer alleging it was a constructive total loss – a position the insurer rejected. The parties then agreed to submit the claim to arbitration before a sole arbitrator at the consent of the English courts.[241] Emphasising that the words of the policy at issue were effectively the same as those addressed in many wartime cases of the past, the arbitrator held that the *Bamburi*'s detention was indeed proximately caused by the Iraqi 'restraint of princes'.[242] In doing so, the arbitrator rejected the argument that the Iraqi motives were 'altruistic' and focused on the safety of the trapped ships. Instead, the arbitrator found that the restraint was 'motivated by a desire to avoid the political embarrassment of ships being sunk in what were, or were claimed to be, Iraqi waters, and to avoid the hazards to future navigation from ships so sunk'.[243] Accordingly, the *Bamburi*'s detention was caused by an insured peril.[244] On the separate issue of whether the shipowner was deprived of the vessel's use sufficient to give rise to a constructive total loss, the arbitrator found the movement of the ship was entirely prohibited as the *Bamburi* 'must remain as idle as a painted ship'.[245] Given that this situation remained unchanged even at the time of the arbitration award in early 1982, the arbitrator found it was 'unlikely' that the shipowner would recover possession of the *Bamburi* within 12 months from the time it submitted the notice of abandonment.[246]

iii. Trading Limits

The insurance consequences of the bombing of a vessel during the Iran-Iraq war was addressed in *Bank of Nova Scotia v Hellenic Mutual War Risks Association (Bermuda) Ltd (The Good Luck)*.[247] The shipowner had chartered the vessel, the *Good Luck*, to an Iranian charterer for the purpose of facilitating oil trades in the Persian Gulf. The vessel was insured with a war risk mutual club, which, by its rules, allowed the club to designate certain regions as additional war risk premium (AWRP) areas, requiring notice before vessels could trade there. The rules also allowed the club to declare 'prohibited areas' that were considered so risky that insured vessels were not allowed to trade there at all. The vessel had been mortgaged by a bank, which required the shipowner to assign the insurance to the bank. To assist in this arrangement, the club had issued a letter of undertaking to the bank indicating that the *Good Luck* was entered with the club and that it would advise the bank 'if the ship ceases to be entered in the association'.[248] In

[241] *The Bamburi* [1982] 1 Lloyd's Rep 312 (Arb) (Staughton J).
[242] ibid, 315.
[243] ibid.
[244] ibid.
[245] ibid, 317.
[246] ibid, 322.
[247] *Bank of Nova Scotia v Hellenic Mutual War Risks Association (Bermuda) Ltd (The Good Luck)* [1991] 2 Lloyd's Rep 191 (HL) (Lord Goff of Chieveley).
[248] ibid, 196.

September 1980, the northern end of the Persian Gulf near the Shatt-al-Arab was declared by the club to be a prohibited area. By the end of 1981, the club discovered that the *Good Luck* was trading in the region without paying an AWRP and was therefore without insurance. In the spring of 1982, the shipowner renegotiated loans with the bank to secure additional financing. At that time, the bank was aware that the *Good Luck* was trading in the Persian Gulf, but it was not aware that it was doing so without insurance. In June of 1982, the *Good Luck* entered the prohibited area approaching Bandar Khomeini and was hit by Iraqi missiles and declared a constructive total loss. The shipowner then made 'a fraudulent claim' with the war risk club 'pretending falsely that they had given an advance declaration of entry into the additional premium area and that they were ignorant of prohibited areas', but the insurer rejected the claim on the basis that the damage had been incurred while the vessel was in a prohibited area and without prior notification of entering an additional premium area.[249] The club never disclosed to the bank what it knew about the 'defects' in the claim made by the shipowner. The bank then sued the insurer for breach of the letter of undertaking that had indicated the *Good Luck* was insured and that the insurer would notify the bank if the insurance lapsed.

The English Commercial Court held for the bank.[250] It reasoned that the club breached the letter of undertaking by failing to alert the bank about the *Good Luck* trading in the Persian Gulf without insurance. Then, the Court of Appeal reversed, finding that the club had no obligation to alert the bank of the *Good Luck*'s lack of insurance until it made the affirmative decision not to cover it.[251] But the House of Lords reversed and reinstated the decision of the trial judge. It reasoned that when a 'promissory warranty is not complied with, the insurer is discharged from liability as from the date of the breach of warranty' because fulfilling the warranty is a 'condition precedent' of the insurer's liability.[252] Deferring to the trial judge's fact findings, the House of Lords explained, 'the vessel ceased to be insured when she entered the prohibited zone', which meant that the club had an obligation to give the bank notice 'long before' it actually did.[253] And since the bank went on to make an advance to the shipowner that it would not have made if the club had been upfront about the lack of cover, 'the bank's loss was accordingly caused by the breach of the club's letter of undertaking'.[254]

A companion case from the era is *Black King Shipping Corp and Wayang (Panama) SA v Mark Ranald Massie (The Litsion Pride)*. There, the *Litsion Pride*

[249] ibid.
[250] *Bank of Nova Scotia v Hellenic Mutual War Risks Association (Bermuda) Ltd (The Good Luck)* [1988] 1 Lloyd's Rep 514 (Comm) (Hobhouse J).
[251] *Bank of Nova Scotia v Hellenic Mutual War Risks Association (Bermuda) Ltd (The Good Luck)* [1989] 2 Lloyd's Rep 238 (CA) (May LJ).
[252] *Bank of Nova Scotia v Hellenic Mutual War Risks Association (Bermuda) Ltd (The Good Luck)* [1991] 2 Lloyd's Rep 191, 202.
[253] ibid, 204.
[254] ibid, 204.

was on a voyage from France to Iran carrying a cargo of sugar through the Persian Gulf in August 1982 when it was attacked by an Iraqi helicopter, caught on fire, ran aground, and sank.[255] The vessel was covered by a policy of war risk insurance, which allowed for worldwide trading, but also contained a provision requiring payment of an AWRP for voyages in certain dangerous areas, including the Persian Gulf. Under the policy terms, the assured was required to give the insurer notice of the intent to enter an additional premium area so that rates could be determined, which would vary depending on 'political conditions and, where applicable, the state of hostilities'.[256] In a letter dated 2 August, the shipowner wrote to the insurance broker instructing it to advise the insurer that the vessel would be 'entering the war zone' in the Persian Gulf later that day. But the letter was not received until 12 August, which was three days after it had been attacked off Bandar Khomeini, Iran, which was well within the AWRP area. The shipowner notified the insurance broker of the event by telex on 11 August and also claimed that it had intended to advise the broker of the plan to enter the war zone, but the 2 August letter 'was not mailed to you immediately as my secretary was on holiday and it was mixed up with other papers'.[257] The shipowner (and its mortgagee) made a claim against the insurer, which it denied on the basis that the shipowner had engaged in fraud and breached the duty of utmost good faith by intentionally aiming to trade in a listed area without paying the AWRP. In the litigation that ensued, the English Commercial Court held for the insurer. It found the shipowner had intended to 'try to slip in and out of the Gulf in the hope that they would not be discovered and avoid paying [the AWRP]'.[258] This was supported by evidence showing that the shipowner was in a 'parlous financial position' and that it was 'unable to afford' the insurance costs.[259] Accordingly, the court also found that the 2 August letter had been 'concocted, and the false information invented, in order to deceive the underwriters, in the hope that they would accept that the failure to give notice was an innocent oversight'.[260]

III. Reflections

Defining the meaning of 'war' has been a recurring task for courts and arbitrators interpreting contract cancellation terms. The *Bantham Steamship* case addressing whether war involving Japan had broken out in China by the autumn of 1937 remains seminal authority recognising that notions of war in the contractual sense

[255] *Black King Shipping Corp and Wayang (Panama) SA v Mark Ranald Massie (The Litsion Pride)* [1985] 1 Lloyd's Rep 437 (Comm) (Hirst J).
[256] ibid, 440.
[257] ibid, 442.
[258] ibid, 506.
[259] ibid, 505.
[260] ibid, 507.

of the term need not mesh identically with the extensive public law commentary relayed by international law scholars nor align with the views expressed by political officials in diplomatic communications.[261] Instead, by acknowledging that contractual references to war are embedded within the confines of private documents, common sense factors such as the scale and level of violence were found to be the more appropriate considerations for weighing the commercial purpose of the wordings, as opposed to the 'technicalities' espoused by contractual outsiders.[262] As reflected in the *Navios Corp* case addressing whether there was a declaration of war by Egypt against a NATO country, courts may still find that a commercial assessment of the nature of a conflict happens to match a parallel understanding in public law.[263] The case also reveals that when a war cancellation clause references a precise action, such as a 'declaration', even the contractual interpretation of the term may require deciphering nuanced political discourse. But taking too much stock in political statements can lead to unrealistic results, as illustrated by the *Manning Brothers* arbitration, which construed the massive conflict in Korea as a mere 'police action' to suppress 'bandits'.[264] This rather improbable holding shows that there may be a tendency to defer to statements made by public officials in evaluating the nature of the conflict under scrutiny in commercial cases, especially when such views are relayed by the political branches of government who are presumed to have foreign relations expertise (in that case, US President Truman). Despite this inclination to abstain from second-guessing the characterisation of the executive on 'political questions', the contrary view regarding the Korean War in the *Seven Seas Steamship* case implicitly acknowledges that political leaders may choose to use tempering messages to cool the rhetoric surrounding a conflict for strategic reasons. Accordingly, in the context of interpreting a war cancellation clause, political characterisations of a conflict may be disregarded or at least viewed cautiously if they are inconsistent with the realities on the ground.[265]

The separate question of how to address contract language requiring an assessment of state attribution adds an additional layer of complexity to the interpretation of war cancellation clauses. Again, the two US arbitration awards addressing the conflict in Korea are instructive. Since the war effort was pursued under UN auspices – a new phenomenon in the 1950s – there was an open question as to whether this meant the US was involved, despite the deployment and active fighting of many thousands of US soldiers. For the purpose of interpreting the clause at issue, the arbitrator in the *Seven Seas Steamship* case determined that the large scale of US contributions to the UN fighting coalition was a more

[261] *Kawasaki Kisen Kabushiki Kaisha v Bantham Steamship Co Ltd* (1939) 63 Lloyd's List Rep 155.
[262] ibid, 164.
[263] *Navios Corp v The Ulysses II* [1958] 161 F Supp 932 (1958).
[264] *Manning Brothers Inc of Delaware, Owners of Steamship Yankee Fighter v Albatross Steamship Co Inc*, 1951 AMC 579 (1951).
[265] *Seven Seas Steamship Corp of New York v Prudential Steamship Corp of New York (The Simon Benson)* 1951 AMC 585 (1951).

important factor than the fact that the US was not fighting the war independently. The counterpoint in the *Manning Brothers* case was that although the US was a key contributor to the coalition military effort, this was a 'peaceful pursuit' to fulfil a fundamental mandate of the UN Charter, rather than World War-style belligerency.[266] The much more contained NATO operation in Kosovo addressed in the *Northern Pioneer* case would seem to make for an easier decision regarding state attribution because the bombing itself and the German contributions to it were more limited. Nevertheless, although the court ultimately found the issue not to be determinative of the outcome, the split nature of the arbitration award at first instance on the point of whether Germany had been involved in a war again demonstrates the challenge of identifying state attribution to military operations performed under the auspices of a coalition. Together, these cases reveal that when assessing rights and obligations under standard contract wordings, the determination as to whether a state has been involved in a war may depend on the scale of its direct contributions to a multilateral security or humanitarian mission, or its participation in training allied fighters or deploying troops. This reasoning raises the additional question of whether state attribution for contract purposes may also flow from a sovereign decision to deploy private contractors or mercenaries to perform belligerent actions.[267] This problem is illuminated further by the contemporary use of hybrid warfare tactics designed in part to evade and conceal state attribution altogether.

Beyond war cancellation clauses, courts and arbitrators have regularly turned to doctrinal principles to determine whether contracts can be avoided due to war-related events. The court in *Pope & Talbot* found that it would be 'impracticable' for the carrier to perform the contract to move lumber between US coasts after a Japanese submarine blew a hole in the side of the ship and the cargo itself was damaged, even though the cargo owner was willing to wait for performance until after the vessel was repaired.[268] In the government requisition cases, frustration and impossibility served as analytical solutions. Both the *Bank Line* and *Earn Line* cases arising during the First World War clarify, for instance, that even if a requisition order financially benefits the shipowner, the governmental decision to require a vessel's use during wartime should be viewed as something so different from what was originally anticipated by the contracting parties that it warrants a dissolution of the contract.[269] Requisition can have similarly disruptive effects in insurance and bill of lading cases. However, courts have resolved them by focusing on contractual and statutory language rather than bare doctrinal reasoning. As demonstrated in the *Calmar* case, although the vessel was requisitioned in the

[266] ibid.

[267] Examples of this phenomenon include the US use of contractors in Iraq and Afghanistan and the Russian use of mercenary fighters in Ukraine.

[268] *Pope & Talbot Inc v Blanchard Lumber Co of Seattle*, 159 F2d 134 (1947).

[269] *Bank Line Ltd v Arthur Capel & Co* [1919] AC 435; *Earn Line Steamship Co Ltd v Sutherland Steamship Co Ltd (The Claveresk)*, 264 F 276 (1920).

midst of a Pacific voyage when the Japanese bombed Pearl Harbor and was then deployed repeatedly in defence of Australia, the language of the insurance policy preserved insurance cover for the Japanese attacks that ultimately destroyed the vessel even though its repeated deployment in war missions in the South Pacific was totally 'inconsistent' with the expectations of the contracting parties.[270] The *Sedco* case arising in the wake of the Falklands War further clarifies that although a requisition order may occur even during more localised conflicts, such measures do not necessarily release a carrier from all of its obligations to the cargo, particularly when the carrier fails to show the loss was sufficiently linked to the requisition order.[271]

Contract clauses and statutory protections referencing 'restraint of princes' in bill of lading cases have been used to address varied forms of wartime disruption. In the *Styria* case, the court found that Spanish contraband control at Gibraltar was an effective restraint that justified the shipmaster's refusal to load cargo subject to the newly announced ban.[272] Likewise, in the *Kronprinzessin Cecilie* case, the shipmaster was found to have acted prudently by abandoning the voyage carrying gold from the US to Europe after hearing rumours of war breaking out following Archduke Ferdinand's assassination in the summer of 1914, which the shipmaster 'prophetically' interpreted as the outbreak of the First World War.[273] In both cases, the US Supreme Court found restraints had occurred when geopolitical events – the onset of contraband control measures and belligerent hostilities – suddenly increased the chances of disruption to the voyages. In the subsequent *Wildwood* case, the court adopted similar reasoning, but rather than characterising the British contraband control risks in the Pacific as a restraint, it excused the carrier for avoiding the voyage on the basis of a liberties clause that referenced the 'judgment' of the shipmaster to assess whether the voyage would be unsafe.[274] In both the *Styria* and the *Wildwood* cases, the courts found the shipmasters had properly used their discretion to turn back despite allegations of over-compliance with contraband controls, suggesting some level of flexibility in interpreting restraint clauses and commercial assessments of unlawful trades. The 'double restraint' of Greek requisition and the threat of attack leading to the spoiled cheese mess in the *Lekas and Drivas* case absolved the carrier of liability for the loss since the cargo owner did not meet the burden to show that the true cause was mishandling of the cargo.[275] This result contrasts with the later *Sedco* requisition case, where the court held the carrier had failed to show that the loss was sufficiently linked to the restraint, which precluded it from benefitting from the statutory exception.[276]

[270] *Calmar SS Corp v Scott*, 345 US 427 (1953).
[271] *Sedco Inc v SS Strathewee*, 800 F2d 27 (1986).
[272] *Steamship Styria v James L Morgan*, 101 F 728 (1900).
[273] *North German Lloyd v Guaranty Trust Co of New York (The Steamship Kronprinzessin Cecilie)*, 37 S Ct 490, 492 (1917).
[274] *Amtorg Trading Corp v The Wildwood*, 133 F2d 765 (1943).
[275] *Lekas & Drivas Inc v Basil Goulandris*, 306 F2d 426 (1962).
[276] *Sedco Inc v SS Strathewee*, 800 F2d 27 (1986).

Both doctrinal reasoning and contract wordings were central to resolving charterparty disputes arising out of the Iran–Iraq War. Courts and arbitrators repeatedly found that frustration had occurred to dissolve existing contracts due to the blockage of the Shatt-al-Arab waterway at the start of the war. As evidenced by the House of Lords decision in the *Evia* case, frustration flowed from the 'abnormal occurrence' of the outbreak of war, but, at the same time, the contract's safe port warranties were not violated because the river was 'prospectively safe' at the time of the charterer's orders.[277] The other cases from the era addressing the operation of safe port warranties during the conflict favoured the charterer's position. In the *Kanchenjunga*, for instance, Kharg Island was known to be a very dangerous port at the time of contracting due to Iraq's repeated attacks on Iran's oil export infrastructure. But since the shipowner had agreed to perform the voyage and even issued a notice of readiness to load when the vessel arrived off Kharg Island, this meant that the shipowner was not within its contractual rights to deny the charterer's orders to perform even after Iraq began bombing the area once again (although, despite the breach, the shipowner was ultimately protected from incurring damages by the language of the contract).[278] Likewise, in the *Chemical Venture*, although the Persian Gulf was held to be unsafe under the meaning of the warranty, after an Iranian jet bombed the vessel off Saudi Arabia en route to Kuwait, the court found the shipowner had waived its right to bring a claim against the charterer for a violation of the safe port provision because it was aware of the situation when it initially agreed to sail into the danger zone.[279]

Courts and arbitrators have treated trading limits clauses similarly in situations where the dangerous conditions were already present before commencement of the voyage. The *Jerom* case demonstrates that provisions appearing to provide the shipowner the freedom to reject orders for risky trades may not necessarily grant a shipowner full discretion when the contract was agreed for the purpose of effectuating voyages in already dangerous conditions. Accordingly, the arbitrators found the shipowner had improperly rejected the charterer's orders to perform a Persian Gulf trade to protect the safety of the crew because it had agreed to the contract with a sober awareness of the Tanker War conditions in the mid-1980s and the contract did not grant the shipowner unilateral discretion to declare that a fundamental change in risk had occurred.[280] The holding for the charterer in the *Product Star* case further illustrates the limitations on shipowner discretion to rely on safety concerns to reject orders to perform voyages when the contract was agreed for the purpose of executing trades within or adjacent to warzones. The court found that for the shipowner to properly invoke the war risk clause to avoid the charterer's orders, it had to meet an objective evidentiary burden of

[277] *Kodros Shipping Corp v Empresa Cubana di Fletes (The Evia)* [1982] 2 Lloyd's Rep 307.
[278] *Motor Oil Hellas (Corinth) Refineries SA v Shipping Corp of India (The Kanchenjunga)* [1990] 1 Lloyd's Rep 391.
[279] *Pearl Carriers Inc v Japan Line Ltd (The Chemical Venture)* [1993] 1 Lloyd's Rep 508.
[280] *Imbar Maritima SA v Palm Shipping Inc (M/T Jerom)*, SMA 2790 (1991).

proof to demonstrate the conditions had substantially changed, and it could not simply rely on its own subjective risk assessment – particularly one that smacked of capriciousness.[281]

The corresponding insurance cases flowing from the Iran–Iraq War further illuminate the practical consequences of contractual trading limits and their interaction with risk designations and disclosure obligations. Following an attack on a vessel by an Iraqi helicopter in the Persian Gulf, the court in the *Litsion Pride* case took issue with the shipowner's lack of transparency and failure to give the insurer proper notice of its trading activity, apparently in an effort to avoid paying the expensive additional war risk premium.[282] The court disregarded the shipowner's fabricated story that its nondisclosure was innocent and instead found that the insurance cover had lapsed by the shipowner's failure to comply with the clear contractual mandate to notify the insurer of its intent to engage in Persian Gulf trading and accept its obligation to pay the additional insurance costs. The House of Lords decision in the *Good Luck* case illustrates that high-risk trading scenarios may also oblige insurers to disclose voyage details to interested stakeholders (namely, ship mortgaging banks) in the event that it affects the status of the insurance cover.[283] The two cases show that although the private war risk insurance market enables the industry to engage in trade even in the midst of active warzones, the functionality of this financial infrastructure depends on transparent and good faith communication between the parties interested in the voyages.

The earlier insurance cases addressing war versus marine perils are in some ways a relic of history given the evolution of warfare strategies and development of war risk policy language. But these cases also provide a window into the nuances of wartime disruption and establish guideposts that continue to inform the balance of liabilities between marine and war risk insurers as they apportion risks between them under corresponding contract wordings. In the *Petersham* and *Matiana* cases, although the vessels were directed to engage in evasive actions under government orders to avoid enemy attack, by zigzagging and sailing without lights, the losses were found to be caused by the marine perils of stranding and collision, respectively. Keeping US and English law aligned for a time, the *Napoli* court followed this authority, but clarified that the inquiry must depend on the nearest cause of the loss for a casualty to shift categories from marine to war peril, which in that case was the collision of the ships sailing in convoy without lights and under military command rather than any hostile attack.[284] The World War II *Coxwold* case illustrates that negligent navigation orders provided by governments to vessels in

[281] *Abu Dhabi National Tanker Co v Product Star Shipping Ltd (The Product Star)* [1993] 1 Lloyd's Rep 397.

[282] *Black King Shipping Corp and Wayang (Panama) SA v Mark Ranald Massie (The Litsion Pride)* [1985] 1 Lloyd's Rep 437.

[283] *Bank of Nova Scotia v Hellenic Mutual War Risks Association (Bermuda) Ltd (The Good Luck)* [1991] 2 Lloyd's Rep 191.

[284] *Queen Insurance Co of America v Globe & Rutgers Fire Insurance Co*, 263 US 487 (1924).

convoy may result in a finding of causation attributable to a warlike operation even when a standard marine peril (in that case, an unexpected tidal set) contributes to the loss.[285] But the *Standard Oil* case reveals that the existence of such dual causes may produce inconsistent results. Although the minesweeping operation off New York in that case was clearly a warlike operation, the collision itself was found to be the 'dominant factor' caused by the marine risk of negligent navigation.[286] The results of these and other cases are fact-intensive and vary in outcome, but in broad strokes they show that during wartime trading, conflict-driven casualties are only a narrow part of the risk exposure, as conventional marine perils – and other external forces – carry the propensity to disrupt commercial activity just as they do during peacetime.

Insurance cases addressing disruption linked to sovereign compulsion have analysed similar challenges but through a decidedly different lens. The court in the *Canadia* case determined that the vessel interception by British contraband control efforts was a warlike operation that caused the grounding because the government 'compelled' the shipmaster to navigate into the path of Scottish islands shrouded by the darkness of extinguished lighthouses.[287] In contrast, the court in the *Baker Castor* case found that orders by the US and Brazilian governments to divert from the voyage intended for New York to New Orleans for the purpose of avoiding German U-boat attack was not a sovereign restraint subject to war risk cover but rather a voluntary and prudent decision by the assured that ultimately resulted in additional transshipment expenses not covered by the war risk policy.[288] The *Bamburi* arbitration addressed a different take on governmental compulsion as the vessel (along with dozens of others) was prohibited from leaving the Shatt-al-Arab warzone by Iraqi authorities, who were apparently concerned about the embarrassment of ships being sunk in its territorial waters and that the wrecks might become future navigation hazards. The arbitrator found the vessel was a constructive total loss even though the waterway was not physically obstructed, demonstrating that sovereign compulsion may trigger classification attributable to a 'restraint of princes' even when the governmental motives for the orders are difficult to decipher.[289] These cases continued to resonate decades later, as dozens of merchant ships became trapped along Ukraine's Black Sea coasts following the full-scale Russian invasion in the spring of 2022, leading to a diplomatic push to secure their release and insurance claims following their abandonment.[290] The temporary UN-backed Black Sea Grain Initiative agreed the following summer allowed some of the trapped ships to depart, with its

[285] *Yorkshire Dale Steamship Co v Minister of War Transport (The Coxwold)* (1942) 73 Lloyd's List Rep 2.

[286] *Standard Oil Co of New Jersey v United States*, 340 US 54 (1950); *Libby, McNeill & Libby v United States*, 340 US 71 (1950).

[287] *Muller v Globe & Rutgers Fire Insurance Co of City of New York*, 246 F 759 (1917).

[288] *Baker Castor Oil Co v Insurance Co of North America*, 157 F2d 3 (1946).

[289] *The Bamburi* [1982] 1 Lloyd's Rep 312.

[290] See R Meade, 'Over 300 Vessels and at Least 1,000 Seafarers Are Stuck in Ukraine' *Lloyd's List* (24 March 2022).

implementation also mirroring arrangements revealed in earlier caselaw through the use of minesweeping, convoys, and government-orchestrated navigation orders. Following the breakdown of the agreement in 2023, government-backed insurance was deployed to facilitate continued trading and offset a potential dearth of commercial war risk options due to the threat of continued attacks – harkening back to the wartime arrangements occurring during the major conflicts of the twentieth century.[291]

[291] See ch 1.

3

Unrest

I. Introduction

War and unrest are not separated by a bright line.[1] This became especially apparent during the Cold War as the two nuclear-armed superpowers and their respective allies engaged in aggressive political confrontation, while also seeking to prevent kinetic engagement between them from escalating out of control. Among the most important events in US–Soviet relations during this complex era was the Cuban Missile Crisis of 1962.[2] Following the US placement of nuclear missile systems at military bases along NATO's eastern borders and the failed attempt by the US government to overthrow Fidel Castro's regime through an invasion at the Bay of Pigs, during the summer of 1962 the USSR secretly delivered intermediate-range ballistic nuclear missiles to a launch site at San Cristobal, Cuba. A US reconnaissance aircraft photographed the sites, which set off a diplomatic crisis in October of that year. On 22 October, the US deployed warships to establish a blockade-like 'quarantine' around Cuba's coast.[3] The US also increased operational readiness for a preemptive attack. Then, with tensions already mounting, on 27 October, a US reconnaissance aircraft was shot down over Cuba, killing the US pilot. This brought the world to the precipice of a major war. But finally, on 28 October, following an exchange of letters between US and Soviet leaders, the USSR agreed to dismantle the missiles and remove them from Cuba. Months later, the US also removed some of its missiles from NATO bases. Although the Cuban Missile Crisis produced only minimal direct physical confrontation between the countries involved, the nearly catastrophic brinkmanship served as a cautionary moment that informed geopolitical techniques in the decades to follow.[4] Recognising that total war was a mutually

[1] The term 'unrest' used in this chapter is not intended to represent a technical category but to describe the varied forms of conflict falling below the threshold of the total world wars and major regional wars examined in ch 2.

[2] See JL Gaddis, *The Cold War: A New History* (Penguin, 2007).

[3] The US was careful not to frame this manoeuvre as a 'blockade' of Cuba, which could have been perceived as an act of war. See JF Kennedy, Presidential Proclamation 3504, Interdiction of the Delivery of Offensive Weapons to Cuba (23 October 1962).

[4] In a reflective speech the following year, US President John F Kennedy candidly remarked that 'total war makes no sense' in the nuclear age. See JF Kennedy, 'Commencement Address at American University' (10 June 1963).

self-defeating proposition, the two sides resorted to more limited proxy fighting, which created its own set of political and commercial problems.

These Cold War proxy conflicts were used opportunistically to assert dominance and define spheres of influence while simultaneously embracing principles of containment and deterrence to stave off direct – potentially nuclear – hostilities. With the US serving as the avatar for Western capitalist democracies and the USSR leading the global communist movement, the Cold War era was packed with ideology-fuelled regional wars, civil wars, rebellions, insurrections, terrorist attacks, and other forms of politically charged unrest spanning across the world. When a civil war in Vietnam spiralled into chaos during the mid-1960s, the US sent hundreds of thousands of troops to fight a violent insurgency in a failed attempt to prevent the spread of communism. This protracted conflict continued until 1975, ultimately spilling into other former French colonies in Laos and Cambodia, which set the conditions for the rise of the Khmer Rouge. In 1979, the US-backed Shah of Iran was deposed during the Islamic Revolution, leading to the establishment of a theocratic anti-American government. This was immediately followed by the Soviet invasion of neighbouring Afghanistan, which was met with a resistance funded by the US. The same year, the US-supported Somoza government in Nicaragua was overthrown by a Soviet-aligned Sandinista incursion. The US then proceeded to secretly support a Contra insurgency against the Sandinistas through the mid-1980s. This pattern repeated itself frequently as the hot nature of the Cold War manifested during civil conflicts in Angola, Chile, Guatemala, Mozambique, and various other countries. Although these regionally confined conflicts were much more limited in scale than the World Wars, they still disrupted international trade, leading to sporadic contract disputes between commercial shipping interests that reconceptualised notions of war risk beyond the direct physical engagement between major powers.

One of the most substantial disruptions to shipping that occurred during the Cold War years took place in Egypt along the Suez Canal. The first Suez Canal crisis emerged when the Egyptian government nationalised the waterway in the summer of 1956. This created immediate tensions between Egypt, Britain, and France.[5] With the UN failing to broker a solution, war broke out with Britain, France, and Israel on one side and Egypt on the other.[6] The conflict resulted in a closure of the Suez Canal for several months from the autumn of 1956 to the spring of 1957, leading to damage to merchant ships and many voyage diversions. But a much longer Suez Canal closure occurred a decade later following the 1967

[5] Although the Suez Canal runs directly through Egyptian territory to connect the Mediterranean Sea to the Red Sea, it was built in the mid-nineteenth century to be operated by a joint British and French Suez Canal Company. When Egypt gained its independence in 1922, it continued to authorise foreign operation of the Canal under a treaty.

[6] The conflict was resolved by the end of 1956 after the US pressured the UK, France, and Israel to withdraw. See US Department of State, Office of the Historian, 'The Suez Crisis 1956'.

Six Day War between Israel and Egypt. This war started when Egypt – apparently acting on false Soviet intelligence regarding Israeli plans to invade Syria – prohibited Israeli-connected ships from navigating through the Strait of Tiran, which blocked Gulf of Aqaba access connecting Southern Israel to the Red Sea.[7] Israel responded to the Egyptian blockade by invading the Sinai Peninsula.[8] Although the fighting was short-lived (as the conflict's name suggests), the Six Day War left Egypt and Israel occupying opposite sides of the Canal Zone. For several years, the two sides engaged in intermittent shelling across the waterway, making Suez Canal passage impossible for commercial voyages. The subsequent Yom Kippur War in the autumn of 1973 resulted in Egypt taking back control of the eastern side of the Canal. Only then was Suez finally cleared of wrecks and debris. It was reopened in 1975 after eight years of closure to commercial traffic. Throughout the closure, merchant ships were forced to divert around the Cape of Good Hope, adding significant time and cost. Many commercial disputes arose to address questions involving damage by missile strikes, liberties to divert, and various other contract challenges.[9]

The recurring hostilities between Israel and neighbouring countries coincided with new forms of politically motivated violence. Non-state militant groups with malicious intentions – which became popularly known (and legally designated) as terrorist organisations – began engaging in infrastructure sabotage, airline and vessel hijackings, and other brazen attacks on civilian targets. Some of these actors were funded or protected by national governments. Following the Islamic Revolution, Iran began funding proxy groups, such as Hezbollah in Lebanon and Hamas in the Palestinian territories, which targeted Israeli and Western interests with attacks, even as a period of détente during the 1980s began to reduce Cold War tensions.[10] These actions performed by militant proxies with support of sovereign governments produced new concerns over the risks of state-sponsored terror.[11] In conjunction with the Iran–Iraq War and the Tanker War period, the maritime dimensions of this emerging threat spurred multilateral efforts to prevent terrorist attacks at sea.[12] These risks also contextualised industry contract reforms reflected in updated wordings. In the London insurance market, for instance, the 1983 Institute Clauses contained an express 'malicious acts' exclusion.[13]

[7] See US Department of State, Office of the Historian, 'The 1967 Arab-Israeli War'.

[8] Israel also took control of Gaza, the West Bank, and other areas that had been controlled by Syria and Jordan.

[9] During the conflict, some vessels were trapped in the Canal Zone itself. In fact, following the outbreak of the Six Day War, a 'yellow fleet' of commercial ships (named as such because they became covered in Sahara Desert dust) remained trapped in the Suez Canal's Great Bitter Lake until 1975. See J Feyrer, 'Distance, Trade, and Income – The 1967 to 1975 Closing of the Suez Canal as a Natural Experiment' *National Bureau of Economic Research* (2009).

[10] A Lane, 'Iran's Islamist Proxies in the Middle East' *Wilson Center* (12 September 2023).

[11] DL Byman, 'Proxy Power: Understanding Iran's Use of Terrorism' *Brookings* (26 July 2006).

[12] R Bowley, *Preventing Terrorist Attacks at Sea: Maritime Terrorism Risk and International Law* (Routledge, 2022).

[13] See Institute Time Clauses (Hulls) 1.10.83, Cl 25.

The corresponding 1983 Institute War and Strike Clauses provided insurance for these exclusions under its enumerated list of covered perils referencing loss caused by 'any terrorist or any person acting maliciously or from a political motive'.[14]

By 1990, the Iran–Iraq War was settled and the Cold War was winding down, but regional conflict reengaged when Iraq started a new conflict by invading Kuwait, sparking concerns of another period of instability and disruption.[15] The US and its allies responded with precision missile attacks on Iraq, which quickly ended the kinetic side of the conflict. Multilateral economic sanctions were then deployed to deter further aggression.[16] Although a Tanker War-style phase of physical disruption to shipping did not materialise as feared, the First Gulf War nevertheless spurred new contractual developments in the vessel-chartering context to address both conventional war risk and the prospect of non-state attacks. Moving beyond the charterparty wordings that had simply mirrored the retired FC&S insurance clause, in 1993 BIMCO circulated new CONWARTIME and VOYWAR provisions to address, in part, the shipowner's liberty to avoid the charterer's orders in the event of war risks broadly defined to include not only war, hostilities, and warlike operations, but also 'acts of terrorists' and 'acts of hostility or malicious damage', regardless of whether the action was performed by 'any person, body, terrorist or political group, or the Government of any state whatsoever'.[17]

This turned out to be a prescient drafting choice as terrorism risk would soon reach crescendo. On 11 September 2001, four teams of Al Qaeda operatives hijacked US civilian aircrafts, crashing two into the twin World Trade Center towers, one into the Pentagon, and another into a field in Pennsylvania. The shocking scale of death and destruction caused by what became known as the '9/11' attacks had profound implications for twenty-first century geopolitics. Following these events, for the first time in its history, NATO invoked its Article 5 collective self-defence commitment.[18] The US and its allies then launched attacks against Al Qaeda and the ruling Taliban in Afghanistan. The shipping community also mobilised. Concerned that terrorist groups might use maritime infrastructure for future attacks, the IMO adopted new regulatory mandates to enhance port security under the International Ship and Port Facility Security (ISPS) Code.[19] The enhanced compliance efforts to align with these new security standards also led to contract modifications. By 2003, BIMCO published ISPS Clauses designed

[14] Institute War and Strike Clauses Hulls-Time, Cl 1.5. The development of these clauses is discussed in K Michel, *War, Terror and Carriage by Sea* (Informa, 2004) ch 5.

[15] Representing a shift from the Cold War era, the US and USSR issued a joint statement condemning the invasion. The geopolitical implications of this moment are discussed in D Ross, *Statecraft 2.0: What American Needs to Lead in a Multipolar World* (OUP, 2025) 13–14.

[16] These sanctions targeting Iraq are discussed in ch 6.

[17] See BIMCO Standard War Risk Clause for Time Charters 1993 (CONWARTIME 1993); BIMCO Standard War Risk Claus for Voyage Chartering 1993 (VOYWAR 1993).

[18] NATO, 'Collective Defense and Article 5' (4 July 2023).

[19] The ISPS Code was imposed through amendments to Chapter XI of the Safety of Life at Sea Convention.

for charterparties to articulate contractual burdens for new regulatory compliance obligations.[20] The same year, the London marine insurance market updated its war risk exclusion language to carve out liability for loss arising from 'any terrorist' or 'any person acting from political motive', with corresponding covered perils mirrored under the revised Institute War and Strike Clauses.[21] The American marine insurance market, which remained an important source of cargo cover, adopted similar revisions. By 2004, it circulated all risk cargo clauses containing a Strikes, Riots & Civil Commotions provision, which expressly excluded cover for both 'malicious acts' and 'acts of one or more persons, whether or not agents of a sovereign power, carried out for political, terroristic or ideological purposes'.[22] This cover could then be reinstated by way of an endorsement using corresponding language.[23]

The military response to these events – rhetorically styled as a 'war on terror' – then escalated into conventional conflicts beyond Afghanistan. In 2003, the US and a coalition of military partners commenced an invasion of Iraq, alleging that it was a state sponsor of terror covertly pursuing the development of weapons of mass destruction.[24] The invasion quickly toppled the Iraqi government, but these attempts at regime change rapidly transformed into a chaotic and deadly nation-building project that created a prolonged period of instability in the region.[25] This Second Gulf War again produced security risks in a strategically significant area for shipping, which generated further industry adaptations reflected in contract wording modifications. In 2004, BIMCO published several new clauses addressing war risk, including updates to its CONWARTIME and VOYWAR clauses, along with a separate War Cancellation Clause.[26] With the war in Iraq turning out to be a politically unpopular undertaking, other threats emanating from the US-described 'axis of evil' (Iran and North Korea) were addressed through multilateral sanctions in attempts to curb those countries' respective nuclear weapons ambitions without direct military intervention. This economic pressure was facilitated by international cooperation driven by a post-Cold War UN Security Council consensus, a progressively influential EU political bloc, and an increasingly integrated China.[27]

Even as the international community seemed to unify in the fight against common threats – including not only terrorism and nuclear non-proliferation,

[20] See BIMCO ISPS Clause for Time Charter Parties 2003; ISPS Clause for Voyage Charter Parties 2004.

[21] See International Hull Clauses, 1.11.03, Cl 30; Institute War and Strike Clauses Hulls-Time, Cl 1.5; see also Michel (n 14) § 5.04.

[22] See American Institute of Marine Underwriters Cargo Clauses All Risks, 1 January 2004.

[23] See American Institute of Marine Underwriters, Strikes, Riots & Civil Commotions (Form 12A), 1 January 2008.

[24] In a speech following the 9/11 attacks, US President George W Bush had described Iraq, Iran, and North Korea as an 'axis of evil'. See 'President Delivers State of the Union Address' (29 January 2002).

[25] See TE Ricks, *Fiasco: The American Military Adventure in Iraq* (Penguin, 2007).

[26] See BIMCO War Risk Clause for Time Charters, 2004 (CONWARTIME 2004); BIMCO War Risk Clause for Voyage Chartering, 2004 (VOYWAR 2004); BIMCO War Cancellation Clause 2004.

[27] These sanctions measures are discussed in ch 5.

but also Somali piracy – the Middle East and North Africa remained turbulent.[28] In the 2010s, an 'Arab Spring' of protestors seeking political reform in Tunisia spilled over into other countries throughout the region and ultimately sparked violent unrest and large-scale wars in Libya, Syria, and Yemen.[29] As these events unfolded, after years of pressure from multilateral sanctions, Iran agreed to roll back its nuclear programme in exchange for sanctions relief. But following a shift in policy priorities, the US withdrew from the agreement in 2018 and unilaterally reimposed sanctions on Iran, occasionally enforcing them by physically seizing vessels and cargo.[30] Iran and its proxies retaliated, including through covert vessel attacks and audacious hijackings – even threatening to close the Strait of Hormuz at the entrance to the Persian Gulf.[31] Regional tensions escalated further when Hamas conducted a large-scale terrorist attack in Israel on 7 October 2023. Israel's heavy military response in Gaza was then followed by further violence against Israeli and Western targets performed by Iran-backed militants. Among them were Houthi rebels who had secured de facto control over large swaths of Yemen following the Arab Spring.[32] In November 2023, the Houthis began hijacking and bombarding commercial ships with missiles and drones as they approached the Bab al Mandeb Strait en route to and from the Suez Canal. Although the Houthis claimed its attacks were designed to effectuate a 'naval blockade' against Israeli interests, they caused largely indiscriminate death, destruction, and environmental pollution.[33] The threat of attacks also gave rise to many voyage diversions, as thousands of ships were forced to avoid the region and navigate around the Cape of Good Hope, cutting annual Suez transits by half.[34] The US, Israel, and other military partners responded by destroying Houthi targets inside Yemen, which quickly escalated into a broader regional conflict with Iran.[35] In the summer of 2025, after the UN International Atomic Energy Agency found Iran to be violating its commitments regarding uranium enrichment, Israel preemptively attacked military targets inside Iran. The US

[28] These piracy challenges and their impact on the modification of contract clauses, including updates to BIMCO's CONWARTIME and VOYWAR clauses in 2013, are discussed in ch 4.

[29] See K Robinson and W Merrow, 'The Arab Spring at Ten Years: What's the Legacy of the Uprisings' *Council on Foreign Relations* (3 December 2020).

[30] See eg US Department of Justice, Press Release: 'Largest US Seizure of Iranian Fuel from Four Tankers' (14 August 2020).

[31] HI Sutton, 'Spate of Attacks on Ships in Middle East Points to Iran-Backed Group' *US Naval Institute News* (6 January 2021).

[32] See CM Blanchard, 'Houthi Attacks in the Red Sea: Issues for Congress' *Congressional Research Service* (6 September 2024).

[33] See E Goksedef, 'Houthis Offer Reassurance to "Compliant" Vessels with Red Sea FAQs' *Lloyd's List* (13 August 2025).

[34] B Diakun and MW Bockmann, 'Falls in Red Sea Ship Traffic Stabilise as Suez Transits Hit Fresh Low' *Lloyd's List* (21 February 2024).

[35] As these Middle East conflicts unfolded, NATO countries continued supporting Ukraine in its defence against Russia. Russia responded with 'hybrid' and 'asymmetric' techniques targeting Western interests, including mysterious sabotage of undersea infrastructure and attacks on maritime assets. This harkened back to Cold War era confrontation. See A Bilal, 'Russia's Hybrid War Against the West' *NATO Review* (26 April 2024).

joined the conflict by sending stealth aircraft across the Atlantic to heavily bomb Iran's nuclear enrichment sites. Iran responded by threatening to close the Strait of Hormuz.[36] In 2025, BIMCO again updated its CONWARTIME and VOYWAR clauses in attempts to contractually address some of these evolving challenges – a sign that the shipping industry had entered yet another precarious age of disruption.[37]

II. Unrest in Commercial Maritime Disputes

A. Chartering and Carriage

i. Rerouting

Many cases involving war and conflict have addressed the impact of vessel re-routing during the multiple closures of the Suez Canal. Among the first was *Glidden Co v Hellenic Lines Ltd*.[38] The parties in that case had agreed to four charterparties to move bulk manufacturing compounds from India to the US in 1956. After the agreements were made but before performance had begun, the Suez Canal route was forced to close by the conflict between Egypt, Britain, and France. The shipowner refused to perform on the basis that taking the ordinary and usual route was impossible since the Suez Canal was unusable, which, it alleged, 'frustrated the adventure'.[39] The shipowner also invoked a *force majeure* clause in the charterparty referencing performance exceptions due to 'restraint of princes' and 'unusual occurrence beyond control of either party'.[40] The shipowner further relied on the 'act of war' carrier liability exclusion contained in US COGSA that had been incorporated into the charterparties by reference.[41] Despite these defences, the charterer sought to enforce the contract. The trial court held that the charterparties were frustrated and dismissed the charterer's action, finding that a voyage via alternative routes would be an 'entirely different undertaking' to the one that had been agreed.[42] But the US Court of Appeals for the Second Circuit reversed on the grounds that alternative routes were still viable despite the Suez closure, which precluded the frustration defence.[43] The court's decision was informed by

[36] See D Osler, 'Strait of Hormuz Closure May Trigger BIMCO Force Majeure Clause' *Lloyd's List* (30 July 2025).

[37] Following on the 2013 updates, these modifications sought, inter alia, to more seamlessly align shipowner and charterer liabilities with their respective insurance obligations. See BIMCO, War Risk Clause for Time Chartering 2025 (CONWARTIME 2025); BIMCO, War Risk Clause for Voyage Charter Parties 2025 (VOYWAR 2025).

[38] *Glidden Co v Hellenic Lines Ltd*, 275 F2d 253 (2nd Cir 1960) (Lumbard J).

[39] *Glidden Co v Hellenic Lines Ltd*, 182 F Supp 172, 174 (SDNY 1959) (Knox J).

[40] ibid.

[41] ibid.

[42] ibid, 180.

[43] *Glidden Co v Hellenic Lines Ltd*, 275 F2d 253 (2nd Cir 1960) (Lumbard J).

the fact that during the contract negotiations the parties had considered including a clause that expressly stated that the charterparty would be frustrated if the Suez Canal were to close, but the parties were ultimately unable to agree on the terms. The court explained that it 'would not be justified in interpreting the agreements as accomplishing by implication the very thing to which the parties declined to agree in express language'.[44] Although the shipowner had alleged that Suez was the 'only economically feasible route', the court found the fact that the parties did not expressly require performance to be through the Suez Canal meant that there was still an obligation to perform by an alternative route around the Cape of Good Hope.[45]

Several English cases also arose out of the first Suez closure, including *Societe Franco-Tunisienne D'Armement v Sidermar SPA (The Massalia)*.[46] The parties in that case had agreed to a voyage charter to move iron ore from northeast India to northwest Italy on the bulk carrier *Massalia*. The parties had agreed to the contract in October 1956 with knowledge that the Canal had already been nationalised by Egypt. Although the Canal remained open for transit at that time, heavy fighting ensued following the contract fixture.[47] As British and French forces launched attacks inside Egypt and occupied both the north and south sides of the Canal, the *Massalia* arrived in India and completed cargo loading. But shortly thereafter, the shipowner claimed that the charterparty had been 'brought to an end by the blocking of the Suez Canal and because of the likelihood of its remaining blocked for a substantial period of time'.[48] The charterer claimed that the shipowner was still obliged to perform the contract via the Cape route but was not entitled to payment beyond what was originally agreed. The parties agreed that this dispute regarding payment should be referred to arbitration following performance around the Cape. As the claim was pending, the *Massalia* sailed via the Cape route and transshipped the cargo to other vessels in Morocco, which later delivered the cargo to the intended destination in Italy. The shipowner maintained that the contract had been frustrated, but since it still performed transport services it sought 'reasonable remuneration', whereas the charterer took the position that the contract had been performed and the previously agreed freight rate governed regardless of the use of the longer Cape route.[49]

Reasoning that the availability of the Suez route was not a basic assumption of the contract and that performance via the Cape was not fundamentally different from the voyage planned by the parties, the arbitration tribunal held in favour of the charterer. But the English Commercial Court reversed, holding that the contract was indeed frustrated. The court determined that the charterparty

[44] ibid, 257.
[45] ibid, 256.
[46] *Societe Franco-Tunisienne D'Armement v Sidermar SPA (The Massalia)* [1960] 1 Lloyd's Rep 594 (Comm) (Pearson J).
[47] ibid, 600.
[48] ibid, 601.
[49] ibid.

language provided evidence the parties had contemplated the Suez route because it contained a clause obliging the shipmaster to send a telegraph 'on passing Suez Canal'.[50] Emphasising 'the simple geography of the matter', the court reasoned that moving cargo from India to Italy via the Suez Canal is a 'fairly direct route', which requires simply going west to the Red Sea, then up through the Canal, and then northwest to Italy.[51] In contrast, the Cape is a 'highly circuitous route' which requires passing the Equator twice.[52] Emphasising the meandering nature of this alternative route, the court explained the Cape route 'is so circuitous, and so unnatural, and so different in a number of respects, from the route via the Suez Canal that it should be regarded as fundamentally different'.[53] Although the contract was deemed frustrated, since the shipowner actually performed an alternative voyage to move the cargo, the court held the shipowner was entitled to reasonable remuneration for the provided services on a quantum meruit theory.[54]

This view was expressly rejected by the English Court of Appeal in *Ocean Tramp Tankers Corp v V/O Sovfracht (The Eugenia)*.[55] In July 1956, as British and French troops began mobilising in the Mediterranean Sea in response to Egypt's nationalisation of the Canal, a Russian state-controlled trading company began negotiating a charterparty to move iron ore from ports in the Black Sea to India on the bulk carrier *Eugenia*. The parties recognised the risk of a potential Suez closure and attempted to negotiate explicit contract terms to deal with the scenario, but they could not come to an agreement on the language. Instead, in the autumn of 1956, the parties fixed a time charter without any explicit clause addressing the prospect of a Suez closure. However, the contract did contain a war clause, which provided that without the consent of the shipowner the charterer could not order a voyage that would bring the vessel 'within a zone which is dangerous as the result of any actual or threatened act of war, war, hostilities, warlike operations'.[56] For the first voyage under the time charter, the charterer gave orders to load the vessel in the Black Sea with cargo to be delivered to India's East Coast. At the time of departure from the loading port, despite the unstable situation developing in Egypt, Suez remained open. But when the *Eugenia* arrived off Port Said at the Mediterranean entrance to the Canal, British and French reconnaissance aircraft were flying over the area and Egypt was deploying anti-aircraft guns against them. Despite this obviously dangerous situation, the charterer arranged for the vessel to enter the Canal in convoy the next morning. The *Eugenia* began to proceed through the Canal, travelling more than 50 km south. Then, English and French aircraft began bombing Egyptian targets in the vicinity. Egypt responded by sinking nearby ships

[50] ibid, 609.
[51] ibid.
[52] ibid.
[53] ibid, 611.
[54] ibid, 613.
[55] *Ocean Tramp Tankers Corp v V/O Sovfracht (The Eugenia)* [1963] 2 Lloyd's Rep 381 (CA) (Lord Denning MR).
[56] ibid, 387.

and blowing up bridges, which blocked passage through the Canal. The *Eugenia* was trapped in place until a ceasefire was agreed. Northbound Canal passage was cleared several months later but southbound passage remained blocked, so the *Eugenia* was forced to turn around in the Canal and head back toward Port Said. At this point, the charterers took the position that the charterparty was frustrated, but the shipowner contested this view. The shipowner then entered into a separate voyage charter with a different charterer to carry the iron ore already on board the *Eugenia* to India via the Cape route. Although this substitute arrangement was actually beneficial to the shipowner because the freight market had 'risen rapidly' due to the Suez crisis, the shipowner sought to recover from the charterer unpaid hire for the time lost when the *Eugenia* was trapped in the Canal.[57]

At first instance, the arbitrators held that the contract was not frustrated, but the English Commercial Court reversed on grounds that the 'voyage round the Cape, is basically or fundamentally different from an adventure involving a voyage via the Suez Canal'.[58] On review, the English Court of Appeal reversed again, finding that the contract was not frustrated. The court reasoned that given that the *Eugenia* was trapped in the Canal by the charterer's own decision to order the vessel to proceed in a dangerous area in breach of the war clause, this amounted to 'self-induced frustration', which is effectively no frustration at all.[59] Describing the basic tenants of frustration, the court explained that if while performing a contract, 'a fundamentally different situation arises for which the parties made no provision – so much so that it would not be just in the new situation to hold them bound to its terms – then the contract is at an end'.[60] Applying this standard, the court found no frustration had occurred in part because the parties had attempted to agree on a clause addressing the Canal closure contingency but were unable to do so. To amount to frustration, the court explained, performance of the contract 'must be more than merely more onerous or more expensive. It must be positively unjust to hold the parties bound'.[61] The voyage from the time of delivery to the time of redelivery would have been 108 days via the Suez Canal, but via the Cape it was 138 days. In addition, the cargo was iron and steel, which would be unlikely to become damaged during the longer voyage; the cargo had already been loaded on board at the time of the canal closure; and the longer voyage around the Cape did not change the basic nature of the contract other than to make it longer and more expensive. For these reasons, the court explained, '[t]he difference over the whole voyage [was] not so radical as to produce frustration'.[62]

[57] ibid, 388.

[58] *Ocean Tramp Tankers Corp v V/O Sovfracht (The Eugenia)* [1963] 2 Lloyd's Rep 155 (Comm) (Megaw J).

[59] *Ocean Tramp Tankers Corp v V/O Sovfracht (The Eugenia)* [1963] 2 Lloyd's Rep 381, 389.

[60] ibid.

[61] ibid, 390.

[62] Lord Denning MR wrote, 'the decision of Mr. Justice Pearson in the *Massalia* … was wrong and should be overruled. It is to be noticed that both in that case and in this the arbitrators held there was no frustration. I think they were right.' ibid, 391.

Following the Six Day War in the summer of 1967, intermittent fighting in the Canal Zone kept it closed to vessel traffic for the next eight years. Among the cases arising out of this much longer closure is *Achille Lauro Fu Giaocchino & C v Total Societa Italiana Per Azioni*.[63] The parties in that case had agreed to a consecutive voyage charter for the tanker *Volere* to move crude oil from the Persian Gulf to various locations in Europe, Africa, and Australia. Under the agreement, the parties aimed to fix as many voyages as possible during a period of one year spanning 1966 to 1967 with the freight rates on an agreed scale. The parties performed many voyages under the contract, until the summer of 1967 when hostilities broke out causing Suez to close without the prospect of re-opening during the remainder of the charter period.[64] The *Volere's* last voyage under the charter involved loading oil in the Persian Gulf and moving it to Portugal by way of the Cape of Good Hope. This caused a dispute between the shipowner and the charterer as to how the freight should be calculated for that voyage. The parties had anticipated the risk of disruption by including a Suez Canal Clause in the charterparty.[65] The clause provided that the freight should be adjusted, 'if the vessel under Charterers' orders or with their consent performs by an alternative route the ballast and/or laden passages which would normally have entailed the transit of the Suez Canal'.[66] The clause further provided that in scenarios that 'would not normally entail transit through the Suez Canal' the freight rate should be calculated 'on the basis of the actual laden passage performed plus a theoretical ballast passage via the Suez Canal to the loading port'.[67] Despite this language, the shipowner contended that the clause should not apply when the Suez Canal was closed because there can only be an 'alternative route' when there is a choice between routes.[68] Since Suez was closed, the shipowner argued that the rate should be calculated based on a laden voyage between the Persian Gulf to Lisbon via the Cape along with a 'notional ballast voyage' back to the Persian Gulf along the same route. But the charterer argued that the freight calculation should not include a notional ballast voyage back to the Persian Gulf and should instead reference a notional ballast voyage from Lisbon to the Persian Gulf via the Suez Canal.

Weighing these technical arguments, the English Commercial Court held for the shipowner.[69] The court explained that if the Suez Canal is closed, the voyage via the Cape is 'indistinguishable in principle from any other voyage and there is not obvious reason for its receiving exceptional treatment' by calculating a

[63] *Achille Lauro Fu Giaocchino & C v Total Societa Italiana Per Azioni* [1969] 2 Lloyd's Rep 65 (CA) (Lord Denning MR).
[64] ibid, 67.
[65] ibid, 67.
[66] ibid.
[67] ibid.
[68] ibid.
[69] *Achille Lauro Fu Giaocchino & C v Total Societa Italiana Per Azioni* [1968] 2 Lloyd's Rep 247 (Comm) (Donaldson J).

notional voyage via the blocked Suez route.[70] Rejecting this view, the English Court of Appeal reversed.[71] The court refused to accept the shipowner's position that the 'alternative route' calculation measure in the Suez Canal Clause did not apply when Suez was closed or that the notional ballast voyage would have to include the Cape route. The court explained that the clause applied regardless of whether the Canal was open or closed. Although the Suez Canal Clause referred to a 'theoretical ballast passage via Suez to the loading port', which could not actually be performed because of the closure, the language of the clause referenced the 'notional' rather than the 'actual' voyage for the purpose of freight calculation.[72] In this context, the court explained, the parties, 'must have intended to cover, not only the case when the Suez Canal is open and storm clouds are gathering, but also the case when the storm clouds have actually come down and closed the Canal'.[73]

The same year, the English Commercial Court decided *Palmco Shipping Inc v Continental Ore Corp (The Captain George K)*.[74] In that case, just before the outbreak the Six Day War, the parties had agreed to a voyage charter to move a cargo of sulphur on the *Captain George K* from the East Coast of Mexico to the West Coast of India. The vessel sailed successfully from Mexico through the Strait of Gibraltar and the Mediterranean Sea, but when it arrived at anchorage outside of Port Said in preparation to make its way south through the Suez Canal, officials operating the Canal pilot station notified the shipmaster that Suez was closed due to fighting in the vicinity. At that point, the shipowner took the position that the contract was frustrated, but – after reserving the right to later pursue its frustration claim – the shipowner accepted the charterer's alternative orders to divert the vessel around the Cape. The *Captain George K* delivered the cargo in India, but the voyage took 44 days longer than expected via the planned route. After performance, the shipowner demanded additional freight for time and costs, but the charterer claimed the freight rate had already been agreed prior to the voyage. An umpire in arbitration held for the charterer, even while expressing sympathy to the shipowner's position, in part because a clause in the charterparty referenced the vessel arriving 'off Suez' and required the shipmaster to send a telegraph after 'passing Suez'.[75] This language, according to the umpire, seemed to show that the parties had intended to go through Suez, which, in any event, was the customary route. The umpire found that there was no expectation that the Canal would become closed at the time of contracting and, for this reason, the voyage performed was different than the one that was contemplated, which had become impossible. Nevertheless, being

[70] ibid, 252.
[71] *Achille Lauro Fu Giaocchino & C v Total Societa Italiana Per Azioni* [1969] 2 Lloyd's Rep 65.
[72] ibid, 68.
[73] ibid.
[74] *Palmco Shipping Inc v Continental Ore Corp (The Captain George K)* [1970] 2 Lloyd's Rep 21 (Comm) (Mocatta J).
[75] ibid, 23.

bound by the *Eugenia* decision (discussed above), the umpire held for the charterer. The English Commercial Court affirmed. The court emphasised that if it had not been bound by the *Eugenia* decision, like the umpire, it would have reached the conclusion that the performed voyage of the *Captain George K* was fundamentally different from that voyage contemplated by the charterparty both in time and mileage, especially given that the vessel had been 'heavily committed to what became the wrong route' when it sailed all the way across the Mediterranean Sea to Port Said before being forced to turn around.[76] Nevertheless, since the facts of the case were aligned with those in the *Eugenia*, there was no precedential basis to find frustration. Thus, 'with a reluctance', the court held in favour of the charterer.[77]

Among the leading American decisions arising out of the second Suez closure is *Transatlantic Financing Corp v United States of America*.[78] There, the parties had agreed to a voyage charter to move wheat on the *SS Christos* from Texas to Iran. After the vessel loaded in Texas, the conflict in Egypt and the Canal zone blocked the Suez route. Although the most direct route from Texas to Iran would have been through the Strait of Gibraltar, the Mediterranean Sea, and the Suez Canal, due to the closure the shipowner performed the voyage via the Cape of Good Hope. This added 18 days and more than 3,000 miles – costs the shipowner sought to recover from the charterer. The charterer (which happened to be the US government) refused to pay additional compensation on the grounds that it had not directed a deviation from the customary route. The US District Court for the District of Columbia held for the charterer.[79] The court reasoned that the closure of Suez was a 'supervening event' that did not make performance impossible, but rather rendered its objective 'more oppressive or more expensive'.[80] In such situations, the court explained, 'the risk of supervening difficulty and expense is for the contractor to bear'.[81] The US Court of Appeals for the District of Columbia Circuit affirmed. It reasoned that the contract did not expressly require the Suez route or allocate the risk in the event that it became closed. The court further found, 'the Cape route is generally regarded as an alternative means of performance'.[82] Given that there was ongoing turmoil in the Suez region at the time of contracting, it was foreseeable that the area might become dangerous. With an appreciation for this danger, the parties still contracted to perform the voyage without allocating the additional perils by explicit terms, which suggested a 'willingness by [the shipowner] to assume abnormal risks'.[83]

[76] ibid, 32.
[77] ibid.
[78] *Transatlantic Financing Corp v United States of America*, 363 F2d 312 (DC Cir 1966) (Wright J).
[79] *Transatlantic Financing Corp v United States of America*, 259 F Supp 725 (DDC 1965) (Corcoran J).
[80] ibid, 728.
[81] ibid.
[82] *Transatlantic Financing Corp v United States of America*, 363 F2d 312, 316 (DC Cir 1966).
[83] ibid, 319.

An even more drastic diversion was at issue in *American Trading & Production Corp v Shell International Marine Ltd*.[84] In that case, the parties had agreed under a voyage charter to move oil on the tanker *Washington Trader* from Texas to India. During the voyage, as the vessel approached the north entrance to Suez, the vessel was forced to abandon the route due to the closure of the Canal.[85] The vessel diverted back across the Mediterranean Sea through the Strait of Gibraltar and down and around the Cape of Good Hope, which added 30 days and nearly 10,000 miles to the expected voyage. The shipowner sought to collect additional freight for the diversion, but the charterer refused to pay. The shipowner argued that Suez was the agreed route and that performance of the contract was impossible, but that by performing a voyage to deliver the cargo via the Cape of Good Hope route instead, 'a benefit was conferred upon the charterer' which should entitle it to compensation assessed through quantum meruit.[86] The US District Court for the Southern District of New York dismissed the shipowner's claim.[87] Affirming the decision, the US Court of Appeals for the Second Circuit first rejected the argument that the Suez Canal was the exclusive method of performance. Instead it found that that the parties contracted under the charter to transport the cargo from Texas to India at an agreed rate with 'absolutely no reference to any fixed route'.[88] Despite the substantial diversion and added costs, the court took the position that the Cape route was 'well recognized' and that it did not make the voyage 'unreasonably difficult, dangerous or onerous'.[89] Accordingly, it found that the increased costs alone did not reach the level of 'commercial impracticability' that might justify modifying the contract to allow the shipowner to recover more than what was originally agreed.[90]

ii. Politically Unsafe Ports

Political unrest has given rise to a number of cases interpreting charterparty safe port warranties. Among them is *Vardinoyannis v The Egyptian General Petroleum Corp (The Evaggelos Th)*.[91] In November 1968, a Greek shipowner time chartered the tanker *Evaggelos Th* for seven months to an Egyptian charterer. At the time of contracting, the parties were aware of the danger of hostilities between Egypt and Israel, which had ebbed and flowed in the region for more than a year following the Six Day War. During 1967 (prior to the execution of the contract at issue),

[84] *American Trading & Production Corp v Shell International Marine Ltd*, 453 F2d 939 (2nd Cir 1972) (Mulligan J).
[85] ibid, 940.
[86] ibid, 941.
[87] *American Trading & Production Corp v Shell International Marine Ltd*, 343 F Supp 91 (SDNY 1971).
[88] *American Trading & Production Corp v Shell International Marine Ltd*, 453 F2d 939, 941.
[89] ibid.
[90] ibid.
[91] *Vardinoyannis v The Egyptian General Petroleum Corp (The Evaggelos Th)* [1971] 2 Lloyd's Rep 200 (Comm) (Donaldson J).

three ships had been sunk by shell fire in the Suez Canal zone. Although the two countries had agreed to a ceasefire in June 1967, they remained on a conflict footing as Israeli troops occupied parts of the Sinai Peninsula along the eastern side of the Canal with Egyptian forces occupying the Western side. In the context of the precarious situation, the *Evaggelos Th* facilitated various trades between the Egyptian refinery at Suez and the Egyptian oil fields in the Gulf of Suez. Even after a near miss by an Israeli shell in March 1968, the parties extended the contract for another six months. But during 25–26 June 1968, the *Evaggelos Th* became caught up in crossfire while discharging into lighter vessels in the Suez Roads near Adabiya, Egypt.[92] The vessel was hit by multiple Israeli shells, caught fire, and became a constructive total loss. The shipowner sued the charterer alleging its orders to trade near Suez breached a safe port provision in the charterparty placing it under an express obligation to discharge only in places where the vessel will 'always lie safely afloat'.[93] The charterer argued that the shipowner had waived the right to complain of the unsafety of the trading area given its knowledge of the risks and its willingness to initially agree to the charter and to later extend its duration even as hostilities intensified.

A panel of London arbitrators held for the charterer and the English Commercial Court affirmed.[94] First, the court explained that the charterparty terms 'safely afloat' were only concerned with the marine characteristics of the discharging place, such as wind or tides, and therefore did not apply in the context of gunfire during hostilities.[95] Second, the court described the implied obligation under the safe port clause as a duty on the time charterer to 'refrain from nominating a place which, by reason of its lack of safety or accessibility would, if nominated, frustrate the charter'.[96] This obligation, the court explained, is relatively broad in that '[s]afety in this context is not confined to physical safety. It extends also to political safety.'[97] However, the court emphasised that the contract at issue was not a 'simple charter' and therefore the implied safe port obligation 'has to be considered against the general business background to the transaction and the express terms of the charter'.[98] Applying this standard, the court found that the Red Sea was expressly permitted for trades under the charter even though it was 'plainly an area involving war risks'.[99] Although Israel itself was excluded under the trading limits, the court found this narrow restriction was 'inevitable' given that the charterer was an Egyptian corporation, and, therefore the court held that this drafting

[92] Lighterage contracts may be used to allow smaller vessels to load from larger ships for onward transport. This practice may be used to facilitate cargo transport from ships that are too large to directly access smaller ports.
[93] ibid, 203.
[94] ibid.
[95] ibid, 203.
[96] ibid, 204.
[97] ibid.
[98] ibid.
[99] ibid.

choice during ongoing hostilities 'does not reflect an acceptance or rejection of war risks'.[100] In addition, the charter provided for redelivery at either Suez or Colombo, which the court found to be evidence that 'the owner seems to have regarded Suez as safe'.[101] Recognising the determination of a safe port is a 'question of fact and degree', the court explained that '[w]hat may be safe in the sense of involving an acceptable degree of hazard, whether war or marine, when carrying cargo in a war zone for one of the parties to the hostilities, may be quite unacceptable and unsafe when carrying other cargo in other areas'.[102] Although the Suez Roads may have been unsafe at the exact time the *Evaggelos TH* was hit by Israeli gunfire, vessels had been freely trading there prior to those events. Since the charterer's employment order had been made before the hostile action, this meant the charterer was not in breach of the safe port warranty.[103]

SMA arbitrations have addressed similar questions. In *Arietta Compania Naviera SA v World Wide Transport Inc*, the parties had contracted in 1970 under a time charter for the tanker *S/T Arietta Venizelos*.[104] The charterparty included terms allowing the vessel to trade 'between safe ports'.[105] In the autumn of 1970, government agencies, shipping publications, and other commercial intelligence sources began alerting the shipping industry of the prospect of attacks or sabotage on tankers by 'guerillas' operating in the eastern Mediterranean Sea.[106] On 17 December 1970, the shipowner sent a telex to the charterer stating that Libya – where the vessel had been trading – had become a dangerous area. The shipowner also emphasised that the vessel's underwriters had declared Libya as excluded from the Institute Warranty Limits, which, it contended, justified a rejection of the charterer's employment orders. The charterer wrote back via telex rejecting the notion that Libya was unsafe and arguing that '[t]here have been no significant changes since this charter was executed and numerous vessels continue to trade there without incident'.[107] Without further consultation with the shipowner on this point, the charterer then directly ordered the shipmaster to proceed to Libya. The shipowner learned of these orders through the shipmaster and intervened to refuse consent to proceed. It requested the charterer nominate an alternative loading port, but the charterer did not do so. Two days later, the shipowner withdrew the vessel. In arbitration, the charterer claimed damages, but the panel majority rejected the claim. It credited expert testimony to find that the security situation in the region was 'of a nature so grave' that the insurers were justified in placing Libya and other

[100] ibid.
[101] ibid, 205.
[102] ibid, 206.
[103] The court remanded the case back to the arbitrators on a separate issue involving the application of an indemnity provision to determine whether the proximate cause of the loss was the charterer's orders to discharge at Suez.
[104] *Arietta Compania Naviera SA v World Wide Transport Inc (The S/T Arietta Venizelos)*, SMA 733 (NY Arb 1972) (Eugene E Murphy, Bruno J Augenti) (Robert P Nash, dissenting).
[105] ibid, 2.
[106] ibid, 4.
[107] ibid.

ports beyond the scope of the Institute Warranty Limits.[108] The panel majority also cited various 'public sources' such as news reports to show the risk of war or terrorism targeting merchant ships was genuine and that the prevailing view in the industry was that 'the Middle East was on the brink of another major outbreak of hostilities'.[109] As a consequence, the panel majority explained, the charterer had 'endangered the vessel by ordering it to a danger zone', which it determined was a breach of the charterparty.[110] Rather than naming an alternative safe port within a reasonable time, the charterer went 'behind the Owner's back' by ordering the shipmaster to go to Libya and was therefore not entitled to recover.[111] A dissenting arbitrator disagreed, reasoning that the shipowner had withdrawn the vessel with 'unseemly haste', likely a pretext to take advantage of spot charter rates that had 'increased astronomically'.[112]

A similar question came before SMA arbitrators after the outbreak of the Yom Kippur War in 1973. In *Marastro Compania Naviera SA v Standard Tankers (Bahamas) Co Ltd*, the parties had agreed to a 10-year time charter for the tanker *M/T Trade Fortitude*.[113] The charterparty addressed safe ports and war risks through several provisions. Under its terms, the charterer had the liberty to employ the vessel anywhere in the world 'between safe ports'.[114] It also provided that the vessel should not be required to enter ports 'where hostilities are in progress, or any war zone, or zone deemed a danger zone in consequence of the existence of war, or actual hostilities, without the consent of the owner'.[115] Additionally, a War Risk clause provided that if 'owing to any war, hostilities, warlike operations', the shipowner determined a port to be dangerous 'in his or their discretion', the charterer 'shall have the right' to order the cargo loaded or discharged 'at any other safe port'.[116] In October 1973, the vessel was in the South China Sea en route from Japan to the Persian Gulf when the Yom Kippur War broke out in Israel, Egypt, and surrounding areas. The shipowner sent a telex to the charterer stating that the vessel should be diverted because the Persian Gulf was 'deemed to be a danger zone' due to 'hostilities in the Middle East'.[117] The charterer wrote back that there was no evidence that the events in Israel and Egypt posed a danger in the Persian Gulf and that it was 'premature at the present time to attempt to judge how the situation might affect this vessel'.[118] Several days later the shipowner again requested re-routing orders, but the

[108] ibid.
[109] ibid, 7.
[110] ibid, 8.
[111] ibid.
[112] ibid, 9.
[113] *Marastro Compania Naviera SA v Standard Tankers (Bahamas) Co Ltd (The M/T Trade Fortitude)*, SMA 1139 (NY Arb 1974) (R Glenn Bauerand Henry C Blackiston) (Captain George Stam dissenting).
[114] ibid, 2.
[115] ibid.
[116] ibid.
[117] ibid, 3.
[118] ibid, 4.

charterer replied with instructions to 'maintain orders for Persian Gulf'.[119] After further disagreement on this point, the charterer relented and ordered the vessel to Muscat, Oman (outside the Persian Gulf). Approximately one week later, the charterer ordered the vessel to Khor Al Amaya, Iraq (inside the Persian Gulf), but the shipowner refused to comply, stating that the regional security situation was 'even more severe', as evidenced by the activation of US and Soviet forces in the region.[120] The charterer replied that the shipowner's refusal was a breach of the charterparty and the shipowner immediately invoked its rights to refer the matter to arbitration.

The majority of arbitrators held for the charterer. Although the panel majority found that the shipowner was 'justifiably apprehensive' about the risks as the vessel headed towards the Middle East from Japan, the 'actual hostilities' were along the borders of Israel, the Eastern Mediterranean Sea, and parts of the Red Sea. The Persian Gulf, on the other hand, was more than 700 miles from Israel. In addition, on the date that the charterer gave orders to proceed to Iraq, there was no longer a reasonable ground for the shipowner to contend that the Persian Gulf was a danger zone. At that point, hostilities in Israel had effectively ceased and UN observers were positioning between the fighting forces. Meanwhile, in the Persian Gulf, hundreds of other tankers had loaded cargo during that same month, and although some Arab countries had enforced an embargo on the export of oil to the West during this period, this 'oil weapon' was being recognised as 'an economic sanction, not a physical threat'.[121] The separate threat of 'sabotage' or 'terrorist acts' by 'Palestinian guerillas' remained viable, but this risk was not worse than it had been prior to the outbreak of the Yom Kippur War.[122] Thus, according to the majority, 'the evidence of danger to shipping in the Persian Gulf was clearly insufficient' to find the charterer breached the contract by ordering the vessel to load in Iraq.[123] Again, however, the decision was not unanimous. Writing separately, a dissenting arbitrator reasoned that the charterparty clauses at issue granted wide discretion for the shipowner to weigh the war risks at the time the charterer's orders were given. Although it was true that many vessels had entered the Persian Gulf during the period in question, the dissent emphasised that the risks remained real given that several regional Arab countries were at war with Israel. The dissent explained that '[t]he decisions of belligerents and other organizations are not known and, within logical limits, are unpredictable'.[124] For this reason, according to the dissent, it was improper to depend on maritime security experts retrospectively second-guessing the commercial risk assessment of the shipowner who had initially relied only on 'information available to the trading

[119] ibid.
[120] ibid, 5.
[121] ibid, 8. These embargos are discussed in ch 6.
[122] ibid.
[123] ibid.
[124] ibid, 9.

world'.[125] Emphasising this point, the dissent remarked, 'the range of Phanom Jets as bombers is not known to businessmen'.[126]

The leading English case on the issue of 'political' safety is *K/S Penta Shipping A/S v Ethiopian Shipping Lines Corp (The Saga Cob)*.[127] In August of 1988, the time-chartered *Saga Cob* was ordered by the charterer to move a cargo of jet fuel north along the Red Sea coast from Assab to Massawa (both ports then controlled by Ethiopia). When the vessel arrived just off Massawa, it was 'attacked by Eritrean guerillas in motor boats using heavy machine guns and rocket grenades'.[128] The shipmaster was injured, the vessel was seriously damaged, and the contract was abandoned. The charterparty contained a clause under which the charterer was obliged to 'exercise due diligence to ensure the vessel is only employed between and at safe ports'.[129] Referencing this clause, the shipowner brought suit against the charterer to obtain damages, which presented the question of whether Massawa was prospectively unsafe when the charterer gave the order to proceed there.[130] The English Commercial court held that the port was unsafe because the risk of attack by Eritrean fighters had become a 'characteristic of the port of Massawa'.[131] Although the court found the risk of an attack was not of a 'high degree' it also was not 'negligible', which was enough to make it prospectively unsafe in August 1988 when the charterer gave the orders to proceed there.[132] But the English Court of Appeal reversed. It determined that although hostilities between the Ethiopian Government and rival Eritrean fighters had been going on for years, most attacks had taken place on inland targets. Acknowledging that there had been one prior attack on a different ship several months prior, this was thought to be 'an isolated abnormal incident'.[133] Since at the time of the charterer's order it appeared that the previous attack had been contained, it was inappropriate to view guerilla attacks by Eritrean fighters as a 'normal characteristic of the port'.[134] Applying the rule that a port will not be held to be unsafe unless 'the "political" risk is sufficient for a reasonable shipowner or master to decline to send or sail his vessel there', the court determined that at the time the charterer ordered the vessel to Massawa in August 1988 the port did not present such political risks as to make the port unsafe.

[125] ibid.
[126] ibid.
[127] *K/S Penta Shipping A/S v Ethiopian Shipping Lines Corp (The Saga Cob)* [1992] 2 Lloyd's Rep 545 (CA) (Parker LJ).
[128] ibid, 546.
[129] ibid.
[130] ibid.
[131] ibid, 549.
[132] *K/S Penta Shipping A/S v Ethiopian Shipping Lines Corp (The Saga Cob)* [1991] 2 Lloyd's Rep 398 (Comm) (Diamond J).
[133] *K/S Penta Shipping A/S v Ethiopian Shipping Lines Corp (The Saga Cob)* [1992] 2 Lloyd's Rep 545, 551.
[134] ibid.

iii. Diversions

Efforts to avoid war risks have also given rise to charterparty disputes involving whether a vessel is on or off hire during the diversion. A leading English case on the issue is *Kuwait Petroleum Corp v I & D Oil Carriers Ltd (The Houda).*[135] The *Houda* was under time charter and performing orders to load oil cargo in Kuwait for delivery to Egypt, when Iraq launched a surprise invasion of Kuwait. When the invasion occurred on 2 August 1990, the *Houda* quickly departed the Kuwaiti terminal only partially loaded, without the bills of lading, and proceeded to anchorage off Fujairah, UAE. On 8 August, the charterer provided employment orders to proceed to the Red Sea with the intention of delivering in Egypt, but the shipowner refused the orders in part because of the uncertainty regarding whether the cargo could be discharged without presenting the bills of lading that had been left in Kuwait and because it was concerned that the vessel's cargo might be subject to the UN sanctions that had been imposed immediately after the war broke out. After several weeks of delays, which included a survey of the cargo and negotiations for the charterer to issue a letter of indemnity, the shipowner agreed to allow the *Houda* to depart the UAE for Egypt, but once the vessel arrived there were further delays in part due to procedural problems for releasing the cargo without the production of the bills of lading that were still in Kuwait. The vessel was not able to discharge the cargo until the end of September. This led to a dispute between the shipowner and charterer as to whether the vessel was on or off hire during this two-month period. The charterer argued the *Houda* was off hire because it was deprived of the use of the vessel due to the shipowner's refusal to follow its orders, and the shipowner argued the *Houda* remained on hire because it was entirely justified in seeking information regarding the risks surrounding the charterer's orders before proceeding to Egypt.

The English Commercial Court held that the vessel was off hire from the time the charterer gave orders to the shipowner on 8 August to the time that the cargo was delivered on 27 September, reasoning that the shipowner's refusal to comply with the charterer's orders was a breach that rendered the time lost.[136] The English Court of Appeal later reversed the decision.[137] The court reasoned that under a 'war situation' the shipowner may have a right or even a duty to 'seek further information about the source of and the validity of any orders', even if the cargo or ship is not subject to an 'immediate physical threat'.[138] When a country has been invaded, the court explained, 'prudent owners may be entitled to guard against the risk that their orders may have come from the "wrong" side'.[139] Furthermore, the court found that any failure to comply with the 8 August orders to deliver the cargo

[135] *Kuwait Petroleum Corp v I & D Oil Carriers Ltd (The Houda)* [1994] 2 Lloyd's Rep 541 (CA) (Neill LJ).

[136] *Kuwait Petroleum Corp v I & D Oil Carriers Ltd (The Houda)* [1993] 1 Lloyd's Rep 333 (Comm) (Phillips J).

[137] *Kuwait Petroleum Corp v I & D Oil Carriers Ltd (The Houda)* [1994] 2 Lloyd's Rep 541.

[138] ibid, 549.

[139] ibid.

to Egypt was not the cause of the delay upon arrival as that was due to the inability to present the bills of lading that had been left behind in Kuwait. Although the court acknowledged a commercial practice of releasing cargo without the production of the bill of lading by way of a letter of indemnity, the existence of the practice does not 'impose on the owners a contractual obligation which does not otherwise exist'.[140] Thus, shipowner was not at fault for the delays and the *Houda* remained on hire throughout the invasion-induced debacle.

Shorter lived geopolitical conflicts also have given rise to hire questions. In *Andros Compania Maritime SA v Mineral Importexport*, during July of 1974, the Greek-flagged vessel *MV Andros Island* was under time charter and preparing to load iron ore for a voyage from Vitoria, Brazil, to the Black Sea port of Constanza, Romania, when a coup d'etat in Cyprus gave rise to a military confrontation between Greece and Turkey.[141] This led to the Turkish invasion of Cyprus. Although a ceasefire was reached quickly, tensions remained high. As a result, the Greek Merchant Marine Ministry issued an advisory to Greek-flagged ships to avoid entering or crossing Turkish territorial waters. The shipowner then contacted the shipmaster and the charterer via telex to place them on notice of the situation and noted that in order to reach Romania, the *Andros Island* would have to pass through the Turkish Straits. With this information, on 22 July, the shipmaster refused to berth and load the cargo. The charterer protested on the grounds that the Turkish authorities were not forbidding any Greek-flagged vessels to pass the Bosphorus. After several days of delay, following the charterer's assurances, the shipowner finally allowed the vessel to berth and load the cargo on 29 July. This gave rise to a dispute regarding whether the vessel was on or off hire during the more than five days between the time of the shipmaster's refusal to berth and the actual berthing and loading. Although the off-hire clause in the charterparty did not expressly address the scenario at issue, a separate War Risk Clause provided that in the event of a discharge port being subjected to blockade, the shipowner 'shall discharge the cargo at any other port covered by this Charterparty as ordered by the Charterers'.[142] In arbitration, the shipowner alleged it would be unreasonable and wrongful to deprive it of hire when the delay in loading was caused by explicit warnings from the flag state's merchant shipping agency that it was not safe to cross Turkish territorial waters.[143] The shipowner further argued the mandatory compliance with this Greek government directive was effectively a 'restraint of princes' under the charterparty that triggered its contractual right and obligation to avoid the risks associated with the planned voyage to Romania via the Turkish Straits.[144] The charterer countered that the warnings issued by the Greek

[140] ibid, 551.
[141] *Andros Compania Maritime SA v Mineral Importexport (The MV Andros Island)*, SMA 1548 (NY Arb 1980) (Joseph Simms and Klaus CJ Mordhorst) (Manfred W Arnold, dissenting in part).
[142] ibid, 11.
[143] ibid.
[144] ibid.

government were mere recommendations, and that even if the political situation resulted in a 'warlike situation', this still would have required the shipowner to load the cargo in Brazil and coordinate with the charterer under the War Risk Clause to determine an alternative discharge port.

The SMA panel majority held for the charterer. The majority first acknowledged that 'the rapidly changing political events in the Eastern Mediterranean Sea gave cause to uncertainties and confusion, both on governmental as well as commercial levels'.[145] However, the majority determined 'this kind of climate of uncertainty must not be allowed to supersede the contractual commitment', particularly when the parties have adopted 'remedial clauses for just such situations'.[146] It explained that under the terms of the charterparty, the shipowner was not authorised to act unilaterally to refuse loading in Brazil and instead was required to operate within the remedial framework of the War Risk Clause. The majority noted that if the shipowner would have operated consistently with the charterparty terms, 'the vessel would have continued to earn hire'.[147] But since the shipowner took a 'preemptive decision' to refuse loading in Brazil, the shipowner acted wrongfully and therefore the vessel was off-hire during the delay.[148] On the separate issue of whether the warning by the Greek government was mandatory and effectively a mutually excepted 'restraint of princes', the majority disagreed with the shipowner's position. It reasoned that these warnings were 'precautionary recommendations based on a prevailing political situation', which, of course, did not escalate into a war due to a quickly negotiated ceasefire and therefore never endangered the *Andros Island* as it was loading on the other side of the world far from the 'troubled seas between Greece and Turkey'.[149]

In *Hellenic Lines Ltd v United States*, the US Second Circuit Court of Appeal addressed the bill of lading consequences of an outbreak of hostilities between Israel and neighbouring Arab countries in 1967.[150] There, a shipment of bagged flour intended for the United Nations Relief and Works Agency had been arranged by the US government on the *MV Italia*. The contract of carriage with the commercial shipowner involved loading the cargo at several ports in the US Gulf of Mexico with the destination at Aqaba, Jordan, which required moving across the Mediterranean Sea and through the Suez Canal. The agreed freight was paid shortly after loading. Although the parties had initially agreed to an estimated date of arrival of 20 May, and the vessel was already behind schedule, the *Italia* stopped to load an additional non-government cargo in Virginia and New York for discharge in Greece, which caused further delays. Shortly after the *Italia* passed Gibraltar on 5 June, the Six Day War broke out between Israel and several other

[145] ibid, 14.
[146] ibid.
[147] ibid.
[148] ibid.
[149] ibid, 15. A dissenting arbitrator agreed the charterer was deprived of the use of the vessel but reasoned that the vessel was only off-hire for two days instead of five.
[150] *Hellenic Lines Ltd v United States*, 512 F2d 1196 (2nd Cir 1975) (Friendly J).

countries. As a consequence, the Suez Canal was temporarily closed to traffic. Acknowledging the dangerous conditions and the inability to move through Suez, the US government requested the *Italia* discharge the cargo in Beirut, Lebanon, or Izmir, Turkey. But the shipowner refused and instead discharged in Piraeus, Greece, along with the non-governmental cargo. The US government charterer then arranged for transportation on a different vessel to Ashdod, Israel. Despite having been prepaid for the freight, the shipowner requested more than $100,000 in additional fees on grounds that the discharge in Greece was subject to higher freight tariff under published liner conference rules. When the US government refused to pay the additional freight, the shipowner sued. The US government counterclaimed alleging the *Italia* had diverted to Piraeus, Greece, without its consent and was liable for the cost of transshipment to Israel.

The US District Court for the Southern District of New York held for the US government.[151] The court determined that not only was it entitled to recover the expenses incurred in arranging alternative transport to Israel, but that the shipowner also had to pay back the pre-paid freight because the delivery was never made. The US Court of Appeals for the Second Circuit affirmed on the merits, but it adjusted the remedy. The court found that the shipowner's decision to load additional non-governmental cargo in Virginia and New York was a voluntary and unreasonable deviation that had the effect of delaying the voyage for 12 days, which ultimately led to further disruption due to the regional hostilities. Supporting this holding, the court construed both the Liberties Clause in the bill of lading and the US Carriage of Goods by Sea Act as only authorising deviations that are not 'pushed beyond reasonableness, in the light of the carrier's duties to cargo'.[152] Given the fact that the shipowner knew the flour needed to reach the refugees in late May but it still decided to pick up non-governmental cargo to make additional profit, the court held that 'it must bear the consequences'.[153] Since the shipowner had categorically engaged in an unreasonable deviation, the court also found 'no significance in the point that the immediate cause of the frustration of the *Italia*'s voyage was the Six Day War'.[154] As a result, the court held the doctrine of 'impossibility of performance' did not excuse the shipowner from its obligations, particularly since the US government did not insist on transporting through Suez or navigating around the Cape but simply requested delivery to alternative Mediterranean ports that were closer to the contractually agreed destination than Piraeus, Greece.[155]

Another case addressing the bill of lading consequences of geopolitical turbulence is *United States of America v Waterman Steamship Corp*.[156] In that case,

[151] The district court decision was unpublished.
[152] ibid, 1207.
[153] ibid.
[154] ibid, 1209.
[155] ibid, 1211.
[156] *United States of America v Waterman Steamship Corp*, 471 F Supp 87 (DDC 1979) (Gesell J).

the US government had contracted with a carrier to move a cargo of humanitarian aid from several US ports to Saigon, South Vietnam, on the *SS Samuel Chase* in April 1975. The US government prepaid in advance after each loading that month. Shortly after the vessel loaded a cargo in New York, Saigon fell to the North Vietnamese Communists. The US government directed the vessel to discharge the cargo in the US and requested repayment of the freight. The carrier discharged the cargo as directed, but resisted returning the payment by invoking a freight-earned clause in the bill of lading, which provided that freight was 'completely earned on receipt of the goods' even if the voyage is 'changed, broken up, frustrated, or abandoned'.[157] In litigation, the US government alleged that the carrier 'could have predicted' that the Communists would take over Saigon before the *Samuel Chase* could arrive there and therefore, with this knowledge, the carrier 'could no longer proceed in good faith, sign bills of lading, and legitimately invoke its freight-earned clause'.[158] The US District Court for the District of Columbia rejected this argument and held in favour of the carrier. It reasoned that the US government was presumed to have a 'far superior knowledge' regarding the situation in Vietnam and therefore must have had 'an equal awareness of the possible risks'.[159] The court, however, limited its holding with a caveat: 'once [the carrier] actually knew or had to have known with certainty that Saigon would fall to the Communists in the immediate future, it could no longer sign bills of lading that properly triggered its freight-earned clause'.[160] Applying this standard to the facts, the court determined that although the carrier's vice president had 'energetically and persistently' aimed to maintain an understanding of the port conditions in Saigon by reading reports and conferring with government officials, these sources suggested the port was considered to be operating normally – at least until 24 April 1975, when international newspapers reported US President Ford's perspective that 'the Indochina war was finished for the United States'.[161] The court noted that as the carrier continued issuing bills of lading, it did so with reasoned judgment, in good faith, and with an awareness that performance of the contract 'would be fulfilling one important objective of the United States' foreign policy'.[162]

B. Marine Insurance

i. Commotion

In *Pesquerias y Secaderos de Bacalao de Espana SA v Beer*, the House of Lords analysed the marine insurance implications of the line between civil unrest and

[157] ibid, 90.
[158] ibid, 91.
[159] ibid, 92.
[160] ibid.
[161] ibid, 94. The court found that freight earned for the carrier bills of lading issued after 24 April had to be returned to the US government.
[162] ibid.

civil war occurring in northern Spain during the 1930s.[163] The shipowner was a fishing and cod-curing company based in Pasajes near San Sebastian, which lost four of its trawlers (the *Mistral*, the *Vendaval*, the *Euskal-Erria*, and the *Hispana*) to seizure by mobs in the autumn of 1936 during a phase of violent conflict between political factions. The vessels were taken by the mobs from Pasajes to Bilbao where they were then requisitioned on order of a newly established Basque Government which opposed the Nationalists in the Spanish Civil War. The *Vendaval* was sunk by a Nationalists cruiser, and the *Mistral*, *Euskal-Erria*, and the *Hispania* were reconstructed by removing the fishing equipment to make the vessels more suitable for military purposes. After the war, the shipowner recovered the three surviving vessels, but they were in a damaged condition due to their conversion into war fighting ships, which gave rise to substantial restoration costs. Each of the vessels were insured under a hull policy that provided cover for loss caused by 'riots or civil commotions' along with 'any other malicious act whatsoever', but the policy expressly excluded cover for 'war risk'.[164] The shipowner claimed the losses were covered under the hull policy as caused by rioting, but the insurer denied the claims, arguing instead that they were caused by war.

The King's Bench held for the shipowner, reasoning that the proximate cause of the loss of the vessels was 'the lawless acts of the mobs'.[165] After weighing the evidence of the political events leading to the losses, the court reasoned that 'it is perfectly clear that these seizures were all malicious acts, and they were acts unlawfully done, without any justification whatsoever'.[166] Rejecting the view that the seizures could be construed as a consequence of hostilities, the trial court explained that '[i]t is extremely difficult to know what is meant by the expression "war risk"' and that '[o]ne could hardly conceive of vaguer language being used'.[167] Rather than categorising the losses within the ambiguous war risk term, the court found the seizures took place as part of an 'extreme state of civil commotion' and were accomplished not by 'military forces' under orders of any authority or 'for the purposes of war to assist the country', but rather by 'disorderly crowds acting on their own'.[168] Regarding the subsequent requisitions by the Basque Government, the court emphasised that these later actions did not change the original source of the loss, which was the mob seizures.

The English Court of Appeal reversed.[169] It reasoned that the trial court had not properly addressed the military motivations of the initial mob seizures in Pasajes. Rejecting the insurer's submission that the vessel seizures were 'merely private acts of robbery, unconnected with any military necessity', the court

[163] *Pesquerias y Secaderos de Bacalao de Espana SA v Beer* (1949) 82 Lloyd's List Rep 501 (HL) (Lord Porter).
[164] ibid, 503.
[165] *Pesquerias y Secaderos de Bacalao de Espana SA v Beer* (1946) 79 Lloyd's List Rep 417 (KB) (Atkinson J).
[166] ibid, 432.
[167] ibid.
[168] ibid.
[169] *Pesquerias y Secaderos de Bacalao de Espana SA v Beer* (1947) 80 Lloyd's List Rep 318 (CA) (Lord Greene MR).

instead found the evidence 'clearly established' that the seizures took place in the midst of the Spanish Civil War.[170] Reframing the evidence that had been submitted to the trial court, it found that the vessels had been seized initially to defend the Basque region from insurgents who were mere kilometres away at the time. Once seized, the vessels were deployed 'for immediate naval operations directed against the insurgents', which demonstrated the timing was not coincidental.[171] The court determined that the *Mistral* was seized with 'knowledge and approval' of the regional governor 'for the urgent needs of coast defense' and the other three vessels were seized 'for the purpose of a large scale evacuation of armed forces and civilians'.[172] Each of the seizures, according to the court, had the effect of preventing the vessels from falling into the hands of the insurgents – an action it described as 'a normal operation of war in the circumstances'.[173] This led the court to hold for the insurer on the grounds that the seizure of each vessel 'was not due to theft but took place as a direct consequence of the warlike operations which were taking place for the urgent purposes of the war'.[174] Aligning with the reasoning of the Court of Appeal, the House of Lords affirmed.[175] It agreed that even if the vessels were initially seized to facilitate the escape from encroaching forces, the vessels were also taken for the civil war purposes of keeping the vessels out of the control of the enemy and for patrolling the coasts. Finding that 'civil war' was reflected in the expression 'war risks', the House of Lords held the loss fell within the exclusion.[176]

In *Flota Mercante Dominicana v American Manufacturers Mutual Insurance Co*, an American court addressed the scope of war risk terms in the context of an isolated military response to an attack by armed rebels in the Dominican Republic in the spring of 1965.[177] In that case, a merchant ship called the *SS Santo Domingo* was engaged in a voyage from New York to the port of Santo Domingo, Dominican Republic, when the shipmaster and crew heard on the radio of major rebellion that had occurred at the intended destination. Once the vessel arrived in the Dominican Republic, US forces were occupying parts of the city across the Ozama River to enforce a US Executive Order to protect US nationals during the fighting. The shipmaster left the vessel to investigate the conditions in town and to get in touch with the shipowner, but due to the danger unfolding in the city, he was unable to return to the ship. Then heavy fighting occurred between police aligned with the ruling government and rebel forces near the ship. Hundreds of police officers briefly went aboard the vessel seeking refuge and food. Some of the police officers

[170] ibid, 324.
[171] ibid, 326.
[172] ibid, 331.
[173] ibid.
[174] ibid, 338.
[175] *Pesquerias y Secaderos de Bacalao de Espana SA v Beer* (1949) 82 Lloyd's List Rep 501.
[176] ibid, 513.
[177] *Flota Mercante Dominicana v American Manufacturers Mutual Insurance Co*, 272 F Supp 540 (SDNY 1967) (Frankel J).

stole lifeboats and other items but they departed the vessel within hours. Shortly thereafter, another large group of armed rebels boarded the vessel and began firing on US military personnel across the river. The US military responded by firing two rounds of large calibre artillery shells at the *Santo Domingo*. The ship caught fire and sank. The *Santo Domingo* was insured under a policy with a war risk rider, which extended cover for 'the risks of hostilities or warlike operations' including damage caused by 'weapons of war'.[178] But it excluded cover for claims 'arising from capture, seizure, arrest, restraint, detainment, preemption, confiscation or requisition by the Government of the United States'.[179] The shipowner brought a claim to recover for the loss of the *Santo Domingo*, but the insurer denied the claim. In litigation, the insurer argued that the events fell within the exclusion because the attack by the US military was effectively a form of capture or restraint. The court rejected this argument and held for the shipowner. First, it reasoned that that the US military's purpose in firing shells into the *Santo Domingo* was 'to end the hostile attacks from those aboard her'.[180] The attack could not be considered a capture or any of the other enumerated cause in the exclusionary clause because the US soldiers who performed the shelling had no interest in acquiring possession of the vessel and were not interested in constraining its movements. Instead, the US soldiers 'would have been entirely content to have the ship go away and cease serving as a source of dangerous gunfire'.[181]

ii. Barratry

One of the leading US decisions on barratry in marine insurance provides a vibrant display of geopolitical disruption in shipping: *National Union Fire Insurance Co of Pittsburgh v The Republic of China*.[182] The central issue in that case was whether a loss fell within marine or war risk insurance policies when the crews of seven vessels owned by a state-run Chinese shipping company defected to the newly founded Communist government in 1949 at a turning point in the Chinese civil war. On 1 October 1949, the opposing Communist government proclaimed the establishment of the People's Republic of China, and the Nationalist government, including some leaders of the state-run shipping company, fled to the island of Taiwan.[183] The shipping company ordered all the vessels in its fleet to sail for Taiwan. The crews on six of the ships were reluctant to do so. Instead, these crews, along with some employees in the government-owned shipping company office

[178] ibid, 543.
[179] ibid, 541.
[180] ibid, 543.
[181] ibid. In a subsequent trial court decision, the court determined that the proximate cause was the occupation of the ship by the rebels who fired at the US soldiers. See *Flota Mercante Dominicana v American Manufacturers Mutual Insurance Co*, 312 F Supp 58 (SDNY 1970).
[182] *National Union Fire Insurance Co of Pittsburgh v The Republic of China*, 254 F2d 177 (4th Cir 1958) (Soper J).
[183] ibid.

in Hong Kong 'publicly defected' to the Communist government.[184] These six vessels were thereafter operated on behalf the People's Republic of China instead of the Nationalist government. A seventh vessel, the *Hai Hsuan*, endured a more complicated situation as it was on a voyage in the Indian Ocean heading east toward Singapore at the time of these developments. When the shipmaster of the *Hai Hsuan* received orders from Nationalist Government to proceed to Taiwan, 'he was anxious to comply but the crew objected'.[185] The crew instead demanded that the vessel stop either in Singapore or Hong Kong rather than Taiwan. The Communists-controlled shipping office in Hong Kong then issued its own orders for the vessel to stop in Singapore. The *Hai Hsuan* officers and crew held a meeting in which the shipmaster relayed his decision to proceed to Taiwan. The chief officer resisted the shipmaster's decision and turned off the engines when the vessel was just off Singapore. Finally, the shipmaster, who had become 'quite ill' during the disagreement, radioed the head office controlled by the Nationalists in Taiwan to request orders. The Taiwan-based office instructed the chief engineer to take control of the vessel and proceed to Taiwan, but the chief engineer refused and put in at Singapore instead where the shipmaster was taken to a hospital. Like the other six vessels, the *Hai Hsuan* was thereafter operated on behalf of the Communist government instead of the Nationalist government.

The Nationalist government and the state-owned shipping company carried both marine and war risk insurance for the vessels. The marine policies were on the 'customary form' and contained the FC&S clause.[186] Accordingly, the marine policies excluded cover for losses caused by 'capture' and 'seizure' along with 'civil war' and 'revolution'.[187] Originally the war risk policies covered the risks of 'barratry', but as the Communists had made headway in the civil war, which increased the risk of capture, the language 'excluding capture and seizure' was added to the war risk policies.[188] The insured (the Nationalist government) made claims for the constructive total loss of the vessels under the policies, which the insurers denied on the basis of the policy language and on the grounds that title to the ships was no longer vested in the Nationalists but rather in the national entity of China itself, which, it claimed, had been assumed by a new de jure government of the People's Republic of China. The central contractual question before the court was whether the loss of the six vessels in Hong Kong and the subsequent loss of the *Hai Hsuan* in Singapore was caused by the covered peril of 'barratry' or excluded from cover

[184] ibid, 181. The district court found the reasons for the defections were not necessarily political: 'They included personal motives, family motives, financial motives and motives resulting from developments in the civil war.' However, the court also noted that the official news agency of the Communist Government described the events on the vessels as a 'righteous uprising' against 'bureaucratic capitalists'. See *National Union Fire Insurance Co of Pittsburgh v The Republic of China* 151 F Supp 211, 223 (D Maryland 1957) (Thomsen J).

[185] *National Union Fire Insurance Co of Pittsburgh v The Republic of China*, 254 F2d 177, 181 (4th Cir 1958).

[186] ibid, 180.

[187] ibid.

[188] ibid.

as 'seizure'. The US District Court for the District of Maryland held the actions involving all seven vessels amounted to barratry.[189] For the six vessels with crews defecting in Hong Kong, this meant the war risk policy provided cover. But the court found that the *Hai Hsuan* was not only lost by the covered peril of barratry, it was simultaneously excluded from the war risk policy as a seizure. However, the court rejected the insurer's position that the assured had no proprietary right to bring a claim, emphasising that the policies had been issued to the Government of the Republic of China, 'as distinguished from the sovereign state or national entity, China'.[190] In any event, the court explained that it was 'bound to accept the political decision of the Department of State that the Nationalist Government is still the de jure government of China' (as of 1950).[191]

The US Court of Appeals for the Fourth Circuit affirmed the trial court's decision regarding the six vessels in Hong Kong, but it reversed the decision regarding the *Hai Hsuan*. It determined that there was no authority to support a holding that barratrous acts of the master or crew of a vessel could fall within the capture and seizure exclusion. The court also reasoned that the crews had engaged in 'voluntary acts' and that the possession of the vessels 'was not compelled by the superior forces of the Communist Government'.[192] With respect to the *Hai Hsuan*, the court found this even more readily apparent given that the crew's defection 'began on the high seas beyond any possible reach of the communist forces'.[193] The Fourth Circuit, however, agreed with the trial court that the insurer's alternative argument regarding ownership rights of China as a state entity was essentially a nonjusticiable political question that required deference to the US executive branch of government. Attempting to side-step the thorny political dimensions of the inquiry, the court emphasised that its task was not resolving a property dispute between rival Chinese governments, but to 'give effect to contracts of insurance' issued to the Nationalist government still in control of a large territory in China. Although that Nationalist government had since been driven from the Chinese mainland, according to the court this did not change the fact that it was 'still in existence and is in complete control of the island of Taiwan and its inhabitants and is still recognised by the United States and other nations as the true representative of the Chinese state'.[194]

Years later, similar questions in the context of civil war in Nicaragua were addressed in *Ope Shipping Ltd v Allstate Insurance Co*.[195] There, four

[189] *National Union Fire Insurance Co of Pittsburgh v The Republic of China*, 151 F Supp 211 (D Maryland 1957). The district court defined barratry as 'any wrongful act wilfully committed by the master or crew to the prejudice of the owner, or, as the case may be, the charterer'. ibid, 227.

[190] ibid, 229.

[191] ibid.

[192] *National Union Fire Insurance Co of Pittsburgh v The Republic of China*, 254 F2d 177, 186 (4th Cir 1958).

[193] ibid.

[194] ibid.

[195] *Ope Shipping Ltd v Allstate Insurance Co*, 521 F Supp 342, 344 (SDNY 1981) (Pollack J).

Nicaragua-flagged vessels were operating by Panamanian corporations under the control of Nicaragua's Somoza government during a time of civil war. In June 1979, the vessels were diverted by revolutionaries among the members of the crews who were armed with weapons and threatened the shipmasters with violence. These actions against the Somoza government were 'direct orders from Sandinista authorities as agents of the insurrection and rebellion in Nicaragua'.[196] At the direction of the Sandinista-sympathising crew members, the vessels were then diverted to Cuba and Panama – countries then friendly to the Sandinista cause – and were returned to Nicaragua in August 1979 after the opposing General Somoza resigned and fled the country. As a final act just before being ousted from power, the Somoza government transferred title of the vessels to corporations based in the Cayman Islands. The vessels were later sold in a judicial sale by the new Sandinista government following an action in rem to satisfy outstanding port fees. When under the control of the Somoza government, the vessels had been covered by separate marine and war risk policies issued by American and British insurers.[197] The plaintiff claimed the marine insurers were liable under a clause referencing 'barratry of the Master and Mariners' or, alternatively, that the war risk insurers were liable because the cause of the loss was a covered 'insurrection' or 'rebellion'.[198] The marine insurer countered that the events were caused by 'civil war', which was excluded from the policy, and the war risk insurer argued that the loss fell within a narrow carve out for capture and seizure 'by the country in which the vessel is owned or registered'.[199]

The US District Court for the Southern District of New York agreed with both insurers and held that the plaintiff could not recover under either policy. First, the court found that although barratry 'as it is classically defined' had taken place and contributed to the loss, '[t]he barratry would not have occurred, however, but for the civil war'.[200] Thus, the 'real underlying cause' or 'proximate cause' of the loss was the Nicaraguan civil war, which was a peril explicitly excluded by the marine policy.[201] As for the war risk insurer, the court reasoned there was no liability because 'the losses of the ships were the result of a confiscation by the Nicaraguan government of Nicaraguan property', which had the effect of placing the loss within the carve out.[202] According to the trial court, the last ditch attempts by the Somoza owners to shift the ownership from a Nicaraguan to a Cayman entity after it had already lost possession to the Sandinistas was 'nothing more than an attempt to evade factors involved in the exclusions of

[196] ibid.

[197] The district court described this as a 'charade of paper transactions attempting to create the semblance of a "sale" of the vessels'. ibid.

[198] ibid.

[199] ibid, 348.

[200] ibid, 349.

[201] ibid.

[202] ibid.

the war risk policy'.[203] The US Court of Appeals for the Second Circuit affirmed the trial court's decision to categorise the loss as caused by civil war excluded from the marine insurance policy, but it reversed the trial court's ruling denying war risk cover. As to the marine policy, the court agreed that the crew had committed barratry, but it found that 'the barratrous acts cannot be viewed in isolation without consideration being given to causative and motivative factors'.[204] Applying a 'common sense' approach, the court found it 'quite obvious' that the commandeering conduct of the Sandinista-aligned crew members was 'a direct result of the Nicaraguan civil war'.[205] With respect to the war risk policy, however, the appeals court found that the trial court had improperly held that the vessels were 'owned or registered' in Nicaragua at the time of the barbarous seizures.[206] Although the Somoza government may have owned the stock of the Panama-registered ship companies, the facts did not warrant 'piercing the corporate veils' to attribute ownership to be based in Nicaragua.[207] The appeals court also disagreed with the trial court's finding that the transfer of the ships to a Cayman Islands corporation was a sham. And critically, it determined that the seizure by the Sandinista rebels was not an action of the country of Nicaragua, in part because the record lacked sufficient proof that Sandinista officials who later gained power ever retroactively validated the crews' actions.[208] Thus, finding the narrow carve-out in the war risk policy inapplicable, the court held the loss was covered by the war risk insurers.

iii. Insurrection

The English Commercial Court addressed the meaning of insurrection under a marine insurance policy in *National Oil Co of Zimbabwe (Private) Ltd v Nicholas Collwyn Sturge*.[209] In that case, an organisation called the Mozambique National Resistance (Renamo) damaged oil pipelines and infrastructure connected to the port of Beria during a period of sectarian fighting. The infrastructure was insured under a marine cargo insurance policy incorporating the Institute Strikes Clauses, which provided cover for damage cause by 'riot' and 'civil commotion', but excluded cover for loss caused by 'civil war', 'rebellion', and 'insurrection'.[210] The assured made a claim under the policy, but the insurer denied cover. This resulted in litigation raising the question of whether

[203] ibid, 350.
[204] *Ope Shipping Ltd v Allstate Insurance Co*, 687 F2d 639, 641 (2nd Cir 1982) (Van Graafeiland J).
[205] ibid, 642.
[206] ibid.
[207] ibid.
[208] ibid, 643. The court emphasised that the government of Nicaragua would not have sued the vessels in rem to force a judicial sale if it had already seized the vessels by the action of the barbarous crews.
[209] *National Oil Co of Zimbabwe (Private) Ltd v Nicholas Collwyn Sturge* [1981] 2 Lloyd's Rep 281 (Comm) (Saville J).
[210] ibid.

Renamo's attack should be categorised under one or more of the exclusions.[211] The court began its analysis by emphasising the exclusions should be interpreted using their 'ordinary business meaning'.[212] It determined that the insurrection term involved, 'organised and violent internal uprising in a country with, as a main purpose, the object of trying to overthrow or supplant the government of that country'.[213] To apply this standard, the court sought to decipher the motivations behind the attack, which required a deep dive into the geopolitical history of the region, including an examination of Portuguese colonialism and the complex relationships between Mozambique and neighbouring countries South Africa and Southern Rhodesia. The court explained that the independent nation of Mozambique sprang from an anti-colonial movement resulting in a military coup in 1974, which placed an organisation called the Front for the Liberation of Mozambique (Frelimo) in charge of a transitional government. The Frelimo government pursued Marxists-Leninists political ideals, including the nationalisation of land, re-education initiatives, and efforts to suppress counterinsurgencies. This led to strained relations between Mozambique and the neighbouring countries.[214] Although its origins were obscure, Renamo was apparently organised to engage in 'specific acts of violence clearly designed to sabotage the economy of Mozambique', which had occurred with regularity during the year of the pipeline attack.[215] Renamo's counterinsurgency efforts were supported by Southern Rhodesia and later by South Africa, but the court rejected the argument that its forces were simply irregular fighters or 'mercenaries' acting on behalf of these neighbouring countries. Instead, the court found that Renamo's true 'immediate aim and purpose' was to 'overthrow the Frelimo government'.[216] Rejecting the 'simplistic and inaccurate propaganda' that Renamo was merely a 'puppet' of Southern Rhodesia or South Africa, the court found the domestic discontent inside the country at the time demonstrated 'a state of insurrection in Mozambique at the material time'.[217] As a result, the court held the attacks were an insurrection, which placed the loss within the insurance policy exclusion.[218]

In *Citgo Petroleum Corp v Starstone Insurance SE*, an American court addressed the marine insurance meaning of insurrection in the context of an 'implosion of democracy' following a disputed election in Venezuela.[219] The assured cargo interest – a US-based subsidiary of the Venezuelan state-owned

[211] ibid.
[212] ibid, 282.
[213] ibid.
[214] ibid, 283.
[215] ibid.
[216] ibid, 286.
[217] ibid, 287.
[218] Since the court found the loss was caused by insurrection, it was unnecessary to determine whether the events were also a rebellion or civil war.
[219] *Citgo Petroleum Corp v Starstone Insurance SE*, WL 2525651 (SDNY 2023) (Woods J).

oil company Petróleos de Venezuela SA (PDVSA) – had chartered a vessel, the *M/T Gerd Knutsen*, to move crude oil from the PDVSA facility in Venezuela to Aruba. This agreement was made during a period of political tumult in Venezuela after a disputed presidential election left the country with two political leaders – Nicolas Maduro and Juan Guaido – claiming victory. Although Guaido was acknowledged by some foreign governments, including the US, as the legitimate victor in the election, Maduro, as incumbent, refused to cede power. With this political instability happening in the background, in January 2019 the parties nevertheless began to perform the contract by loading the cargo on the *Gerd Knutsen*. After the cargo was loaded, the shipmaster requested clearance to depart the port, but the Maduro-aligned Venezuelan port officials refused to provide authorisation claiming that the US-based buyer had not paid PDVSA for the cargo due to banking disruption caused by trade sanctions imposed by US officials in the wake of the disputed election. Instead of authorising the vessel to depart, PDVSA requested that the cargo be returned, but the buyer asserted that payment for the cargo had already been processed. This standoff resulted in a delay of more than a year, during which the *Gerd Knutsen* was stuck at anchorage on the Venezuelan coast. Finally, in February 2020, PDVSA ordered the shipmaster to bring the *Gerd Knutsen* to a different port under escort by Venezuelan military vessels where armed military personnel and PDVSA representatives demanded the cargo be discharged. The cargo was insured under an insurance policy referencing the Institute War Clauses, which expressly provided cover for enumerated war risk losses, including 'insurrection, or civil strife arising therefrom'.[220] The assured brought a claim against the insurer, which the insurer denied. In the litigation that followed, the assured alleged that Maduro's refusal to accept the election and efforts to retain power fell within the insurrection term. The insurer countered that the events in Venezuela did not amount to an insurrection because an insurrection cannot occur where the party alleged to have performed it never lost its governmental power.

The US District Court for the Southern District of New York held for the assured. It defined insurrection under the contract as requiring 'a violent uprising' with a group acting for the purpose of 'overthrowing the constituted government and seizing its powers'.[221] Applying this standard, the court agreed with the assured's position that Guaido (the newly elected President) had been recognised by the US executive branch as the legitimate government of Venezuela – a political position that, according to the court, 'conclusively binds the judiciary'.[222] At the same time, however, the court was sympathetic to the insurer's position that Maduro (the former President attempting to hang on his authority) never truly lost his power over the Venezuelan military, while Guaido 'wielded little-to-no de facto power' irrespective of the fact the US recognised him as the legitimate

[220] ibid, 4.
[221] ibid, 10.
[222] ibid, 11.

leader of Venezuela.[223] The court admitted that these facts made for a 'trickier fit' to insurrection as a contract term.[224] However, finding that there was a reasonable basis for each interpretation of whether an insurrection had occurred, the court held this warranted a conclusion that favoured the assured. Accordingly, the actions by the Maduro government 'constituted an insurrection within the meaning of the Policy', which meant they were covered under the war risk clauses.[225]

iv. Terrorism

A line of insurance cases addressing terrorism and malicious acts emerged out of a 'Chilean Grape Crisis' occurring in the US in 1989. Among them is *New Market Investment Corp v Fireman's Fund Insurance Co.*[226] That case involved a dispute between a cargo owner (a fruit importer) and its insurer due to an emergency US customs prohibition on fruit from Chile. In the spring of 1989, the US Embassy in Santiago received anonymous telephone calls relaying threats that Chilean fruit bound to the US had been 'injected with cyanide'.[227] At first, these threats were thought to be a hoax, but the US government enhanced its visual inspections on Chilean fruit arriving at US ports. When a ship called the *Almeria Star* arrived in Philadelphia, an FDA laboratory inspection of 'two seedless red Chilean grapes' with a 'suspicious appearance' revealed that they had, in fact, been poisoned with cyanide.[228] US officials seized all Chilean fruit at or en route to US ports. As a result of the seizures, the fruit importer suffered significant damage due to destruction by customs officials, spoilage, and credits to third party customers who could not sell the fruit they had purchased from the importer. The importer made a claim with its insurer under an open marine cargo policy containing a Strikes, Riots, and Civil Commotions Endorsement covering losses caused by 'malicious act' as well as acts 'carried out for political, terroristic or ideological purposes'.[229] The insurer resisted liability on grounds that the endorsement to the policy only covered physical damage to the fruit rather than the impact of governmental restrictions. After dismissing the insurer's motion for summary judgment and presiding over a jury trial on the merits, the US District Court for the Eastern District of Pennsylvania held in favour of the cargo owner. The court reasoned that physical damage is not a 'prerequisite to liability' under the endorsement and that the jury verdict was supported by evidence to find terrorism, rather than governmental detention, as the proximate cause of the loss.[230]

[223] ibid, 11.
[224] ibid.
[225] ibid, 15.
[226] *New Market Investment Corp v Fireman's Fund Insurance Co*, 774 F Supp 909 (ED Penn 1991) (Broderick J).
[227] ibid, 911.
[228] ibid.
[229] ibid, 912.
[230] ibid, 913. The cargo owner recovered more than $200,000 from the insurer.

In *IF P&C Insurance Ltd (Pbl) v Silversea Cruises Ltd*, the English Court of Appeal discussed – albeit in obiter dicta – whether the 9/11 terror attacks in the United States could be considered 'acts of war' under a policy of business interruption insurance held by a cruise line.[231] In the immediate aftermath of the attacks, governmental authorities around the world – including the US State Department – issued advisories warning travellers of the potential for additional attacks in the US and elsewhere. A cruise line company alleged that both the attacks and the governmental travel advisories caused existing customers to cancel cruise bookings and deterred new customers. The cruise line brought claims under its business interruption insurance policy, invoking a clause providing cover for loss due to the vessel being 'deprived of income' as a consequence of 'acts of war' or 'armed conflict' that 'interfere with the scheduled itinerary of the insured vessel, whether actual or threatened'.[232] The insurer resisted the claims arguing, in part, that the 9/11 attacks were not acts of war or armed conflict under the policy. The English Commercial court held for the insurer on other grounds, namely the assured's failure to demonstrate the losses were caused by the attacks or the travel advisories.[233] The English Court of Appeal affirmed the result. Although it agreed with the trial court that it was not dispositive to the outcome in the case, the Court of Appeal relayed the parties' submissions addressing whether 9/11 was an act of war or armed conflict under the insurance terms.[234] On one hand, Al Qaeda and the West could be identified as the relevant sides with opposing objectives. Al Qaeda aimed to defeat the US and force its withdrawal from Middle East. Moreover, the scale of the 9/11 attacks were 'unprecedented in any terms of mere terrorism'.[235] But on the other hand, the 9/11 attacks had been described by testifying experts as a 'terrorist attack' perpetrated by a 'terrorist organization'.[236] Arguably then, the attacks themselves might not constitute an armed conflict between opposing sides since they directly involved 'only the hijackers and their victims'.[237] Furthermore, Al Qaeda could not be viewed as having sovereignty or even sovereign aspirations nor did it have the objective of 'undermining [US] territorial integrity or of wresting power from it'.[238]

Addressing these distinct views, two of the Court of Appeal judges expressed slightly different opinions on the matter. The author of the principal judgment explained three reasons to support the position that 9/11 was at least 'a candidate for an act of war'.[239] First, the attacks had led to the US invasion of Afghanistan

[231] *IF P&C Insurance Ltd (Pbl) v Silversea Cruises Ltd* [2004] Lloyd's Rep IR 696 (CA) (Rix LJ).
[232] ibid, 703.
[233] *IF P&C Insurance Ltd (Pbl) v Silversea Cruises Ltd* [2004] Lloyd's Rep IR 217 (Comm) (Tomlinson J).
[234] *IF P&C Insurance Ltd (Pbl) v Silversea Cruises Ltd* [2004] Lloyd's Rep IR 696, 722.
[235] ibid, 723.
[236] ibid.
[237] ibid.
[238] ibid.
[239] ibid. This view was presented by Lord Justice Rix.

within a month, and experts had explained when Afghanistan was under the Taliban, it was a 'state sponsor of Al Qaeda'.[240] Second, in the commercial context, it was not 'particularly helpful to think of war in its international law sense as armed conflict between sovereign states'.[241] Given that the insurance policy covered a fleet of vessels operating around the world, 'considerable weight has to be given to the concern of business men and their insurers over the scale and ramifications of the conflict'.[242] Third, the simple fact that 9/11 was a terrorist attack does not directly answer the separate question of 'whether it amounted to something more'.[243] A concurring judge wrote separately to express reservations with this approach, reasoning that it was doubtful that the insurer or the assured, as business people, 'would have said as they watched those aircraft smash into the Twin Towers, "That's an act of war!"'.[244] The concurring judge further found it persuasive that the US travel advisories indicated that the attacks were 'terrorist actions from extremist groups' and 'retaliatory actions by terrorists … who harbor grievances against the United States'.[245] The subsequent 'war on terror' declared by US authorities, was merely a 'rhetorical response serving only to emphasize that there was no identifiable "side" against whom the war could be waged'.[246] Although the war in Afghanistan 'truly was a war against that state', it was not a war against Bin Laden and his organisation because 'war is not conducted against an individual and his wicked henchmen, however real a threat they pose to the security of a state'.[247] Finally, according to the concurring judge, the attacks lacked the continuity of an armed conflict.[248] Although the threat of more violence from Al Qaeda remained, its 'essentially random attacks' would not be viewed by an ordinary business person as presenting the 'persisting fighting between military groups which is the hallmark of armed conflict'.[249]

III. Reflections

The Suez closure cases are key to understanding how courts and arbitrators respond to doctrinal reasoning in the context of diversions caused by political unrest. The court in the *Glidden Co* case rejected the argument that the Suez closure frustrated

[240] ibid.
[241] ibid.
[242] ibid.
[243] ibid.
[244] ibid. This view was relayed by Lord Justice Ward.
[245] ibid, 724.
[246] ibid.
[247] ibid.
[248] ibid.
[249] ibid. The leading US insurance cases addressing this line between war and terrorism do not contain a maritime component but offer rich discussion mirroring the above debate. See eg *Pan American World Airways Inc v Aetna Casualty & Surety Co*, 505 F2d 989 (2nd Cir 1974); *Universal Cable Productions v Atlantic Specialty Insurance Co*, 929 F3d 1143 (9th Cir 2019).

the charterparty because the Cape route remained a viable alternative for navigation between India and the US and because the parties had been unable to agree on a contract provision addressing the prospect of a closure.[250] The *Massalia* court took a different view regarding a planned voyage between India and Italy by finding the contract was frustrated following the Suez closure because the Cape was a substantially more 'circuitous' route.[251] This perspective was expressly rejected in the subsequent *Eugenia* case, which reasoned that although the vessel in that case had intended to move from the Black Sea to India via Suez and was forced to backtrack northbound to the Mediterranean Sea, past Gibraltar, and then to the Cape after the Canal became blocked, the contract was not frustrated because the charterer had 'self-induced' the scenario by insisting the vessel proceed through Suez when the area had already become embroiled in a major military conflict.[252] Addressing a similar set of facts, the *Captain George K* case provides a distinct assessment of the doctrine of impossibility alongside frustration, as the court highlighted the umpire's initial finding that performing the anticipated voyage from Mexico to India through Suez was physically impossible due to the Canal closure, but it also (reluctantly) rejected the shipowner's frustration argument on grounds that the *Eugenia* precedent required it to do so.[253] In both the *Transatlantic Financing* and the *American Trading & Production* cases, the voyages (from the US to Iran and the US to India, respectively) were found not to be excused by impossibility or impracticability after the Suez closure because the Cape alternative remained physically viable to facilitate performance even though it was more burdensome and expensive.[254] This meant the shipowners in those cases were liable to absorb the additional costs because the Suez disruption was foreseeable at the time of contracting. In assessing the application of avoidance doctrines, the Suez cases collectively show that frustration, impossibility, and impracticability each involve high hurdles to clear, even in the event of a major navigation artery being physically obstructed by conflict.

These and other cases examining the Suez closures also provide evidence of commercial solutions through contract language. Along with its frustration analysis, the court in the *Glidden Co* case rejected contractual arguments based on a *force majeure* clause referencing 'restraint of princes', as well as the US COGSA's 'act of war' excepted peril provision incorporated into the charterparty under a clause paramount.[255] Similarly, the court in the *Eugenia* case found that the war clause contained in that charterparty was inapplicable to the Suez closure, in part

[250] *Glidden Co v Hellenic Lines Ltd* 275 F2d 253 (2nd Cir 1960).

[251] *Societe Franco-Tunisienne D'Armement v Sidermar SPA (The Massalia)* [1960] 1 Lloyd's Rep 594, 609 (Comm).

[252] *Ocean Tramp Tankers Corp v V/O Sovfracht (The Eugenia)* [1963] 2 Lloyd's Rep 381, 389 (CA).

[253] *Palmco Shipping Inc v Continental Ore Corp (The Captain George K)* [1970] 2 Lloyd's Rep 21 (Comm).

[254] *Transatlantic Financing Corp v United States of America*, 363 F2d 312 (DC Cir 1966); *American Trading & Production Corp v Shell International Marine Ltd*, 453 F2d 939 (2nd Cir 1972).

[255] *Glidden Co v Hellenic Lines Ltd* 275 F2d 253 (2nd Cir 1960).

because the parties had failed to assent to a proposed Suez Canal clause that would have addressed the prospect of a blockage more directly.[256] The inability to agree on a clause fixing the route or addressing rights and responsibilities in the event of a Suez closure was also found relevant in both the *Transatlantic Financing* and *American Trading & Production* cases, where the courts determined that the shipowners had assumed the risk of a customary route closure by agreeing to fixed freight voyage charters without any contractual safeguards addressing the possibility of diversion costs.[257] Other courts have found such clauses indicative of the parties' intentions. Although the decision was expressly criticised in the later *Eugenia* case, the court in the *Massalia* case found the contractual reference to a telegraphic message required to be sent by the shipmaster upon 'passing Suez Canal' was sufficient evidence that the parties had intended to use that route rather than the Cape.[258] The *Captain George K* court referenced a similar provision to show the parties had intended to proceed through Suez, although the court held this was immaterial as it was bound by the outcome of the *Eugenia* decision.[259] The parties in the *Achille Lauro Fu Giacocchino* case successfully agreed to a more explicit Suez Canal Clause, but its language was ambiguous on how freight should be adjusted in the event of a closure under a nebulous reference to calculations to be made based on a 'theoretical voyage'.[260] Collectively, the cases point to the need for contracting parties to address the prospect of route disruptions through explicit and carefully drafted provisions.[261]

Since many of these re-routing cases involve fixed price voyage charters, they have limited implications for how these principles should apply in the context of time charters or other agreements that do not involve lump sum pricing. Absent the application of an avoidance doctrine or exceptions clauses, the risk of delays in the context of a voyage charter is generally placed on the shipowner, while similar disruption in other contractual scenarios has produced diverging solutions. The *Andros Island* arbitration benefitted the charterer, as the vessel was found to be off hire following the shipowner's 'preemptive decision' to reject the charterer's orders during the short-lived conflict between Greece and Turkey over Cyprus because it went beyond the liberties expressed in the charterparty's war risk clause.[262] The panel rooted its analysis in equitable considerations to fashion a remedy for the charterer, rather than rigidly applying the standard off-hire language, which did not expressly contemplate such scenarios. The *Houda* case provides an additional

[256] *Ocean Tramp Tankers Corp v V/O Sovfracht (The Eugenia)* [1963] 2 Lloyd's Rep 381 (CA).

[257] *Transatlantic Financing Corp v United States of America*, 363 F2d 312 (DC Cir 1966); *American Trading & Production Corp v Shell International Marine Ltd*, 453 F2d 939 (2nd Cir 1972).

[258] *Societe Franco-Tunisienne D'Armement v Sidermar SPA (The Massalia)* [1960] 1 Lloyd's Rep 594, 609 (Comm).

[259] *Palmco Shipping Inc v Continental Ore Corp (The Captain George K)* [1970] 2 Lloyd's Rep 21 (Comm).

[260] *Achille Lauro Fu Giaocchino & C v Total Societa Italiana Per Azioni* [1969] 2 Lloyd's Rep 65 (CA).

[261] Several of these provisions are discussed in ch 4.

[262] *Andros Compania Maritime SA v Mineral Importexport (The MV Andros Island)* SMA 1548 (NY Arb 1980).

illustration as the court found the vessel remained on hire and accruing costs to the time charterer's account when the vessel encountered delays after the emergency departure from Kuwait caused by Iraq's 1990 invasion forced the vessel to sail without the bills of lading.[263] Again, the court in that case focused on policy considerations to resolve the dispute, namely the need to protect a shipowner's ability to reassess risks to the vessel, cargo, and crew following an emergency departure due to the outbreak of conflict.

Bill of lading cases have relied on solutions applying both doctrinal principles and express contract language. In the *Hellenic Lines* case, the court rejected the carrier's argument that the Six Day War made performance of the voyage to carry humanitarian goods on behalf of the US government impossible or frustrated because it was the shipowner's own voluntary choice to take on additional cargo before the intended voyage to Jordan, which delayed the vessel and forced a diversion.[264] Despite language in the bill of lading granting the carrier 'liberties' to deviate, the court determined it would be unreasonable to apply it to allow recovery of additional transshipment costs. The freight earned clause in the *Waterman Steamship* case, however, reveals that bill of lading clauses providing for the recovery of freight even in the event of voyages that become frustrated may entitle the carrier to protection when military developments prevent performance.[265] Although the contracted voyage to support the US government operations was prevented by the fall of Saigon to North Vietnam, the court found that the freight earned clause preserved the carrier's right to payment because at the time of contracting it believed in good faith that the voyage would be successful and, in any event, the US government shipper was in a better position to assess the political conditions in Vietnam and the viability of the voyage when it loaded the cargo.

Disputes over the application of safe port warranties add an instructive layer on commercial case law addressing the disruption caused by political unrest. The cases show courts and arbitrators place a high burden on the shipowner to demonstrate a scale and scope of unsafety to justify invoking contractual rights to deny a charterer's orders. The *Evaggelos Th* case is revealing on this point, as the court found that even when a vessel is destroyed by shelling after being caught in a crossfire, the safe port warranty is not necessarily breached when the shipowner is aware of the risks at the time of contracting and nevertheless consents to trading in a dangerous area. Although Israel and Egypt had agreed to a ceasefire, the parties had knowledge that the Suez Roads where the damage took place remained a high risk zone as the soldiers from the two countries continued to engage in sporadic fighting during the Suez Canal closure, which limited the shipowner's ability to rely on the safe port warranty.[266] Applying a similarly high standard for proving unsafety, in

[263] *Kuwait Petroleum Corp v I & D Oil Carriers Ltd* (*The Houda*) [1994] 2 Lloyd's Rep 541 (CA).

[264] *Hellenic Lines Ltd v United States* 512 F2d 1196 (2nd Cir 1975).

[265] *United States of America v Waterman Steamship Corp*, 471 F Supp 87 (DDC 1979).

[266] *Vardinoyannis v The Egyptian General Petroleum Corp (The Evaggelos Th)* [1971] 2 Lloyd's Rep 200 (Comm).

the *Saga Cob*, the court refused to find the charterer's order to an Ethiopian port a violation of the safe port warranty even though the vessel was attacked by Eritrean guerilla fighters shortly after another vessel had suffered the same fate. Despite the prospect of attack, the court found that the political risk had not been so prevalent that unsafety became part of the port's characteristics.[267] Likewise, in the *Trade Fortitude* case, the arbitral panel majority was unwilling to accept the shipowner's argument that the Persian Gulf had become unsafe due to the outbreak of the Yom Kippur War hundreds of miles away.[268] At least in some cases, however, sudden changes in port conditions have given rise to a finding of unsafety. The *Arietta Venizelos* case is illustrative as the arbitral panel was persuaded that threats of guerilla attacks on tankers in the Mediterranean evidenced by Libya's insurance designation as outside the Institute Warranty Limits demonstrated enough risk to warrant the shipowner's refusal to deny the charterer's orders.[269]

Cases addressing insurance cover questions have revealed the complexity of delineating between the various forms of hostility falling short of war and the resulting implications for classifying vessel attacks and seizures under standard contract categories. Solutions have often depended on an assessment of the political motivations of the actors involved. In the *Pesquierias y Secaderos* case, the House of Lords emphasised the political aims of the factions fighting in the Spanish Civil War when holding that the vessel seizures fell within the contractual conception of a war rather than theft, riot, or civil commotion.[270] The court in *Flota Mercante Dominicana* engaged in a similar assessment of the US military's peacekeeping motivations when deciding that the sinking of a merchant vessel by US forces in the Dominican Republic was not a capture or restraint under a war risk clause because it was compelled by a purely defensive motive after the US troops were fired upon.[271] Motivative assessments were also found critical in the *Ope Shipping* case, as the court determined that although the vessel seizure by Nicaraguan Sandinista sympathisers was a form of barratry, it was still an action falling under the contractual category of civil war when viewed through the lens of proximate cause.[272] The complex interaction between contract categories examined in the *National Union* case is particularly striking, as the court found that the crew's defection to the Communists after the Nationalists were forced to flee from Mainland China to Taiwan was barratry but not seizure under the terms of the insurance policies.[273] This finding hinged not only on the apparent political

[267] *K/S Penta Shipping A/S v Ethiopian Shipping Lines Corp (The Saga Cob)* [1992] 2 Lloyd's Rep 545 (CA).

[268] *Marastro Compania Naviera SA v Standard Tankers (Bahamas) Co Ltd (The M/T Trade Fortitude)*, SMA 1139 (NY Arb 1974).

[269] *Arietta Compania Naviera SA v World Wide Transport Inc (The S/T Arietta Venizelos)*, SMA 733 (NY Arb 1972).

[270] *Pesquerias y Secaderos de Bacalao de Espana SA v Beer* (1949) 82 Lloyd's List Rep 501 (HL).

[271] *Flota Mercante Dominicana v American Manufacturers Mutual Insurance Co*, 272 F Supp 540 (SDNY 1967).

[272] *Ope Shipping Ltd v Allstate Insurance Co*, 687 F2d 639 (2nd Cir 1982).

[273] *National Union Fire Insurance Co of Pittsburgh v The Republic of China*, 254 F2d 177 (4th Cir 1958).

agnosticism of at least some of the defecting crew members, but also the court's resistance to turning the insurance dispute into a 'political question' of property ownership between rival governments.

This inclination to abstain from entertaining political questions has also materialised in cases addressing the contractual classification of insurrection. In the *Citgo Petroleum* case, for instance, the court determined it was bound by the expressed position of the US executive branch, which had officially acknowledged a singular victor in a disputed presidential election in Venezuela even though he never actually wielded power in that country.[274] Since the US government had already made this finding in political contexts, the court determined the vessel seizure at issue was caused by an insurrection under the insurance policy term, even while acknowledging that such a finding was a 'trickier fit' when there was no overthrow of a constituted government to seize its powers but rather an existing government attempting to maintain the status quo.[275] Other cases addressing purported insurrections, however, have focused on the assessment of competing political motivations. In the *National Oil Co of Zimbabwe* case, the court found that the insurrection term required weighing the aims of the actors engaged in unrest to determine whether they actually sought to overthrow the existing government or had some other form of political agenda such as to stir chaos or to fulfil strategic objectives of neighbouring countries.[276] In finding that the Renamo militants that caused the damage to the oil pipeline in that case were not 'mercenaries' or 'puppets' of external actors but rather were aiming to overthrow the existing government, the court held the organisation's actions fell within the ordinary business meaning of insurrection.[277] A similar inquiry was used to resolve the *Ope Shipping* case involving the seizure of vessels by Nicaraguan Sandinista sympathisers, as the court found that despite allegations of barratry and insurrection, the broader context of civil war demonstrated 'motivative factors', which caused the loss to shift from the marine to the war risk insurers.[278] In each of these cases, the courts were careful to consider not only the meaning of the insurrection term, but also the surrounding geopolitical dynamics, making them particularly useful illustrations of how insurance wordings may push contract questions beyond the typical nuances of commercial law.

The terrorism cases raise yet another element of complexity in insurance classification. In the *New Market Investments* case involving the mass seizure of Chilean grapes, the court found that the insurance policy referencing 'malicious acts' covered not only direct cargo damage but also governmental acts aiming to avert the public poisoning plot.[279] The larger scale of indirect losses arising out of

[274] WL 2525651 (SDNY 2023).

[275] ibid, 11.

[276] *National Oil Co of Zimbabwe (Private) Ltd v Nicholas Collwyn Sturge* [1981] 2 Lloyd's Rep 281 (Comm).

[277] ibid, 287.

[278] *Ope Shipping Ltd v Allstate Insurance Co*, 687 F2d 639 (2nd Cir 1982).

[279] *New Market Investment Corp v Fireman's Fund Insurance Co*, 774 F Supp 909 (ED Penn 1991).

the 9/11 attacks led to a different outcome in the *Silverseas Cruises* case, but also produced illuminating, albeit contrasting, lines of reasoning between concurring judges addressing the philosophical question of whether major terror attacks can be considered equivalent to war risks.[280] In one sense the 9/11 attacks could be considered a form of war under insurance terms irrespective of the fact that the events were perpetrated by non-state actors rather than a sovereign government since the events caused significant loss of life, property damage, and ultimately led to the invasion of Afghanistan. But on the other hand, the notion of the 'war on terror' flowing from the 9/11 attacks did not necessarily mean that the initial violence would be construed by a business person as an 'act of war', especially since they were isolated events that lacked the continuity of conventional belligerent conflict. Unfortunately, the perplexing contract questions stirred up by terrorism continue to confound in the contemporary era. The many attacks performed by Houthi militants on merchant ships in the Bab al-Mandab Strait and Red Sea since 2023 are a remarkable case in point as they implicate many of the same kinds of questions raised in earlier cases, including not only how the attacks should be categorised on a spectrum of insurance terms, but also their implications for justifying widespread diversions from the Suez Canal route to the Cape of Good Hope and the application of safe port warranties throughout the region. Existing case law and new contract clauses, including the BIMCO CONWARTIME and VOYWAR 2025 clauses, may provide some guidance. But the ongoing Houthi threat represents a relatively novel conundrum in which the lines between war and terrorism – and perhaps even other categories – are fundamentally blurred.

[280] *IF P&C Insurance Ltd (Pbl) v Silversea Cruises Ltd* [2004] Lloyd's Rep IR 696 (CA).

4

Piracy

I. Introduction

Although piracy may be viewed as an international crime of seemingly tenuous geopolitical consequence, over centuries it has held a close connection to sea power struggles. In its early forms along coastal settlements in the Mediterranean Sea, piracy was understood to be a type of raid warfare performed by bands of maritime gangs of a character that scholars have described as akin to the Vikings of the Middle Ages.[1] As global trade expanded through colonial conquests fuelled by shipbuilding innovations and navigation technology, merchant traders moved valuable cargo on voyages across long distances far from the safety of their home ports, leaving them vulnerable to attack by actors willing to steal opportunistically for financial gain. By the late seventeenth century – considered by some as piracy's 'golden age' – perpetrators of this form of apolitical profit-motivated plundering were commonly branded with the indelicate title 'enemies of all mankind'.[2] Suppression efforts facilitated by naval patrols and diplomatic agreements with piracy-prone coastal states sent this form of menace into steady decline during the eighteenth century.[3] But, rather paradoxically, a basically equivalent state-sanctioned practice was viewed differently, as national governments deputised 'privateers' – effectively maritime militias – with express authorisation to seize and capture 'enemy' vessels and cargo under letters of marque. These official documents purported to transform what were essentially piratical acts into lawful seizures to claim war prizes on behalf of sovereign powers. Even as conventional piracy was condemned and contained, privateering flourished in phases tracking wars and conflicts, with pronounced increases during the American Revolutionary War and the Napoleonic Wars. Although the practice was eventually banned by major European powers under the Paris Declaration following the Crimean War in the mid-nineteenth century, privateering continued even into the steamship era, notably during the US Civil

[1] See generally J Kraska, *Contemporary Maritime Piracy: International Law, Strategy, and Diplomacy at Sea* (Bloomsbury, 2011).

[2] This designation apparently has Roman origins and was often referenced using the Latin phrase *hostis humani generis*. See C Harding, '"Hostis Humani Generis" – The Pirate as Outlaw in the Early Modern Law of the Sea' in C Jowitt (ed), *Pirates? The Politics of Plunder 1550–1650* (Palgrave, 2007).

[3] Limited phases of piracy transpired in the early nineteenth century as Barbary Corsairs in North Africa demanded tribute before allowing safe passage in the Mediterranean Sea.

War – with the Union invoking piratical terms in political rhetoric to rebuke the tactics of the rebelling Confederate states.[4]

In the early twentieth century, faster ships and increased vessel traffic supporting a rapidly globalising economy further reduced exposure to piracy risk.[5] Bigger and better warships protected freedom of navigation and also served as a piracy deterrent. These military vessels – and especially their submarine counterparts – were themselves the more pervasive physical threat to shipping during the two World Wars. In fact, emphasising the brazen character of wartime attacks on merchant ships, the havoc imposed by submarine warfare was sometimes described with piracy analogies.[6] Following the Second World War, the looming threat of confrontation between nuclear superpowers continued to trump piracy concerns. Counterintuitively, Cold War-era military initiatives may have even indirectly suppressed piracy as a maritime security threat, as the US and the Soviet Union projected power in the maritime domain with globe-trotting naval presences and increasingly sophisticated systems of technology-fuelled surveillance. However, even during the Cold War, occasional attacks by state and non-state actors were described as piracy. Reflecting back on the Cuban Missile Crisis in 1962, the Soviet head of state described the US 'quarantine' of Cuba not only as a 'blockade' but also 'piracy on the High Seas'.[7] In 1975, when Khmer Rouge forces seized a US government-chartered container ship off Cambodia, the US President described the event as an 'act of piracy'.[8] And after a 1985 attack by members of the extremist Palestinian Liberation Front on an Italian passenger vessel, the *Achille Lauro*, which resulted in the death of an American citizen, this event was described by US officials as both terrorism and piracy.[9] Beyond the rhetoric, at least one outbreak of conventional piracy did occur during the Cold War following the US withdrawal of its forces from Vietnam. As large numbers of refugees fled Vietnam by sea in attempts to reach safe havens in Malaysia and elsewhere, some vessels were attacked by maritime criminals.[10] But barring these isolated events, piracy was a relatively rare occurrence until the end of the Cold War.

Contractual references to piracy remained fluid throughout trading history. In the insurance context, for instance, the Lloyd's SG form expressly contemplated cover for loss caused by 'pirates' as well as 'enemies', 'rovers', 'letters of mart and countermart', and other piracy-related (or privateering-related) perils.[11] After

[4] Scholars have noted the term piracy has been used as a 'vague pejorative' for political actions pursued by force. See AP Rubin, *The Law of Piracy* (2nd edn, Transnational Publishers, 1998) 313. This notion of state-sanctioned piracy continues to linger in contemporary political discourse.

[5] See ED Dickinson, 'Is the Crime of Piracy Obsolete?' (1925) 38 *Harvard Law Review* 334.

[6] See Rubin (n 4) 313–18.

[7] N Khrushchev, 'Statement on the Cuban Crisis of 1962' (12 December 1962).

[8] CJ Lamb, *The Mayaguez Crisis, Mission Command, and Civil-military Relations* (US Joint Chiefs of Staff, 2018).

[9] See M Halberstam, 'Terrorism on the High Seas: The Achille Lauro, Piracy and the IMO Convention on Maritime Safety' (1988) 82(2) *American Journal of International Law* 269.

[10] See Rubin (n 4) 383.

[11] The Lloyd's SG form is attached as an Annex to the English Marine Insurance Act 1906.

the FC&S Clause emerged for voluntary adoption in its early forms, it typically did not exclude piracy from the marine cover.[12] Following major wars during the nineteenth century, the FC&S language in the London market was modified to reference the broad war risk category of 'hostilities and warlike operations', yet it continued to remain silent on piracy.[13] But by the time the FC&S Clause was mandated by a Lloyd's resolution in 1898, the FC&S Clause treated piracy differently than other war risks by excluding cover for 'capture, seizure and detention, and of the consequences thereof, or any attempt thereat, piracy excepted'.[14] Representing a shift in cover priorities, updates to the FC&S Clause just prior to the Second World War then removed this 'piracy excepted' language and instead referenced piracy along with other war risks excluded from the marine policy.[15] After the 1980s London market reforms, this 'piracy excepted' language reappeared with the new hull clauses, which again shifted piracy from the war risk policy back to the marine policy.[16] The accompanying 1983 Institute War and Strikes Clauses confirmed that piracy was not covered by the war risk policy under the London wordings.[17] Conversely, in the American hull and cargo insurance market, piracy remained excluded from the marine policy.[18] Naturally, the corresponding American Institute war risk clauses expressly covered piracy.[19] This is obviously a complex and technical history. The point is that in the insurance context piracy has been moved back and forth between the marine policy and the war risk policy as maritime security challenges have evolved over the last 200 years, reflecting the difficulty of categorising its unusual combination of criminal and political characteristics.[20]

Following the end of the Cold War, maritime trade continued to increase while global security priorities pivoted away from the heavy naval presence that had characterised a decades-long war footing between major powers. Perhaps without coincidence, piracy began to rise again. These attacks took place in hotspots around the world, but especially in Southeast Asia off the coasts of China, Indonesia, Malaysia, Singapore, and Vietnam. The piracy occurring during this era generally took the form of nighttime thievery by small groups

[12] One version of the FC&S Clause during the Napoleonic Wars read: 'Warranted free from capture, seizure and detention, and all the consequences thereof, or any attempt thereat, and free from all consequences of hostilities, riots, or commotions.' M Davey, J Davey, and O Caplin, *Miller's Marine War Risks* (4th edn, Informa, 2020) § 1.10.

[13] ibid.

[14] ibid § 1.11.

[15] ibid § 1.18–1.19.

[16] Institute Time Clauses (Hulls) 1.10.83. The subsequent iterations also kept piracy as a marine risk.

[17] Institute War and Strike Clauses Hulls-Time.

[18] American Institute Hull Clauses (2 June 1977); American Institute of Marine Underwriters Cargo Clauses All Risks (1 January 2004).

[19] American Institute Hull War Risks and Strikes Clauses (29 September 2009); American Institute of Marine Underwriters, War Risk Open Policy (Cargo) (2 December 1993).

[20] This phenomenon is discussed in P Todd, *Maritime Fraud and Piracy* (2nd edn, Lloyd's List, 2010) § 1.055.

of sea robbers.[21] There were also isolated instances of serious violence toward crew members perpetrated to confiscate vessels to then be used in smuggling operations as 'phantom ships'.[22] Coinciding with these events, new charter-party clauses were adopted with explicit reference to piracy. BIMCO's 1993 CONWARTIME and VOYWAR clauses, for instance, expressly recognised 'acts of piracy' under its definition of 'war risk'.[23] As with other war risks defined under the clauses, the shipowner was granted – subject to its 'reasonable judgment' – the liberty to deny the charterer's orders to proceed to any place that exposed the vessel, crew, and cargo to piracy risk (or any other listed form of war risk).[24] Following the 9/11 attacks and the substantial counterterrorism initiatives that ensued, increases in piracy incidents in the Malacca Straits caused the Lloyd's Joint War Committee to (temporarily) add the region to its list of high risk areas in 2005.[25] Despite piracy's limited resurgence, in the early years of the twenty-first century, governmental and industry attention remained fixated on the fight against terrorism.

Throughout this period, another form of piracy threat was developing. Following the ouster of Somalia's socialist government in 1991, civil unrest had been so severe that UN peacekeepers and US troops were sent to execute a humanitarian mission in Mogadishu. By 1994 violence forced their withdrawal (illustrated by the infamous Black Hawk Down incident), which contributed to Somalia sliding further into political fragmentation.[26] In this central governance void, armed groups began 'patrolling' Somalia's coasts claiming to act as guardians of its fisheries while seeking financial gain through theft, bribery, or ransom.[27] By 2007, this phenomenon had spiralled into a full-fledged piracy threat in the Gulf of Aden and beyond. Over the next several years, fishing vessels, container ships, tankers – even bulk carriers carrying humanitarian aid to the region on behalf of the UN World Food Programme – were hijacked by

[21] See IMO Doc MSC 623 (1993) Guidance to Ship-owners and Ship-operators, Shipmasters and Crews on Preventing and Suppressing Acts of Piracy Armed Robbery Against Ships.

[22] Scholars have described allegations from this era as state-sponsored piracy performed as 'interdictions' by actors appearing to be Chinese or Indonesian governmental agents. See N Renwick and J Abbot, 'Piratical Violence and Maritime Security in Southeast Asia' [1999] 30(2) *Security Dialogue* 183; K Zou, 'Piracy at Sea and China's Response' (2000) *Lloyd's Maritime and Commercial Law Quarterly* 364.

[23] See eg BIMCO Standard War Risk Clause for Time Charters 1993 (CONWARTIME 1993), Cl 1(b); BIMCO Standard War Risk Clause for Voyage Chartering 1993 (VOYWAR 1993), Cl 1(b). Note that earlier charterparties also included piracy in war risk definitions. See T Young et al, *Voyage Charters* (5th edn, Informa, 2022) § 26.13.

[24] The 2004 updates to CONWARTIME and VOYWAR modified the shipowner's liberty to avoid areas that 'likely to be or to become dangerous'. See eg BIMCO Standard War Risk Clause for Time Charters 2004 (CONWARTIME 2004), Cl (a)(ii).

[25] The listing was removed the following year. See 'Malacca Straits Removed from War Risk List' (2006) *Insurance Journal* (9 August).

[26] S Biddle, *Nonstate Warfare: The Military Methods of Guerillas, Warlords, and Militias* (Princeton University Press, 2021) ch 7.

[27] J Kraska and B Wilson, 'Maritime Piracy in East Africa' (2009) 26(2) *Journal of International Affairs* 55, 58.

men armed with automatic weapons and rocket-propelled grenades who hijacked vessels from small manoeuvrable skiffs. Rather than attempting to confiscate the vessels or their cargos, these pirates took crews hostage and demanded ransom payments routinely in the millions of US dollars. Ship operators re-routed from high-risk areas, but the pirates continued their attacks with increasingly daring tactics facilitated by 'motherships' serving as launches hundreds of miles from the Somali coasts in the Western Indian Ocean. This pattern repeated frequently with hundreds of attacks carried out primarily between 2007 and 2012.[28] The crisis spurred a flurry of multilateral initiatives and military interventions. Members of NATO and the EU, along with China, India, Japan, and other countries deployed security resources to patrol the area.[29] Shipping industry actors also adjusted protocol to carry security advisers or armed personnel.[30] After several years of relentless hijackings, hostage scenarios, and ransom payments, piracy off East Africa declined precipitously by 2013.

The Somali piracy experience spurred new contractual responses. Although in the London hull insurance market piracy was still considered a marine risk, not a war risk, an optional clause was available for addition to hull policies, which could shift piracy out of the marine cover and potentially back to the war risk cover (as had been the case before the 1980s reforms).[31] In May 2008, the Joint War Committee designated the Gulf of Aden as a listed area, signalling implications for the assessment of an additional war risk premium for vessels trading there. Even with these industry adjustments, given that many of the Somali piracy-related losses were ransom payments, losses were not necessarily covered by the marine or war risk hull underwriters. For this reason, shipowners began procuring supplementary kidnapping and ransom insurance to address this unique form of loss.[32] Other costs were allocated by the terms of charterparties. As some vessel operators chose to take on armed guards or to navigate around the Cape of Good Hope to avoid the Gulf of Aden altogether, these operational decisions raised contractual questions, including the liability for hire, demurrage, and responsibility to pay for any additional insurance costs. Aiming to supplement its recently revised CONWARTIME and VOYWAR 2004 language, in 2009, BIMCO circulated Piracy Clauses for time and voyage charterparties.[33] Based

[28] IMO Reports on Acts of Piracy and Armed Robbery Against Ships: Annual Report – 2013, MSC.4/Circ.208 (1 March 2013).

[29] See eg NATO, *Counter-piracy Operations (2008–2016)* (19 May 2022).

[30] These industry adjustments were aided by the publication of Best Management Practices. See BIMCO et al, 'BMP5: Best Management Practice to Deter Piracy and Enhance Maritime Security in the Red Sea, Gulf of Aden, Indian Ocean and Arabian Sea' (June 2018).

[31] This could be accomplished by the adoption of a 'Violent Theft, Piracy and Barratry Exclusion Clause'. J Gilman et al, *Arnould Law of Marine Insurance and General Average* (20th edn, Sweet & Maxwell, 2021) § 23–24.

[32] K Lewins and R Merkin, 'Piracy, Ransom and Marine Insurance' (2011) 35 *Melbourne University Law Review* 717.

[33] BIMCO Piracy Clause for Time Charter Parties 2009; BIMCO Piracy Clause for Consecutive Voyage Charter Parties and COAs 2009.

on feedback on these clauses, BIMCO issued updates in 2013 to more clearly establish the shipowner's liberties to take precautions when the vessel is moving through dangerous sea areas, such as by complying with best practices mandated by its insurers or by bringing on board armed security personnel and equipment.[34] Other industry organisations, including INTERTANKO, produced alternative versions.[35] New case law addressing these and other contractual matters led to further revisions of BIMCO's CONWARTIME and VOYWAR Clauses in 2013.[36]

Although Somali piracy effectively disappeared for more than a decade, as fears rise over its potential resurgence, the prospect of renewed commercial disruption alongside the other compounding forms of war risk continue to shape industry discourse. Even as conventional piracy remains a legitimate concern, contemporary political rhetoric reveals an ongoing inclination to invoke piratical analogies in the context of governmental intervention. When the US seized a vessel carrying Iranian oil in violation of US sanctions, Iran's Foreign Minister described it as an 'act of piracy'.[37] The Foreign Minister of the Philippines claimed the Chinese Coast Guard 'acted like pirates' when it physically confronted operators of a Philippine supply vessel in disputed waters in the South China Sea.[38] After Russia fired on merchant ships following the diplomatic breakdown of the Black Sea Grain Initiative, a Ukrainian official described the actions as 'an act of piracy'.[39] When the Estonian Coast Guard escorted a Russia-connected 'dark fleet' vessel without flag registration out of its Exclusive Economic Zone, a Russian official described the action as 'comparable to piracy'.[40] As the US seized oil tankers, including a Russia-flagged vessel, to enforce a 'quarantine' of Venezuela, Russian politicians branded the maneuvers as 'outright piracy'.[41] And in attempts to justify military action against the Houthi militia in Yemen, a public statement circulated by the office of the US President described the group both as 'terrorists' and a 'band of pirates'.[42] There are many other examples of this phenomenon. Most – perhaps all – of these events fall beyond the meaning of piracy in the public international law or the contractual sense of the term. Nevertheless, this legally muddled discourse calls back perplexing questions at the intersection of piracy and geopolitics that have materialised over centuries of commercial jurisprudence.[43]

[34] BIMCO Piracy Clause for Time Charter Parties 2013; BIMCO Piracy Clause for Consecutive Voyage Charter Parties and COAs 2013.

[35] A comprehensive survey of these clauses is included in Todd (n 20) ch 4.

[36] These updates are discussed in section III of this chapter.

[37] 'Iran Calls US Move to Seize Oil Shipment an "Act of Piracy"' *Reuters* (15 February 2021).

[38] M Flores and NJ Morales, 'Philippines tells Beijing Words Must Match Actions in South China Sea' *Reuters* (19 June 2024).

[39] JC Tramazzo and I Santicola, 'Russia's Interdiction of Neutral Merchant Vessels and the Law of the Sea' *Articles of War* (11 September 2023).

[40] R Meade, 'Russia Lashes Out at NATO "Pirates" as UN Addresses Escalating Maritime Security Concerns' *Lloyd's List* (21 May 2025).

[41] L Papachristous and M Trevelyan, 'Russia Says US Seizure of Oil Tanker is Illegal, Lawmaker Calls it Piracy' *Reuters*, 7 January 2026.

[42] US White House, 'Trump Administration's Actions Made Houthi Terrorists Pay' (25 March 2025).

[43] See D Osler, 'Somalia Piracy Resurgence Makes Kidnap & Ransom Cover Necessary' *Lloyd's List* (13 March 2024).

II. Piracy in Commercial Maritime Disputes

A. Chartering and Carriage

i. Piracy and Governmental Restraint

Some cases involving governmental restraint have led to difficult questions involving state attribution and allegations of piracy. In *Luigi Monta v Cechofracht Co Ltd*, an Italian shipowner agreed to a voyage charter with Czechoslovakian company to move iron ore, silk, and groundnut cake from China to Europe on the steamship *Marilu*.[44] The events giving rise to the dispute took place in 1953, just several years after the civil war in China resulted in the Communists taking control of the Chinese mainland while the defeated Nationalists fled to the island of Taiwan, which was then known by some in the Western world as Formosa.[45] The *Marilu* successfully loaded the cargo in China, but as the vessel sailed south toward Singapore, it was intercepted by a warship operated by Chinese Nationalists. The vessel was then diverted to Keelung where the cargo was confiscated by officials purporting to represent the Chinese Nationalist government of Formosa. The charterparty contained a 'war risk' clause that granted the shipowner the liberty 'to comply with any orders or directions' from 'any Government' or 'any person acting or purporting to act with the authority of such Government'.[46] The clause further provided that compliance with such orders, 'shall be a fulfilment of the contract voyage and the freight shall be payable accordingly'.[47] Invoking the war risk clause, the shipowner sought to collect freight from the charterer, which it refused to pay since the voyage was never completed. In arbitration, the charterer argued in part that since the war risk clause used the capital 'G' in 'Government', this meant that it only applied to orders from authorities that were formally recognised as nations by the British Foreign Office.[48] Since the British government did not recognise the Chinese Nationalists as the official government of Formosa, the charterer contended, both the orders to divert the vessel and the subsequent seizure of the cargo was more akin to 'piratical activity' than a governmental act.[49] The shipowner countered that that the express terms of the war risk clause did not require the directing government to be a formally recognised nation, and that commercial document should not be interpreted through the lens of 'technicalities' such as the political views of the British government.[50]

[44] *Luigi Monta v Cechofracht Co Ltd* [1956] 2 Lloyd's Rep 97 (QB) (Sellers J).
[45] The name Formosa is apparently of Portuguese origin.
[46] ibid.
[47] ibid.
[48] ibid, 103.
[49] ibid, 104.
[50] ibid, 101. The shipowner further argued that the Italian shipmaster could not have been expected to know the nuanced foreign policy perspective of the British government at the time of the intervention, and that, in any event, there was no real choice but to comply with the orders of the soldiers operating the warship or officials on the ground in Keelung.

The umpire in arbitration found that irrespective of whether the officials purporting to govern the island of Formosa were acting on behalf of a nation, the practical reality was that in 1953 the Chinese Nationalists who had operated the warship and intervened in the *Marilu*'s voyage were in fact controlling Formosa and other smaller islands off the coast of the Chinese mainland. For this reason, the actors carrying on the administration of the island of Formosa at the time had to be considered a government under the language of the clause. Since their actions disrupted the performance of the charterparty, this triggered the contractual protections, which entitled the shipowner to recover the freight even though the cargo had been seized and the voyage was never fully performed. Affirming the decision on appeal, the Queen's Bench highlighted the umpire's findings that the events were not piracy and were instead performed in the context of 'hostilities' that had been occurring in 'somewhat spasmodic fashion' between the government in mainland China and the de facto administration governing Formosa.[51] The court found that although the war risk clause should not be read broadly to include 'subservient authority such as municipal or provincial government', a proper interpretation should also consider the 'qualities and character' of the authority giving orders, including whether it had the power to 'exercise … full executive and legislative power over an established territory'.[52] Dismissing the relevance of political disharmony between the British and Italian positions as to whether to officially recognise the government in Formosa, the court emphasised that the charterparty at issue was a 'commercial document in common use by traders of many nationalities'.[53]

Another case raising questions of governmental involvement in piratical acts is *Petroships Pte Ltd v Petec Trading and Investment Corp.*[54] In that case, the tanker *Petro Ranger* was carrying gasoil and kerosene under a voyage charterer from Singapore to Vietnam when it was hijacked by pirates who forcefully subdued the crew, took control of the vessel, and sailed north into Chinese territorial waters just off the city of Haikou in Hainan Island. In attempts to avoid detection, the pirates painted over the name of the vessel with a fake name, disabled the radio equipment, and created false registration and bills of lading. Despite the pirates' efforts to conceal what they had done, less than 10 days after the hijacking the vessel was discovered by Chinese authorities discharging cargo in a ship-to-ship transfer at sea. The Chinese authorities suspected both vessels of smuggling, so they escorted them to anchorage under armed guard and demanded the remainder of the cargo be discharged into shore tanks. More than one month after the hijacking, the Chinese authorities allowed the *Petro Ranger* to depart without

[51] ibid, 105.
[52] ibid.
[53] ibid.
[54] *Petroships Pte Ltd v Petec Trading and Investment Corp* [2001] 2 Lloyd's Rep 348 (Comm) (Cresswell J).

its cargo. The cargo itself was later sold at auction in China. The voyage charterer, who was also the cargo owner, brought a claim in arbitration against the shipowner alleging it was liable for the cargo loss. Although the charterer acknowledged that the initial loss of some of the cargo by the pirates was subject to an exception in the charterparty relieving the shipowner of liability for 'act of public enemies, pirates, or assailing thieves', it claimed that the shipowner was liable for the remainder of the cargo seized by the Chinese authorities.[55] The shipowner countered that that the intervention of the Chinese authorities occurred as a result of the initial piracy, so the exceptions clause referencing piracy still applied to the subsequent government confiscation. Alternatively, the shipowner argued it had no liability under the doctrine of frustration.[56]

The arbitral tribunal rejected these arguments and held for the charterer. It found that there was 'at least an unspoken understanding' between the shipowner and the Chinese government regarding the detention of the vessel and subsequent seizure of the cargo.[57] In fact, the arbitrators noted that 'there was a very high probability that the piracy took place with the knowledge and approval of certain Chinese government officials', which meant that the shipowner could not rely on the piracy exception.[58] The arbitrators further rejected the shipowner's argument of frustration, finding that since the vessel and cargo were quickly discovered in Chinese waters after the pirate hijacking, the contractual performance would still have been possible, albeit with some delay, if not for the subsequent confiscation by the Chinese authorities. On appeal, the English Commercial Court affirmed the award. However, the court did order the tribunal to more clearly articulate the reasons for determining that the charterparty was not frustrated by the governmental seizure in China, reasoning that the standard of frustration is 'radical change' in the circumstances – a criterion which was not mentioned in the award.[59]

Without directly mentioning the term piracy, the US Court of Appeals for the Ninth Circuit addressed the commercial consequences of a commandeered and confiscated vessel in *Wong Wing Fai Co v United States of America*.[60] In that case, the Military Sealift Command of the US Navy agreed with a shipowner for the use the *Vira 8* to facilitate fuel supply to US Navy ships during the evacuation of South Vietnam on 9 April 1975. Due to the emergency military situation that existed at the time, the parties did not enter into a standard charterparty and instead expressed their charter intentions via a 'letter agreement', which did not specify a termination date.[61] Several weeks after the agreement was reached, the shipowner expressed

[55] ibid, 355.

[56] ibid, 356. The shipowner also referenced a 'restraint of princes' exceptions clause, but this position was not pursued on appeal following arbitration.

[57] ibid.

[58] ibid.

[59] ibid, 355. Instead, the tribunal's reasoning used language describing the frustration standard as measured by impossibility of performance.

[60] *Wong Wing Fai Co v United States of America*, 840 F2d 1462 (9th Cir 1988) (Stephens J).

[61] ibid, 1464.

the desire to terminate the charter because of the cost of its private war risk insurance and the need to make the vessel available for another charterer in Singapore the following month. The government charterer agreed to terminate the charter effective 25 April, pending the discharge of its remaining cargo. However, due to a 'rapidly deteriorating military situation', the parties were unable to discharge the cargo by the agreed date of 25 April, so the vessel remained off the coast of Vietnam while the charterer attempted to find a safe place for discharge.[62] On 30 April 1975, South Vietnam fell to the North Vietnamese. At that time, the *Vira 8* was five miles off the shore of Vietnam awaiting instructions when suddenly 110 fleeing South Vietnamese soldiers 'commandeered the ship' and ordered the shipmaster to sail to Singapore. The shipmaster complied under duress, but when the vessel arrived in Singapore, the Singaporean authorities refused to allow the ship to enter the port, so it returned to Vietnam where the North Vietnamese government confiscated the ship and its cargo. The shipowner brought a claim against the government charterer for the loss of the vessel, unpaid hire, and lost profits from the inability to perform the subsequent charter in Singapore.

The US District Court for the Northern District of California held that the shipowner could recover for the unpaid hire up through 25 April – the date of the agreed contract termination – but it rejected the shipowner's other claims.[63] The US Court of Appeals for the Ninth Circuit affirmed the trial court's decision denying recovery for the loss of the vessel since the agreement between the parties did not task the charterer with the obligation to procure war risk insurance. But the Ninth Circuit modified the trial court's decision on the unpaid hire issue. It found that the shipowner was entitled to a further recovery for the unpaid hire between 25 April and 30 April because the *Vira 8* had been waiting at anchorage due to the inability to discharge the charterer's cargo. However the court found that once the fleeing Vietnamese soldiers commandeered the vessel on 30 April, this 'frustrated the charter' and therefore at that moment 'the obligation to pay charter hire ceased on that date'.[64] Defining frustration in the context of a charterparty as 'a change of conditions so radical that accomplishment of the commercial object of the charter is made impossible', the court referenced US case law in which government wartime requisition had resulted in the frustration of a charterparty. Drawing an analogy to these requisition cases, the court determined that '[t]he commandeering of the vessel in the instant case was an event squarely within the range of events giving rise to the frustration doctrine'.[65]

ii. Delays

These cases laid analytical foundations for the string of charterparty disputes following the outbreak of the Somali piracy in the early twenty-first century. The

[62] ibid.
[63] The District Court decision was unpublished.
[64] ibid, 1471.
[65] ibid.

first case to make its way to the English courts was *Cosco Bulk Carrier Co Ltd v Team Up Owning Co Ltd (The Saldanha).*[66] In 2009, the bulk carrier *Saldanha* was under time charter fulfilling the charterer's orders to load a cargo of coal in Indonesia for carriage to Slovenia. Although the shipowner initially raised the issue of whether the voyage should be via the Cape of Good Hope due to piracy risk along the Suez route, the charterer requested that the vessel sail through the Suez instead. The shipowner reserved the right to refuse to comply with the orders unless the charterer confirmed it would pay an additional war risk premium under the language of the charterparty, which the charterer agreed to do. As feared by the shipowner, Somali pirates seized the vessel in the Gulf of Aden and compelled the shipmaster to divert to Somali waters where the vessel remained for more than two months. In the aftermath of the piracy attack, a dispute arose between the shipowner and charterer as to whether the charterer owed hire and other expenses incurred during the delay. In arbitration, the tribunal held for the shipowner on the grounds that hire continued to run throughout the charter period given that the standard off-hire clause used in the charterparty did not list piracy as an off-hire event. On appeal in the English Commercial Court, the charterer argued that the vessel should have been considered off-hire under the off-hire clause's references to 'detention by average accidents to ship or cargo', 'default and/or deficiency of men', or 'any other cause'.[67] The court rejected these arguments and agreed with the arbitral tribunal's position that the seizure of the ship by 'external actors' is not a peril contemplated by the contract's standard off-hire language.[68] Although the charterparty also contained a 'bespoke' clause addressing seizures, the court found that the language of the clause 'did not extend to cover seizure by pirates' and instead appeared to reference arrest and detention by governmental authorities and, in any event, carried no direct implications for the off-hire clause.[69] The court noted the outcome may have been a 'misfortune' for the charterer, but emphasised a lesson for future contract drafting: 'Should the parties be minded to treat seizures by pirates as an off-hire event under a time charter-party, they can do so straightforwardly and most obviously by way of an express provision in a "seizures" or "detention" clause.'[70]

In a subsequent case, *Osmium Shipping Corp v Cargill International SA (The Captain Stefanos)*, the parties agreed to a time charter for the bulk carrier *Captain Stefanos*.[71] As the vessel was under the charterer's orders to move a cargo

[66] *Cosco Bulk Carrier Co Ltd v Team Up Owning Co Ltd* (*The Saldanha*) [2011] 1 Lloyd's Rep 187 (Comm) (Gross J).

[67] ibid, 189. The court agreed with the arbitral tribunal that the 'any other cause' language should be construed in a limited way to reflect the general context of the contract. Under the principle of *ejusdem generis*, the court found it relevant that the other named causes in the off-hire clause deal with the physical condition or efficiency of the vessel and crew, rather than any 'extraneous' cause of disruption such as piracy.

[68] ibid, 194.

[69] ibid.

[70] ibid.

[71] *Osmium Shipping Corp v Cargill International SA (The Captain Stefanos)* [2012] 2 Lloyd's Rep 46 (Comm) (Cooke J).

of coal from South Africa to Italy by way of the Suez Canal in the autumn of 2008, it was hijacked by pirates off the coast of Somalia. The pirates detained the vessel for more than two months until the shipowner paid a ransom for its release. Again, the central issue was whether the vessel was off hire during the pirate detention. Alleging the vessel was off-hire, the charterer not only relied on the standard off-hire clause, but also a rider clause that allowed for the suspension of hire in the event of 'capture/seizure, or detention or threatened detention by any authority'.[72] The shipowner argued that 'by any authority' did not explicitly include pirates and, alternatively, that the off-hire language should be viewed alongside the accompanying CONWARTIME provision that 'taken as a whole' placed the risk of piracy on the charterer.[73] The arbitral tribunal rejected the shipowner's arguments and held for the charterer, and the English Commercial Court affirmed the award. On the issue of whether the CONWARTIME provision should affect the interpretation of the off-hire clause, the court found that the clauses do not necessarily tie together.[74] The court explained that 'standard form charterparties are often used with a series of "add-on" special clauses which do not always fit together immaculately or happily'.[75] The court found that the CONWARTIME clause 'cannot bear the weight which the shipowners wish to give it' as it relates to 'performance of the charterparty and to breach, and not to off-hire'.[76] Rather than trying to fit the two clauses together, the court determined that it was most appropriate to focus on the off-hire clause language, including the 'particular words used and the grammatical structure and syntax of the clause in question'.[77] Engaging in a meticulous analysis of the use of punctuation and grammatical structure of the various 'distinct off-hire events' embedded within the clause, the court found that under its 'plain and obvious meaning' the off-hire clause included 'capture/ seizure' by pirates, which ultimately benefitted the charterer.[78]

A more specific 'piracy clause' was at issue in *Eleni Shipping Ltd v Transgrain Shipping BV (The Eleni P)*.[79] In that case, the bulk carrier *Eleni P* was under time charter when the charterer gave orders to load a cargo of iron ore in Ukraine for delivery in China. The vessel sailed through the Suez Canal and Gulf of Aden, but as it moved through the Arabian Sea many miles off the coast of Oman it was hijacked by Somali pirates who detained the vessel for seven months. The charterparty contained several clauses addressing the prospect of seizure, including the CONWARTIME clause as well as a bespoke piracy clause, which provided that the charterer was authorised to order the vessel to transit

[72] ibid, 47.
[73] This was the CONWARTIME 2004 clause.
[74] ibid, 49.
[75] ibid, 49.
[76] ibid, 52.
[77] ibid, 50.
[78] ibid, 52.
[79] *Eleni Shipping Ltd v Transgrain Shipping BV (The Eleni P)* [2019] 2 Lloyd's Rep 265 (Comm) (Popplewell J).

the Gulf of Aden subject to reimbursement of additional war risk premiums, kidnap and ransom insurance, and crew war bonuses.[80] But the piracy clause also provided that '[i]n case vessel should be threatened/ kidnapped by reason of piracy, payment of hire shall be suspended'.[81] Relying on this piracy clause, the charterer refused to pay hire during the detention. The shipowner brought a claim in arbitration seeking unpaid hire accrued throughout the seven-month ordeal, arguing in part that the piracy clause should not apply because the capture occurred outside the Gulf of Aden. The arbitral tribunal held in favour of the charterer and the English Commercial Court affirmed.[82] The court reasoned that the piracy clause was not intended to define the phrase 'Gulf of Aden' as an ascertainable geographic region that would limit the application of the off-hire provision.[83] Instead, it determined that the reference to the Gulf of Aden in the clause had the purpose of facilitating transit passage through an area known to be dangerous due to piracy. In this way, the piracy clause carved out a risk regime for the purpose of enabling the charterer 'to trade the vessel through the Suez Canal'.[84] According to the court, the piracy clause effectively modified the general right of refusal to proceed in dangerous waters as articulated by the CONWARTIME clause.[85] The court explained that the choice of including the explicit piracy clause in the charterparty was actually beneficial to the shipowner because it made the contract terms more attractive to potential charterers. According to the court, by agreeing to allow Gulf of Aden transit and addressing the risks by direct language, this was a 'quid pro quo for the commercial advantage in being able to offer their vessel for such service, which was no doubt reflected in the other terms including the rate of hire'.[86]

iii. Avoiding Piracy

Other cases have addressed the piracy dimensions of the CONWARTIME clause from a different angle. In *Pacific Basin IHX Ltd v Bulkhandling Handymax AS (The Triton Lark)*, during the autumn of 2008, the time charterer of the bulk carrier the *Triton Lark* instructed the shipowner to perform a voyage moving potash from Germany to China via the Suez Canal.[87] But after receiving warnings

[80] This was the CONWARTIME 2004 clause.

[81] ibid, 270.

[82] The shipowner also argued that other clauses in the charterparty, including a 'capture, seizure, and arrest' clause did not apply to place the vessel off-hire because its reference to 'any authority or by any legal process' did not relate to piracy. The court agreed with the shipowner on this point, but due to the separate piracy clause this holding was not dispositive. ibid, 268.

[83] ibid, 271.

[84] ibid.

[85] ibid. On this point, the court explained that without the piracy clause, the shipowner 'would otherwise be entitled to refuse voyage orders to make a transit of the Gulf of Aden, which would preclude trading between Europe and Asia, without having to go around the Cape of Good Hope'. ibid.

[86] ibid.

[87] *Pacific Basin IHX Ltd v Bulkhandling Handymax AS (The Triton Lark I)* [2012] 1 Lloyd's Rep 151 (Comm) (Teare J).

of pirate attacks in the Gulf of Aden, the shipowner proceeded via the Cape of Good Hope route, while placing the charterer on notice of its position that '[t]he only safe route is round the Cape' as the Gulf of Aden route was 'manifestly unsafe'.[88] The shipowner later sought to recover the additional costs of the diversion from the charterer, including hire and bunkers. In the arbitration proceedings, the shipowner justified its position by referencing the CONWARTIME clause, which granted the shipowner the freedom to avoid orders 'where it appears that the Vessel, her cargo, crew or other persons on board the Vessel, in the reasonable judgment of the Master and/or the Owners, may be, or are likely to be, exposed to War Risks'.[89] The arbitral tribunal ruled in favour of the shipowner on grounds that there was a 'serious risk' that the vessel would be exposed to pirate hijacking in the Gulf of Aden.[90] The English Commercial Court reversed, finding that the tribunal had misapplied the clause as a matter of law. The court found that the tribunal applied the notion of 'serious risk' to mean 'an important event, demanding consideration'.[91] This, the court determined, was an incorrect reading of the CONWARTIME clause. The court found that its key language, 'may be, or are likely to be', connotes 'as serious risk in the sense of one of which it could be said that there was a real likelihood or real danger that the vessel would be exposed to acts of piracy'.[92] Following the publication of the court's first judgment, the parties requested additional clarification from the court on the meaning of 'exposed to War Risks' in the CONWARTIME clause.[93] The shipowner contended that the phrase meant 'being exposed to the risk of piracy' while the charterer argued it meant 'being exposed to acts of piracy having an actual effect on the vessel'.[94] Rather than untangling the subtle nuances of the parties' diverging interpretations, the court explained that the clause should be read to assess 'whether there is a real likelihood that the vessel will be exposed to acts of piracy in the sense that the place will be dangerous on account of acts of piracy'.[95] The court found this to be consistent with the 'overriding priorities' expressed in the BIMCO circular distributed with the CONWARTIME clause in 1993.[96] The court explained: '[W]hether or not the Gulf of Aden was dangerous to *Triton Lark* on account of acts of piracy will depend upon the degree of likelihood that they will occur and the gravity of the consequences to the vessel, cargo and crew should they occur.'[97] This question, the court noted, was a matter for the arbitrators to determine based on the evidence.

[88] ibid, 155.
[89] ibid, 153. This was the CONWARTIME 1993 clause.
[90] ibid, 158.
[91] ibid.
[92] ibid.
[93] *Pacific Basin IHX Ltd v Bulkhandling Handymax AS (The Triton Lark II)* [2012] 1 Lloyd's Rep 457 (Comm) (Teare J).
[94] ibid, 458.
[95] ibid.
[96] ibid.
[97] ibid.

A further interpretive challenge relating to the 2004 version of the CONWARTIME clause was raised in the English Commercial Court in *Taokas Navigation SA v Komrowski Bulk Shipping KG (GMBH & Co) (The Paiwan Wisdom)*.[98] The *Paiwan Wisdom* was under a sub-sub time charter containing the CONWARTIME clause along with a clause requiring the vessel to 'always trade within IWL [Institute Warranty Limits]' and expressly excluded Eritrea, Ethiopia, and Somalia, but not Kenya.[99] The clause also read, 'passing Gulf of Aden always allowed with H&M [Hull and Machinery] insurance authorization'.[100] After the vessel was delivered into the charterer's services, in April 2010, the charterer gave employment orders to load a cargo of cement clinker in Taiwan for discharge in Kenya. Invoking the CONWARTIME clause on grounds that piracy in the Indian Ocean and waters off East Africa was 'getting more severe', the shipowner refused the charterer's orders to go to Kenya.[101] As a result, the charterer had to charter a different vessel to perform the voyage, leading to costs of more than $800,000. The charterer brought a claim in arbitration, but the arbitrators held for the shipowner on the grounds that the CONWARTIME clause granted it the authority to refuse to proceed to Kenya, especially given the parties were aware of the threat of piracy at the time of contracting. On appeal, the charterer argued that on the true construction of the contract, there had to be a 'material change in the relevant war risk' in order for the shipowner to have the liberty to refuse the charterer's orders.[102] It further contended that the trading limits clause, which expressly permitted passing the Gulf of Aden, contained an 'implicit reference to the risk of piracy' that indicated the shipowner's acceptance of the risk in exchange for the payment of hire.[103] The court rejected these arguments and affirmed the arbitral tribunal's decision for the shipowner. The court found that although Kenya was within the IWL and not excluded by the specific list in the charterparty, the CONWARTIME clause still gave the shipowner a basis to refuse orders to navigate through the Indian Ocean to Kenya if there was 'a real likelihood of the vessel being exposed to the acts of piracy on such route'.[104] According to the court, it was not necessary for this likelihood to have materially increased from the time that the charterparty was agreed. Instead, although in general trading to Kenya was permitted under the charterparty, the CONWARTIME clause enabled the shipowner 'to avoid danger from war risk which may be encountered en route to Kenya'.[105]

[98] *Taokas Navigation SA v Komrowski Bulk Shipping KG (GMBH & Co) (The Paiwan Wisdom)* [2012] 2 Lloyd's Rep 416 (Comm) (Teare J).

[99] ibid, 418. The contract contained the CONWARTIME 2004 clause.

[100] ibid.

[101] ibid, 418.

[102] ibid, 419.

[103] ibid, 420. The charterer further contended that the inclusion of the trading limits clause indicated that the parties had given careful consideration to the issue of piracy and decided only to exclude certain countries in East Africa, which did not include Kenya.

[104] ibid.

[105] ibid, 421.

An SMA award, *Precious Ornaments Ltd v Helena Chartering Inc*, addressed the separate question of rerouting for the purpose of taking on security guards in waters of high risk of piracy attack.[106] The parties had agreed to a time charter for the *Manisamut Naree* during a period running from 2007–2008. The vessel was on a voyage from Indonesia to Ireland in December 2008, when the shipowner notified the charterer that due to 'lots of piracy incidents' off Somalia, it intended to deviate to board unarmed security experts in Oman as a counter-piracy measure before proceeding through the Gulf of Aden.[107] It later sought to collect for the time lost during the diversion. In arbitration, the charterer argued that taking on the guards was not necessary and that it was sufficient that the parties had agreed to a specific route to avoid piracy attack. It contended that it should not be left to bear the financial burden of the shipowner's unilateral decision to deploy armed guards. The shipowner countered that the deviation to take on the security personnel was made in efforts to protect the vessel, the crew, and the cargo and that these measures fell within a clause in the charterparty explicitly granting the shipowner the liberty to deviate to safeguard life and property. This, it argued, was supported by the fact that advisories from governments and industry organisations had recommended the use of security guards to deter pirates in the region. The arbitration panel held in favour of the shipowner. It reasoned that the deviation to take on the security guards was reasonable under the circumstances and that the charterer therefore owed hire for any lost time. To support its position that the deviation and the use of the security personnel were 'reasonable exercises of due diligence and good seamanship', the panel referenced section 4(4) of the US Carriage of Goods by Sea Act and the Hague Rules (incorporated into the charterparty by a clause paramount), which provide that the carrier shall not be liable for 'any deviation in saving life or attempting to safe life or property at sea'.[108] The panel also found that the cost of the security guards should be divided between the parties.

iv. Cargo Loss

In *Trafigura Beheer BV v Navigazione Montanari Spa*, a vessel called the *Valle di Cordoba* was under a voyage charter to transport motor oil from Cort d'Ivoire to Nigeria.[109] In 2010, while the vessel was waiting for discharge instructions in the Gulf of Guinea just off the coast of Benin, a group of 15 armed men took control of the vessel and executed a ship-to-ship (STS) transfer of some of the cargo onto a lightering vessel. The charterparty contained an 'in-transit loss' clause,

[106] *Precious Ornaments Ltd v Helena Chartering Inc (The Manisamut Naree)*, SMA 4088 (NY Arb 2010) (Manfred W Arnold, Thomas F Fox, and James N Hood).

[107] ibid, 3.

[108] ibid, 4.

[109] *Trafigura Beheer BV v Navigazione Montanari Spa (The Valle Di Cordoba)* [2014] 1 Lloyd's Rep 550 (Comm) (Andrew Smith J).

which provided that the shipowner 'will be responsible for the full amount of any in-transit loss' measured by the difference between net cargo volume after loading and before discharge.[110] Invoking this clause, the charterer brought a claim against the shipowner for the lost cargo in the English Commercial Court. Although it was apparently immaterial to the resolution of the claim, the parties agreed by stipulation that the men who attacked the vessel were 'pirates'.[111] Instead, the central point of contention in the litigation was whether the in-transit loss clause applied to the cargo confiscation. The charterer contended that since there was a difference in net volume between the cargo at the time of loading and then after the pirate seizure, the shipowner was liable for the loss under the plain terms of the clause. The shipowner countered that this broad interpretation of the clause would lead to 'unusual' strict liability for cargo loss. Holding for the shipowner, the English Commercial Court found the more narrow view was consistent with the 'natural business sense' and the 'commercial background' of the clause.[112] Crediting evidence that the clause was designed to address other forms of loss such as evaporation during transport, the court found that the expressions used in the clause 'connote loss that is incidental to the carriage of oil products, and does not extend to losses such as those that occurred in this case because of the action of the pirates'.[113] Although the court declined to precisely define the full scope of what kinds of loss might fall within the clause, the court unequivocally held that '[l]oss from the pirates' activities clearly is not covered'.[114]

v. Ransom

Most recently, the UK Supreme Court addressed the charterparty implications of piracy in *Herculito Maritime Ltd v Gunvor International BV*.[115] That case involved a vessel called the *MT Polar*, which was seized by Somali pirates in October 2010 while moving fuel oil through the Gulf of Aden under a voyage charter between Russia and Singapore via the Suez Canal. The *Polar* was detained by the pirates for 10 months until the shipowners paid a ransom of $7.7 million. After paying the ransom, the shipowner claimed general average, seeking to collect $4.8 million from the Singapore-based cargo interests who were bill of lading holders. The cargo interests issued a general average bond guaranteed by its cargo insurers for the release of the cargo, but they resisted liability on the merits in LMAA arbitration. The arbitral tribunal held in favour of the cargo interests, reasoning that the bills of lading did not allow recovery in general average for the ransom payments.

[110] ibid. The clause applied only 'if in-transit loss exceeds.05%'.
[111] ibid.
[112] ibid, 555.
[113] ibid.
[114] ibid, 556.
[115] *Herculito Maritime Ltd and Others v Gunvor International BV and Others (The Polar)* [2024] 1 Lloyd's Rep 85 (UKSC) (Hamblen LJ).

The arbitral tribunal found that the exclusive means of recovering was by way of the kidnap and ransom insurance policy or war risk policy, because under the charterparty the charterer had agreed to pay the premium for this additional insurance and the bills of lading incorporated the terms of the charterparty. The arbitral tribunal found this contractual arrangement created an exclusive 'fund' or 'code' that prevented the shipowner from claiming contribution from the charterer for any of the perils covered by the additional insurance.[116] According to the arbitral tribunal this charterparty code encapsulating piracy risks was incorporated into the bills of lading, which had the effect of precluding the general average claim against the cargo interests as well.[117]

The English Commercial Court reversed the decision.[118] The court held that although the bills of lading did incorporate the terms of the charterparty, this did not have the effect of binding the cargo interests to pay the additional ransom or war risk insurance premiums. As a result, the bills of lading did not create an exclusive code that would preclude other avenues for recovery against the cargo interests and therefore the shipowner could proceed in seeking general average for the ransom payment. In the English Court of Appeal, the cargo interests argued that the decision was incorrect because it meant that the holders of the bills of lading 'took the burden of the charterparty regime (eg the various liberties given to the owner to deviate from the proposed voyage through the Suez Canal or to deliver the cargo at an alternative port) but without the benefit of insurance cover'.[119] The Court of Appeal rejected this argument and affirmed the decision below. It reasoned that 'the risk of piracy and the potential need to pay a ransom were not only foreseeable but were foreseen by the parties to the bills of lading contract and dealt with expressly by them'.[120] Since the vessel was allowed to transit through the dangerous waters of the Gulf of Aden, the court found this meant the cargo interests knew or should have known that 'payment of such a ransom would give rise to general average'.[121] The UK Supreme Court affirmed.[122] Scrutinising the charterparty language and examining applicable case law on the notion of insurance codes, the Supreme Court found that 'there was no insurance code which could be incorporated into the bills of lading contracts'.[123] Furthermore, the court explained, there was no basis to 'manipulate' the terms of the bills of lading to find the holders were protected from general average.[124]

[116] *Herculito Maritime Ltd and Others v Gunvor International BV and Others (The Polar)* [2021] 1 Lloyd's Rep 150 (Comm) (Teare J).

[117] ibid, 159.

[118] ibid.

[119] *Herculito Maritime Ltd and Others v Gunvor International BV and Others (The Polar)* [2022] 1 Lloyd's Rep 375, 381 (CA) (Males J).

[120] ibid, 387.

[121] ibid.

[122] *Herculito Maritime Ltd and Others v Gunvor International BV and Others (The Polar)* [2024] 1 Lloyd's Rep 85.

[123] ibid, 99.

[124] ibid, 103.

B. Marine Insurance

i. Piracy and War

Marine insurance cases addressing the geopolitical dimensions of piracy include several American judgments arising out the US Civil War (1861–1865).[125] The first is an 1863 decision by the Supreme Judicial Court of Maine: *Dole v Merchants' Mutual Marine Insurance Co.*[126] In the summer of 1861, a vessel called the *Golden Rocket* was attacked by a group of soldiers acting under the authority of the Navy of the Confederate States who were operating another vessel called the *Sumter*. The men claimed the *Golden Rocket* as a 'prize of war', stripped its sails, took its provisions and stores, and destroyed it by fire. The shipowner sought recovery under an insurance policy covering 'perils of the seas, enemies, pirates, assailing thieves, restraints, and detainments of all kings, princes, or people'.[127] The insurer resisted payment on grounds that the loss fell within a form of FC&S exclusion, which read: 'Warranted free from capture, seizure, or detention, or the consequences of any attempt thereat, any stipulation to this policy to the contrary notwithstanding.'[128] This raised the question of whether the events were covered as acts of enemies or pirates, or whether they were excluded as capture or seizure. Refusing to allow evidence of the status of the perpetrators as 'belligerents' that might be capable of 'carrying on hostilities against the United States', the trial court held for the plaintiff assured.[129]

The Supreme Court of Maine reversed. The court first found that the plaintiff's claim could not be maintained without a finding that the actions amounted to piracy. The insurer had argued that the term should be understood by reference to the crime as defined by 'the law of nations', which it alleged could not apply to the acts of the Confederate solders because they did not 'seize, without discrimination, every vessel which they chose to seize, regardless of national character'.[130] The court rejected this restrictive view and instead found that the parties to the insurance contract could be presumed to have understood the term to embrace a broader class of risks, including 'any kind of *piracy*, whether by the statutes or by the law of nations'.[131] However, the court found that it was not necessary to untangle such distinctions because the alleged acts, if proven, were 'clearly acts of piracy' whether defined by the law of nations, statutes, or the common law.[132]

[125] There are even older cases addressing piracy and marine insurance. A thorough treatment of these early cases is provided in R Merkin, *Marine Insurance: A Legal History* (Edward Elgar, 2021) § 9-093. See eg *Dean v Hornby* [1854] 3 E&B 180; *Palmer v Naylor* [1854] 10 Exch 382; *Kleinwort v Shepard* [1859] 1 E&E 44.

[126] *Dole v Merchants' Mutual Marine Insurance Co* [1863] 51 Me 465 (SC Maine) (Davis J).

[127] ibid, 465.

[128] ibid, 471.

[129] ibid, 466.

[130] ibid, 467–68.

[131] ibid, 467 (emphasis in original).

[132] ibid, 467.

The court also found that 'indiscriminate hostility' is not necessary to form the crime of piracy, just as the crime of robbery on land does not require a 'general purpose to rob everybody'.[133] The court also held that the attack could be viewed as being committed by 'enemies', although that this would imply 'the existence of "war."'[134] To contextualise this point, the court emphasised that 'every forcible contest between two governments, de facto, or de jure, is war'. In that sense, the court reasoned, '[w]ar is an existing fact, and not a legislative decree'.[135] Although the US Congress had the power to declare war, the court explained, it may still be 'initiated by other nations, or by traitors; and then it exists, whether there is any declaration of war or not'.[136] Consequently, in a civil war, the 'traitors' who engage in rebellion and hostilities against the 'established government' may commit acts of war. At the same time, the court noted, 'their acts are not only acts of war, but also of robbery, murder, or piracy'.[137] Thus, it held the actions of the soldiers 'were not the less piratical because they were belligerent'.[138] Simultaneously, however, the court found that the loss fell within the policy's exception for capture and seizure. Accordingly, the court rejected the plaintiff's argument that the contract terms must be viewed restrictively in the context of a marine insurance policy, explaining instead that '[t]here can be no doubt that the words "capture and seizure," in their general significance, are broad enough to embrace a taking by pirates'.[139] The events, being both 'piratical and belligerent', constituted a capture and seizure, which placed the loss within the FC&S exclusion to the benefit of the insurer.[140]

A similar question was addressed in *Fifield v Insurance Co of the State of Pennsylvania*.[141] While on a voyage carrying sugar from Cuba to England in the summer of 1861, a brig called the *John Welsh* was captured approximately 250 miles off the coast of Nantucket Shoals, Massachusetts, by privateers sailing under letters of marque issue by the Confederate States. The Confederate privateers had approached the *John Welsh* sailing the French flag, quickly switched to the secession flag, plundered the *John Welsh*, and transferred the crew to another ship. The *John Welsh* was then taken over by a prize crew and headed south. It was never recovered. Shortly thereafter, the privateers committed the same offence against other vessels in the region. The perpetrators were eventually arrested and brought to Philadelphia, where they were tried and convicted for the crime of piracy. The men were never sentenced and were instead exchanged by the US government as Confederate prisoners of war. The shipowner of the *John Welsh*

[133] ibid, 468.
[134] ibid, 470.
[135] ibid.
[136] ibid.
[137] ibid.
[138] ibid, 471.
[139] ibid.
[140] ibid, 477. Justices Cutting and Barrows dissented on grounds that 'the taking was piratical, but not a capture, seizure or detention, as understood in contracts of insurance'. ibid, 478.
[141] *Fifield v Insurance Co of the State of Pennsylvania*, 47 PA 166 (SC Penn 1864) (Woodward J).

filed a claim against its marine insurer.[142] The policy expressly insured the vessel against losses caused by pirates, rovers, and assailing thieves, but the insurer resisted cover by invoking an FC&S clause that provided it 'shall not be liable for any claim for or loss by seizure, capture, or detention, or the consequences of any attempt thereat'.[143] Again, this raised the contractual question of how the civil wartime events should be classified under the conflicting terms of the insurance policy.

The trial court held for the insurer and the Supreme Court of Pennsylvania affirmed. In its analysis, the court framed the central question as whether the loss of the *John Welsh* was a 'piratical loss or capture jure belli'.[144] The court first noted that the conviction of the perpetrators showed that the acts constituted the 'crime of piracy, unless the commission under which they were committed was such as to take away their piratical character'.[145] On this point, the court examined evidence that the President of the Confederate States had apparently commissioned private armed vessels, including the privateering crew, with letters of marque and general reprisal, which authorised them to engage in a 'war on the commerce of the United States' and with instructions not to impede the 'rights of all neutral powers'.[146] The court reasoned that (at the time) privateering and piracy were generally distinguishable as privateering involved 'captures jure belli under colour of governmental authority and for the benefit of a political power organized as a government de jure or de facto' whereas piracy was 'mere robbery on the high seas committed from motives of personal gain'.[147] Privateering was committed for the benefit of the 'commissioning power' while the other benefits the 'perpetrators merely'.[148] Moreover, piracy was a crime as described by acts of the US Congress, while privateering had been considered 'lawful warfare on public enemies', including during the US 'revolutionary struggle' against the British.[149] The court found that whether the capture of the *John Welsh* was performed by privateers or a pirates depended on the 'legal effect' of the commission issued by the Confederacy. Although it rejected the notion that the Confederate States acted as a legitimate de jure government, the court found that 'any government, however, violent and wrongful its origin, which is in the actual exercise of sovereignty over a territory and people large enough for a nation, must be considered a government de facto'.[150] The court reasoned that determining when to recognise a 'new power' may be complicated or delayed if there has not yet been a period of peace for it

[142] ibid.
[143] ibid, 168.
[144] ibid. *Jure belli* roughly means 'under the laws of war'.
[145] ibid.
[146] ibid, 169.
[147] ibid.
[148] ibid.
[149] ibid, 169. Although European countries had declared privateering to be abolished by the Declaration of Paris in 1856, according to the court, the US had not acceded to this declaration as not to 'surrender our right of privateering' to be used in domestic and foreign wars. ibid.
[150] ibid, 170.

to 'consolidate its administration'.[151] The court emphasised that the Confederate States had carried on war for more than three years, that its 'belligerent rights' had been recognised by major powers in Europe, and, most importantly, that it was 'exercising sovereignty over a territory larger and a people more numerous than those of our original thirteen states'.[152] Taking care not to imply that the US government accepted the Confederacy as a legitimate government, the court held that the capture of the *John Welsh* was 'a capture jure belli and not piratical'.[153] In doing so, the court found that US President Lincoln's decision to exchange the crew of the privateering vessel as prisoners of war must be interpreted as support for the notion that the men were not pirates, even if the President did not intend to establish an inference that the Confederacy was a de facto government. The consequence for the marine insurers was that events giving rise to the loss of the *John Welsh* were excluded from the policy under the FC&S exception for 'capture' and were not covered as a loss caused by pirates.[154]

A third US Civil War-era dispute was decided by the US Supreme Court in *Mauran v Alliance Insurance Co*.[155] That case involved the 1861 seizure of a vessel called the *Marshall* by the crew of a steamer called the *Music*, which took place at the mouth of the Mississippi River below New Orleans, Louisiana, where the river releases into the Gulf of Mexico. At the time of the seizure, the *Music* crew 'hoisted the Confederate flag to the mast-head of the *Marshall*, and informed the captain and pilot that the ship was "a prize to the Confederate States."'[156] The shipowner of the *Marshall* made a claim against its insurer. The policy covered losses caused by pirates and thieves but also contained an FC&S exclusion barring recovery for capture and seizure.[157] Accordingly, the insurer denied the claim on the grounds that the events should be categorised under the exclusion. The central issue in litigation was whether the loss was caused by 'assailing thieves' or 'pirates', which would be covered by the body of the insurance policy, or whether it was caused by 'capture', which would be excluded from cover.[158] The trial court held for the insurer and the shipowner appealed to the US Supreme Court. The shipowner argued that the events should be classified as piracy under the policy as they fell within the criminal definition laid out by US legislation, which referenced

[151] ibid. As an analogy, the court noted that although the original 13 states organised a confederation in 1777, the US was in 'constant war' with the British until 1783. The court wrote: '[W]ho doubts now – who ever did doubt – that in all that interval they were a government de facto.' ibid.

[152] ibid.

[153] ibid, 173.

[154] ibid, 174. Three Justices issued separate concurring opinions. Among them was Justice Read, who expressed the view that in the context of an insurance policy 'the word pirates is used in the sense known to the commercial world'. He wrote: 'Here was a rebel cruiser, not committing a single act of robbery, but capturing vessels under rebel authority, and we cannot say that this is piracy in the sense in which it is understood by the world at large.' ibid, 181.

[155] *Mauran v Alliance Insurance Co*, 73 US 1 (USSC 1867) (Nelson J).

[156] ibid, 2.

[157] ibid, 1–2.

[158] ibid, 2.

'any act of hostility against the United States, or any citizen thereof under color of any commission from any foreign prince or state, or any pretence of authority from any person'.[159] The shipowner also cited an 1861 Presidential Proclamation by Abraham Lincoln, which read: 'If any person, under the pretended authority of said (Confederate) States, or under any other pretence, shall molest a vessel of the United States, or the persons or cargo on board of her, such a person will be amenable to the laws of the United States for the prevention and punishment of piracy.'[160] Since representatives of both political branches of government had proclaimed that the soldiers of the Confederate States had acted as pirates (with some of the offenders actually convicted of the piracy crime), the shipowner alleged the court was obliged to classify the seizure of the *Marshall* as a covered act of piracy. The insurer countered that regardless of these criminal definitions and political pronouncements suggesting the actions were akin to piracy, the seizure on behalf of the Confederacy was plainly excluded from the policy as a wartime capture.

The US Supreme Court agreed with the insurer and affirmed the decision of the trial court. The court acknowledged that 'the United States have never admitted the so-called "Confederate States" to be a government' and that 'it may well treat every citizen of the United States who aided in the rebellion as committing treason or piracy'.[161] But the court found that '[t]he fact remains that here was a great power capable of levying war against us, which did so levy and wage war, and which made a capture'.[162] The court found that it should not matter whether the capture was lawful or whether the Confederate States was a 'perfectly lawful government'.[163] The more relevant factor was whether the capture was performed by a de facto government, defined as 'one in possession of the supreme or sovereign power', even if it was 'founded perhaps in crime, and in the violation of every principle of international or municipal law, and of right and justice'.[164] The court found that the question of whether the actions amounted to capture rather than piracy depended on whether the Southern Confederacy was a 'government in fact'.[165] While emphasising that the Confederate States was organised in a 'wholly illegal and void' manner from the perspective of the US Constitution, the court recognised that the territory controlled by the Confederate States was greater than 'many of the old governments in Europe' and contained millions of people.[166] Moreover, the court found it relevant that the war carried on by the Confederate States was expansive, including blockaded ports, property seizures, and 'vessel captures recognized as

[159] ibid.
[160] ibid, 4.
[161] ibid, 8.
[162] ibid.
[163] ibid, 9.
[164] ibid, 6.
[165] ibid, 13.
[166] ibid, 14.

prizes of war'.[167] These actions exhibited 'war as a matter of fact' that showed that the Confederate States acted with the 'attributes of government'.[168] Accordingly, regardless of whether the actions were also piracy, the court found the 'captures' under the commission of the Confederacy were 'among those excepted out of the policy by the warranty of the insured'.[169]

Following these three decisions, the Supreme Court of Louisiana addressed a similar problem by distinguishing similar facts and avoiding the notion of piracy altogether. In *Babbit, Goode & Co v The Sun Mutual Insurance Co*, a steamboat called the *Mars* was carrying a cargo of sugar along the Mississippi River from New Orleans, Louisiana, to Cincinnati, Ohio, in April 1861, when a 'mob of citizens' fired a cannon from the shore of Helena, Arkansas, as the ship attempted to pass.[170] The mob then ordered the shipmaster to land and seized the cargo. These events occurred just 12 days before the state of Arkansas succeeded from the Union to join the Civil War on the side of the Confederacy. The Ohio-based cargo owner made a claim against its insurer, which it denied on grounds that the loss was excluded as 'capture or detention by enemies of the United States'.[171] Holding for the plaintiff, the lower court rejected this argument and the Supreme Court affirmed. Despite the wartime context, the court found that the group that had seized the cargo acted 'under no pretext of authority, but simply as a mob'.[172] Although the court acknowledged that the motive of the seizure may have been that the cargo belonged to someone in Ohio (well within Union territory), the court explained that 'the reason of the outrage does not necessarily determine its character'.[173] The court found that the mob 'neither represented nor claimed to represent any State or government, real or imaginary, actual or pretended'.[174] The court used this factual distinction to contrast with the other previous cases in which the capture was found to have been performed by Confederate soldiers or privateers.[175]

ii. Piracy and Unrest

English courts have also addressed questions at the intersection of piracy and civil conflict in the marine insurance context. In *Republic of Bolivia v Indemnity Mutual*

[167] ibid.
[168] ibid.
[169] ibid.
[170] *Babbit, Goode & Co v The Sun Mutual Insurance Co*, 23 La Ann 314 (SC Louisiana 1871) (Howe J).
[171] ibid, 315.
[172] ibid.
[173] ibid.
[174] ibid.
[175] Other cases involving attacks on vessels during the US Civil war include *Sinnerton v Columbian Insurance Co*, which found that a vessel sunk in a channel by mob on behalf of State of Virginia was performed by men who 'were not *hostes humani generis*, nor did they act *causa lucri*' – meaning they were not pirates acting as enemies of all mankind nor for their own personal gain but rather in pursuit of civil war aims. *Sinnerton v Columbian Insurance Co* [1867] 37 NY 174 (Court of Appeals NY).

Marine Assurance Co, the central issue was whether a marine insurance policy or an accompanying war risk policy covered goods seized from a ship as it moved along a tributary of the Amazon River on the boundary between Bolivia and Brazil.[176] The vessel was en route to transport supplies to Bolivian soldiers based in a remote inland outpost called Puerto Alonzo accessible only by the Acre River. As the vessel moved along the river in December 1900, a group of 'malcontents' acting as part of a political movement to resist Bolivian rule used an armed vessel to detain the ship and take possession of the cargo, which was owned by the Republic of Bolivia and insured under a policy of insurance subject to English law.[177] The marine insurance policy provided cover for loss caused by 'piracy', but the policy excluded 'capture' and 'seizure' under an FC&S clause. The assured cargo owner argued that the actions giving rise to the loss fell within the definition of piracy, and the marine insurer argued the events were not piracy and instead should be categorised as an excluded war risk under the FC&S clause.

The King's Bench held for the insurer. It reasoned that the term 'piracy' in an insurance policy should be interpreted in its 'popular' or 'business meaning'.[178] Although the assured had referenced definitions of piracy provided by writers on criminal law and international law, the trial court found these definitions to be 'very wide'.[179] The court expressed doubt on the idea that 'what might be piracy in international law is necessarily piracy within the meaning of the term in a policy of insurance'.[180] Instead, the court explained, '[o]ne has to look at what is the natural and clear meaning of the word "pirate" in a document used by business men for business purposes'.[181] In doing so, the court explained, 'one must attach to it a more popular meaning, the meaning that would be given to it by ordinary persons, rather than the meaning to which it might be extended by writers on international law'.[182] Nevertheless, the trial court recognised that a passage from an international law treatise – Hall's International Law – encapsulated the 'popular or business meaning' by explaining that piratical events must involve the pursuit of a 'private, as contrasted with public, ends'.[183] Citing another passage from the same international law treatise, the court acknowledged a distinction between politically motivated attacks that might be viewed as piracy by victims who have a particular State interest versus piracy 'in its coarser forms' through indiscriminate attack without a political objective.[184] The court found this kind of

[176] *Republic of Bolivia v Indemnity Mutual Marine Assurance Co* [1909] 1 KB 785 (KB) (Pickford J).
[177] ibid. According to the trial court judgment, the men who attacked the steamer had also stopped other vessels along the river, but these vessels were released once they ascertained that the vessels were not carrying goods for the Bolivian government. This fact supported the notion that the attack was targeted and political rather than indiscriminate and piratical. ibid, 789.
[178] ibid.
[179] ibid, 790.
[180] ibid.
[181] ibid.
[182] ibid.
[183] ibid, 791.
[184] ibid, 792.

piracy in the 'coarser sense' to be its meaning in an insurance policy.[185] Applying this rule to the cargo loss at issue, the court found that it was not covered under the insurance term because the seizure was performed as a targeted and politically motivated act with intent to disrupt the Bolivian government's efforts to supply its troops. The English Court of Appeal agreed.[186] It found that a 'business' meaning of the term piracy hinged on its use 'in this particular policy' rather than definitions under international or municipal law. The court also found that even if one were to apply a broader international law definition there was 'no pretence for calling this that happened on the borders of Brazil and Bolivia piracy'.[187] Since the events took place on a tributary branch of the Amazon River far from the location where it runs into the ocean, this was 'not the theatre on which piracy could be committed'.[188] Instead, the events were more similar to the other war risk perils referenced in the FC&S clause, such as riots, civil commotions, hostilities, or warlike operations.

An English court addressed the insurance meaning of piracy in another dynamic geopolitical context in *Banque Monetaca & Carystuiaki v Motor Union Insurance Co Ltd*.[189] In the summer of 1920, a Greek-owned schooner called the *Filia* was on a voyage in the Black Sea when it encountered engine trouble and anchored off the coast of Turkey for repairs and replenishment of stores. The area was in a place called Kerassounde, which was controlled by a 'notorious Nationalist leader called Osman Agha'.[190] A group of men acting on his behalf took possession of the *Filia*, captured the crew, and raised the Turkish flag. Neither the vessel nor the crew was ever found. The *Filia* was subject to a policy of war risk insurance, which covered capture, seizure, arrest, and warlike operations, but – as in the other previous cases – the war risk policy did not cover loss caused by piracy. The shipowner made a claim against the war risk insurer, which it denied on the basis that the actions giving rise to the loss was piracy, rather than any other category described by the terms of cover, which included only 'capture, seizure, hostilities, warlike operations'.[191] Following litigation on the issue, the King's Bench held for the shipowner on grounds that the events fell within the war risk policy cover as a seizure. Although the court recognised that Osman Agha was commonly believed to be 'a person of low character' who had previously acted as a 'brigand', he was also 'at a position of considerable authority' who was 'virtually controlling, as dictator, the region in which this seizure took place'.[192] In addition, the court found that at the time of the seizure the Greek army

[185] ibid.

[186] *Republic of Bolivia v Indemnity Mutual Marine Assurance Co* [1909] 1 KB 785 (CA) (Vaughan Williams LJ).

[187] ibid, 798.

[188] ibid, 799.

[189] *Banque Monetaca & Carystuiaki v Motor Union Insurance Co Ltd* (1923) 14 Lloyd's List Rep 48 (KB) (Roche J).

[190] The court noted that Osman Agha later became governor of Kerassounde.

[191] ibid.

[192] ibid, 50.

was 'engaged in carrying on active hostile operations' against the Nationalist Turks in the region.[193] Throughout this period of 'active warfare' between the Greeks and Turks, Osman Agha had been on the side of the Turks, which, according to the court, meant that 'he did capture and seize this Greek vessel under cover of and largely upon motives of a political character'.[194] Although the court acknowledged that there may have also been 'personal gain' motivating the seizure, it was 'dominantly political and military'.[195] The court also found the events were part of a broader 'political movement' and therefore the seizure could not be viewed simply as a 'scheme of brigandage'.[196] At the same time, the court highlighted that Osman Agha had committed other similar acts that were 'piratical in their nature', such as boarding a French vessel and stealing property from it.[197] According to the court, the seizure of the Greek vessel at issue was different from the previous attack on the French vessel, in part because it was done as part of a broader Turkish Nationalist movement. This distinction supported the court's view that 'the seizure of the *Filia* was so dominantly a military matter as to move it from the position of piracy within the meaning of the clause'.[198]

iii. Contemporary Piracy

Although the piracy peril was added to the British FC&S clause in the mid-twentieth century, judicial scrutiny over its meaning in marine insurance policies continued. In *Athens Maritime v Hellenic Mutual War Risk Association (Bermuda) Ltd (The Andreas Lemos)*, a vessel called the *Andreas Lemos* was anchored about 12 miles from the coast of Chittagong, Bangladesh, in the summer of 1977, when a gang of men armed with long knives boarded the vessel and stole some of the vessel's equipment, including mooring ropes. The crew discovered what was happening and chased the assailants away.[199] The shipowner had insured the vessel under a standard H&M policy and enrolled the vessel with a war risk insurance mutual. The war risk association rules provided that the vessel was insured against loss of machinery and equipment caused by 'the risks excluded from the Standard Form of English Marine Policy' by way of the FC&S clause, which at the time referenced 'piracy' along with various other war risks.[200] The shipowner

[193] ibid.
[194] ibid.
[195] ibid.
[196] ibid.
[197] ibid, 51. The court found it relevant that the Turkish government had apologised to the French Government for Osman Agha's seizure of the French vessel, while there was no evidence of such an apology to the Greek Government for the attack on the *Filia*.
[198] ibid, 51. Evidence was also provided that the Greek authorities had considered an exchange of prisoners for the crew of the *Filia*, further suggesting the attack was part of a political controversy not simply an indiscriminate act of piracy.
[199] *Athens Maritime v Hellenic Mutual War Risk Association (Bermuda) Ltd (The Andreas Lemos)* [1982] 2 Lloyd's Rep 483 (Comm) (Staughton J).
[200] ibid, 486.

argued the loss should fall to the war risk mutual as either 'piracy', 'riot', or 'persons acting maliciously'. But the war risk insurer resisted cover on grounds the actions were performed by 'thieves' which would fall within the H&M cover instead. It contended that the casualty could not be considered piracy because it occurred within the territorial waters of Bangladesh and since there was no threat of force giving rise to the loss.

The English Commercial Court agreed with the war risk insurer that the events were not piracy. First, the court referenced various public international law treatises to find that piracy (in the public law sense) can only take place outside the jurisdiction of any state, namely on the high seas. The reason for this, according to the court, is that when such actions take place outside the jurisdiction of any particular state it is necessary under international law to grant special law enforcement authority. In contrast, however, when robbery is performed within the jurisdiction of a state it is not necessary to grant universal jurisdiction to all states to prosecute and punish offenders. But the court noted that considerations in public international law do not necessarily inform the definition of piracy 'for the interpretation of a contract of insurance'.[201] The court found that various authorities defining piracy in the domestic criminal contexts also did not provide a definitive answer on the meaning of the term in an insurance policy. Instead, drawing from previous English case law, the court emphasised the need to ascertain piracy's meaning by using 'commercial sense'.[202] In doing so, the court noted that '[t]he very notion of piracy is inconsistent with clandestine theft'.[203] According to the court, '[i]t is not necessary that the thieves must raise the pirate flag and fire a shot across the victim's bows before they can be called pirates. But piracy is not committed by stealth.'[204]

Other modern cases interpreting piracy as an insurance term have addressed the issue through the lens of the Institute Clauses adopted as part of the wholesale London insurance market reforms during the 1980s. In *Bayswater Carriers Pte Ltd v QBE Insurance (International) Pte Ltd*, during January 2003, a Singapore-registered tug called the *BW Wisdom* was hijacked by armed men while waiting at anchorage on the south side of the Singapore Strait less than a mile from the harbour of Batam, Indonesia.[205] The crew of the *BW Wisdom* were held hostage for two days before they were released on an island and later rescued by the Indonesian Navy. The hijackers sailed away on the tug, which was never recovered. The *BW Wisdom* had been insured under a policy of insurance subject to the 1983 Institute Time Clauses Hulls, which expressly provided cover for piracy. The shipowner made a claim under the policy, but the insurer

[201] ibid, 488.
[202] ibid, 491.
[203] ibid.
[204] ibid. However, the court did acknowledge that '[t]his case is very near the borderline'.
[205] *Bayswater Carriers Pte Ltd v QBE Insurance (International) Pte Ltd* [2005] SGHC 185 (Singapore HC) (Belinda Ang Saw Ean J).

resisted cover on grounds that the hijacking was not piracy because it did not occur on the high seas. The High Court of Singapore rejected the insurer's position and ruled in favour of the shipowner. Following the English approach, the court found that the term 'piracy' should be interpreted under its plain, ordinary, and popular sense rather than any technical meaning. The court then examined the definition of piracy as referenced in international law, including under the United Nations Convention on the Law of the Sea (UNCLOS), Article 101, which provides that piracy must occur on the high seas. But the court determined that the distinction between the high seas and territorial waters in international law was a 'matter of jurisdiction'.[206] Since in the case of an act of piracy occurring in territorial waters jurisdiction would be assumed, the court explained, the UNCLOS definition of piracy would not be appropriate for construing its meaning in an insurance policy. Furthermore, the court found that the definitions of piracy in both customary international law and domestic criminal law suggested piracy does not have to take place on the high seas. Since the insurance policy at issue was for a vessel whose trading patterns were mainly between Singapore and Batam Island – and because the policy itself contained trading limits expressly stating this purpose – the insurer could not reasonably contend that the piracy term was only intended to cover actions performed on the high seas.[207] Moreover, the court found that even if the hijacking did not amount to piracy it would still fall within the policy as violent theft by outside persons. The court highlighted that the two perils overlapped, which pointed to piracy's evolving history as an insured peril. The court explained that '[t]he distinction between the two perils in the past was necessary when piracy was excluded as a marine peril and was insured by the war risk underwriter under a war risk cover'.[208]

A leading insurance case issued during the height of the Somali piracy crisis is *Masefield AG v Amlin Corporate Member Ltd* in which the English Commercial Court and Court of Appeal examined whether a cargo insurance provider was liable for total loss to a cargo of biodiesel when Somali pirates seized the ship, the *Bunga Melati Dua*, during a voyage from Malaysia to the Netherlands.[209] In the summer of 2008, the pirates boarded the vessel in the Gulf of Aden and diverted it to Somali waters where it remained for more than a month during ransom negotiations.[210] The cargo was insured under an all risk open cover policy with terms based on the London Institute Cargo Clauses.

[206] ibid, 82.
[207] The trading limits clause read: 'Warranted trading within Singapore home trade principally between Singapore, Batam Island, Pasir Gudang and Tanjong Pelepas and or/ held covered at additional premium to be agreed.' The named ports are in Singapore, Indonesia, and Malaysia within the Singapore Straits or its surrounding waters.
[208] ibid, 83.
[209] *Masefield AG v Amlin Corporate Member Ltd (The Bunga Melati Dua)* [2010] 1 Lloyd's Rep 509 (Comm) (David Steel J).
[210] ibid, 509.

The policy contained a war risk exclusion referencing 'capture, seizure, arrest, restraint or detainment (piracy excepted)'.[211] There was common ground that the policy covered piracy and that the attackers were pirates. The central point of contention was whether the cargo owner was entitled to claim a total loss on the basis that it was irretrievably deprived of the cargo. One month after the vessel seizure, while the vessel was still under control of the pirates, the cargo owner served a notice of abandonment to the defendant cargo insurer, which it declined. Shortly thereafter, the pirates released the vessel, crew, and cargo when the shipowner paid a ransom. The vessel then continued on to Rotterdam where it discharged its cargo The cargo owner brought a claim against the insurer in the English Commercial Court, alleging that the cargo had become either an 'actual total loss' or a 'constructive total loss' when the assured was 'irretrievably deprived' of it when the vessel was seized by the pirates, even though the cargo was restored at a later date.[212] The English Commercial court held for the insurer. Addressing whether the cargo owner's notice of abandonment was valid, the court emphasised the geopolitical context. It first reasoned that 'Somalia is a failed state with no effective government or law enforcement' creating a 'fertile breeding ground for piracy'.[213] The court explained that since there was effectively no diplomatic avenue for negotiation with the Somali government, 'the only realistic and effective manner of obtaining the release of a vessel is the negotiation and payment of ransom'.[214] The court noted that many other ships had been seized in the region during the period leading up to the attack on the *Bunga Melati Dua*, all of which were released along with their cargo on the payment of ransoms, totalling tens of millions of US dollars. For this reason, there were actually good prospects of recovering the cargo at the time when the notice of abandonment was submitted to the insurer. The court found there was insufficient evidence for the cargo owner to expect the pirates intended to seize or sell the cargo. In fact, the opposite was demonstrated by contemporaneous circulars provided by maritime security consultants as well as publicly available media reporting demonstrating the 'modus operandi' of the pirates was to ransom the vessel, cargo, and crew for payment based on an 'economic proportion of the value of the property at stake'.[215] Expert witnesses concurred that there was a 'high expectation' that the cargo would be recovered in a relatively short period of time after paying ransom.[216] This, of course, turned out to be an accurate prediction, as the vessel was released with all of its cargo upon payment of ransom less than six weeks after being seized. Consequently, the court found that the evidence demonstrated that the cargo owner was not

[211] ibid, 511.
[212] Although the cargo was recovered, it had allegedly diminished in value given that the biofuel market was seasonal.
[213] ibid, 511.
[214] ibid.
[215] ibid, 512.
[216] ibid, 513.

'irretrievably deprived' of the cargo because there was a clear intention by the pirates to return the property after receiving the ransom.[217]

The English Court of Appeal affirmed.[218] The cargo owner had argued that the payment of ransom was undesirable from a public interest and morality perspective and therefore the insured property must be considered irretrievably lost if the only means of recovering it was to engage in such unlawful or unethical action. Rejecting this argument, the court reasoned that there was no basis to find a capture or seizure automatically as an actual total loss or to support the claim of a constructive total loss. Instead, the pirate seizure was not an irretrievable deprivation of property but a 'typical "wait and see" situation'.[219] Furthermore, on the issue of ransom, the court explained that '[p]irates have been spoken of as the enemies of mankind. On the other hand, there is no universal morality against the payment of ransom, the act not of the aggressor but of the victim of piratical threats, performed in order to save property and the liberty of life of hostages'.[220] While acknowledging that the payment of ransoms to pirates arguably encourages their activities and contributes to 'morally muddied waters', the court recognised that there was not yet an 'international consensus as to a solution' other than deploying additional naval forces to the region.[221] Irrespective of the alleged immorality of the shipowner's ransom payment to the pirates, the court held that there was no justification in overturning the decision below.[222]

III. Reflections

In evaluating the line between piracy and governmental seizures, the US Civil War insurance cases illustrate that the classifications referenced in early contract clauses do not necessarily comport with political realities. As soldiers, privateers, and political sympathisers repeatedly seized commercial vessels – sometimes authorised under official orders and sometimes acting as vigilantes – shipowners, insurers, and ultimately the courts were challenged to examine these events through a contractual lens that did not clearly distinguish the nature of piracy from wartime seizure. In the *Dole* case, the court found a solution by classifying

[217] ibid, 514.
[218] *Masefield AG v Amlin Corporate Member Ltd (The Bunga Melati Dua)* [2011] 1 Lloyd's Rep 630 (CA) (Rix LJ).
[219] ibid, 642.
[220] ibid, 644.
[221] ibid, 645. The court also emphasised that it was the shipowner, not the cargo owner, who ultimately paid the ransom, which suggested the matter of the ethics of ransom had limited relevance to the cargo owner's situation.
[222] In another fascinating case, the Somali piracy crisis was used as pretext in a complex and highly orchestrated vessel scuttling operation. The court found the events did not amount to the covered peril of piracy. *Suez Fortune Investment Ltd v Talbot Underwriting Ltd (The Brilliant Virtuoso)* [2019] 2 Lloyd's Rep 485 (Comm).

the Confederate seizure as both piratical and belligerent, which, it determined, placed the events within the FC&S exclusion.[223] The court in the *Mauran* decision was less definitive, taking the position that regardless of whether the seizure at issue in that case was also piracy, it was a capture excluded from the marine cover because the Confederacy had de facto power to wage war even if it was organised as a rebellion against the legitimate US government.[224] The *Fifield* court focused instead on untangling the significance of piracy versus privateering in the peculiar context of explicit authorisation for seizures granted by an unlawful government.[225] The court in the subsequent *Babbit* case addressed the seizure by a mob aligned with the Confederate movement by separating the events from the notion of a wartime seizure by diminishing the connections to political motivations or possible endorsement by rebel leadership.[226] Together the cases illustrate judicial perceptions of entities with attributes of sovereignty, such as de facto control over territory, in efforts to conceptualise piracy alongside other forms of war risk.

The reasoning in the *Banque Monetaca* case largely aligns with this approach by focusing on the perpetrators' political aims and control over territory, as the court zeroed in on the backdrop of the Turkish War of Independence to contextualise the vessel seizure by a group who had performed acts of piracy in the recent past but were also acting within the scope of the political movement of the time.[227] This Turkish Nationalist movement, which involved the leader of the group becoming a governor of the region, was determined to be a critical factor in characterising the motive of the seizure as a belligerent wartime act rather than a piratical scheme, which had the effect of shifting its classification within the framework of the insurance clauses. Political context was also central to the court's analysis in the *Republic of Bolivia* case, which determined that the primary purpose of the seizure along the river running through the Bolivian forest was to promote a political movement.[228] Even though the attackers were 'malcontents' without evidence of de facto control over the region, their political motive, which was to prevent supplies from reaching Bolivian soldiers in the Amazon interior, marked a distinction from the indiscriminate brand of attacks for private ends that typically characterise piracy.[229] Charterparty case law has reflected similar analysis, as demonstrated by the *Luigi Monta* case involving the seizure by Nationalists authorities in Formosa (Taiwan).[230] Turning to political context to

[223] *Dole v Merchants' Mutual Marine Insurance Co*, 51 Me 465 (1863).

[224] *Mauran v Alliance Insurance Co*, 73 US 1 (1867).

[225] *Fifield v Insurance Co of the State of Pennsylvania*, 47 PA 166 (1864).

[226] *Babbit, Goode & Co v The Sun Mutual Insurance Co*, 23 La Ann 314 (1971).

[227] *Banque Monetaca & Carystuiaki v Motor Union Insurance Co Ltd* (1923) 14 Ll L Rep 48.

[228] *Republic of Bolivia v Indemnity Mutual Marine Assurance Co* [1909] 1 KB 785.

[229] ibid. Recall the implications for a finding of piracy in the *Republic of Bolivia* case is different than that of the *Andreas Lemos* case because of shifting revisions to the FC&S clause. See Todd (n 20) § 1.055.

[230] *Luigi Monta v Cechofracht Co Ltd* [1956] 2 Lloyd's Rep 97.

examine liability between the shipowner and the charterer, the court reasoned that the de facto sovereignty of the Nationalists government in 1953 was enough to classify the action as seizure rather than piracy even though it occurred years after the Communists had defeated the Nationalists in the Chinese Civil War and claimed to be the legitimate power over all of China, including its barrier islands. Rather than deferring to technical distinctions between internationally recognised and unrecognised governments or examining the diplomatic propriety of treating the Nationalists as a legitimate government, the court instead emphasised the quality and character of the authority it actually asserted, which fundamentally depended on the fact that the group that performed the seizure exercised genuine control over Taiwan in 1953.

In delineating between piracy and other risk categories, some courts have endeavoured to technically define the term. In doing so, they have generally viewed piracy in the commercial law sense to be broader than the international law definitions or those embedded in municipal criminal codes.[231] The *Republic of Bolivia* case remains a standard bearer on this point in directing the focus to the views of an ordinary business person rather than deferring only to definitions outside the context of commercial law. Of course, even the *Republic of Boliva* court found certain descriptions in public international law useful as a starting place, particularly those passages referencing the way that piracy generally involves indiscriminate attacks for private financial gain as opposed to targeted political attacks for public ends.[232] This distinction is also manifested in the US Civil War cases with only subtle differences between them. Referencing US criminal statutes, the court in the *Fifield* case, for instance, found that piracy was robbery committed for personal gain and was distinguishable from an attack in the aid of a political rebellion authorised by a commissioning power.[233] Without referencing public law definitions, a similar notion of private versus public ends supported the court's decision in the *Banque Monetaca* case, since the Turkish Nationalists there appeared to be acting in support of a broader political movement rather than the profit-centred 'brigandage' that the same group had performed on other occasions.[234] Even with more contemporary forms of piracy, standards derived from public law sources have served as a relevant means of defining piracy in commercial documents, including in the *Andreas Lemos* case, in which the court referenced domestic criminal statutes to distinguish piracy from clandestine theft under the insurance terms.[235]

[231] See Todd (n 20) § 1.043.

[232] *Republic of Bolivia v Indemnity Mutual Marine Assurance Co* [1909] 1 KB 785.

[233] *Fifield v Insurance Co of the State of Pennsylvania*, 47 PA 166 (1864). The court in *Dole*, however, rejected the notion that piracy in the insurance context had to be understood through the lens of domestic statutes or 'the law of nations'. Instead 'any kind of *piracy*' was captured under the clause at issue. (emphasis in original). See *Dole v Merchants' Mutual Marine Insurance Co*, 51 Me 465, 467 (1863).

[234] *Banque Monetaca & Carystuiaki v Motor Union Insurance Co Ltd* (1923) 14 Lloyd's List Rep 48.

[235] *Athens Maritime v Hellenic Mutual War Risk Association (Bermuda) Ltd (The Andreas Lemos)* [1983] 2 Lloyd's Rep 843.

In referencing public law definitions, the location of the attack has been a contentious factor in classifying events as piratical or not. Some of the seizures in the US Civil War cases took place within riparian contexts or territorial waters far from the high seas, including the *Babbit* case involving the mob attack by cannon performed from the riverbank of the Mississippi River within the otherwise landlocked state of Arkansas.[236] Perhaps in part for this reason, the *Babbit* court did not appear to entertain the piracy classification – instead focusing on whether the event was a wartime seizure or a mob attack – despite the obvious analogy to other cases of the era that had considered similar acts as piracy. A more probable explanation for this distinct approach, however, is that the decision was made by the Supreme Court of Louisiana, which is one of the Southern states that had seceded from the US to join the Confederacy (although the decision had been made after the end of the war and Louisiana's reunification into the US in 1868). Locality also played a role in identifying the seizure as something other than piracy in the *Republic of Bolivia* case, as the court acknowledged that the events had occurred on a river deep in the Amazon jungle nowhere near the ocean and even further from the high seas as required by some public law piracy definitions.[237] In contrast, although the *Andreas Lemos* court found that the theft in that case occurring just beyond the territorial waters of Bangladesh was not piracy, it addressed the locality question by first acknowledging the high seas jurisdictional aspect of the public international law definition before dismissing its relevance in the context of insurance contract interpretation.[238] The *Bayswater* court likewise rejected the relevance of the UNCLOS-based high seas requirement, reasoning instead that this feature of the public law definition of piracy is for jurisdictional purposes under international law with little crossover significance to defining the term's limits in an insurance contract.[239]

The separate question of whether a seizure by a sovereign or quasi-sovereign actor can be properly considered piracy in the contractual sense of the term remains an open question. The US Civil War cases remain important sources of authority on this point, as courts repeatedly found that the seizures performed by Confederacy-aligned actors were equivalent to governmental seizures, even as the same actions were branded piracy by the executive branch of the US government. Although it would seem that US President Lincoln's proclamation that the seizures performed by Confederate soldiers were acts of piracy would be granted some level of deference given he was the constitutionally declared head of state and Commander in Chief of the US military, the courts recognised that these political pronouncements were aimed at characterising the events as unlawful rebellion rather than to guide insurance classifications.

[236] *Babbit, Goode & Co v The Sun Mutual Insurance Co*, 23 La Ann 314 (1871).

[237] *Republic of Bolivia v Indemnity Mutual Marine Assurance Co* [1909]1 KB 785, 799.

[238] *Athens Maritime v Hellenic Mutual War Risk Association (Bermuda) Ltd (The Andreas Lemos)* [1983] 2 Lloyd's Rep 483.

[239] *Bayswater Carriers Pte Ltd v QBE Insurance (International) Pte Ltd* [2005] SGHC 185.

Accordingly, these political positions were found less important than the reality that the Confederate states had amassed control over a significant portion of land inhabited by millions of people, which justified findings in multiple cases that the events were also properly categorised as governmental seizures. The court in *Luigi Monta* likewise recognised that the seizure carried out by Nationalist authorities off Taiwan should not necessarily be classified only by deference to political branches of government influenced by diplomatic pressures and should instead consider the de facto powers of the entity performing the seizure.[240] This line of cases is critical authority for categorising the actions of non-state actors in the contemporary era, as state and non-state actors with de facto control over territory continue to seize vessels for varied motivations.

The charterparty cases reveal further argument regarding the application of principles-based avoidance and modification doctrines. In the *Petroships* case, the seizures by pirates and later Chinese authorities did not persuade the arbitral tribunal that the doctrine of frustration should relieve the shipowner of its obligations (although the court reviewing the award was ultimately not convinced the tribunal had applied the proper standards of frustration).[241] In contrast, in the *Wong Wing Fai* case, the court found that the seizure and confiscation of the vessel by Vietnamese soldiers did frustrate the charter and placed it off hire (although it did not explicitly classify the seizure as piratical).[242] The doctrine of illegality was also invoked, albeit unsuccessfully, in the *Bunga Melati Dua* case in efforts to show the payment of ransom to release the cargo would have been unlawful or at least as a violation of public policy. In the modern era, however, other doctrines, such as impossibility of performance, have not been raised in piracy-related cases, as parties have instead chosen to frame their positions based on explicit contract wordings.

Especially in the cases arising during the Somali piracy crisis, litigants relied primarily on the language of charterparty clauses addressing hire. In the *Saldanha* case, the court was not persuaded that the seizure at issue fell within the terms of the standard off-hire clause or a separate bespoke clause referencing governmental detention, which compelled the court to suggest more explicit language to address the issue in subsequent charters.[243] The more specific off-hire language in a rider clause addressing capture and seizure led to a different outcome in the subsequent *Captain Stefanos* case, where the court found the Somali pirate seizure placed the vessel off hire even though the contract also contained a CONWARTIME provision that burdened the charterer with at least some of the

[240] *Luigi Monta v Cechofracht Co Ltd* [1956] 2 Lloyd's Rep 97.

[241] *Petroships Pte Ltd v Petec Trading and Investment Corp* [2001] 2 Lloyd's Rep 348.

[242] *Wong Wing Fai Co v United States of America* [1988] 840 F2d 1462.

[243] *Cosco Bulk Carrier Co Ltd v Team Up Owning Co Ltd (The Saldanha)* [2011] 1 Lloyd's Rep 187. Similarly, in the *Valle di Cordoba* case, the court was not persuaded that the 'in-transit loss' clause in the charterparty applied to cargo loss by pirates who confiscated motor oil via ship-to-ship transfer off of Nigeria. That clause was designed for an entirely different purpose. *Trafigura Beheer BV v Navigazione Montanari Spa (The Valle Di Cordoba)* [2014] 1 Lloyd's Rep 550.

piracy-related risks.[244] The more explicit piracy clause in the *Eleni P* case made for an easier interpretive task as the court found the parties intended to place the vessel off-hire during pirate seizures, although this case provides a lesson on drafting technique as the parties squabbled over the scope of the clause due to its geographically ambiguous reference to the Gulf of Aden, even as the Somali pirate operations had been encroaching further east into the Indian Ocean.[245]

Other charterparty cases addressing piracy provide further insight into the scope of re-routing liberties. In the *Precious Ornaments* case, without referencing any specific piracy clause, the SMA panel found that the shipowner was justified in its decision to divert from the intended course to take on security guards before proceeding through the Gulf of Aden in part because governments and industry organisations had issued new warnings of pirate risks affecting the region.[246] Other cases have hinged on the interpretation of explicit war risk clauses. In the *Triton Lark* cases, the court sought to clarify the contractual standards authorising the shipmaster to re-route under the CONWARTIME 1993 clause referencing exposure to war risks, which ultimately required an assessment of whether the area was dangerous according to the 'degree of likelihood' of piracy attack and the 'gravity of the consequences' that might affect the vessel, crew, and cargo.[247] The subsequent *Paiwan Wisdom* case clarified the meaning of the revised CONWARTIME 2004 clause, which granted the shipowner the liberty to avoid a route giving rise to a real risk of piracy off the coast of Kenya, even though the risk had not necessarily increased since the time the contract was agreed.[248] Following these cases, in 2013, BIMCO revised the CONWARTIME clause to streamline the risk assessment standard, along with its revised Piracy Clauses. Although the CONWARTIME and VOYWAR clauses were revised again in 2025, the language regarding re-routing liberties remains similar to the 2013 iterations.[249]

With modern pirates changing tactics to focus on extracting ransom payments, vessel or cargo confiscation is a less likely outcome. These distinct factual scenarios have led to restructured contractual arrangements and raised policy questions left unaddressed by much of the early piracy jurisprudence. The UK Supreme Court decision in the *Polar* is unique in finding the multi-million dollar ransom payment flowing from a Somali pirate seizure gave rise to viable general average claims against the cargo interests.[250] The court found that general average included sharing the burden of the ransom, despite the fact that the underlying charterparty had

[244] *Osmium Shipping Corp v Cargill International SA (The Captain Stefanos)* [2012] 2 Lloyd's Rep 46.

[245] *Eleni Shipping Ltd v Transgrain Shipping BV (The Eleni P)* [2019] 2 Lloyd's Rep 265 (Comm).

[246] *Precious Ornaments Ltd v Helena Chartering Inc (The Manisamut Naree)*, SMA 4088 (2010).

[247] *Pacific Basin IHX Ltd v Bulkhandling Handymax AS (The Triton Lark II)* [2012] 1 Lloyd's Rep 457.

[248] *Taokas Navigation SA v Komrowski Bulk Shipping KG (GMBH & Co) (The Paiwan Wisdom)* [2012] 2 Lloyd's Rep 416.

[249] War Risk Clause for Time Chartering 2025 (CONWARTIME 2025); War Risk Clause for Voyage Charter Parties 2025 (VOYWAR 2025).

[250] *Herculito Maritime Ltd and Others v Gunvor International BV and Others (The Polar)* [2024] 1 Lloyd's Rep 85.

addressed piracy liabilities between the shipowner and charterer through express language. The *Bunga Melati Dua* case further highlights the contractual implications for ransom-based piracy, as the court examined (but ultimately rejected) the argument that ransom payments to pirates were unlawful or a violation of universal public morals.[251] Instead, the court acknowledged that ransom exchange could save life and property, although it might simultaneously incentivise future attacks – a balance of policy considerations that led the court to find there was not yet an international consensus on the issue. As other commentators have noted, however, the payment of ransom to pirates may cause additional illegality and public policy challenges. For instance, during the Somali piracy crisis, US officials took regulatory action to prohibit ransom payments when there is a connection to terrorist groups, despite the fact that ascertaining such a nexus would be difficult to determine.[252] Although there may be some natural resistance to the notion of US law limiting the ability for foreign enterprises to engage in ransom negotiations when the stakes are high – as demonstrated by the application of US coercive techniques in other contexts such as the enforcement of economic sanctions, including against international financial institutions – the practical impact of foreign illegality remains a legitimate barrier for piracy ransom payments, despite the *Bunga Melati Dua* holding that ransom payments do not presumptively run counter to public morals. Such questions have become even more pronounced not only as Somali piracy re-emerges as a possible threat, but also due to the attacks and hijackings performed by Houthi militants in the Red Sea. The Houthis have claimed their actions are to promote an anti-Israel political agenda rather than to seek financial benefit, yet at times their actions have resembled piracy tactics, especially given the largely indiscriminate nature of their civilian targets. Complicating matters – and mirroring the discourse surrounding previous conflicts – even as US officials brand the Houthis as both 'terrorists' and 'pirates', the Houthis themselves have claimed to act as the Yemeni armed forces implementing 'sanctions' and 'blockade'.[253] What this rhetorical theatre means for contract interpretation is an unresolved and unfortunately relevant question.

[251] *Masefield AG v Amlin Corporate Member Ltd (The Bunga Melati Dua)* [2011] 1 Lloyd's Rep 630.
[252] See Lewins and Merkin (n 32).
[253] US White House, 'Trump Administration's Actions Made Houthi Terrorists Pay' (25 March 2025); R Wright, 'Houthis Vow to Escalate Attacks in Red Sea' *Financial Times* (28 July 2025).

5

Sanctions

I. Introduction

Modern sanctions are often described as a form of economic warfare, but history shows they were first developed to preserve the peace. Following the vast destruction of the First World War, where the coercive economic tactics of blockade, embargo, and contraband control were widely implemented by nations still embroiled in belligerent conflict, the political architects of the post-war reconstruction era sought to deploy similar techniques to respond in the event of any state taking affirmative steps to breach the Treaty of Versailles. Legal justification for this approach was embedded in the Covenant of the League of Nations, as multilateralism was pursued as a means of diminishing the likelihood of future hostilities.[1] This confidence in sanctions to restrain state behaviour in the interwar period was met with a different reality, as the League of Nations failed to curb Japanese, Italian, and German aggression. Despite concerted attempts to channel economic tools into a form of peace-keeping weaponry, only 20 years after the end of the First World War much of the world again plunged into a global conflict. As the Second World War unfolded, any previous optimism regarding sanctions as a peacetime solution was buried under the rubble, as the levers of economic statecraft returned to their former role in simultaneous deployment alongside belligerent hostilities.

By the end of the Second World War, as political leaders began to envision a new rules-based order, sanctions re-surfaced as a potential route to maintain an uncertain peace – yet with a greater sense of urgency under the cloud of the nuclear age. This led to the creation of new multilateral institutions, including the UN. Like the Covenant of the League of Nations, the 1945 UN Charter recognised economic sanctions as a means of international law enforcement. The Charter established a Security Council with the power to make binding recommendations and decisions regarding threats to international peace and security, explicitly granting it the authority to respond through the 'interruption of economic relations'.[2] Almost

[1] See Covenant of the League of Nations, Art 16. See N Mulder, *The Economic Weapon: The Rise of Sanctions as a Tool of Modern War* (Yale University Press, 2022).

[2] See Charter of the United Nations, Art 41. Under Art 23, the Security Council is made up of 15 members, with 10 rotating members and five permanent members. Under the UN Charter, the permanent five members are: 'The Republic of China, France, the Union of Soviet Socialist Republics, the United Kingdom of Great Britain and Northern Ireland, and the United States of America.' In 1971, the People's Republic of China replaced the Republic of China (Taiwan) in the Security Council. After the USSR dissolved in 1991, its place on the Security Council became occupied by the Russian Federation.

immediately, however, hopes of a sanctions-fuelled peace were again derailed by the resumption of the Chinese Civil War and the outbreak of the Korean War, both of which exhibited the nascent struggle over political ideology that hardened into a Cold War that shaped geopolitics for the next four decades. Following the Cuban Missile Crisis, where the US had pushed the boundaries of provocation by temporarily restricting maritime access to Cuba under its blockade-like 'quarantine', the US continued enforcing economic reprisals against the communist stronghold through its less aggressive but still coercive unilateral embargo.[3] These trade restrictions on the largest nation in the Caribbean became a flashpoint in the development of unilateral sanctions, as US law forbade Cuba-connected trades even though the two countries were not at war and the Security Council had not mandated or approved of their application.

Of course, this was due in part to Cold War divisions that obstructed Security Council consensus. But even during the Cold War UN sanctions were put to the test in the mid-1960s when the white minority ruling party of Southern Rhodesia – a then self-governing colony of Great Britain – declared independence in efforts to stave off progressive constitutional reforms.[4] Although two permanent members of the Security Council – France and the USSR – abstained from the vote, in 1966 the Security Council agreed for the first time to mandate economic sanctions.[5] These sanctions included restrictions on vessels 'reasonably believed to be carrying oil destined for Southern Rhodesia'.[6] Subsequent Security Council mandates further restricted the inward and outward trade of commodities.[7] Although the maritime dimensions of these sanctions would appear to be limited given that Southern Rhodesia was landlocked, the ban was enforced at the Mozambique port at Beria, which the British monitored by naval patrol – mirroring the notion of wartime blockade, but without the war.[8] The uncertain results of these UN sanctions and the continued challenge of multilateral consensus tempered expectations over sanctions during an otherwise turbulent 1970s and 1980s. Wars, civil wars, rebellions, and revolutions around the world contributed to a fraught geopolitical climate during the final decades of the Cold War era, yet no mandatory Security Council sanctions were issued. At the same time, this period incubated the innovation of other forms of non-belligerent economic statecraft measures implemented outside of Security Council auspices, notably through national boycotts targeting South Africa for its apartheid practices, and

[3] See JF Kennedy, Presidential Proclamation 3447: Embargo on All Trade with Cuba (3 February 1962).

[4] The turmoil in Southern Rhodesia was caused by what the UN Security Council described as a 'racist minority' regime. See UNSC Res 216 (12 November 1965); UNSC Res 217 (1965 20 November).

[5] See UNSC Res 221 (9 April 1966).

[6] ibid.

[7] See UNSC Res 232 (16 December 1966); UNSC Res 253 (29 May 1968).

[8] The Beria Patrol continued for nine years from 1966 to 1975. See J Kraska and R Pedrozo, *International Maritime Security Law* (Martinus Nijhoff, 2013) § 24.1.

oil export controls imposed by Arab states against Israeli allies following the Yom Kippur War.[9]

It was not until after the Cold War concluded that multilateral sanctions truly began to flourish. During the 'sanctions decade' of the 1990s, Iraq, Haiti, and the former Yugoslavia were each subjected to mandatory UN Security Council sanctions.[10] The sanctions targeting Iraq after its invasion of Kuwait were particularly onerous. These measures mandated UN Member States to prevent the import, export, and transshipment of Iraqi commodities.[11] They also called on states to regulate shipping traffic for the purpose of inspecting and verifying compliance with UN mandates.[12] Eventually, however, the Iraq sanctions began to create humanitarian concerns due to perceived impediments on the flow of food and medicine to civilians.[13] These shifting sentiments led to the establishment of the UN Oil-for-Food Programme, under which the Security Council authorised the export of Iraqi oil under a tightly regulated framework in which the proceeds of the transactions were submitted to an escrow account to be used to 'meet the humanitarian needs of the Iraqi population' by purchasing medicine, food, and supplies for 'essential civilian needs'.[14] Ethical concerns about sanctions harming civilian populations shaped policy discourse regarding the need for 'smart' or 'targeted' measures crafted to more carefully channel economic pressure to individuals, such as political and business elites, rather than the innocent people simply living in the sanctioned states.[15] This movement not only informed the work of the Security Council, but also the emerging EU-level sanctions framework, under which EU Member States sought to bolster economic and political integration through a Common Foreign and Security Policy flowing from the 1992 Maastricht Treaty.[16]

The 9/11 terror attacks incentivised the rapid sophistication of sanctions tactics, as US regulators sought to halt the flow of illicit financing that supported international terrorist networks. US agencies, especially the Office of Foreign Assets Control (OFAC) of the US Department of Treasury, reconfigured regulatory processes that had been previously used for anti-money laundering and anti-drug trafficking initiatives into new methods of targeting the finances of non-state actors like Al-Qaeda.[17] These methods included blacklisting individuals and entities

[9] These statecraft measures are discussed in ch 6.

[10] See generally D Cortright and GA Lopez, *The Sanctions Decade: Assessing UN Strategies in the 1990s* (Lynne Rienner Publishers, 2000).

[11] See UNSC Res 661 (6 August 1990).

[12] See UNSC Res 665 (25 August 1990).

[13] See UNSC Res 666 (13 September 1990).

[14] See UNSC Res 986 (14 April 1995); Memorandum of Understanding Between the Secretariat of the United Nations and the Government of Iraq on the Implementation of Security Council Resolution 986 (1995), S/1996/356.

[15] See J Gordon, 'Smart Sanctions Revisited' (2011) 25 *Ethics & International Affairs* 315.

[16] This EU-level cooperation sought to establish an autonomous sanctions policy that could achieve EU objectives. See European Parliamentary Research Service, 'EU Sanctions: A Key Foreign and Security Policy Instrument' (May 2018).

[17] See J Zarate, *Treasury's War: The Unleashing of a New Era of Financial Warfare* (Public Affairs, 2013).

suspected of terrorism financing, which burdened them with travel bans and asset freezes and barred them from access to integral US banking infrastructure. To enforce these restrictions, OFAC began mandating third parties, such as banks, to refrain from facilitating transactions with those on its Specially Designated Nationals (SDN) list under the threat of 'secondary sanctions' penalties. These regulatory approaches expanded 'know your customer' obligations throughout the private sector, especially in the international banking and finance industry, which the US government viewed as a coercive chokepoint for leveraging access to the US financial system as a means of mandating extraterritorial compliance.[18]

Over the next two decades, similar sanctions methods were adopted not only by national governments but also multilateral institutions, including the UN and EU, in response to threats to international peace and security, especially nuclear weapons proliferation concerns involving North Korea and Iran. In addition to sectoral restrictions on the flow of designated commodities, North Korea-linked individuals, entities, and vessels were placed on blacklists, while financial service providers and marine insurers were forbidden from engaging in associated transactions. National governments, including the US, enforced these sanctions by criminally prosecuting violators, seizing vessels and cargo, and imposing civil penalties on third party private actors.[19] In part due to its interconnectedness with the global economy as a leading oil exporter, the sanctions targeting Iran during this period were particularly consequential. Measures included the blacklist designation of Iranian companies and banks, marine insurance bans covering the entire fleet of Iran's national shipping lines, and an EU-wide Iranian oil import prohibition.[20] These measures seemed to pay off, as Iran agreed with the permanent five members of the Security Council (plus Germany) to halt its nuclear programme in exchange for sanctions relief under the 2015 Joint Comprehensive Plan of Action (JCPOA). Following the models of the sanctions placed on North Korea and Iran, humanitarian concerns arising out of violent crackdowns on civil unrest in Libya and Syria, and later disputed elections in Venezuela, led to further action by sanctioning authorities (especially the US) through restrictions on the maritime transport markets. As these measures proliferated, shipping industry organisations adopted revised wordings to address sanction compliance obligations and allocate enforcement risks. BIMCO and INTERTANKO published multiple iterations of sanctions clauses designed for incorporation into charterparties, which expressed the rights and obligations arising out of sanctions exposure incidents, including cancellation options in

[18] See E Fishman, *Chokepoints: American Power in the Age of Economic Warfare* (Portfolio/Penguin, 2025).

[19] See eg US Department of Justice, Press Release: 'Department of Justice Announces Forfeiture of North Korean Cargo Vessel' (21 October 2019).

[20] See eg UNSC Res 1737 (23 December 2006); UNSC Res 1747 (24 March 2007); UNSC Res 1803 (8 March 2008); UNSC Res 1929 (9 June 2010).

the event of counterparty designation on sanctions blacklists.[21] Likewise, marine insurers – including all of the IG P&I clubs – began using sanctions exclusion language in their policies and rules, allowing them to cancel cover in the event of unlawful or suspicious activity.[22] Further complicating the sanctions compliance landscape, in 2018, the US announced it would withdraw from the Iran nuclear deal, even as the remaining parties sought to hold the JCPOA together.[23] This led to a fractious period of disharmony between US and EU sanctions rules, which burdened the private sector with conflicting obligations flowing from the divergent regulatory approaches of traditional Western allies.

As sanctions techniques evolved throughout the twenty-first century, circumvention tactics kept pace within nefarious corners of the shipping industry. Sanctions-busting vessel operators engaged in vessel location manipulation and identity laundering techniques designed to conceal their trading activities and avoid regulatory enforcement penalties. In response, regulators began demanding more compliance scrutiny from the private sector by imposing enhanced due diligence processes aimed at combatting 'deceptive shipping practices'.[24] By 2020, sanctioning authorities issued regulatory guidance describing new obligations on shipping industry participants to vigilantly monitor counterparty behaviour, including through the use of vessel tracking technology designed to scrutinise Automatic Identification System (AIS) signals for sanctions-busting manipulation in real time. These regulatory changes set off a flurry of compliance reactions as private actors scrambled to adjust risk allocation methods. A new generation of contract clauses and accompanying technology-driven compliance products and service providers emerged. New sanctions clauses, including a BIMCO AIS Switch Off Clause, were published in attempts to more explicitly address sanctions circumvention tactics by articulating recourse in the event of counterparties engaging in suspicious behaviour such as deactivating mandatory vessel tracking transmitters or engaging in unauthorised ship-to-ship cargo transfers that could be viewed by sanctions enforcing authorities as a red flag for attempts at concealment.[25]

Sanctions expanded further in the wake of Russia's 2022 full-scale invasion of Ukraine. With the UN Security Council unable to react due to Russia's permanent seat and corresponding veto power, new sanctions coalitions formed with

[21] See eg BIMCO Sanctions Clause for Time Charter Parties 2010; BIMCO Designated Entities Clause 2013; BIMCO Sanctions Clause for Time Charter Parties 2020; BIMCO Sanctions Clause for Voyage Charter Parties 2020; INTERTANKO Sanctions Clause 2011.

[22] A survey of these early sanctions clauses are discussed in RL Kilpatrick, Jr, 'Maritime Sanctions Clauses' (2020) *Lloyd's Maritime and Commercial Law Quarterly* 565.

[23] See Office of the US President, Press Release: 'President Donald J Trump is Ending United States Participation in an Unacceptable Iran Deal' (8 May 2018).

[24] See US Department of Treasury, Department of State, Coast Guard, 'Sanctions Advisory for the Maritim Industry, Energy and Metals Sectors, and Related Communities' (14 May 2020); UK HM Treasury Office of Financial Sanctions Implementation, 'Maritime Guidance: Financial Sanctions Guidance for Entities and Individuals Operating within the Maritime Shipping Sector' (December 2020).

[25] See BIMCO AIS Switch-Off Clause 2021.

leadership by the G7 nations.[26] Together, the G7, EU, and various other national authorities imposed comprehensive sanctions targeting Russian state-owned enterprises, politically connected individuals and entities, and broad sectors of the Russian economy. In December 2022, this sanctions coalition established a Russian oil price cap regime, which required 'maritime service providers' to maintain compliance with an artificial cargo price mandate.[27] Its rules required industry actors spanning across the commercial chain to scrutinise their business dealings by investigating cargo pricing data or otherwise promise compliance through the exchange of attestation documents. These new mandates were followed by enforcement actions, which resulted in further efforts to mitigate risk exposure through contract wordings.[28] At the same time, an expanding 'dark fleet' sector of the shipping industry continued to engage in sanctions circumvention activity to facilitate illicit trades in contravention of Western pressure.[29] Throughout this period, a barrage of case law began to build addressing the contractual consequences arising out of these scenarios – telling a complex story of geopolitics and commerce that is still unfolding.

II. Sanctions in Commercial Maritime Disputes

A. Chartering and Carriage

i. Compliance Burdens

Among the early sanctions-related charterparty arbitration awards is *Dundas Shipping & Trading Co Ltd v Stravelakis Brothers Ltd.*[30] The parties had entered into a contract of affreightment for a period of two years in which the charterer agreed to arrange for the movement of a series of cargoes on vessels controlled by a Greece-based shipowner. At the time of the charter negotiations, the parties were aware that the UN Security Council had imposed sanctions on Southern Rhodesia and various national authorities had implemented them. As the contract of affreightment was under negotiation, the parties agreed under a separate voyage charter to move iron ore lifted from Beria, Mozambique. During loading for that voyage, stevedores at the port alerted the shipmaster that some of the cargo was from Southern Rhodesia, even though the certificates of

[26] Russia's political alliance with China also obstructed any prospect of Security Council sanctions.

[27] See Statement of the G7 and Australia on a Price Cap for Seaborne Russian-origin Crude Oil (2 December 2022).

[28] See eg BIMCO Russian Oil Price Cap Scheme Clause 2024.

[29] See IMO, Resolution A.1192(33), Adopted 6 December 2023, Urging Member States and All Relevant Stakeholders to Promote Actions to Prevent Illegal Operations in the Maritime Sector by the 'Dark Fleet' or 'Shadow Fleet'.

[30] *Dundas Shipping & Trading Co Ltd v Stravelakis Brothers Ltd*, SMA 1174 (NY Arb 1977) (Donald L Caldera, John Hance, and Koll L Biornstad).

origin referenced the cargo as 'lawful merchandise'.[31] The shipmaster authorised loading of the cargo under the voyage charter, but later advised the shipowner that there may be further compliance problems with future shipments under the longer-term contract of affreightment. The contract of affreightment was agreed shortly thereafter, but the shipowner refused to nominate a vessel for the first loading. The shipowner explained to the charterer that there was a risk of civil and criminal sanctions from Greek authorities for executing the previous voyage charter and alleged that this risk could be replicated under the contract of affreightment. The charterer responded with assurances the cargo would not be Southern Rhodesian, but the shipowner refused to perform, which led to a dispute referred to SMA arbitration. During the arbitration, the shipowner alleged that the contract was unenforceable because it involved the movement of unlawful cargo and compelled performance of an illegal act. Since the charterer had allegedly shipped Southern Rhodesian origin cargo under the previous voyage charter, the shipowner claimed this amounted to 'probable cause' that the charterer would attempt to do so again, which could trigger sanctions exposing the shipowner.[32] The charterer contended that the shipowner's reference to sanctions risk was pretext to take advantage of a changing and favourable freight market, and that the certificate of origin indicating the cargo was 'lawful' should be accepted at face value.

The SMA panel agreed with the charterer and found the shipowner breached the contract by failing to present the vessel or give the charterer the opportunity to load lawful cargo. The panel noted the unique commercial challenge created by the sanctions, describing how it added the 'novel hazard of politically motivated "law" to the more conventional hazards usually faced by maritime ventures'.[33] Beyond the expected risks of moving bulk commodities by sea, such as cargo damage and fire, the arbitrators described the sanctions as an 'extra cargo hazard, that of lifting illegal Rhodesian ore rather than non-sanction cargoes from acceptable origins'.[34] But the panel also expressed scepticism regarding the legal nature of the sanctions and their impact on commercial dealings. The panel wrote: 'There is a lack of known governmental prosecution or commercial arbitration involving these "sanction" laws, notwithstanding the large volume of Rhodesian cargo known to move worldwide'.[35] Since the sanctions were 'stimulated by political rather than economic-moral rationales, and erratically applied (or not at all)' the panel determined that it 'cannot void a serious transaction merely because the "laws" exist'.[36] Demonstrating the incredulous attitude toward the commercial impact of sanctions at the time, the

[31] ibid, 2.
[32] ibid.
[33] ibid, 4.
[34] ibid.
[35] ibid.
[36] ibid.

arbitrators explained, '[i]t would pain the Panel to elevate this "laws" theoretical existence … to control over the time hallowed law and practice that dignifies Maritime Agreements'.[37]

Sanctions proliferation during the 1990s created a series of charterparty disputes arbitrated under SMA auspices. In *Gulf Group Panama SA v Conti-lines SA (Brasca)*, the parties had agreed to a voyage charter to move bulk cargo on the *M/V Coral I* from the Dominican Republic to Haiti.[38] After the execution of that voyage, the parties agreed to a time charter trip intended to load in Florida. Implementing UN-mandated sanctions on Haiti, US law at that time restricted vessel access to US ports if the vessel had previously called to Haiti unless the vessel was granted a licence from OFAC. When the shipowner applied for an OFAC licence, OFAC discovered that the vessel had previously carried merchandise violating the trade restrictions on Haiti. OFAC not only refused to issue a licence for the vessel to load in Florida but also assessed a civil penalty against the shipowner for moving prohibited cargo in violation of US law. The vessel was forced to depart the port in Florida and secure substitute employment elsewhere.

The shipowner commenced arbitration against the charterer to recover for the time lost and the penalty settlement it paid to OFAC. In arbitration, the shipowner argued that the charterer was aware that some of the cargo on the vessel was in violation of US law in part because the charterer had been provided with advisories from US authorities describing the compliance obligations flowing from the Haiti sanctions. The shipowner claimed the charterer breached rider clauses in the charterparty referencing liability for non-compliance with cargo documentation, contraband, and sanctions rules, including a clause requiring the carriage of 'lawful general cargo … according to the rules and regulations prescribed by the U.N. Haitian blockade'.[39] The shipowner argued this imposed an obligation of compliance with US law because the US was the 'principal promoter and enforcer' of the UN sanctions.[40] The charterer countered that it did not breach the charterparty because these clauses did not explicitly reference compliance with US law. It further contended that the vessel had regularly traded to US ports and the shipowner was in a better position to ascertain OFAC rules and procedure regarding clearance for vessels that had previously called to Haiti. The arbitration panel held in favour of the shipowner on the grounds that the charterer breached the charterparty by shipping cargo that was not in compliance with OFAC regulations. It reasoned that documentation provided by OFAC demonstrated that some of the cargo carried on the vessel indeed violated the UN sanctions targeting Haiti and that '[i]t is unlikely that OFAC, the U.S. Government agency charged with the responsibility for compliance with the Haiti regulations, would incorrectly apply

[37] ibid. The capital letters emphasising 'Maritime Agreements' are in the original award.

[38] *Gulf Group Panama SA v Conti-lines SA (Brasca) (The M/V Coral I)*, SMA 3287 (NY Arb 1996) (Donald Zubrod, Jack Berg, and Dean Tsagaris).

[39] ibid, 2.

[40] ibid.

them'.[41] Accordingly, the panel found that the charterer had breached the charterparty clauses warranting the cargo to be lawful and in compliance with the UN trade restrictions on Haiti. It awarded the shipowner damages, including reimbursement of the settlement the shipowner had paid to OFAC.

The US trade restrictions on Cuba also caused charterparty problems landing in SMA arbitration. In *Belship Navigation Inc v Sealift Inc*, a Greece-based shipowner and US-based charterer had agreed to a short-term (30-day) time charter of the *M/V Huntsville* for the purpose of lifting US origin wheat cargo from a large bulk carrier onto the smaller vessel to effectuate delivery to a small port that was then controlled by Ethiopia.[42] This short-term charter was actually a sub-charter of another time charter subject to a longer 12-month term, and the identity of the beneficial owner of the *M/V Huntsville* was apparently not disclosed during the sub-charter fixture. The day after the commencement of the charter period, just before the cargo was loaded onto the *M/V Huntsville*, the US-based charterer learned that the vessel was beneficially owned by 'Cuban interests'.[43] The charterer immediately cancelled the charterparty on the basis that the contract was illegal, null, and void. Subsequently, US OFAC assessed a civil penalty against the charterer for violating US law prohibiting trade with Cuba. The shipowner then commenced arbitration against the charterer to recover damages alleging that it had partially performed the contract by delivering the vessel to the loading port. In arbitration, neither party contested that the performance of the charterparty would be unlawful. Instead, the question was where the economic losses should fall. The shipowner argued that the charterer failed to exercise due diligence to comply with US law or to seek an OFAC licence, which ultimately led to the termination of the charterparty. The shipowner emphasised that as a Greek national it was not subject to US sanctions on Cuba, while the US-based charterer was obviously bound by the sanctions and should have known the intricacies of compliance with US law. The charterer argued that there was no realistic basis to believe that OFAC would have granted a licence to perform the charterparty even if it would have solicited one.

The SMA panel majority held in favour of the charterer. First, the majority found that the charterer did not have prior knowledge of the vessel's Cuban ownership, which was evidenced by its 'open and undisguised' efforts to pay hire through a US bank that presumably would have denied payment to a Cuban entity.[44] It further held it immaterial that the charterer did not apply for an OFAC licence because there was no realistic possibility of receiving one. The majority also rejected the shipowner's contention that it should not be expected to be

[41] ibid, 4.

[42] *Belship Navigation Inc v Sealift Inc (The M/V Huntsville)*, SMA 3429 (NY Arb 1998) (Henry Engelbrecht and Jack Berg) (Richard A Zimmerman dissenting). Complicating matters by enhancing the repercussions of non-compliance with US law, this transaction was financed by the US Agency for International Development.

[43] ibid, 5.

[44] ibid.

aware of the US sanctions since it was based in Greece. It reasoned that '[t]he U.S. embargo against Cuba has been in place for almost 40 years and is a cornerstone of U.S. foreign policy. It is well known and understood throughout the international community, particularly in the shipping industry.'[45] The majority further explained: 'The Cuban boycott statute is not an obscure piece of legislation quietly tucked away in the public archives. A commercial shipping organization would have to be operating in a vacuum not to be aware of it and its impact.'[46] The shipowner, being subject to a longer term time charter agreement, had a due diligence obligation to ascertain the true beneficial owner of the vessel for the purpose of checking 'reputation, financial status and operational reliability'.[47] Irrespective of any sanctions compliance burden, the majority explained, if this investigation would have been performed properly, the Cuban nexus could have been discovered before the contract fixture, which might have prevented the loss. However, a dissenting arbitrator dismissed the proposition that the charterer had met its due diligence obligation and instead found that the charterer did not properly check the 'pedigree' of the vessel subject to the short-term charter, while the Greece-based shipowner had no comparable obligation under US law.[48] To meet this standard, the dissent reasoned, the charterer should have engaged in more intensive interaction with OFAC, which could have been contacted directly by phone, fax, or through its website.[49]

ii. Cargo Restrictions

The UN sanctions flowing from Iraq's invasion of Kuwait raised a series of commercial disputes. Among those that landed in SMA arbitration is *Great Beluga Shipping Inc v Bayoil Inc*, which arose out of a voyage charter of the *M/T Energy Explorer* to move crude oil within a flexible loading range in the Middle East.[50] To perform the charter, the US-based charterer ordered the vessel to load oil at an Iraqi port. But the next day, before the vessel arrived, Iraq invaded Kuwait. US President George HW Bush immediately issued an Executive Order restricting trade with both Iraq and Kuwait, and less than a week later the UN Security Council issued a corresponding Resolution mandating trade restrictions which were implemented broadly by national authorities. As a result, the charterer cancelled the charterparty, invoking the defence of frustration and *force majeure*. The shipowner contested this position and demanded the charterer nominate an alternative loading port, but the charterer refused. In arbitration,

[45] ibid.
[46] ibid.
[47] ibid.
[48] ibid, 7.
[49] ibid, 8.
[50] *Great Beluga Shipping Inc v Bayoil Inc (The Energy Explorer)*, SMA 3033 (NY Arb 1993) (Alfred E Yudes Jr, Jack Berg, and Lloyd C Nelson).

both parties agreed that Iraq's invasion of Kuwait prevented the vessel from lawfully loading Iraqi origin oil. The question was whether the charterer was obliged under the charterparty to nominate an alternative loading port. The shipowner argued that the charterer had failed to seek alternative employment for the vessel once it became impossible to load in Iraq. The charterer argued that the initial nomination of the Iraqi port made the contract a 'named port' charter, and that there was no longer any obligation to nominate an alternative loading port. The charterer also claimed that there were no other viable cargoes within the designated contractual range, which made performance both impossible and frustrated, further warranting a *force majeure* declaration. The arbitration panel agreed with the shipowner. It found that although Iraq's invasion of Kuwait and the resulting 'legal barriers' imposed by the US and UN sanctions made it impossible to load cargo in Iraq, these events did not have the effect of frustrating the charterparty.[51] Under the express terms of the contract, the charterer had other options, including to secure a substitute cargo in a different location within the contractual range or to sub-charter the vessel. The panel found there were at least some viable commercial opportunities available for the vessel, but that the charterer wrongfully terminated the charterparty and 'left the Owner to market his own vessel'.[52] Accordingly, the panel ordered the charterer to pay damages to the shipowner for lost time and revenue to secure substitute employment for the vessel.

An SMA panel reached a different result in *Nordic American Shipping A/S v Bayoil (USA) Inc.*[53] In that case, both the shipowner and charterer were US-based companies which had contracted under two tanker lighterage voyage charters to facilitate the movement of Iraqi crude from the Middle East to the US. The charterparties were agreed the month before Iraq's invasion of Kuwait and were impacted by the subsequent US Executive Order blocking the import of Iraq-origin goods into the US. However, the Executive Order delegated OFAC the authority to implement the sanctions. OFAC developed a legal framework including 'Transition Rules' outlining interim procedures to lessen the immediate commercial disruption on US importers caused by the ban. Despite these rules, the two vessels encountered delays offloading the cargo in the US. The shipowner sought additional freight, overtime, and port expenses incurred during the delays, but the charterer resisted on the basis that the sanctions disrupted the lawful discharge of the cargo. In arbitration, the shipowner claimed that the charterer could have avoided losses caused by the delays if it had quickly acted to obtain clearance under OFAC's Transition Rules. The shipowner alleged that the OFAC rules provided for options

[51] ibid, 5.

[52] ibid, 6. Note that the arbitration award did not separately address the charterer's *force majeure* argument.

[53] *Nordic American Shipping A/S v Bayoil (USA) Inc*, SMA 2972 (NY Arb 1993) (Jack Berg, Klaus CJ Mordhorst, Thomas E Murphy).

including offloading the cargo into temporary discharge tanks, but that the charterer did not take the initiative to perform under those procedures. The charterer responded that the shipowner made no attempt to propose this or any other alternative arrangement that might have allowed the cargo to be lawfully discharged more quickly. The charterer also argued that at the time the cargo arrived performance of the contract would have been temporarily impossible and temporarily illegal, triggering a general exceptions clause in the charterparty absolving it of overtime claims caused by 'restraint of princes' or *force majeure*.[54]

The panel held in favour of the charterer. First, the panel explained that this US regulatory response to Iraq's invasion was 'precipitous and unexpected', and that its 'impact was universal and swift'.[55] Recognising this disruption, OFAC's Transition Rules were implemented '[t]o ease the harsh impact of government policy on companies that traded with Iraq prior to the invasion and who were now directly affected by the embargo'.[56] Nevertheless, the panel concluded that despite these measures to blunt the commercial consequences of the ban, 'the Executive Order prohibited by law the discharge and importation of Iraqi and Kuwaiti cargoes into the United States and that this prohibition temporarily reduced [the charterer's] ability to perform'.[57] For this reason, it would not make 'commercial sense' for the charterer to incur substantial additional costs in attempts to comply with the OFAC exceptions.[58] Without examining the *force majeure* argument or 'restraint of princes' language in detail, the panel held that the exceptions language in the charterparty 'affords [the charterer] the right to temporarily suspend performance in accordance with the Executive Order'.[59]

SMA arbitrators addressed similar challenges arising out the Iraq sanctions in *Repsol Petroleo SA v Sun International Ltd*.[60] There, the parties agreed to a voyage charter to move Iraqi crude loaded from a pipeline in Eastern Turkey to be delivered to the US. After Iraq's invasion of Kuwait, Turkey joined the US and other nations in implementing the UN-mandated restrictions on the export of Iraqi crude, including the closure of a pipeline that had been designated for loading the cargo under contract.[61] The charterer cancelled the charterparty on grounds that the export prohibition by Turkish authorities was 'an obvious *force majeure*'.[62] The shipowner arranged substitute employment for the vessel but claimed losses from the charterer for wrongful cancellation.[63] In arbitration, the shipowner argued that the charterparty cancellation was improper because the export restrictions

[54] ibid, 4.
[55] ibid, 5.
[56] ibid.
[57] ibid, 6.
[58] ibid.
[59] ibid, 6.
[60] *Repsol Petroleo SA v Sun International Ltd (M/T Orduna)*, SMA 2967 (NY Arb 1993) (Herbert Sondheim, Richard H Sommer, and Donald E Zubrod).
[61] ibid, 2.
[62] ibid.
[63] ibid.

did not render performance impossible or commercially impractical but rather more expensive and time consuming. It further contended that since the charterparty at issue was not a 'named port charter' the charterer could have arranged the loading of similar cargo from within a broad geographic range that would not have been subject to the Iraqi crude restrictions. The charterer provided evidence that not only had it attempted to secure an alternative cargo within the contractual range, but it had even approached the shipowner about the prospect of securing a cargo in the Black Sea or Red Sea, which was well beyond the Eastern Mediterranean region described in the contract. Based on this evidence, the charterer argued that the Turkish pipeline subject to the export ban was the only source of crude in the region and that its attempt to load there was 'nullified by the impact of the Kuwait invasion and embargo against Iraq'.[64] Referencing 'exceptions' provisions in the charterparty and the doctrine of impossibility, the charterer further submitted that it was exonerated of liability by contract and operation of law.[65] The arbitration panel held for the charterer. It determined that the language of the contract placed a 'burden' on the charterer to show that it 'exerted reasonable effort' to secure a substitute cargo once the nominated port was closed by the Turkish authorities. But the panel held that the charterer had met that evidentiary hurdle by witness statements and affidavits showing that it had attempted to find an alternative cargo within the contractual range and even beyond. Highlighting that frustration of purpose may be viewed under standards of 'impracticability', the panel found that the invasion of Kuwait had an 'immediate impact' on the ability to obtain a substitute cargo, which justified the charterer's cancellation as a *force majeure* event.[66]

A different kind of controversy flowing from the Iraq sanctions was at issue in *Tankers International LLC v Bayoil Supply and Trading Ltd*.[67] That case involved a voyage charter of the *M/T Rafael* to move oil from Iraq to several possible discharge ports at the option of the charterer. Although the charter was on a standard form, a rider clause contained an Iraqi Cargo Warranty Clause reading in relevant part: 'This charter, and the cargo to be loaded under this charter, will at all times conform with United Nations Resolutions in force with regard to loading crude oils in Iraq'.[68] At the time of the charter, UN Security Council resolutions restricted oil exports of Iraqi origin with the exception of those complying with the Oil-for-Food Programme. To employ the vessel under charter in accordance with the UN programme, the charterer had contracted with an Iraqi entity to move crude from Iraq to discharge at US ports. But due to a dispute between Iraq and United Nations officials regarding the price of oil under the programme, Iraq

[64] ibid, 3.
[65] ibid.
[66] ibid, 4.
[67] *Tankers International LLC v Bayoil Supply and Trading Ltd (The M/T Raphael)*, SMA 3739 (NY Arb 2002) (Raymond A Connel, Manfred W Amold, and Thomas E Murphy).
[68] ibid, 2.

paused oil exports until a solution was achieved following 10 days of negotiations. This temporary suspension led to a backlog in vessel arrivals, which caused a delay in the *Rafael*'s loading. Although the vessel was ultimately able to load the cargo and perform the voyage to the US, albeit loading seven days late, the shipowner sought demurrage for the delay. In arbitration, the shipowner contended that the warranty clause mandated the charterer only to provide cargo consistent with the UN Resolution, and since no such cargo was available during the short-lived diplomatic dispute between Iraq and the UN, the charterer was responsible to bear the losses flowing from the delay. It also argued that although the suspension of exports by Iraq delayed loading, this was only a temporary measure. The charterer countered that it should be absolved of liability because the delay was caused by a 'restraint of princes' identified by a general exceptions clause.[69] The charterer further contended that the period of delay due to the Iraqi export restrictions should not count against laytime due to 'temporary impossibility of performance' and because it would have required the charterer to make an 'illegal payment' of a surcharge in violation of the Oil-for-Food Programme rules.[70]

The arbitral panel found the charterer liable for the demurrage costs. The panel reasoned that there is an 'absolute liability' for the payment of demurrage, subject to only a few exceptions.[71] Although the charterparty did provide contractual reductions in demurrage liability for 'stoppage or restraint of labor', the demurrage clause did not include an exception for 'restraint of princes'.[72] Finding that the delay was caused by 'the act of the Iraqi government directing the suspension of loading operations pending resolution of its dispute with the Security Council', the panel held that this event did not fall within the exclusionary language of the contract.[73] The panel also found that since the delay caused by the Iraqi government was not permanent, this brief disruption could not excuse the charterer's obligation to pay demurrage on the basis of arguments framed as 'temporary illegality' or 'temporary impossibility'.[74] Addressing the explicit language of the compliance warranty, the panel explained that its language was not static but also designed to address 'conditions from the time of contracting through completion of discharge' including the evolution of the diplomatic situation involving Iraq and the UN.[75] The panel explained that the clause represented 'a contractual recognition by the parties that the United Nations sanctions, and a restive Iraqi government, were a combination that could complicate smooth lifting' during the negotiations over the extension of the Oil-for-Food Programme.[76]

[69] ibid, 3.
[70] ibid.
[71] ibid.
[72] ibid, 5.
[73] ibid.
[74] ibid.
[75] ibid.
[76] ibid.

Among the first English cases addressing the contractual consequences of economic sanctions is *Ullises Shipping Corp v Fal Shipping Co Ltd (The Greek Fighter)*.[77] In that case, without prior arbitration, the English Commercial Court examined the charterparty implications of a vessel and cargo seizure administered by UAE authorities aiming to enforce UN-level sanctions on Iraq, which had been incorporated into UAE domestic law. The parties had agreed to a time charter to use the *Greek Fighter* as an oil storage facility off the coast of the UAE. During the charter period and while the *Greek Fighter* was at anchorage, the UAE Coastguard detained the vessel, alleging it had taken on illicit Iraqi oil in contravention of the UN Oil-for-Food Programme.[78] The UAE authorities later sold the vessel and cargo. The shipowner sued the charterer seeking indemnity for extensive losses. In litigation, the shipowner alleged that the charterer breached charterparty clauses warranting that the vessel would not carry 'unlawful merchandise' or engage in voyages that 'would expose the vessel' to government seizure.[79] The shipowner further argued that even if the cargo was lawful and the UAE detention was unjustified, the charterer had still breached a 'safe port warranty' by ordering the vessel to store oil at anchorage in UAE territorial waters where it was at risk of seizure.[80] The charterer contended that it did not breach the lawfulness warranty because it had no knowledge of Iraqi origin crude stored on the vessel and it did not violate the safe port warranty because it had no reason to expect that the UAE authorities would engage in the sanctions enforcement action against the vessel. The charterer further contended that it should be absolved of liability under the charterparty's mutual exceptions clauses referencing 'restraint of princes', and that the shipowner did not properly mitigate its losses by failing to intervene in the judicial sale. The court held for the shipowner. It first reasoned that the lawfulness warranty was 'absolute' and applied under the facts regardless of whether the charterer was aware of the existence of illicit Iraqi crude on the vessel. The court also determined that other similar language in the charterparty 'reinforces and expands' the shipowner's protection against the breach of the lawfulness warranty.[81] On the application of the safe port warranty, the court agreed with the shipowner that this includes 'political and similar risks'.[82] And rejecting the charterer's 'restraint of princes' argument, the court explained 'the safe port warranty would supersede the general exception'.[83]

More recently, SMA arbitrators have addressed charterparty disputes affected by sanctions by evaluating the impact of express sanctions clauses. Among these

[77] *Ullises Shipping Corp v Fal Shipping Co Ltd (The Greek Fighter)* [2006] 1 Lloyd's Rep Plus 99 (Comm) (Colman J).

[78] The same vessel had been detained previously by the UAE Coastguard and UN Maritime Intervention Force on grounds that it was involved in smuggling Iraqi oil.

[79] ibid, para [9].

[80] ibid, para [19].

[81] ibid, para [283].

[82] ibid, para [317].

[83] ibid.

cases is a consolidated arbitration award: *Brujo Finance Co v Sea Energy Co.*[84] That case addressed a preliminary motion regarding whether a shipowner had properly invoked a sanctions clause under a voyage charterparty when it demanded the charterer provide alternative orders in response to sanctions risk. The charterparty at issue provided for two consecutive voyages of the *MT Alkimos* from Cristobal, Panama, to either Curacao or Aruba, or to discharge the cargo by ship-to-ship (STS) transfer. The charterparty was agreed on a standard form, but it also contained a sanctions clause rider granting the shipowner 'absolute discretion' to refuse orders that 'could expose' it to US or EU sanctions and provided that in such circumstances the 'charterers shall be obliged to provide alternative voyage orders'.[85] Just before the vessel arrived at the loading port for the first voyage, the charterer instructed the shipowner to perform an STS transfer near Aruba. The shipowner immediately messaged the charterer explaining that it 'WILL NOT participate in any illegal trading' involving Venezuela and that any transshipment vessel would be subject to 'strict anti-sanctions scrutiny'.[86] The shipowner then sent a request for additional details regarding the proposed STS transfer. The charterer responded with information, including an unsigned charterparty, indicating that the vessel that would participate in the STS transfer was called the *MT Beauty One*. The shipowner requested additional information about the beneficial ownership of the *Beauty One*. The charterer clarified that the *Beauty One* was not on OFAC's list of sanctioned vessels, and requested to perform the STS operation outside of Aruba's territorial waters just off the coast of Venezuela. The shipowner then raised additional concerns, including information that it had received from a 'tracking service' indicating that the *Beauty One* had previously made multiple calls to Venezuela and suggested that engaging in an STS transaction with the vessel could result in sanctions enforcement by OFAC.[87] Invoking the language of the sanctions clause and referencing the 'recent trading history exclusively in Venezuelan waters', the shipowner requested assurances that the charterer would comply with the terms of the charterparty, including documentation regarding the cargo origin, the beneficial ownership of the *Beauty One*, its onward destination, and the ultimate consignee of the cargo.[88] The charterer did not provide this information and instead suggested that the shipowner contact OFAC to determine whether the STS operation would give rise to US sanctions. The shipowner responded that the charterer was in breach of the sanctions clause and refused performance unless the charterer provided alternative voyage instructions, which it did not.[89]

In SMA arbitration, the shipowner alleged that it had properly invoked the sanctions clause, which gave it a contractual basis to refuse the STS transaction

[84] *Brujo Finance Co v Sea Energy Co (The MT Alkimos)*, SMA 4388 (NY Arb 2020) (Sandra Gluck, David W Martowski, and Robert G Shaw).
[85] ibid, 2.
[86] ibid, 4.
[87] ibid, 5.
[88] ibid.
[89] ibid.

and request alternative orders. It further argued that performing the STS transaction as directed would have exposed it to US sanctions, and that the charterer breached its obligation to provide adequate assurances of lawful performance. The charterer countered that there was no evidence that the cargo had a Venezuela nexus. It argued that the trading history of the *Beauty One* was not a relevant basis to determine that the proposed STS transfer would trigger an OFAC enforcement action, that the shipowner should have sought clearance from OFAC to perform the transactions, and that the sanctions clause did not give the shipowner 'unfettered discretion' to refuse STS transactions and demand alternative orders.[90] The panel held for the shipowner. It reasoned that the terms of the sanctions clause provided for the absolute discretion to refuse trades and demand alternative orders if the charterer sought performance that 'could expose' the shipowner or other entities to US sanctions.[91] The panel found that this language allowed the shipowner to exercise discretion under the clause as long as there was 'any discernible risk' that the STS transaction could give rise to sanctions. The panel determined that the documentary evidence provided by the parties was sufficient to establish such a risk. This included information such as the published OFAC regulations outlining the rules for Venezuela-connected trades, the suspicious trading history of the *Beauty One* transshipment vessel, and the charterer's failure to provide clear answers to the shipowner's compliance concerns.

Other cases involving Venezuela sanctions have examined charterparty allocation of compliance mandates affecting payment processing. In *Star Tankers Inc v Citgo Petroleum*, the parties had agreed to a voyage charter to move petroleum from Houston to Venezuela.[92] The parties performed the contract and the charterer paid the primary freight invoice in full, but it did not pay four subsequent invoices for demurrage, port fees, and other costs on the basis that it was 'prevented from making a payment by sanctions and related restrictions imposed upon [it] as a result of a dispute between the governments of the United States and Venezuela'.[93] The point of contention between the parties in arbitration was whether the payment of the invoices required an OFAC licence and who – the charterer or the shipowner – should bear the obligation of obtaining it. As claimant, the shipowner alleged that the type of payment at issue did not fall within the sanctions prohibitions and contested the proposition that payment would cause problems of access to the banking system. Even if payment did require an OFAC licence, the shipowner alleged, the charterer must assume the obligation to obtain it. The charterer did not dispute the validity of the invoices but instead argued that explicit OFAC authorisation was necessary because, although it was not subject to US sanctions directly, attempts to transfer funds in previous transactions had

[90] ibid, 7.
[91] ibid.
[92] *Star Tankers Inc v Citgo Petroleum Corp*, SMA 4399 (NY Arb 2020) (David Gilmartin, LeRoy Lambert, and William Quinn).
[93] ibid.

been rejected by international banks due to their internal compliance concerns. The charterer further argued that the shipowner, as creditor, bore the burden of obtaining the OFAC assurances. The arbitral panel held for the shipowner. First, the panel declined to 'attempt to interpret' whether the US sanctions applied or to 'hazard an opinion' on which party would bear the burden of securing a licence, if needed.[94] Instead, although the panel acknowledged that it was 'not unreasonable' for the charterer to wait to make payment until an OFAC licence was issued, this complication did not excuse the charterer from responding to 'commercially reasonable requests' to facilitate this process.[95] The panel resolved the issue by finding the charterer was the 'more knowledgeable party with regard to U.S. sanctions since [it] must deal with them on an ongoing basis'.[96] It found that to hold otherwise by requiring the shipowner to 'shoulder the trouble and expense of obtaining a license' would be 'unreasonable'.[97]

Another SMA panel decision addressing charterparty performance involving Venezuela is *Playa Shipping Corp v Citgo Petroleum Corp*.[98] In that case, the parties had contracted under two consecutive voyage charters to transport diesel from the US to Venezuela on the *M/T Mambo*. The parties performed as agreed, but the charterer later refused to pay invoices for demurrage and port expenses incurred during the voyages, on the basis that US sanctions on Venezuela prevented payment due to rejections by the shipowner's bank. The shipowner sought collection in arbitration and moved for an interim award for security to ensure that it could be paid if it later prevailed on the merits. The charterer argued that the US sanctions targeting Venezuela's state-owned oil companies prevented it from lawfully engaging in transactions with a US nexus unless OFAC granted a specific licence authorising it to do so. It cited guidance on the OFAC website to support this position and claimed that the shipowner bore the burden of obtaining such a licence. The charterer further argued that it had attempted to make payments to the shipowner's bank, but the bank refused to process the payments and instead flagged the transactions during its own internal sanctions compliance procedures. The shipowner contended that the US sanctions did not apply to the collection of debt from the Venezuelan charterer, in part because OFAC had issued general licences that expressly authorised such transactions. The SMA panel held in favour of the shipowner. First, it found that OFAC had already issued a general licence that 'specifically authorizes transactions and activities by [the charterer or its affiliates] that would otherwise be prohibited by various Executive Orders'.[99]

[94] ibid, 5. The panel noted that as part of the proceedings it took the initiative to investigate the process of compliance with the Venezuela sanctions through direct contact with OFAC. It wrote: 'The only reply was verbal advice from OFAC to look on the OFAC website, which was of little help.'

[95] ibid, 6.

[96] ibid, 5.

[97] ibid, 6.

[98] *Playa Shipping Corp v Citgo Petroleum Corp (The M/T Mambo)*, SMA 4418 (NY Arb 2021) (Lucienne Carasso Bulow, Louis Epstein, and William Quinn).

[99] ibid, 9.

Since the general licence applied to the payment at issue, it was not necessary to separately seek an additional specific licence from OFAC. To support this position, the panel referenced an email exchange between OFAC and the shipowner's counsel in which OFAC explained that it does not approve applications for specific licences when there is already a general licence in place authorising the transaction at issue. The panel found that this correspondence with OFAC 'strongly supports the Owner's position that the payments in question are authorized' by the general licences.[100]

iii. Blacklists

Other sanctions cases have addressed the contractual implications of a party or affiliate being named to a blacklist. In *OCM Maritime Nile LLC v Courage Shipping Co*, the shipowner and charterer had agreed to two bareboat charters for bulk carriers, the *Courage* and the *Amethyst*, which included the right for the charterer to purchase the vessels at any time during the charter and also mandated the purchase at the end of the charter.[101] Hire payments would be credited toward the purchases. During the charter period, the beneficial owner controlling the chartering companies was sanctioned by US authorities and named to the SDN List for providing financing to Iran's Islamic Revolutionary Guard Corps-Qods Force and shipping sanctioned Iranian crude oil to Hezbollah. These activities, OFAC determined, violated the US Global Terrorism Sanctions Regulations. When the shipowner discovered this sanctions designation, it terminated the contracts and sought repossession of the vessels.[102] The charterer refused to return the vessels and instead argued it should be entitled to exercise the right to purchase. In litigation, the shipowner sought declarations that the charterparties had been lawfully terminated and that it was entitled to repossession of the vessels. It argued that the sanctions designation was an event of default under the charterparty that warranted repossession and forfeiture of any hire paid which would otherwise have been credited toward the charterer's purchase of the vessels. The charterer accepted that an event of default had occurred, but it argued it was still entitled to purchase the vessels in accordance with the charterparty, that OFAC might have allowed the purchase by way of a specific licence, and that it was entitled equitable relief from forfeiture because it would grant a windfall to the shipowner.

The English Commercial Court held for the shipowner, reasoning that the charterparty clauses contained an unqualified right to possession in the event of termination caused by default. Although the purpose of the transaction was to provide a structure for the charterer to finance the purchase of the vessels, the decision to use a bareboat charter to accomplish this meant that the shipowner

[100] ibid, 9.
[101] *OCM Maritime Nile LLC v Courage Shipping Co* [2022] 2 Lloyd's Rep 619 (Comm) (Sir Andrew Smith).
[102] The P&I and H&M insurers also cancelled cover due to the sanctions. ibid, 627.

would maintain a right of possession. The court also rejected the relevance of the argument that the charterparties could be performed lawfully if the parties were to obtain an OFAC licence. On this point, referencing expert witnesses on US sanctions law, the court found that there was 'little prospect' of securing a licence.[103] Without such authorisation, the court determined, restoring the charterparties would demand the shipowner to perform contracts with an SDN-listed entity, which could cause the shipowner to become at risk of being placed on the sanctions list. Reinforcing the conclusion that the charterer should not be entitled to equitable relief from forfeiture, the trial court also found that the charterer had engaged in serious misconduct, including switching off the vessels' AIS transponders to prevent the shipowner from tracking their locations, and sailing one of the vessels into Syrian waters, which blatantly violated the contractual trading limits. The English Court of Appeal affirmed.[104] Aligning with the reasoning of the trial court, it agreed that the shipowner was entitled to take repossession of the vessels due to the charterer's sanctions designation, regardless of whether the shipowner gave any formal notice of default. It also agreed with the trial court's assessment regarding the serious commercial risks imposed by the US sanctions, which effectively precluded the lawful execution of the charterparties. The court credited the trial court's findings that OFAC would be unlikely to grant a licence to authorise the sale and that the charterer had engaged in misconduct, such as switching off the vessels' AIS transponders, that warranted a dismissal of its claims to equitable relief. The court also added the point that doing business with a person on the SDN list 'would be likely to damage [the shipowner's] reputation with investors, banks and others with whom they do business'.[105]

In *O v C*, the English Commercial Court addressed the impact of US sanctions on a charterparty cancellation and subsequent sale of cargo on board the vessel.[106] The parties had agreed to move a cargo of Naphtha from Singapore, but on the same day that the cargo was loaded on the vessel the charterer was named to the OFAC SDN list due to violations of US sanctions targeting Iran. Invoking a BIMCO Sanctions Clause contained in the charterparty, the shipowner terminated the contract. Additionally, since the cargo had already been loaded on the vessel, the shipowner refused to discharge the cargo to the benefit of the charterer. The charterer brought a claim in arbitration for damages alleging that the shipowner's actions amounted to conversion. The shipowner sought a judicial order allowing it to sell the cargo and place the proceeds in a blocked account pursuant to an OFAC licence. Although the charterer did not resist the sale of the cargo, it argued the proceeds should be paid to the court rather than a blocked account while the arbitration claim on the merits was pending. On the narrow issue of whether the proceeds of the sale could be submitted to the court rather than a blocked US

[103] ibid, 649.
[104] *OCM Maritime Nile LLC v Courage Shipping Co* [2023] 1 Lloyd's Rep 13 (CA) (Males LJ).
[105] ibid, 21.
[106] *O v C* [2024] EWHC 2838 (Comm) (Sir Nigel Teare).

account, the English Commercial Court held for the charterer. Taking care to 'avoid trespassing upon the agreed jurisdiction of the arbitral tribunal', the court found that based on the conflicting views of expert witnesses on US sanctions law there was potentially a risk that payment of the proceeds of the cargo sale to the court would be regarded by OFAC as a breach of sanctions.[107] Nevertheless, the court found that there was a 'very powerful argument' that OFAC would not prosecute the shipowner by paying the proceeds to the court rather than a blocked account: the shipowner was 'not seeking to breach US sanctions but to comply with them'.[108] After comparing conflicting expert testimony and reviewing OFAC guidance documents, the court explained that there was 'no real prospect of a prosecution'.[109] This finding was bolstered by the fact that payment into the court would be compelled by judicial order (rather than a voluntary act by the shipowner) and that the purpose of paying into the court would be to preserve the proceeds of the cargo sale pending the results of the arbitration on the merits instead of any attempt to 'avoid or frustrate the effect of US sanctions'.[110]

Other blacklisting cases have addressed Russia-related sanctions. In *Gravelor Shipping Ltd v GTLK Asia M5 Ltd*, a bareboat charterer of two vessels sought to exercise a purchase option against the registered shipowner whose parent company, the Russian Ministry of Transportation Leasing Co, became subject to EU and US sanctions in the aftermath of Russia's full-scale invasion of Ukraine in 2022.[111] As soon as the war began, referencing the 'difficult political situation', the charterer expressed its intention to exercise a purchase option of the vessels.[112] Then, after the shipowner's parent company became subject to EU-level sanctions, the charterer missed hire payments, alleging that international banking institutions would not process the payments due to sanctions compliance concerns. As a result, the shipowner claimed this as a default that warranted termination of the charterparty. The charterer again sought to exercise the purchase option, but only into a frozen account. Subsequently, the US also sanctioned the shipowner's parent company, which caused the charterer to refuse to make the payments into the frozen account in US dollars, but the charterer offered Euros instead. When the shipowner resisted, arguing it had no obligation to transfer title or accept payment into a frozen account, the charterer sought specific performance to enforce the contract. The English Commercial Court agreed with the charterer and granted it specific performance to purchase the vessels by way of payment in Euros into a frozen account. It made this determination based

[107] ibid, para [7].
[108] ibid, para [30].
[109] ibid, para [33]. The experts for both the shipowner and the charterer agreed that as 'allied' jurisdictions the relative geopolitical harmony between the US and UK was a relevant factor in the determination of whether OFAC might prosecute the shipowner for paying into court according to a UK court order. ibid, paras [26]–[27].
[110] ibid.
[111] *Gravelor Shipping Ltd v GTLK Asia M5 Ltd* [2023] 2 Lloyd's Rep 239 (Comm) (Foxton J).
[112] ibid, 244.

on careful scrutiny of various charterparty clauses, including the default clause, the purchase option clause, and other clauses referencing sanctions. The court also took notice of the 'incapability' of payment caused by banking institutions being 'cautious and careful' in processing payments that might violate sanctions.[113] For this reason, although the charterparty originally contemplated payment in US dollars, the court found that the sanctions warranted an alternative reading of the obligation that would comport with 'commercial good sense'.[114] The court found payment in Euros into a frozen account for the purpose of complying with EU and US sanctions would satisfy the charterer's obligation under the charterparty. According to the court, any difficulty or even impossibility in accessing the funds would not be caused by the payment process but rather 'it would be the result of an entirely external limitation arising from a perceived characteristic of the payee' – the fact that the shipowner or its parent company had been sanctioned.[115]

In another Russia-connected case, *Tonzip Maritime Ltd v 2Rivers Pte Ltd*, the parties had agreed to a voyage charter to move oil on the tanker *Catalan Sea* from Russia to Turkey in 2021.[116] The contract contained a sanctions clause under which the charterer warranted that no person or entity with an interest in the cargo was 'designated or subject to any national, international or supranational law or regulation imposing trade and economic sanctions' and that performance of the charterparty 'is not and will not be prohibited or restricted by law, and will not expose' the shipowner, the vessel, or its insurers to sanctions.[117] The clause also granted the shipowner the right to deny orders for the vessel's employment, which 'in the reasonable judgment of the owners, is prohibited by sanctions or will expose' the shipowner, vessel, insurers, or others connected to the voyage, and that the charterer would be obliged to provide alternative orders 'in the event that such risk arises in relation to a voyage the vessel is performing'.[118] Prior to performance, the EU and UK had imposed sanctions on Russia following the annexation of Ukrainian Crimea by blacklisting certain Russia-connected businesses and individuals. After the vessel arrived for loading in Russia in November 2021, the shipowner conducted a sanctions due diligence check using third party screening tools, which revealed that the company that owned the cargo was associated with a Russian businessman who had been designated under EU and UK sanctions. Invoking the sanctions clause and claiming the blacklisted businessman was the 'indirect owner' of the cargo, the shipowner refused loading and requested the charterer to provide alternative orders.[119] The charterer offered assurances and evidence that the blacklisted businessman named by the shipowner had no

[113] ibid, 252.
[114] ibid.
[115] ibid, 254.
[116] *Tonzip Maritime Ltd v 2Rivers Pte Ltd* [2025] EWHC 2036 (Comm) (Andrew Hochhauser KC).
[117] ibid, para [28].
[118] ibid.
[119] ibid, para [21].

controlling stake in the cargo owning company and therefore did not violate the sanctions. When the shipowner refused to perform, the charterer cancelled the charterparty and fixed a different vessel to move the cargo.

The shipowner brought a claim in the English Commercial Court for wrongful breach and the charterer counterclaimed for its own losses. The shipowner alleged that the sanctions clause granted it the discretion to avoid orders in a 'fast moving commercial environment' where 'decisions need to be made quickly, for both financial and operational reasons, and without the luxury of time to investigate the sanctions issues in great detail'.[120] The charterer countered that the sanctions clause's language ('is prohibited' and 'will expose') required an objectively higher standard of proof than permissive drafting alternatives ('may be exposed') that had been at issue in earlier case law.[121] Holding for the charterer, the court found that the shipowner had not used 'reasonable judgment' in refusing the charterer's orders to load the cargo.[122] The court reasoned that the third party information the shipowner used to perform its sanctions risk screening was inconclusive as to whether the blacklisted Russian businessman actually had a controlling stake in the cargo-owning company under the standards laid out by the EU and UK sanctions. Accordingly, the shipowner failed to satisfy the evidentiary burden embedded in the sanctions clause, as it 'did not make a reasonable objective decision that the listed persons were subject to the risk of sanctions or were open to the danger of sanctions'.[123]

Another recent English case addressed the contractual implications of a ship management company's efforts to avoid blacklisting exposure by refusing to facilitate trades linked to both Iran and Venezuela. In *Ceto Shipping Corp v Savory Shipping Inc*, the tanker *Victor I* was under a three-year bareboat charter in which the shipowner was obliged to transfer title to the vessel at the expiration of the agreement provided that all sums had been paid under the charter and an accompanying ship management agreement.[124] In April 2020, the bareboat charterer sub-chartered the vessel to move Iranian-origin gasoline to Trinidad and Tobago (although the intended destination was actually Venezuela). When the bareboat charterer ordered the ship management company to facilitate this sub-charter, it refused by invoking a 'legality clause', which provided that the ship manager, 'shall not be obliged to comply with the provisions of this Agreement if in the reasonable judgment of the Parties it will expose them or their insurers, re-insurers, crew, registered owners, to any sanction'.[125] The bare-boat charterer then terminated the ship management agreement, but when it later attempted to enforce the charterparty provisions to transfer title to the

[120] ibid, para [40].
[121] ibid, para [60].
[122] ibid, para [69].
[123] ibid, para [131].
[124] *Ceto Shipping Corp v Savory Shipping Inc* [2025] EWHC 2033 (Comm) (Cockerill J).
[125] ibid, Appendix.

vessel, the shipowner refused, alleging that the termination of the ship management agreement precluded the automatic transfer of title. The bareboat charterer sued to enforce the obligation, but the English Commercial Court held for the shipowner. The court's reasoning centred on whether the bareboat charterer was entitled to terminate the ship management agreement following the refusal to perform the sub-charter to Venezuela. To answer the question, the court focused on the 'reasonable judgment' of the ship management company under the legality clause[126] It first held that the reasonableness inquiry does not require 'virtual certainty' of sanctions being imposed because the language 'will expose' is not a wording requiring an objective 'result' given that 'such a level of certainty would seem inapt to civil commercial events'.[127] Applying this less-than-certain standard to measure the sanctions exposure, the court weighed expert testimony regarding the likelihood of enforcement action from US authorities and determined that the risk was indeed 'high'.[128] Based on this finding, the court determined that the ship management company had properly and reasonably invoked the legality clause in good faith, which meant that the bareboat charterer had wrongly terminated the ship management agreement, and therefore the shipowner was correct that payments were outstanding, which justified its refusal to transfer title of the vessel to the bareboat charterer.

iv. Practical Barriers

An English court addressed the knock-on effects of broadly applied US sanctions in *Laysun Service Co Ltd v Del Monte International GmbH*.[129] In that case, the parties had entered into a contract of affreightment covering a series of voyages to move refrigerated bananas from the Philippines to Iran on behalf of a third-party purchaser based in the UAE. These transactions were agreed to be performed at a time when multilateral sanctions on Iran had been rolled back as part of the JCPOA. However, when the US announced its intention to withdraw from its participation in the JCPOA, the UAE-based buyers claimed they were unable to receive payments from the Iran-based receivers because of sanctions compliance scrutiny by UAE-based banks. In addition, in response to the renewed sanctions, Iran's government imposed new regulations to control the outflow of foreign currency, which included a requirement to obtain import permits for goods arriving at Iran's ports. At the time when the banana shipments were scheduled to arrive, there was already a de facto moratorium on the issuance of such import permits. On these two bases – the payment issue and the permit issue – the charterer invoked

[126] ibid, para [238].

[127] ibid, para [243]. The court explained that '[w]hat matters is whether the judgment was objectively reasonable, not whether the process of reaching it was reasonable or sensible'. ibid, para [241].

[128] ibid, para [260].

[129] *Laysun Service Co Ltd v Del Monte International GmbH* [2023] Lloyd's Rep Plus 15 (Comm) (Calver J).

a *force majeure* provision in the contract and stopped providing cargos for shipment or paying for the transport. The dispute was referred to London arbitration. During the proceedings, the shipowner sought to collect damages on the basis that the charterer had breached the contract of affreightment. The charterer argued it was impossible to perform the contract and that it was excused from performance under the *force majeure* clause. The arbitral tribunal held in favour of the charterer. It found that the payment issue alone justified the charterer's reference to the *force majeure* clause because the ultimate buyer could not make payments due to UAE banks being unwilling to process them. It also found that it would have been impossible to perform the contract once the Iranian government stopped authorising imports by permits. And finally, it determined that there was nothing 'reasonably practicable' that the charterer could have done to resume performance prior to the expiration of the agreement. The shipowner sought review by the English Commercial Court, but the court held that 'the appeal is doomed' because the challenge hinged on the tribunal's factual findings that could not be re-opened.[130]

The most authoritative decision addressing sanctions disruption in the context of a vessel chartering contract is *RTI Ltd v Mur Shipping BV* – a case that moved from London arbitration all the way to the UK Supreme Court.[131] In that case, a Netherlands-based shipowner and Jersey-based charterer had agreed to a contract of affreightment to move seven shipments of bauxite from Guinea to Ukraine, with payment of freight to be made in US dollars. During the contract period, OFAC named the charterer's parent company to the SDN List. The shipowner alleged this was a breach of the charterparty and invoked a *force majeure* clause in the contract on the grounds that the sanctions prevented freight payment in US dollars. The charterer rejected the shipowner's *force majeure* notice and proposed to pay freight in Euros and to absorb any relevant exchange rate losses when converting them into US dollars. The shipowner accepted some payments in Euros as arranged by the charterer when OFAC issued a temporary licence, but out of concern that US intermediary banks would delay processing payments due to sanctions compliance risks, the shipowner eventually refused to nominate vessels under the contract, again relying on the *force majeure* defence. The charterer then commenced arbitration and the arbitral tribunal ruled in favour of the charterer. The tribunal accepted the contention that the impact of the sanctions would be 'drastic', and that it was 'highly likely' that this would impede the charterer's ability to make payment in US dollars because US banks were cautious not to facilitate transactions that might expose them to secondary sanctions from OFAC.[132] However, since the *force majeure* clause contained language requiring the affected party

[130] ibid. The judge wrote: 'In any event, in my judgment, the Tribunal correctly interpreted [the *force majeure* clause].'
[131] *RTI Ltd v Mur Shipping BV* [2024] 1 Lloyd's Rep 621 (UKSC) (Hamblen and Burrows LJJ).
[132] *RTI Ltd v Mur Shipping BV* [2022] 2 Lloyd's Rep 297 (Comm) (Jacobs J).

to engage in 'reasonable endeavours' to overcome the *force majeure* situation, the tribunal reasoned that the shipowner should have accepted the charterer's proposal to pay freight in Euros instead of US dollars as this was a 'completely realistic alternative' to contractual performance.[133] But the English Commercial Court overturned the decision of the tribunal on appeal. The court determined that the charterer was contractually required to pay freight in US dollars, not Euros, and that the 'reasonable endeavours' language of the *force majeure* clause did not burden the shipowner with an obligation to accept a non-contractual currency. The court rejected the charterer's argument that payment in Euros was effectively equivalent to payment in dollars because the funds could be readily converted by intermediary banks. Instead, the court explained, 'the obligation to pay freight in the agreed currency is an important contractual obligation'.[134] Consequently, the 'reasonable endeavours' language embedded in the *force majeure* clause did not require the shipowner to 'sacrifice' this contractual right.[135]

A majority of the English Court of Appeal restored the decision of the arbitral tribunal.[136] The majority explained that the *force majeure* clause contemplated both an 'event' and 'state of affairs' which 'suggests an element of flexibility in the application of the clause'.[137] The question was whether the event or state of affairs could be 'overcome' by the 'reasonable endeavours' of the affected party – in this case the shipowner. Read in a 'common sense way', the clause is designed to help achieve the underlying obligations of the parties, which includes the shipowner receiving the contractual amount of US dollars.[138] Applied to the proposal to pay in Euros to be immediately converted into US dollars, the court found that there was 'no reason why a solution which ensured the achievement of this purpose should not be regarded as overcoming the state of affairs resulting from the imposition of sanctions'.[139] If the shipowner had accepted the charterer's proposal, the court reasoned, this 'would have achieved precisely the same result as performance of the contractual obligation to pay in US dollars, namely the receipt in [the shipowner's] bank account of the right quantity of dollars at the right time'.[140] Although the charterparty required payment of freight to be made in US dollars, the charterer's proposal to pay in Euros and convert them immediately into US dollars would have 'overcome the state of affairs caused by the imposition of sanctions' with 'no detriment' to the shipowner.[141] A carefully reasoned dissent aligned with the decision of the Commercial Court judge below.[142] The dissenting judge took the position that the alternative payment option proposed

[133] ibid, 304.
[134] ibid, 316.
[135] ibid, 319.
[136] *RTI Ltd v Mur Shipping BV* [2023] 1 Lloyd's Rep 463 (CA) (Males LJ).
[137] ibid.
[138] ibid.
[139] ibid, 471.
[140] ibid, 472.
[141] ibid.
[142] ibid, 472 (Arnold LJ, dissenting).

by the charterer was 'non-contractual'.[143] According to the dissent, irrespective of whether this alternative payment arrangement would have helped solve the disruptive state of affairs created by the sanctions, the *force majeure* clause did not demand that the shipowner accept non-contractual performance as this would not 'overcome' the barrier to contractual performance.[144]

In a unanimous decision, the UK Supreme Court reversed the judgment below and – once again – overturned the award of the arbitral tribunal.[145] The UK Supreme Court explained that the 'reasonable endeavours' concept is a 'very common feature' of a *force majeure* clause that would be read as an implied matter of principle even if the clause did not contain such express language.[146] The court explained that since the 'impediment to performance' was the likelihood of banking delays arising out of the US sanctions, this could have been overcome by, for instance, an OFAC licence that allowed the contract to be performed by the payment of US dollars. However, this was not the same as the charterer's proposal of non-contractual payment in Euros. Under such an arrangement, the court reasoned, '[t]he banking delay for US dollar payments resulting from the imposition of sanctions remained in place and was not "overcome" by offering non-contractual performance'.[147] Furthermore, although freedom of contract principles would theoretically allow a party to give up the right to accept contractual performance in lieu of non-contractual alternatives to overcome disruption, this requires an explicit agreement. The court explained, 'parties do not forego valuable rights without it being made clear that that was their intention'.[148] To imply an obligation to accept an extra-contractual solution to the inability to perform, the court reasoned, 'would introduce uncertainty contrary to the expectations of reasonable business people'.[149]

B. Marine Insurance

i. Cover Restrictions

In *Islamic Republic of Iran Shipping Lines (IRISL) v Steamship Mutual Underwriting Association (Bermuda) Ltd*, the English Commercial Court examined whether a P&I club properly terminated insurance cover in reaction to UK sanctions restricting P&I insurance for vessels operated by Iran's state-owned shipping line.[150] More than two dozen of these vessels, including the bulk carrier *M/V Zoorik*, were entered with a P&I club operated out of the UK. The club

[143] ibid, 473.
[144] ibid.
[145] *RTI Ltd v Mur Shipping BV* [2024] 1 Lloyd's Rep 621.
[146] ibid, 626.
[147] ibid, 628.
[148] ibid, 629.
[149] ibid, 631.
[150] *Islamic Republic of Iran Shipping Lines (IRISL) v Steamship Mutual Underwriting Association (Bermuda) Ltd* [2011] 1 Lloyd's Rep IR 145 (Comm) (Beatson J).

had provided a 'Blue Card' to the UK CLC Bunkers Maritime and Coastguard Agency evidencing that it would provide the vessel's compulsory cover for oil pollution liabilities under the International Convention for Bunker Oil Pollution Damage 2001 (the 'Bunkers Convention'). But then UK HM Treasury officials issued an order prohibiting UK-connected insurers from providing P&I cover to the Iranian shipowner's vessels. HM Treasury also issued multiple rounds of temporary licences, with a final iteration of the licence limiting authorisation for three months to 'continue to provide insurance cover in accordance with the Blue Cards issued to [the shipowner]'.[151] Concerned that the updated licence had the effect of prohibiting insurance cover for claims made directly by the shipowner, the club sought guidance from HM Treasury regarding the scope of the sanctions.[152] When it did not receive a response, the club wrote to the shipowner immediately cancelling cover for all of its entered vessels, including the *Zoorik*. Less than 24 hours after the club terminated cover, the *Zoorik* ran aground off the coast of China, causing the vessel to break apart and emit extensive bunker oil pollution. Third party claimants, including the Chinese Maritime Safety Administration, a helicopter rescue bureau, a wreck removal company, and various Chinese fishing companies each made claims directly against the shipowner. The shipowner paid those third-party claims and then sought reimbursement from the P&I club, alleging that it had improperly terminated cover. The club refused to reimburse the shipowner, taking the position that it would be unlawful to do so.

The shipowner filed suit in the English Commercial Court seeking to recover under the terminated insurance contract. In the litigation, the club argued that it bore no liability to reimburse the shipowner because due to the UK sanctions it was prohibited from performing the insurance contract on the basis of supervening illegality and frustration. The shipowner countered that the payment of claims within the scope of the Bunkers Convention were not rendered illegal by the sanctions because the licence expressly allowed for continued cover regarding bunker oil pollution-related liabilities reflected in the Blue Card the club had issued on behalf of the *Zoorik*. The court held for the shipowner. It reasoned that despite the UK sanctions broadly prohibiting P&I cover for the shipowner's vessels, the licences authorising insurance according to the 'Blue Cards' permitted cover for all relevant bunker oil pollution liabilities, including third-party claims made directly against the insurer contemplated under the Bunkers Convention, which encapsulated subsequent claims made by the insured against the insurer to reimburse it for the claims it had paid to third parties. The court explained that the Bunkers Convention as incorporated into English law mandates cover for the 'costs of preventative measures and reinstatement regardless of whether they are initially borne by the shipowner or a third party'.[153] Although the court recognised that

[151] ibid, 153.
[152] ibid.
[153] ibid, 159.

the sanctions rendered the P&I cover partially unlawful, it determined that reimbursement of the pollution-related claims at issue were still authorised under the UK sanctions licence, which made the P&I club's contract termination wrongful. The court also rejected the club's frustration defence. Applying a 'multi-factorial' approach, the court determined that sanctions and corresponding licence 'did not render the Club's obligations radically different so as to frustrate the contract of insurance'.[154] Although the sanctions narrowed the scope of cover permitted, the court found the fundamental purpose of the contract remained, which was 'to provide indemnity insurance on a mutual basis to those who enter their ships with the Club'.[155]

The implications of sanctions-based illegality were also addressed in *Sea Glory Maritime Co v Al Sagr National Insurance Co (The M/V Nancy)*.[156] In that case, a fire broke out on a bulk carrier while at anchorage off a port in Eastern Russia, which rendered the vessel a constructive total loss. The shipowner made a claim for insurance cover under the vessel's hull and machinery policy. Although it was undisputed that fire was an insured peril under the policy, the insurer refused to pay the claim on grounds that the vessel's previous voyage moving a cargo of sulphur between Iran and China was unlawful under US sanctions. When the shipowner pursued the claim in the English Commercial Court, the defendant insurer argued that this unlawful voyage amounted to a breach of warranty of legality at common law and under English legislation. The court rejected these defences and ruled in favour of the shipowner. It found that the vessel had indeed facilitated an Iran-connected trade, which had apparently violated US sanctions at the time of performance in late 2008. However, the court determined that such foreign illegality had no effect on the insurance policy, which was governed by English law. Although the English marine insurance legislation cited by the insurer did create an implied warranty of lawfulness, case law interpreting its provisions referenced lawfulness based on domestic English law rather than foreign law. The court also noted that the planned commercial voyage when the fire occurred – moving steel billets and wires from Russia to Taiwan and the Philippines – was entirely lawful, which compelled the court to find that there was 'no causative connection between the illegality and the claim for indemnity'.[157] Although, at that time, Iran was also subject to other less onerous sanctions from the UN, EU, and UK due to its nuclear programme, the court rejected the argument that a 'general principle of public policy' should entitle the insurer to resist payment.[158] While acknowledging the situation raised 'an important policy issue' the court noted that the UK had implemented its own sanctions on Iran, which were not referenced as the basis for any

[154] ibid, 167.
[155] ibid.
[156] *Sea Glory Maritime Co v Al Sagr National Insurance Co (The M/V Nancy)* [2014] 2 Lloyd's Rep 14 (Comm) (Blair J).
[157] ibid, 149.
[158] ibid.

alleged illegality. For this reason, the court explained it would be inappropriate to use public policy to allow the insurer to invoke such a defence when the contract at issue was 'completely unconnected' to a breach of US sanctions.[159] On this point, the court noted that the timing was relevant because the sanctions were enacted rapidly, suggesting any illegality was inadvertent. The court explained, '[a] case of inadvertence is very different from a case of deliberate unlawful conduct'.[160] Finally, the court rejected the insurer's argument that the shipowner had an obligation to disclose information regarding the vessel's previous voyages to Iran. While the court referenced expert testimony suggesting the sanctions laws at the time were evolving so fast that 'it was so difficult for underwriters to understand them', it ultimately found that the defendant insurer had 'at least as much opportunity to appraise the effect' of the US sanctions as the shipowner claimant.[161]

ii. Exposure

Other marine insurance cases addressing restricted insurance cover have hinged on the interpretation of explicit sanctions clauses embedded in the insurance policies. *Arash Shipping Enterprises Co Ltd v Groupama Transport* examined the impact of a sanctions clause in a policy of hull and machinery insurance affected by EU sanctions on Iran.[162] In 2010, the insurer had contracted to provide hull and machinery cover for a fleet of oil tankers owned by entities connected to the Iranian state. The policy period was for one year, but the insurance contract also contained a clause that provided for automatic renewal for an additional year if the policy holder maintained a designated credit balance during the first 10 months of the policy. Since the policy holder was controlled by an entity based in Iran, which was increasingly the subject of multilateral sanctions at the time, the insurance policy contained an 'Iran Sanctions Clause', which provided that the insurer 'may cancel' the insurance 'where the Assured has exposed or may, in the opinion of the Insurer, expose the Insurer to the risk of being or becoming subject to any sanction' by the UN, EU, US, UK, or the flag state.[163] During the policy period, the EU Council issued a new round of sanctions prohibiting insurance cover for certain entities connected to Iran, including extensions or renewals of insurance agreements that had been concluded before the sanctions entered into force.[164] Before the policy lapsed, citing the EU sanctions and the sanctions clause, the insurer gave the policy holders notice of cancellation at the end of the policy period, effectively refusing to honour the automatic renewal provision.

[159] ibid, 150.
[160] ibid.
[161] ibid.
[162] *Arash Shipping Enterprises Co Ltd v Groupama Transport Sveriges Angfartygs Assurans Forening* [2011] 2 Lloyd's Rep 607 (CA) (Stanley Burnton LJ).
[163] ibid, 609.
[164] ibid, 610.

The assured filed an action in the English Commercial Court seeking a declaration to invalidate the insurer's decision to cancel the policy. The court held that the cancellation was contractually permitted, and that the EU sanctions prohibited the extension of the policy period.[165]

In the English Court of Appeal, the assured argued that the sanctions clause could not be invoked unless the assured affirmatively exposed the insurer to a specific risk of sanctions by an act or omission. It also contested the finding that EU sanctions prohibited the extension of the policy under the renewal clause. The insurer argued that it would be an unduly narrow reading of the sanctions clause to require an act or omission by the assured, that instead its language provided a broad right to refuse renewal, and that, in any event, the sanctions prohibited the extension of the policy. The appeals court agreed with the insurer's position that the sanctions clause did not require an act or omission by the assured. Instead, the court found the sanctions clause was flexibly drafted using permissive 'may' language, which allowed it to apply if the insurer had the subjective opinion that it would be exposed to sanctions, as long as this opinion was genuine and reasonable. This meant that the court itself did not have to make an explicit finding of sanctions exposure. The court reasoned that 'the policy confers the right of cancellation on the insurer if it is of the specified opinion, not if the court is of that opinion. Once the Insurer is genuinely and reasonably of the requisite opinion, it has a contractual right to serve notice of cancellation.'[166] On the separate issue of whether the EU sanctions prohibited the renewal of the policy, the court sidestepped the question, describing the matter as 'academic'.[167] The court explained that English judges adjudicating civil cases do not have the authority to provide a definitive answer on the application of the EU sanctions, as the 'court of final decision' on such matters is instead the Court of Justice of the European Union.[168]

An English court reached a different result on a similar question in *Mamancochet Mining Ltd v Aegis Managing Agency Ltd*.[169] In that case, the central issue was whether a cargo insurer could avoid or suspend the obligation to pay a claim on the basis of a sanctions clause contained in its policy. In 2012, a cargo of several million US dollars of steel billets was carried from Russia to Iran on two vessels. On arrival, due to payment problems attributed to the consignee, the cargo was placed in bonded storage at an Iranian port. Shortly thereafter, the cargo was stolen from the warehouse. The assured made a claim under the cargo insurance policy, which explicitly covered the risk of theft during multimodal transport to the final destination. Although the insurer did not dispute that the claim fell within the policy coverage, it resisted payment of the claim by invoking a sanctions clause,

[165] This trial court decision was apparently unpublished.
[166] ibid, 614.
[167] ibid, 615.
[168] ibid.
[169] *Mamancochet Mining Ltd v Aegis Managing Agency Ltd* [2018] 2 Lloyd's Rep 441 (Comm) (Teare J).

which provided that '[n]o (re)insurer shall be deemed to provide cover and no (re)insurer shall be liable to pay any claim' if doing so 'would expose that (re)insurer to any sanction' under UN, EU, US, or UK rules.[170] The insurer contended that if it paid the claim this 'would expose' it to sanctions. The assured acquiesced regarding the claim during the period of multilateral sanctions targeting Iran. However, several years later, these sanctions were largely rolled back as part of the JCPOA. After the diplomatic agreement went into effect in January 2016, the assured again sought to collect on the basis that the payment would no longer expose the insurer to sanctions. But before the insurer paid the claim, in May 2018, the US unilaterally withdrew from the JCPOA and re-imposed sanctions on Iran by ending a temporary licence, subject to a wind-down period of six months. In response to the US withdrawal from the JCPOA, some other national and supranational parties to the deal attempted to preserve the diplomatic agreement, including through an EU-level 'Blocking Regulation' that purportedly blunted the impact of US sanctions.[171]

The claimant brought an action on an expedited basis in the English Commercial Court seeking to recover the claim prior to the end of the six-month wind-down period before the US sanctions went into full effect. The insurer argued that the sanctions clause gave it the liberty to avoid paying claims that would put it at 'risk' of violating US sanctions.[172] Since the US sanctions at issue prohibited services to Iranian entities, the insurer alleged that these rules placed it at risk of exposure to sanctions if it paid the claim, even during the wind-down period. The assured countered that the sanctions clause required a definitive showing on the 'balance of probabilities' that payment of the claim would put it in breach of the sanctions, which it alleged the insurer could not do given that the wind-down period was still in effect.[173] The court held in favour of the assured. Addressing the meaning of the contractual term 'expose', the court determined that the language 'does not refer in terms to being exposed to *the risk* of a sanction or prohibition. It refers to a payment which "would expose" the insurer "to any sanction, prohibition, or restriction."'[174] The court reasoned that as a whole the language of the sanctions clause objectively 'provides that the insurer is not liable to pay a claim where payment would be prohibited under one of the named systems of law and thus "would expose" the defendants to a sanction'.[175] Applying this objective standard, the court considered the testimony of US legal experts, US regulatory guidance, and even statements of US political officials, to ultimately find that the OFAC general waiver authorising payments of claims during the wind-down period demonstrated that 'payment of the insurance claim in question is not prohibited by the US so payment by that date would not expose the defendants to sanctions'.[176] For that reason, as long as

[170] ibid, 443.
[171] ibid, 446.
[172] ibid.
[173] ibid.
[174] ibid, 446 (emphasis in original).
[175] ibid, 447.
[176] ibid, 450.

the insurer paid the claim before the end of the wind-down period, which it was obliged to do, it would not be exposed to sanctions under the meaning of the clause. On a separate point, although the court acknowledged that the issue was not dispositive, it rejected the claimant's alternative argument hinging on the EU Blocking Regulation, reasoning that it was 'not engaged' when the liability was suspended under a sanctions clause, as this was a question of the terms of the insurance policy rather than of compliance with foreign sanctions.[177]

iii. Third Parties

In a dispute arising out of a collision and subsequent ship arrest, the English Court of Appeal addressed another insurance-related sanctions clause issue in *M/V Pacific Pearl Co Ltd v Osios David Shipping Inc.*[178] In that case, three vessels were involved in a July 2018 collision in the Suez Canal. As is customary in the industry, the parties agreed under a collision jurisdiction agreement to each provide a Letter of Undertaking (LOU) from their respective P&I insurers to serve as security to avoid the vessels being arrested in response to collision liabilities. These LOUs were generally provided on a standard form developed in industry practice. However, since one of the vessels, the *Panamax Alexander*, had an 'Iranian nexus' because the consignee of the cargo was based in Iran, its P&I club amended the LOU form to include a sanctions clause. The terms of the sanctions clause broadly provided that the club would bear no liability to make payments under the LOU if doing so would be 'unlawful, prohibited or sanctionable' or if a bank involved in the payment chain was 'unable or unwilling' to make payments, including due to its own 'internal policies'.[179] The P&I club included this language because the US had recently announced its intention to withdraw from the JCPOA and instead planned to reimpose sanctions on Iran unilaterally. One of the other claimants, the shipowner of the *Osios David*, did not accept the P&I club LOU containing the sanctions clause as adequate security, and arrested an affiliated ship called the *Panamax Christina* in South Africa.[180] The shipowner of the *Panamax Christina* secured an LOU from that vessel's P&I club that did not contain a sanctions clause, and the vessel was released, but the shipowner of the *Panamax Christina* sought to recover damages incurred as a result of the arrest. In litigation, the claimant shipowner argued that the ship arrest of the *Panamax Christina* was unjustified because the initial LOU issued by the shipowner of the *Panamax Alexander* provided 'reasonably satisfactory' security under the collision jurisdiction agreement, even though it contained a sanctions clause.[181] The respondent shipowner argued that the sanctions clause diminished the security of the LOU and thus the

[177] ibid, 451.

[178] *M/V Pacific Pearl Co Ltd v Osios David Shipping Inc* [2022] Lloyd's Rep 261 (Comm) (Sir Nigel Teare).

[179] ibid, 265.

[180] This vessel was owned by a company associated with the shipowner of the *Panamax Alexander*.

[181] ibid, 263.

ship arrest of the *Panamax Christina* was necessary to assure adequate security while the underlying collision liabilities were assessed on the merits.

The English Commercial Court held for the respondent shipowner of the *Osios David*. It first explained the purpose of the sanctions clause, noting that P&I clubs adopt them in reaction to governmental decisions to 'conduct foreign policy through the use of sanctions' that might 'render the performance of the obligations of P&I Clubs under LOUs unlawful' or at least 'create difficulties in performance of those obligations'.[182] As a consequence, the inclusion of the sanctions clause in the LOU 'recognizes an inevitable commercial reality' of enhanced risk associated with transactions involving an Iranian nexus.[183] Although the court found that the insurer's use of a sanctions clause in the LOU was objectively reasonable, it held that this did not mean that the LOU had to be accepted by the other party as adequate security. Instead, the court held, it was permissible for the party seeking security to do so alternatively by way of arrest. On this point, the English Court of Appeal reversed the decision in favour of the claimant shipowner.[184] It affirmed the trial court's holding that the inclusion of the sanctions clause was objectively reasonable. But the court rejected the proposition that an LOU reasonably containing a sanctions clause could be disregarded by the other party. The court explained that if reasonable security is provided in accordance with the collision jurisdiction agreement, 'it is not open to the receiving party to seek alternative or better security by means of an arrest; and that if a ship has been arrested, it must be released once reasonable security is provided'.[185] To hold otherwise, the court explained, 'turns well established Admiralty practice on its head' by allowing ship arrest despite the provision of reasonable and adequate security that is designed to prevent the inconvenience of such disruption.[186]

Security for a pending claim was also at issue in the Singaporean case *Oghiaanous Khoroushan Shipping Lines Co of Kish v Owner of the Vessel 'Tina I'*.[187] That case arose out of a collision between the Greek-owned *Tina I* and the Iranian-owned *Shahraz* just off the coast of Jakarta, Indonesia. Following a claim for collision liabilities, the shipowner of the *Tina I* agreed to accept responsibility under a collision liability agreement, which included an obligation to provide security to the court on an agreed quantum. The parties subsequently agreed on the quantum of security but they disagreed on the terms because the Iran-based shipowner of the *Shahraz* had been subject to US sanctions and was named on the OFAC SDN list. To address the possible application of US secondary sanctions, the shipowner of the *Tina I* aimed to include a sanctions clause in its security provided to the court, which would allow it to refuse payment in the event of exposure to US sanctions.

[182] ibid.
[183] ibid, 270.
[184] *M/V Pacific Pearl Co Ltd v Osios David Shipping Inc* [2022] 1 Lloyd's Rep Plus 91 (CA) (Males LJ).
[185] ibid, para [39].
[186] ibid, para [41].
[187] *Oghiaanous Khoroushan Shipping Lines Co of Kish v Owner of the Vessel 'Tina I'* [2024] SGHCR 12 (Singapore HC) (AR Navin Anand J).

The shipowner of the *Shahraz* contested the legitimacy of the sanctions clause, which led to a dispute in the High Court of the Republic of Singapore on 'the narrow but novel issue of whether the payment out from court should be subject to the Sanctions Clause'.[188] The court found that the sanctions clause was invalid. It justified this holding on the grounds that there was no genuine evidentiary basis for including the sanctions clause as a term of the security, that the sanctions clause was inconsistent with the legal consequences of payment into court, and that it would prevent the claimant from obtaining adequate security. The court emphasised the fact that the sanctions clause was 'phrased subjectively, and confers a discretion on the Defendant to deny payment of the security to the Claimant based on the Defendant's own subjective risk assessment'.[189] This made the prospect of the shipowner of the *Shahraz* receiving payment 'significantly in the hands of the Defendant'.[190] For this reason, the court explained, the Claimant would actually be in a better position to enforce the collision liability by ship arrest as compared to the security agreement containing the sanctions clause. In this sense, by accepting the sanctions clause, the Claimant 'would have relinquished a substantial security for a comparatively uncertain one'.[191] Distinguishing the *M/V Pacific Pearl* case discussed above, the court found that it must reject the inclusion of the sanctions clause to 'ensure that the security the Claimant is ordered to accept is an adequate replacement for what it is giving up'.[192] Otherwise, the court explained, the 'right to arrest and obtain pre-judgment security for its claim should not be lightly curtailed'.[193]

While not directly tied to marine insurance, several other recent decisions have addressed the impact of sanctions affecting third parties in the banking and trade finance context associated with shipping transactions. Among them is *DVB Bank SE v Shere Shipping Co Ltd* in which the English Commercial Court examined whether a borrower under a ship financing arrangement could avoid its contractual obligations on the basis that Iran sanctions made it impossible to make the payments.[194] In 2006, an affiliate of Iran's national shipping line had borrowed $50 million as part of a post-delivery financing arrangement to acquire four vessels. Under the loan agreement, the borrowers agreed to make scheduled payments and to keep the vessels insured and properly registered. Shortly after the borrowers began making the payments, international business activities with an Iranian nexus started to be affected by multilateral economic sanctions. Repayment under the loan agreement was apparently authorised in exceptions to the sanctions and the

[188] ibid, 6.
[189] ibid, 14.
[190] ibid.
[191] ibid, 15.
[192] ibid, 18. The court reasoned that the Club LOU containing a sanctions clause at issue in the *M/V Pacific Pearl* case was not equivalent to the security of paying into court in the present case. The court explained that '[p]ayment into court is governed by the domestic rules of court, while the enforcement of an undertaking, being a contract between the issuing law firm or P&I Club and the beneficiary, is based on contractual principles'. ibid, 13.
[193] ibid.
[194] *DVB Bank SE v Shere Shipping Co Ltd* [2013] EWHC 2321 (Comm) (Simon J).

borrowers continued making scheduled payments for a short period. But eventually the borrowers and its affiliated guarantors sought to avoid performance on the basis that the contract had been 'rendered impossible' due to EU-level sanctions.[195] In litigation, the claimants sought to enforce the loan agreement, alleging that the borrowers were using the sanctions as 'an excuse not to honour their contractual obligations'.[196] The claimant applied for summary judgment on the basis that the sanctions were subject to exceptions that authorised repayment of existing loans and that the borrowers had in fact continued to make payments after the sanctions came into effect, which demonstrated that performance was not impossible. The borrowers acknowledged default of the loan agreement but contended that the sanctions had the effect of discharging, frustrating, or suspending the contractual obligations due to supervening illegality. The English Commercial Court held in favour of the claimant lender. The court interpreted the EU sanctions to allow the repayment of the loan in the event that a licence was granted by the sanctioning authorities. Since the borrowers had previously obtained such permissions and even made payments, this demonstrated that it was not impossible for them to obtain a licence again. This meant that the defence of supervening illegality and frustration had 'no real prospect of success' at trial.[197] Accordingly, the court granted summary judgment in favour of the claimant lender.

Another important case decided in Singapore highlights the commercial maritime dimensions of sanctions-based banking complications and their intersection with shipping practice. In *Kuvera Resources Pte Ltd v JPMorgan Chase Bank NA*, a Singaporean trading company held two confirmed letters of credit relating to coal shipments between Indonesia and the Middle East.[198] When it attempted to collect as the beneficiary by providing documents compliant with the letters of credit, the confirming bank – a US bank branch based in Singapore – issued its own confirmations. Each of the bank's confirmations contained a bespoke sanctions clause, which read: 'Should documents be presented involving any country, entity, vessel, or individual listed in or otherwise subject to any applicable restriction, we shall not be liable for any delay or failure to pay.'[199] During the bank's internal post-presentation sanctions screening procedures, the bank discovered a 'red flag' as one of the vessels that had moved coal in the underlying trade, the *Omnia*, had apparently used a different name, the *Lady Mona*, and had been owned by a Syrian national, making the transaction subject to US sanctions targeting Syria. Taking the position that the documents issued in accordance with the letters of credit demonstrated the involvement of a vessel subject to US sanctions, and referencing the sanctions clause, the bank refused to pay the confirmed letters of credit. The claimant filed an action in the High Court of

[195] ibid, para [16].
[196] ibid.
[197] ibid, para [55].
[198] *Kuvera Resources Pte Ltd v JPMorgan Chase Bank NA* [2023] 1 Lloyd's Rep 604 (Singapore HC) (Vinodh Coomaraswamy J).
[199] ibid, 606.

the Republic of Singapore on the basis that payment of the confirmed letters of credit was wrongfully rejected. The claimant argued that it was not bound by the sanctions clause because the bank's confirmations were not a contractual term. Alternatively, it alleged that the sanctions clause was 'fundamentally inconsistent' with the purpose of the bank's confirmations because it made 'illusory' the irrevocable nature of the confirmed letters of credit.[200] The defendant bank argued that the clause was both binding and narrow enough not to interrupt its role as an alternative payor to the beneficiary because it could be invoked only if there was an objective risk of exposure to sanctions. Relying on expert testimony supporting its position of US sanctions exposure, along with direct albeit retrospective correspondence with OFAC officials for the purpose of the litigation, the bank alleged that the facts demonstrated an objective sanctions risk and warranted reliance on the sanctions clause.

The trial court held for the bank. It reasoned that the sanctions clause was a binding and enforceable contractual term that did not disrupt the bank's role as an independent payor to the beneficiary.[201] It also credited the expert testimony describing the likelihood of US sanctions exposure, emphasising that OFAC had published regulatory guidance that specifically warned shipping industry participants of the risk of 'red flags' such as concealed vessel ownership structures, changed vessel names, and other 'deceptive shipping practices' commonly deployed to evade sanctions, including those targeting Syria.[202] The court found that OFAC would have regarded payment under the confirmed letters of credit a breach of sanctions. For this reason, the questionable vessel ownership history of the *Omnia* supported the bank's determination under its 'risk-based approach to sanctions compliance' to invoke the sanctions clause and avoid contractual performance.[203] But the Singapore Court of Appeal reversed the decision below, ruling that the bank breached its obligations under the confirmed letters of credit by refusing to pay against fully compliant documents.[204] Although the court affirmed the trial court's position that the sanctions clause in the bank's confirmation was a binding contractual term, it found that the clause imposed a burden on the bank to objectively establish the involvement of a vessel subject to sanctions – in this case showing that the *Omnia* was 'Syrian-owned at all material times'.[205] The court found that the bank had not met this burden through the circumstantial evidence it provided, including its retrospective correspondence with OFAC for the purpose of the litigation. The court reasoned that OFAC was not mentioned in the sanctions clause itself and that since an OFAC enforcement action theoretically could be appealed and reviewed through the US court system, the OFAC

[200] ibid, 616.
[201] ibid.
[202] ibid, 624.
[203] ibid.
[204] *Kuvera Resources Pte Ltd v JPMorgan Chase Bank NA* [2024] 2 Lloyd's Rep 541 (Singapore CA) (Steven Chong J).
[205] ibid, 546.

correspondence was not enough to show through evidence admissible in a judicial proceeding that payment on the confirmed letters of credit would have definitively amounted to a sanctions breach. Although the court acknowledged that the OFAC correspondence and expert testimony provided in support of the bank's position may have demonstrated a legitimate sanctions risk, this was not enough to meet the objective burden implicit in the sanctions clause. For the bank to successfully invoke its own sanctions clause, the court explained, it had to overcome a *prima facie* inference that the shipowner was not Syrian during the relevant period, which the court described as 'an issue capable of objective determination' through commercially available compliance tools.[206]

III. Reflections

Arbitral awards and court judgments issued in response to sanctions-related disputes demonstrate a stark evolution in perception towards their effects on maritime transactions. The earliest cases illustrate a palpable scepticism over the legal status of sanctions – especially those imposed under UN auspices. The SMA award in *Dundas Shipping* evidences this perspective as the arbitral panel described sanctions as a 'novel hazard' running parallel to other 'conventional' perils affecting maritime trade, but then conceptually resisted their interference with 'hallowed' contractual agreements and even questioned the 'theoretical existence' of sanctions as enforceable legal mechanisms.[207] In the decades that followed, suspicion faded as UN-level sanctions were framed through national implementation under more familiar domestic legal instruments. This is evident in the *Gulf Group Panama* case as the arbitrators recognised the genuine commercial barriers imposed by the US Executive Orders and OFAC regulations implementing UN sanctions on Haiti, and later in the *Respol Petroleo* case affected by Turkish enforcement of UN limitations on Iraqi crude exports.[208] Especially in scenarios in which national authorities assessed financial penalties for sanctions violations, this was presumptively recognised as a legitimate commercial barrier, such as in the *Belship Navigation* case, where the arbitral panel found that the US sanctions targeting Cuba were so well known that they had to be understood in the international shipping community as a 'cornerstone' of regulatory policy that warranted legal compliance reactions worldwide.[209]

But not all of this perception shift can be attributed to the implementation of sanctions into national law. As sanctions proliferated during the 1990s and early 2000s, contracting parties began to more commonly reference sanctions

[206] ibid, 550.
[207] *Dundas Shipping & Trading Co Ltd v Stravelakis Brothers Ltd*, SMA 1174 (NY Arb 1977).
[208] *Gulf Group Panama SA v Conti-lines SA (Brasca) (The M/V Coral I)*, SMA 3287 (NY Arb 1996); *Repsol Petroleo SA v Sun International Ltd (M/T Orduna)*, SMA 2967 (NY Arb 1993).
[209] *Belship Navigation Inc v Sealift Inc (The M/V Huntsville)*, SMA 3429 (NY Arb 1998).

directly in charterparty agreements, which had the effect of converting disputes arising out of sanctions barriers into questions of contract interpretation. For instance, although the SMA arbitral panel in *Tankers International* found that the delays caused by Iraq's stalled negotiations with the UN over the execution of the Oil-for-Food Programme did not excuse the charterer from bearing the resulting costs, this was not due to any finding that the UN sanctions lacked legitimate legal status; rather, the result hinged on the interpretation of an express provision that allocated the risks of loading delays on the charterer if caused by the inability to load cargo 'conforming to United Nations resolutions'.[210] Likewise, the arbitral panel in *Gulf Group Panama* not only found a genuine barrier to performance in the US implementation of the Haiti sanctions, but also through the contract's reference to lawfulness obligations 'prescribed by the U.N. Haitian blockade'.[211] The flood of more recent cases evidence that this anticipation of sanctions-based disruption expressed through explicit clauses is now standard practice for compliance and risk-shifting purposes, reflecting the contemporary sentiment that sanctions are an incontrovertible variable in the commercial maritime landscape.

On the merits, cases addressing sanctions-related issues reveal common patterns in contractual and principle-based argumentation. Relying on standard form provisions and explicit sanctions clauses, the contractual arguments can be divided into two primary categories: those relying on clauses that excuse performance by way of mutual exceptions, and those relying on clauses that directly allocate liability between the parties. Within the first category are *force majeure* and 'restraint of princes' clauses. Judicial and arbitral reactions to these mutual exceptions clauses have been mixed. For instance, in *Great Beluga Shipping*, the SMA arbitration panel rejected the charterer's argument that the legal barriers imposed by UN and US restrictions on the export of Iraqi crude mutually excused the parties from performance on the basis of a *force majeure* provision because it could have loaded from a different port or sub-chartered the vessel.[212] And in *Tankers International*, the SMA panel was unmoved by the charterer's argument that the loading delays caused by stalled diplomatic negotiations amounted to a 'restraint of princes' even though the charterparty at issue contained an explicit sanctions compliance warranty.[213] Similarly, the *Greek Fighter* case shows that 'restraint of princes' language embedded in a broad *force majeure* provision will not necessarily release the charterer from its fundamental obligations to engage in lawful trades and nominate safe ports, which the charterer did not fulfil in that case when it stored sanctioned Iraqi crude on the vessel just off the coast of the UN-compliant UAE.[214] In each of these cases, the determinations favoured

[210] *Tankers International LLC v Bayoil Supply and Trading Ltd (The M/T Raphael)*, SMA 3739 (NY Arb 2002).

[211] *Dundas Shipping & Trading Co Ltd v Stravelakis Brothers Ltd*, SMA 1174 (NY Arb 1977).

[212] *Great Beluga Shipping Inc v Bayoil Inc (The Energy Explorer)*, SMA 3033 (NY Arb 1993).

[213] *Tankers International LLC v Bayoil Supply and Trading Ltd (The M/T Raphael)*, SMA 3739 (NY Arb 2002).

[214] *Ullises Shipping Corp v Fal Shipping Co Ltd (The Greek Fighter)* [2006] Lloyd's Rep Plus 99 (Comm).

the shipowner. However, SMA arbitrators reached a contrary result favouring the charterer in *Respol Petroleo*, as the panel found that the UN sanctions on Iraq as enforced via the Turkish pipeline closure did amount to a *force majeure* event.[215] A similar result in the *Laysun Service Co Ltd* case demonstrates that a *force majeure* argument can also resonate when there are practical barriers that arise as a more remote consequence of the sanctions, such as the inability to obtain customs permits and the unwillingness of third-party banks to process payments.[216] But, as shown by the seminal *MUR Shipping* decision, a finding of *force majeure* may still favour the shipowner if the clause at issue defines a limited measure of 'reasonable endeavours' that the affected party must pursue in efforts to overcome sanctions barriers.[217]

As for clauses that aim to directly allocate liability between the contracting parties, these may take the form of either standard boilerplate provisions or bespoke sanctions clauses. For instance, in the charterparty context, the standard risk-assigning clauses commonly referenced in sanctions-related disputes include language addressing freight, demurrage, and hire during delays. Again, the cases vary in outcome. In *Tankers International*, the SMA panel applied an 'absolute' demurrage liability approach favouring the shipowner when a dispute between Iraq and the UN led to delayed loading, despite the fact that the charterparty contained a tailored provision contemplating disruption caused by sanctions.[218] The arbitral panel in *Nordic American* reached a different result on similar facts, holding that it would not make 'commercial sense' to find the charterer responsible for the costs of delays caused by US sanctions on Iraq following its invasion of Kuwait because the barriers were unexpected and swift, making the cargo discharge temporarily impossible, irrespective of the underlying performance obligation expressed in the charterparty.[219]

As sanctions clauses have evolved with more sophisticated wordings, this has affected the methods of dispute resolution. Contemporary sanctions clauses not only include language that explicitly shift liability between the contracting parties in the event of risk exposure but may also demand pre-and-post contract due diligence such as vessel vetting, real-time tracking, and cargo origin and destination verification. The *Brujo Finance* case is a key illustration of how these clauses function in practice, as the SMA panel found that the language of the sanctions clause gave the shipowner wide discretion to avoid contractual performance ordered by the charterer that 'could expose' it to sanctions, which it found was a distinct possibility given that the charterer requested the shipowner to perform an STS transaction with a vessel that had a recent trading history of engaging in suspicious activity just off the coast of the heavily sanctioned state of Venezuela.[220] But again,

[215] *Repsol Petroleo SA v Sun International Ltd (M/T Orduna)*, SMA 2967 (NY Arb 1993).

[216] *Laysun Service Co Ltd v Del Monte International GmbH* [2023] Lloyd's Rep Plus 15 (Comm).

[217] *RTI Ltd v Mur Shipping BV* [2024] 1 Lloyd's Rep 621 (UKSC).

[218] *Tankers International LLC v Bayoil Supply and Trading Ltd (The M/T Raphael)*, SMA 3739 (NY Arb 2002).

[219] *Nordic American Shipping A/S v Bayoil (USA) Inc*, SMA 2972 (NY Arb 1993).

[220] *Brujo Finance Co v Sea Energy Co (The MT Alkimos)*, SMA 4388 (NY Arb 2020).

these clauses do not always favour the shipowner. In *Gravelor Shipping*, it was the bareboat charterer who benefitted from the sanctions-attuned contract drafting, as the court found that the clauses at issue warranted commercially reasonable modifications to performance rather than outright cancellation when the shipowner suddenly became subject to sanctions, which complicated the processing of hire payments.[221] In the *Tonzip Maritime* case, the charterer was the beneficiary of the sanctions clause because it used objective language that required the shipowner to establish that in its 'reasonable judgment' the alleged blacklisted connection to the cargo-owning company made it subject to the risk of enforcement or at least 'open to the danger of sanctions', which was a burden the shipowner failed to meet.[222] At the same time, the *Ceto Shipping* case illustrates that although a clause's reference to reasonableness may add an objective component to the required risk assessment, it does not mandate absolute certainty, in part because such a high standard would be unworkable in the context of measuring the likelihood of an enforcement action subject to some level of prosecutorial discretion.[223]

The marine insurance and trade finance cases add further guidance on sanctions clause drafting, as courts have reached diverging results dependent on whether the language grants the insurer or service provider subjective discretion to assess sanctions exposure or whether it demands an objective demonstration of sanctions risk. As with the discretionary charterparty language in *Brujo Finance*, which granted broad authority to the shipowner to invoke the sanctions clause, the marine insurer in *Arash Shipping* successfully relied on similarly permissive language to avoid paying a claim that 'may, in the opinion of the Insurer, expose' it to sanctions.[224] In juxtaposition, the court in *Mamancochet Mining* reached a different result due to the objective language in the insurance policy, which required the insurer to demonstrate payment of the claim 'would expose' it to sanctions.[225] Similarly, the sanctions clause in the letters of credit in *Kuvera* imposed an objectively high burden on the bank to establish the likelihood of a sanctions violation.[226] However, at least in the context of security paid to court as part of a collision liability agreement, as demonstrated by the *Tina I* case, even a subjective and discretionary sanctions clause might not provide the intended contractual protection if it runs counter to the overriding purpose of the agreement.[227] Together, these cases show both the value and the limits of sanctions clause wordings. Objective clauses may appear balanced but they tend to impose a high burden of proof that may defeat the purpose of the clause to offer more than a contractual unlawfulness defence, while subjective language provides the needed

[221] *Gravelor Shipping Ltd v GTLK Asia M5 Ltd* [2023] 2 Lloyd's Rep 239 (Comm).
[222] *Tonzip Maritime Ltd v 2Rivers Pte Ltd* [2025] EWHC 2036 (Comm).
[223] *Ceto Shipping Corp v Savory Shipping Inc* [2025] EWHC 2033 (Comm).
[224] *Arash Shipping Enterprises Co Ltd v Groupama Transport Sveriges Angfartygs Assurans Forening* [2011] 2 Lloyd's Rep 607 (CA).
[225] *Mamancochet Mining Ltd v Aegis Managing Agency Ltd* [2018] 2 Lloyd's Rep 441 (Comm).
[226] *Kuvera Resources Pte Ltd v JPMorgan Chase Bank NA* [2023] 1 Lloyd's Rep 604 (SGCA).
[227] *Oghiaanous Khoroushan Shipping Lines Co of Kish v Owner of the Vessel 'Tina I'* [2024] SGHCR 12 (SGHC).

flexibility to react to sanctions uncertainty but are one-sided and could be abused to justify opportunistic avoidance. Although clauses granting discretion limited by reasonableness may occupy the middle ground, case law has already revealed uncertainty over their interpretation.

Beyond these clause-based arguments, the cases also relay doctrinal reasoning relying on principles of illegality, impossibility, and frustration. In some cases, the breach of the lawfulness obligation was self-evident by the enforcement action taken by national authorities, such as in the *Greek Fighter* case in which UAE officials seized the vessel and cargo.[228] But when illegality has been contested, courts and arbitrators have been challenged to weigh in on the scope of the sanctions to determine whether contractual performance meets the lawfulness threshold. This can be a perplexing scenario, as answering the question has often required courts and arbitrators to predict how sanctioning authorities – sometimes based in foreign jurisdictions – might enforce trading restrictions under a patchwork of rules embedded in multilateral commitments, legislation, executive action, administrative regulations, and regulatory guidance, subject to carve-outs, derogations, and exceptions via licences. This task is particularly challenging if sanctions require the application of foreign law or involve fragmented approaches, as evidenced by the various cases addressing the Iran sanctions following the US withdrawal from the JCPOA while the remaining state parties sought to hold the diplomatic deal together.[229]

In part for this reason, litigation and arbitration on the legality issue has often referenced direct correspondence with sanctioning authorities as a basis to ascertain whether contractual performance would be permitted.[230] Courts and arbitrators have reacted to this evidence (or lack thereof) in different ways. In the *IRISL v Steamship Mutual* case, the P&I club worked closely with UK authorities to ascertain whether cover was authorised by the Iran sanctions and licences, but when it did not receive a definitive answer the insurer preemptively cancelled cover. Due to this acquiescence, it was the court, not HM Treasury, which ultimately evaluated the legality of the insurance contract. In contrast, in *Star Tankers*, the arbitral tribunal expressed frustration that OFAC officials provided 'little help' in explaining the scope of the Venezuela sanctions, which led it to sidestep the matter altogether.[231] In contrast, the SMA arbitrators in the *Playa Shipping* case were more willing to assess OFAC licensing rules, including by analysing direct correspondence with OFAC.[232] While in *Kuvera*, although OFAC provided a letter for the purpose of the litigation to clarify that, if performed, the banking transaction would have run afoul of the sanctions, the court found this retrospective assessment was not dispositive in

[228] *Ullises Shipping Corp v Fal Shipping Co Ltd* (*The Greek Fighter*) [2006] 1 Lloyd's Rep Plus 99 (Comm).
[229] *Mamancochet Mining Ltd v Aegis Managing Agency Ltd* [2018] 2 Lloyd's Rep 441 (Comm).
[230] *Playa Shipping Corp v Citgo Petroleum Corp (The M/T Mambo)*, SMA 4418 (NY Arb 2021).
[231] *Star Tankers Inc v Citgo Petroleum Corp*, SMA 4399 (NY Arb 2020).
[232] *Playa Shipping Corp v Citgo Petroleum Corp (The M/T Mambo)*, SMA 4418 (NY Arb 2021).

answering the question of lawfulness.[233] Even if performance is likely to attract an enforcement action, the lawfulness inquiry does not end there, as it may be possible to obtain a specific licence from a sanctioning authority. The outcome then hinges on weighing the prospect of obtaining such a licence, which in the charterparty context raises the secondary question of who – shipowner or charterer – is responsible for navigating the licensing process. This, of course, may be dictated by contract, but when it is not, courts and arbitrators have instead relied on equitable principles to allocate the responsibility by considering – as in the *Star Tankers* and *Gulf Group Panama* cases – which party is more likely to have the superior knowledge of sanctions compliance processes.[234] As in the *DVB Bank* case, it also may be relevant to consider whether a licence has been successfully obtained in the past, or, as in the *OCM Maritime* case, whether it is likely that a licence would be granted in the future.[235]

Beyond lawfulness, alternative arguments framed as contractual impossibility may still resonate, especially in scenarios where the complications arise from intermediary banks self-regulating payment processing in efforts to broadly avoid sanctions risk or any perception of impropriety. In fact, due to the over-compliant practices of financial institutions, the impossibility argument may exceed the scope of illegality because even if a transaction is unlikely to result in a sanctions enforcement action, the practical challenge of making payments may create genuine barriers to contractual performance. A finding of impossibility, however, does not necessarily result in performance discharge, as the sanctions disruption due to impossibility may only be temporary, which can have the effect of suspending rather than excusing the obligation to perform.[236] Furthermore, as demonstrated by the *Gravelor Shipping* case, the party whose performance is disrupted by sanctions-related payment complications may still be able to overcome this barrier through alternative means, such as making payment in non-contractual currencies or into a frozen account.[237] Consequently, although the impossibility argument is potentially wider in scope than illegality, its effectiveness is limited by the high burden of proving its application.[238] The alternative argument of frustration has been unsuccessful so far as a basis to address the consequences of sanctions

[233] *Kuvera Resources Pte Ltd v JPMorgan Chase Bank NA* [2023] 1 Lloyd's Rep 604 (SGCA).

[234] See eg *Star Tankers Inc v Citgo Petroleum Corp*, SMA 4399 (NY Arb 2020). Of course, if there is already a general licence in place, performance would be lawful so there would be no basis to seek a specific licence. See *Playa Shipping Corp v Citgo Petroleum Corp (The M/T Mambo)*, SMA 4418 (NY Arb 2021).

[235] *DVB Bank SE v Shere Shipping Co Ltd* [2013] EWHC 2321 (Comm); *OCM Maritime Nile LLC v Courage Shipping Co* [2022] 2 Lloyd's Rep 619 (Comm).

[236] See eg *Tankers International LLC v Bayoil Supply and Trading Ltd (The M/T Raphael)*, SMA 3739 (NY Arb 2002).

[237] See eg *Gravelor Shipping Ltd v GTLK Asia M5 Ltd* [2023] 2 Lloyd's Rep 239 (Comm). Recall, however, that in *Mur Shipping* the UK Supreme Court held this was a 'non-contractual' solution. *RTI Ltd v Mur Shipping BV* [2024] 1 Lloyd's Rep 621 (UKSC).

[238] A trend in this sanctions-related argument of impossibility has recently appeared in banking contexts as well. See generally RL Kilpatrick Jr, 'Sanctions-based Impossibility' (2024) *Lloyd's Maritime and Commercial Law Quarterly* 221.

disruption, as courts and arbitrators have recognised its narrow application. As shown in the *Great Beluga* case, performance may be unlawful and impossible due to sanctions yet the contract is not frustrated.[239] The same principle applied in the *IRISL* case, as the court accepted that the insurance contract was partially unlawful but not frustrated.[240] In any event, frustration and the other principle-based theories are not likely to be considered in isolation. Rather, parties tend to invoke these doctrines alongside boilerplate or tailored clauses for a multi-pronged argument.

Case law and industry trends suggest parties are increasingly turning to due diligence investigations both to comply with sanctions mandates and to protect their contractual rights. In the *Belship* case, the burden of investigation into the 'pedigree' of the vessels was a point of contention that led to a split in the arbitration award over whether a shipowner was required to have detailed knowledge of all of the parties in a sub-chartering chain.[241] A parallel question of vessel ownership led the court in *Kuvera* to explain that due to the availability of commercial intelligence products the vessel ownership history was 'objectively ascertainable'.[242] Moreover, the *Brujo Finance* case shows that a 'tracking service' or other commercial intelligence provider might provide an important source of evidence when determining whether to invoke contractual argument on sanctions grounds. However, the inadequate screening deployed in the *Tonzip Maritime* case that turned up inconclusive evidence to justify invoking the sanctions clause serves as a warning of the level of sophistication that may be necessary to meet the implicit burdens created by contractual solutions.[243] As regulatory authorities increasingly mandate counterparty identity investigations, know-your-cargo inquiries, and the examination of vessel trading histories including real-time scrutiny of geolocation data, these burdensome measures are likely to demand the expertise of third-parties specialising in sanctions compliance. These techniques will undoubtedly improve over time with advances in artificial intelligence and machine learning, especially given the multilateral synergy seeking to reign in the 'dark fleet' through transparency tools. With a dynamic body of case law now establishing guideposts, courts and arbitrators will be poised to react to the inevitable contractual innovations incorporating these advances.

[239] *Great Beluga Shipping Inc v Bayoil Inc (The Energy Explorer)*, SMA 3033 (NY Arb 1993).
[240] *Islamic Republic of Iran Shipping Line (IRISL) v Steamship Mutual Underwriting Association (Bermuda) Ltd* [2011] 1 Lloyd's Rep 195 (Comm).
[241] *Belship Navigation Inc v Sealift Inc (The M/V Huntsville)*, SMA 3429 (NY Arb 1998).
[242] *Kuvera Resources Pte Ltd v JPMorgan Chase Bank NA* [2023] 1 Lloyd's Rep 604 (Comm).
[243] *Tonzip Maritime Ltd v 2Rivers Pte Ltd* [2025] EWHC 2036 (Comm).

6

Statecraft

I. Introduction

Sanctions are not the only form of weaponised trade policy. Various other economic measures are routinely deployed by governments to promote geopolitical objectives, including embargos, boycotts, tariffs, and export controls, as well as positive 'soft power' approaches, such as the provision of humanitarian aid, infrastructure financing, or targeted procurement of goods and services.[1] These tools may be utilised to enhance national security, protect domestic industries, combat smuggling, promote political values, build rapport with diplomatic or military allies, or to execute economic confrontation popularly characterised as 'trade wars'.[2] Like other forms of geopolitical disruption, the origins of these strategies and the commercial responses to their implementation have a rich history. A fascinating phase in this story occurred during the Napoleonic Wars. After France was defeated by the British Navy in the Battle of Trafalgar, which deterred Napoleon from attempting an invasion across the English Channel, France announced a 'Continental System', which purported to prohibit neutral ships from trading with Britain.[3] Since France did not have the resources to establish a true naval blockade to consistently enforce these restrictions, it instead threatened third countries with ground invasions if they refused to abide. These trade rules spurred clever contract innovations in the marine insurance markets. For instance, a 'Napoleon Clause' – effectively an early version of the FC&S clause – specifically relieved insurers of liability for seizures caused by customs enforcement 'in any river, port or place under the jurisdiction of Napoleon, or under the jurisdiction of any power under his control, or in alliance with him'.[4] Britain countered the French restrictions with parallel measures by raising fees on European ships arriving at British ports that had previously called in France and by seizing American vessels trading in the French West Indies.[5] Insurers adapted again through broader clauses excluding

[1] See DA Baldwin, *Economic Statecraft* (Princeton University Press, 2020); other scholars have described this toolkit of economic levers as 'geoeconomics'. See RD Blackwill and JM Harris, *War by Other Means: Geoeconomics and Statecraft* (Belknap / Harvard University Press, 2016).

[2] See NO Oermann and HJ Wolff, *Trade Wars: Past and Present* (OUP, 2022).

[3] See generally LE Davis and SL Engerman, *Naval Blockades in Peace and War: An Economic History Since 1750* (CUP, 2009).

[4] See eg *Black and Burke v The Marine Insurance Co*, 11 Johns 287 (SC New York, 1814).

[5] The US responded to these French and British trade restrictions by imposing its own 'embargo' on trade with both nations. See DA Irwin, *Clashing Over Commerce: A History of US Trade Policy* (Chicago University Press, 2017).

cover for loss 'on account of any illicit or prohibited trade'.[6] Frustrated with Napoleon's antics, Russia eventually refused to comply with French trade rules, which (just as Napoleon had threatened) led to war. The Russians defeated the French, bringing the Continental System to an end, but its legacy lived on to contextualise trade wars and commercial adaptations in the many decades that followed.

During the First World War, Germany's economy relied substantially on foreign inputs for domestic manufacturing. Deploying trade policy as a means of warfare, both the US and UK adopted 'Trading with the Enemy' legislation to curb economic engagement with Germany and the Central Powers using a flexible statutory basis to impose embargos, export controls, and other restrictive measures.[7] Following the Treaty of Versailles, economic pressure was then used to subject Germany to harsh reparations for its role in the war. In the interwar period, a trend in isolationism and trade protectionism began to take hold, especially in the US, reflecting a countermovement to the nascent internationalist views of those advocating for multilateral initiatives such as the League of Nations. This shift was exacerbated by the Great Depression, which spurred the US Congress to pass the Smoot-Hawley Tarriff Act of 1930 to substantially increase import taxes on foreign goods.[8] These measures spawned trade policy retaliation, which compounded economic troubles, leading the US Congress to reverse course by the mid 1930s. By that point German resentment towards economic reprisals imposed after the First World War had mobilised a resurgent nationalism reflected in the rise of the Nazi cause in Europe, while the security situation in Asia and Africa was already unravelling with Japan's continued annexation of Chinese territory and the Italian incursion into Ethiopia. As the Second World War began to rage on multiple fronts, the US initially deployed trade policy to support Britain, China, France, and the Soviet Union under a Lend-Lease programme, while simultaneously aiming to portray a neutral position.[9] But after the 1941 Japanese attack on Pearl Harbor, this illusion of neutrality was abandoned as the US joined its allies in direct hostilities and economic warfare against the Axis Powers until 1945.[10]

[6] See *Duerhagen v United States Insurance Co* [1816] 2 Serg & Rawle 309 (SC Pennsylvania).

[7] These measures included multilateral export controls on manganese used in steel production. See N Mulder, *The Economic Weapon: The Rise of Sanctions as a Tool of Modern War* (Yale University Press, 2022). These Trading with the Enemy statutes were later used for other coercive economic purposes. See N Mulder, 'The Trading with the Enemy Acts in the Age of Expropriation, 1914–1949' (2020) 15 *Journal of Global History* 81.

[8] See Irwin (n 5).

[9] The Lend-Lease programme initially allowed for the finance of war supplies on credit if beneficiary countries could not pay, but this eventually evolved into a form of aid with no expectation of repayment. See US Department of State, Office of the Historian, 'Lend-Lease and Military Aid to the Allies in the Early Years of World War II'.

[10] See J Scherner, 'Germany, Blockade and Strategic Raw Materials in the Era of the Two World Wars' (2024) 46 *The International History Review* 515; S Garon, 'Operation STARVATION, 1945: A Transnational History of Blockades and the Defeat of Japan' (2024) 46 *The International History Review* 535.

In the postwar era, the international community vigorously pursued multilateralism through the creation of new institutions. This included not only the UN but also the Bretton Woods institutions (the International Monetary Fund and the World Bank), which were designed to provide access to capital for reconstruction. Trade policy, however, remained a pricklier subject. Although there were negotiations and proposals to establish an International Trade Organization akin to the other post-war institutions, it never fully materialised.[11] Instead, the General Agreement on Tariffs and Trade (GATT), which had entered into force as a temporary measure in 1947, remained the framework for international trade rules until it was replaced by the World Trade Organization (WTO) decades later.[12] The GATT contained basic aspirational rules, including national commitments to refrain from trade discrimination; to maintain a baseline for unconditional 'most favoured nation' treatment of imports; to convert non-tariff barriers into more transparent tariffs; and to commit to regular negotiations for further concessions to promote freer trade. The GATT, however, allowed for exceptions, including the right to impose countervailing measures in response to unfair trade practices, such as subsidies and dumping, or to take actions necessary for the protection of 'essential security interests'.[13] Recognising the potential for political abuse, however, this national security exception was rarely invoked.

Despite these lofty ambitions to reduce economic barriers, the Cold War obstructed the multilateral trade agenda. In conjunction with its ideology-driven proxy conflicts, throughout the Cold War various forms of statecraft were deployed to promote competing political objectives. Continuing on with the investment strategy that had driven the wartime Lend-Lease programme, the US helped finance reconstruction in Western Europe under the Marshall Plan and similar programmes in Asia, which involved the distribution of large amounts of humanitarian aid and financial assistance to allies and even former wartime foes.[14] Following the cessation of hostilities in the Chinese Civil War and the Korean War, the US and other allies within the NATO alliance coordinated to impose import bans and export controls on the Soviet Union, the People's Republic of China, and other aligned communist countries, through policies aimed at preventing strategic 'dual use' technologies from reaching their ideological rivals.[15] The Soviet Union and the Warsaw Pact countries embraced parallel barriers through their own

[11] See AF Lowenfeld, *International Economic Law* (2nd edn, OUP, 2008) ch 3.

[12] The GATT was replaced by the WTO in 1995.

[13] This exception is provided in Article XXI of GATT.

[14] The US simultaneously ended its Lend-Lease aid to the Soviet Union, which may have contributed to ideological confrontation. See DC Copeland, *A World Safe for Commerce: American Foreign Policy from the Revolution to the Rise of China* (Princeton University Press, 2024).

[15] Dual-use items were targeted because they could be used for either civilian or military purposes. In efforts to control export of these goods to the Soviet-aligned bloc, in 1949, the US, the UK, France and other Western countries established a Coordinating Committee for Multilateral Export Controls (CoCom). See M Mastanduno, *Economic Containment: CoCom and the Politics of East-West Trade* (Cornell University Press, 1992).

multilateral institutions, including limitations on travel, trade, and information exchange with the West.[16]

Even countries not directly embedded within the Cold War ideological dichotomy engaged in creative forms of economic statecraft during this period. Among the most consequential of such measures was the oil embargo imposed by a coalition of Arab states under the Organization of Arab Petroleum Exporting Countries following the Yom Kippur War in 1973.[17] During the war, the US and other Western states had supported Israel by resupplying its military. In response, a bloc of Arab states acted in concert to reduce oil production and implement an oil embargo to impede shipments to the US and other Israeli allies, including the UK, Canada, Japan, and the Netherlands. Using the embargo as a bargaining chip, the Arab state coalition demanded that Israel withdraw from certain occupied territories and that third countries like the US stop supporting Israel militarily, financially, and diplomatically. This export restriction strategy dubbed the 'oil weapon' created a global energy shortage and placed substantial stress on the global economy, which at the time depended on Middle East oil exports. It also produced a remarkable body of case law examining the contractual implications of the restrictions and their wide-ranging knock-on effects.

Despite these disruptions, technological developments, especially the invention and proliferation of the shipping container in the second half of the twentieth century, greatly enhanced the physical ability to move cargo through multimodal transport processes, which bolstered the belief that trade liberalisation and open market reforms could provide new opportunities for economic development.[18] Among the most significant evolutions of this era was the rise of China. Following open market reforms initiated during the 1970s, China's economy grew exponentially while it pursued a modified brand of 'capitalism with Chinese characteristics'.[19] Demonstrating its newfound commitment to free trade principles, China joined the GATT in observer status in 1987. Following the controversial government crackdown on pro-democracy protesters at Tiananmen Square in 1989, the US and other Western governments targeted China with trade controls intended to limit its access to arms and strategic technologies.[20] However, after the dissolution of the Soviet Union in 1991 and the overall reductions in ideology-driven tensions, even with relations damaged by human rights concerns, Western democracies continued forging a path towards mutually beneficial trade

[16] See L Crump and S Godard, 'Reassessing Communist International Organisations: A Comparative Analysis of COMECON and the Warsaw Pact in Relation to their Cold War Competitors' (2017) 27 *Contemporary European History* 85.

[17] See FA Verrastro and G Caruso, 'The Arab Oil Embargo – 40 Years Later' (*Center for Strategic & International Studies*, 16 October 2013).

[18] See M Levinson, *The Box: How the Shipping Container Made the World Smaller and the World Economy Bigger* (Princeton University Press, 2008).

[19] See Y Huang, *Capitalism with Chinese Characteristics: Entrepreneurship and the State* (CUP, 2010).

[20] See H Meijer, *Trading with the Enemy: The Making of US Export Control Policy toward the People's Republic of China* (OUP, 2016).

with China, which fuelled its path to join the WTO and established the conditions for unprecedented commercial interdependence in the following decades.[21] Other post-Cold War free trade initiatives, including the expansion of EU trade liberalisation and integration and the North American Free Trade Agreement (NAFTA), further solidified the trade policy sentiments of the 1990s. Even the newly organised Russian Federation began pursuing a years-long accession process to join the WTO in the final years of the twentieth century.

These trends began to shift with the post-9/11 threat of transnational terrorism, which burdened travel and trade with security-attuned priorities. Then, the 2008 financial crisis destabilised markets worldwide, providing tangible evidence of the risks of economic interconnectivity. After formally joining the WTO in 2012, Russia annexed Crimea within two years, which initiated the first wave of Western trade sanctions against Russia. Populist backlash to the economic shifts from globalisation was also catching up.[22] By the mid 2010s, the Doha 'Development Round' of WTO negotiations was effectively abandoned after years of negotiations failed to reach multilateral consensus on steps for new trade barrier concessions. In a 2016 referendum, the UK voted to end its participation in the EU through Brexit. Shortly thereafter, the US withdrew its advocacy for a major regional trade agreement: the Trans-Pacific Partnership.[23] China, meanwhile, engaged in 'positive' statecraft tactics by cultivating alliances through large-scale aid, lending, and infrastructure projects under its Belt and Road Initiative.[24] In part to counter China's influence and to combat what was perceived to be its abuse of WTO rules, the US began establishing new restrictions on the import of Chinese goods – even invoking the contentious 'national security' exception – sparking market fears of a 'de-coupling' between what were by then the world's two largest economies.[25] The US then began imposing further trade barriers on imports from Canada, the EU, and other traditional allies, calling into doubt the free trade principles that had been central to Western economic policy since the end of the Second World War.[26] Aggravating these isolationist trends, the Covid-19 pandemic followed, with borders across the world suddenly shut in the spring of 2020. These incremental changes mobilised shipping industry organisations to update contract wordings.[27]

[21] During this period, market reforms occurred in other communist countries, including Vietnam, which joined the WTO in 2007.

[22] See E Braw, *Goodbye Globalization: The Return of a Divided World* (Yale University Press, 2024).

[23] However, in 2020 the US did agree to an updated version of NAFTA in the United States-Mexico-Canada Agreement.

[24] See J Reilly, *Orchestration: China's Economic Statecraft Across Asia and Europe* (OUP, 2021).

[25] See BJ Murrill, 'The National Security Exception and the World Trade Organization' (Congressional Research Service, 28 November 2018).

[26] See JB Heath, 'The New National Security Challenge to the Economic Order' (2020) 129 *Yale Law Journal* 1020.

[27] Following the outbreak of the Covid-19 Pandemic, BIMCO and INTERTANKO both published new clauses addressing infectious diseases. See eg BIMCO Infectious or Contagious Diseases Clause for Time Charter Parties 2022. A version of this clause has already been examined in case law. See *Bunge SA v Pan Ocean Co Ltd (The Sagar Ratan)* [2025] EWHC 193 (Admiralty).

In 2022, BIMCO produced a new Force Majeure Clause triggered in enumerated situations that 'prevents a party from performing one or more of its contractual obligations', including not only war, terrorism, piracy, and various forms of unrest, but also statecraft measures falling outside the scope of sanctions – namely 'embargo', 'generally imposed trade restriction', 'boycott', and 'act of government or public authority whether lawful or unlawful'.[28]

After years of cultivating mutually beneficial trade, including investment in multiple large-scale undersea natural gas pipelines, the war in Ukraine (literally) damaged the physical and institutional infrastructure for economic integration between Europe and Russia.[29] Russia meanwhile pursued trading opportunities elsewhere, including with China and India, while seeking to avoid the consequences of Western sanctions and export controls. Protectionist policies expanded further in 2025, when the US announced major cuts to humanitarian assistance programmes and imposed widespread tariffs on many of its trading partners at levels not seen since the Smoot-Hawley era.[30] These measures were rationalised on the basis of wide-ranging policy justifications, including national security, the protection of domestic manufacturing, and alleged failures to regulate illegal immigration and illicit drug supply lines. China, in particular, was targeted by the US, not only with tariffs and export controls but also with a controversial regulatory proposal to apply 'service fees' on China-linked ships accessing US ports.[31] China responded by weaponising its own trade controls, including threats to limit access to its coveted rare earth minerals needed for high tech manufacturing.[32] These burgeoning trade wars confirmed that the world had entered a new phase of protectionism. As it had done throughout trading history, the shipping industry worked inventively to adapt by finding contractual solutions, including through new clauses allocating risks arising out of US–China adversarial dynamics.[33]

[28] See BIMCO Force Majeure Clause 2022. Since sanctions issues are covered under BIMCO's sanctions clauses, a background note published along with its Force Majeure Clause clarifies that it is not designed to cover sanctions but instead addresses other 'restrictions placed on imports/ exports by a country/ EU to protect domestic markets/ products. It could be a general ban on imports of goods or raw materials from other countries or the application of tariffs or a ban on exports to protect, for example, domestic supplies.' ibid.

[29] See United Nations, 'At Security Council Meeting on Sabotage of Nord Stream Pipeline, Many Speakers Condemn Attacks on Critical Infrastructure, Stress Need for Accountability' (4 October 2024).

[30] See E Prasad, 'The Age of Tariffs: Trump is Launching a Turbulent New Era for the Global Economy' *Foreign Affairs* (3 April 2025). These US tariffs were imposed by the executive rather than the legislative branch of government. Consequently, some were challenged in the courts. See eg *VOS Selections Inc v Trump*, 149 F4th1312 (Fed Cir 2025), 607 US (USSC 2026).

[31] See US Trade Representative, 'Notice of Action and Proposed Action in Section 301 Investigation of China's Targeting the Maritime, Logistics, and Shipbuilding Sectors for Dominance', 90 Federal Register 17114 (23 April 2025).

[32] See H Farrell and A Newman, 'The Weaponized World Economy: Surviving the New Age of Economic Coercion' *Foreign Affairs* (19 August 2025).

[33] See BIMCO USTR Clause for Time Charter Parties 2025; INTERTANKO Model Clauses for US Chinese Nexus Fees 2025.

II. Statecraft in Commercial Maritime Disputes

A. Chartering and Carriage

i. Embargos

A series of cases from the 1970s addressed the contractual impact of embargos and protective export controls relating to a global energy crisis flowing from conflict between Israel and neighbouring states in the Middle East. In *Sicula Oceanica SPA v Corco Tankers Inc*, the parties had contracted under a voyage charter to move oil from Libya to Italy in two consecutive voyages on the *Auriga Primo*.[34] Before the agreement was finalised, the Libyan government nationalised its oil sector. Then, in response to the outbreak of the Yom Kippur War on 6 October 1973, the Libyan government announced it would cut oil production, increase the price of oil exports, and establish an embargo on all shipments destined for the US. However, at that time, Libyan authorities still authorised vessel nominations for oil exports to non-US destinations, including Italy. After the completion of the first voyage in November of that year, the Libyan state-controlled oil exporter notified the charterer that there would be no additional loadings available for a period of at least one month, but it also communicated that it 'shall advise you soon' regarding the possibility of loading the following month.[35] The charterer responded by refusing to participate in the second voyage. The shipowner obtained alternative employment for the vessel and brought an action in arbitration to recover for its losses. In arbitration, the charterer argued it was excused from performing the second voyage under the doctrine of frustration and by reference to a 'restraint of princes' clause since the Libyan state-controlled oil exporter refused to authorise cargo loading 'for an indefinite period'.[36] The shipowner argued that even though the Libyan restrictions had changed the expected timeline for cargo loading, the charterparty could still be performed but with some delays. It alleged that despite the delays, the charterer's obligation to perform remained intact. The panel agreed with the shipowner. First, it held that the Libyan authorities had implied that loading would be authorised at a later date. The panel explained that '[a]n obstacle which merely delays performance is not one that frustrates performance, unless the delay is so lengthy as to frustrate the commercial object of the venture'.[37] Second, it reasoned that the 'restraint of princes' defence did not apply to the dispute because the temporary restrictions 'never fully prohibited shipments from Libya' and, therefore, the cargo loading was not restrained under the meaning of the clause.[38]

[34] *Sicula Oceanica SPA v Corco Tankers Inc (The Auriga Primo)*, SMA 1096 (NY Arb 1977) (Richard H Sommer, R Glenn Bauer, and Martin J McHugh).

[35] ibid, 3.

[36] ibid.

[37] ibid.

[38] ibid.

SMA arbitrators reached the same result but for different reasons in *Academy Tankers Inc v Phillips Petroleum Co.*[39] In that case, the parties agreed to move crude oil from North Africa to the US on two vessels under voyage charters. The charterer instructed the shipowner to load the vessels in Libya, but before the vessels were able to take on cargo, Libya declared an embargo on oil shipments to the US. The charterer cancelled the charterparties on grounds of frustration and refused to nominate alternative loading ports. The shipowner then secured alternative employment for the vessels and commenced arbitration against the charterer. The shipowner alleged that the charterer breached its obligations under the contracts on the basis that the Libyan restrictions did not amount to frustration or impossibility, and that the charterparties contained a 'special provision' that held the charterers liable for demurrage, bunkers, and other expenses if it is 'unable to load the Vessel for political or whatever other reasons'.[40] The charterer contended that since the Libyan port had been nominated, once the Libyan embargo was imposed this ended the contracts 'by operation of law'.[41] It further argued that the charterparties' 'restraint of princes' clauses shielded it from liability for losses caused by such restrictions.[42] The panel held for the shipowner. The panel noted that due to the timing of the fixtures, the contracts were affected by 'a state of great turmoil' in the oil sale and transportation markets following the outbreak of the war.[43] Accordingly, the panel explained that the 'threat of an Arab oil embargo directed toward pro-Israel countries was a distinct possibility' during the time of contracting.[44] For this reason, the panel rejected the argument that the Libyan embargo brought an end to the contracts by frustration. Instead, it found that this eventuality was 'clearly anticipated by the parties' as evidenced by the special provision referencing the possibility of 'political' reasons for delay costs that must be absorbed by the charterer.[45] Since the parties 'foresaw such an event occurring', the charterer could not be relieved of its contractual obligations.[46]

An English court, in *Seabridge Shipping Ltd v Antco Shipping Ltd (The Furness Bridge)*, addressed a similar factual scenario by focusing on whether it was 'commercially practicable' for a charterer to procure an alternative cargo to perform a contract disrupted by the 1973 Libyan oil embargo.[47] The parties had agreed to a voyage charter to move oil from a 'European Mediterranean'

[39] *Academy Tankers Inc v Philips Petroleum*, SMA 1342 (NY Arb 1978) (Harry G Webber, Lloyd C Nelson, and Michael A VanGelder).
[40] ibid, 2.
[41] ibid, 6.
[42] ibid.
[43] ibid.
[44] ibid.
[45] ibid.
[46] ibid, 7. The panel explained that the charterer disregarded viable options to perform, such as waiting until the embargo was lifted and paying demurrage in the interim. The panel did not separately address the charterer's 'restraint of princes' argument.
[47] *Seabridge Shipping Ltd v Antco Shipping Ltd (The Furness Bridge)* [1977] 2 Lloyd's Rep 367 (Comm) (Kerr J).

port to Freeport, the Bahamas. The charterer had previously established a pattern of loading oil from Libya, which was also the expectation for this transaction, even though the contract contained a broader contractual loading range.[48] The shipowner nominated the vessel for loading, but on the same day Libya and other Arab countries imposed an oil embargo on the US as well as Caribbean nations where US importers regularly sourced refined oil products. As a result, the charterer claimed that 'the Arab boycott prevented Libyan oil from being shipped to Freeport for ultimate use in the USA'.[49] The shipowner treated this as a wrongful repudiation and withdrew the vessel. The charterer contended, conversely, that it was excused under a mutual exceptions clause referencing 'restraint of princes' or that the contract was already void on grounds of frustration or commercial impossibility. In London arbitration, the umpire held for the shipowner. Although the umpire acknowledged that there was a restraint of princes preventing loading in Libya and there were also 'commercial and practical difficulties' in finding an alternative cargo from a non-Libyan port within the permitted loading range, the charterer failed to meet the burden to establish no such alternative cargo was available.[50] The English Commercial Court affirmed the result favouring the shipowner, but it took issue with the lack of clarity in the umpire's award, reasoning that taken as a whole the facts, 'do not amount to a finding that the shipment from any contractual non-Libyan port or ports was commercially impossible'.[51] Nevertheless, irrespective of the umpire's ambiguous findings, considering the 'whole tenor' of the award, the court found that the charterer did not meet its evidentiary burden to show that the contract could not have been performed by loading at ports outside of Libya.

This line of embargo cases has not always resulted in favourable results for the shipowner. In another case impacted by the Libyan embargo, *Alma Shipping Corp v Amerada Hess Shipping Corp*, the parties had agreed to a voyage charter to move crude oil on the *SS Calliopi Carras* from Libya to St Croix, US Virgin Islands.[52] By the time the vessel had completed discharge of cargo for a previous voyage to Yugoslavia, the Yom Kippur War had broken out. The *Calliopi Carras* arrived at anchorage off Libya on 17 October 1973, just before Libya issued a decree suspending oil shipments to the US. Once the shipmaster received notice that the vessel could not load the cargo bound for St Croix, the charterer engaged in 'hurried negotiations' to arrange for the Libyan cargo to be loaded for delivery to England, which was still permitted under Libyan law. The shipmaster performed this alternative voyage, but a dispute later arose regarding the amount of freight the charterer owed the shipowner, which resulted in additional delays. In arbitration,

[48] The court explained that the range described as 'European Mediterranean' was unusual and may have been a broker's error.

[49] ibid, 371.

[50] ibid, 376.

[51] ibid, 379.

[52] *Alma Shipping Corp v Amerada Hess Shipping Corp*, SMA 1111 (NY Arb 1977) (Aelred Joseph Slattery and John C Moore) (J Bond Smith dissenting).

citing a war risk clause, the shipowner argued that the charterer was liable for the originally agreed freight for the voyage to St Croix, plus demurrage. The charterer countered that the charterparty was frustrated by the Libyan embargo to the US and that the terms of the contract released both parties from liability because the embargo was a 'restraint of princes'. The panel majority held for the charterer on the basis that the Libyan embargo 'constituted a frustration of the purpose of the Charter'.[53] The panel majority explained that since the original charter had been frustrated, the charterer's alternative orders to England had the effect of making 'a new charter'.[54] To justify its holding that the war risk clause was not relevant to resolving the dispute, the panel majority reasoned that the 'Libyan embargo did not compel the Owner to load the cargo nor to discharge at [England]. Nor did it compel the Charterer to ship the cargo.'[55] But because the contract had been frustrated, the shipowner was not entitled to freight for the originally planned voyage to St Croix and was instead entitled to a reasonable freight rate based on quantum meruit principles. A dissenting arbitrator expressed the position that the frustration doctrine should not apply because the contract had adequately allocated such risks and provided that the shipowner should be entitled to freight.[56]

Other cases from this era reveal how oil export hubs beyond Libya were disrupted as oil export policy was deployed for diplomatic leverage. In *Mobil Shipping and Transportation Co v Michail A Karageorgis SA*, the parties agreed to a voyage charter to move crude oil on the *M/T Corona* from a flexible loading range in the Persian Gulf to the Netherlands.[57] During the contract period, several Arab states, including Algeria, Kuwait, and Saudi Arabia, had placed embargos on oil exports to Western states, including the Netherlands. These measures prevented the charterer from obtaining a cargo within the contract's trading limits. The charterer eventually found a partial cargo with a destination of Brazil and the parties agreed to an addendum to the charter expanding the trading limits to facilitate the voyage.[58] After performance, the charterer refused to pay for deadfreight, demurrage, and other costs related to the Brazil shipment on grounds that the original contract had been frustrated by the various regulatory actions restricting oil exports to the Netherlands. The shipowner commenced SMA arbitration to collect the unpaid invoices, and the panel held in its favour. The panel found that the charterer was well aware of the '"chaotic" conditions that existed in the Persian Gulf area prior to and up to the date the charter was concluded'.[59] For this reason, as a 'prudent' charterer, it should have known at the time of contracting that there was a possibility that Persian Gulf states would

[53] ibid, 2.
[54] ibid, 3.
[55] ibid.
[56] ibid, 3.
[57] *Mobil Shipping and Transportation Co v Michail A Karageorgis SA (M/T Corona)*, SMA 961 (NY Arb 1975) (Arthur E Ferris, William H Yost, and Charles G Herbermann Jr).
[58] The award does not specify the country of export for the shipment to Brazil.
[59] ibid, 2.

prohibit oil exports to the Netherlands, especially since other regional states had already done so. According to the panel, the charterer's knowledge that certain exporting states may resort to the 'oil weapon' precluded a finding of charterparty frustration.[60]

Another embargo-adjacent case from the era is *Kawasaki Steel Corp v Sardoil SPA (The Zuiho Maru)*.[61] In the autumn of 1973, the parties had contracted under a voyage charter to move oil from Saudi Arabia to Italy on the tanker *Zuiho Maru*. Before the cargo was loaded, the Saudi Arabian Minister of Petroleum announced a decision to cut production and place embargos and quotas on certain Israeli-aligned countries. At the direction of the Saudi Arabian government, the Saudi-based oil exporters instituted a rationing schemes affecting individual oil tankers attempting to load cargo for export. These restrictions prevented the charterer's ability to secure a full cargo, with a shortage of 7.52 per cent after loading. The shipowner alleged the charterer was liable for deadfreight and demurrage incurred during a related loading delay. The charterer argued that it was excused from performance on the basis of illegality and frustration and that it only owed the shipowner for the voyage on a quantum merit basis. The arbitral tribunal held for the shipowner. On appeal, the English Commercial Court affirmed. It reasoned that the charterer had an 'absolute obligation to supply a cargo of the contractual description and quantity'.[62] The court explained that the charterer's inability to secure the cargo 'because of difficulties or delays in the country of shipment' was not 'capable of bringing the doctrine of frustration into operation'.[63] The fact that the vessel actually did perform the voyage carrying the vast majority of the cargo demonstrated that there was 'nothing like a sufficiently fundamental change of circumstances' that could give rise to a frustrating event.[64] On the issue of lawfulness, the court found the argument 'equally untenable' because the cause of the inability to load the full cargo was 'due indirectly' to the Saudi regulations and the resulting rationing scheme by the oil exporters, which meant '[i]llegality is therefore irrelevant'.[65] To excuse the charterer for the shortfall, the court explained, 'would require some express and sufficient exemption clause', which was not present in the contract.[66]

Also examining the knock-on impacts of embargos, in *Skibs A/S Suderoy v Joc International BV*, an SMA panel assessed the impact of a Turkish oil export ban motivated by the aim of stabilising domestic supply rather than an overtly political rationalisation.[67] The dispute involved a voyage charter of the tanker

[60] ibid.
[61] *Kawasaki Steel Corp v Sardoil SPA (The Zuiho Maru)* [1977] 2 Lloyd's Rep 552 (Comm) (Kerr J).
[62] ibid, 555.
[63] ibid.
[64] ibid.
[65] ibid.
[66] ibid.
[67] *Skibs A/S Suderoy v JOC International BV (M/T Tore Knudsen)*, SMA 1108 (NY Arb 1977) (Ferdinand E Sauer and Lloyd C Nelson) (Harry B Chassen dissenting).

M/V Tore Knudsen, which had been expected to load petroleum products in Bulgaria and Turkey for discharge in the Netherlands in the autumn of 1973. The vessel successfully loaded in Bulgaria, but the Yom Kippur War broke out before the second loading in Turkey. When the vessel arrived off Turkey, the Turkish authorities refused to authorise loading as the Turkish government had issued an immediate ban on the export of all petroleum products for the purpose of conserving domestic supplies. After several days, the charterer directed the vessel to go ahead and sail to the Netherlands without the second Turkish cargo. The shipowner sought recovery for demurrage and deadfreight, which the charterer refused to pay. In arbitration, the charterer argued that the inability to load in Turkey was caused by a 'restraint of princes' in the form of the Turkish embargo, or, alternatively, that it was relieved of liability under the doctrines of frustration and commercial impossibility.[68] The shipowner countered that the charterer had failed to formally seek an embargo exception from Turkish authorities, and claimed that there were alternative cargoes available in Italy that could have mitigated the loss. The panel majority held for the shipowner. It reasoned that the refusal of the Turkish authorities to permit the loading did not excuse the charterer from the obligation to load a 'full and complete cargo'.[69] It explained that the charterer's inability to secure a cargo in Turkey as intended did not relieve it from contractual liability to fully compensate the shipowner for its losses, especially given that a mitigating alternative cargo from Italy appeared to be a 'feasible solution to the supply problem'.[70] A dissenting arbitrator expressed the view that the 'restraint of princes' clause should have excused the charterer from performing due to the 'unexpected intervention of the Turkish government in banning the export of all petroleum products' at a time when oil was in short supply due to widespread embargos.[71]

A final case from the era demonstrates how these various embargos and export restrictions created bunkering challenges that generated charterparty disputes. In *Amax Mineral Sales Corp v Interocean Shipping Co*, the parties had agreed to a one-year time charter for the use of the *SS Nagano* when the oil embargos imposed by various exporting states started to take hold on the bunker supply markets.[72] In response to the embargos, while the vessel was in Japan at the port of Kobe preparing to leave on a voyage to Dunkirk, France, by way of the Cape of Good Hope, the Japanese Petroleum Board imposed quota regulations that substantially raised the price of bunkering, causing 'some difficulty with the bunker nomination'.[73] In addition, with inadequate bunkering available off South Africa, the shipmaster slowed the vessel's speed to reduce bunker consumption and eventually diverted

[68] ibid, 2.
[69] ibid, 3.
[70] ibid.
[71] ibid, 6.
[72] *Amax Mineral Sales Corp v Interocean Shipping Co (The SS Nagano)*, SMA 1233 (NY Arb 1978) (Ferdinand E Sauer and Lloyd C Nelson) (Hammond L Cederholm dissenting).
[73] ibid, 3.

to Spain to obtain bunkers before resuming at normal speed for the remainder of the voyage to France. This caused delays, which the charterer argued justified an adjustment of hire, in part because at the time the charter was agreed the shipowner 'must have known of the potential disruption of international bunker supplies'.[74] The shipowner contested this view, contending instead that the difficulties in bunkering due to the embargos meant it 'had no choice but to reduce speed on the voyage in order to conserve the remaining fuel'.[75] In arbitration, the SMA panel majority held for the charterer. Although the panel acknowledged the oil embargos imposed were 'the culprit for the subsequent refueling concern', if the shipmaster would have properly refuelled in Japan, the slow steaming and 'unnecessary prolongation of the voyage' would have been avoided.[76] As a result, the majority awarded the charterer an amount equivalent to 4½ days of the daily hire rate. A partially dissenting arbitrator expressed the opinion that the charterer should have recovered even more compensation for the shipowner's failure to procure bunkers, reasoning that the shipowner had not reacted swiftly to the 'rumble of unrest and possible war' and the 'pending threat of oil embargo'.[77]

ii. Boycotts

Trade restrictions styled as boycotts have given rise to analogous challenges. In *Universe Tankships Inc v Burmah Oil Tankers Ltd*, SMA arbitrators addressed the question of whether a vessel was off hire during a delay caused by a Nigerian boycott on South Africa implemented to protest its apartheid policies.[78] The parties had agreed to a time charter for the oil tanker *Universe Explorer*. In 1979, at the charterer's direction, the vessel commenced a voyage from the Middle East to Rotterdam around the Cape of Good Hope, with the intention of partially loading oil in the Middle East, topping off in Nigeria, and then discharging in the Netherlands. As the vessel sailed around the Cape, it received stores by helicopter off of Cape Town, South Africa. When the vessel later arrived in Nigeria, a pilot boarded to help aid local navigation. When the shipmaster offered him a beer, the pilot noticed that it was a South African brand and told the shipmaster that Nigerian law prohibited access to ships that had previously called at South Africa.[79] The shipmaster then disclosed to the Nigerian authorities that the vessel had loaded stores near Cape Town. The Nigerian authorities ordered the vessel to

[74] ibid, 4.
[75] ibid.
[76] ibid, 5.
[77] ibid, 7.
[78] *Universe Tankships Inc v Burmah Oil Tankers Ltd (The Universe Explorer)*, SMA 2016 (NY Arb 1984) (Richard H Sommer and Nicholas J Healy Jr) (Donald M Kennedy partially dissenting).
[79] ibid, 1. The award described the Nigerian boycott in this way: 'The Nigerian regulation prohibits ships from entering Nigerian waters if, within the six weeks preceding arrival to a Nigerian Terminal, the ship had called at a port in South Africa, Namibia or Israel. A port call, as defined in this regulation, includes receipt of services from shore by helicopter or launch.'

leave the berth and refused to authorise loading for several weeks. This forced the charterer to contract for a different vessel to load the cargo in Nigeria, although it arranged a second cargo for the *Universe Explorer* once the Nigerian authorities eventually authorised port access. The charterer alleged that the *Universe Explorer* was off-hire during the delay, which the shipowner contested and demanded hire for the entire voyage.[80] In arbitration, the charterer claimed the shipowner's decision to take on stores in South Africa was a breach of navigating limits that led to a 'restraint' that frustrated the main purpose of the charterparty and that the events fell within the 'interference of authorities' language of the off-hire clause.[81] The charterer further argued that when the shipmaster provided information to the Nigerian authorities regarding the vessel's contact with South Africa, this was a violation of US anti-boycott rules. The shipowner disputed these positions and alleged that by directing the vessel to load in Nigeria, the charterer had nominated a 'politically unsafe port'.[82] With respect to the US anti-boycott regulations, the shipowner claimed the vessel's customary trading patterns 'created a duty on the Vessel to continue the practice of storing off South Africa' because the anti-boycott rules prohibited 'adherence to Nigeria's boycott of South Africa'.[83] The SMA panel majority held for the charterer. It found that the charterer had properly placed the vessel off-hire as the off-hire clause expressly contemplated events like the actions of the Nigerian officials through its reference to 'interference of authorities'. It also rejected the notion that the charterer's nomination of Nigeria was a 'politically unsafe port' because it was the shipowner, not the charterer, who was aware that the vessel had received stores in South Africa, which ultimately gave rise to the 'Nigerian sanction'.[84] The panel further found that the shipmaster created the risk of restraint by taking on South African provisions and 'inadvertently "informing" the port authorities of the contact with South Africa'.[85] It also noted that the shipowner did not alert the charterer about the contact with boycotted South Africa, which could have allowed it to 'make an informed decision' about whether to risk a port call to Nigeria.[86] Finally, the panel majority rejected the shipowner's argument that anti-boycott regulations compelled the shipowner to take on South African stores and instead found that the vessel could have done so anywhere within the designated trading limits. Although the panel majority agreed that under the language of the charterparty and the US regulations the shipowner 'had to comply with both contractual obligations and public regulations', the panel held, '[t]hese requirements did not necessarily conflict'.[87]

[80] ibid.
[81] ibid.
[82] ibid, 4.
[83] ibid.
[84] ibid, 5.
[85] ibid.
[86] ibid.
[87] ibid, 7. The panel majority, however, limited the charterer's remedy to placing the vessel off-hire, finding that the charterer could not recover additional damages for alleged breach of the navigation limits. A partially dissenting arbitrator expressed the view that the shipowner should be liable 'for all foreseeable losses' sustained by the charterer.

Beyond the charterparty context, another form of boycott leading to shipping disruption is action taken by labour unions to achieve geopolitical objectives. In *International Longshoremen's Association v Allied International Inc*, the US Supreme Court addressed the fallout from a labour union's decision in January 1980 not to handle cargo arriving from or destined for the Soviet Union after its invasion of Afghanistan.[88] After the labour union imposed the boycott, which affected major ports along the US east and gulf coasts, a US-based importer of Russian wood products sued the union under a US labour statute creating a private right of action for the victims of 'secondary boycotts'.[89] In first instance, the US District Court for the District of Massachusetts held for the union finding that the activity was not within the scope of activity barred by the statute.[90] The US Court of Appeals for the First Circuit reversed, reasoning that US law did not allow unions to use its powers over neutral parties 'in aid of a random political objective far removed from what has traditionally been thought to be the realm of legitimate union activity'.[91] The US Supreme Court affirmed and held that the union's activity was a clear violation of US law, which prohibits unions from 'inducing employees to refuse to handle goods with the object of forcing any person to cease doing business with any other person'.[92] Noting that the union's purpose of boycotting was to protest the 'foreign and military policy of the Soviet Union', the court reasoned that 'as understandable and even commendable as the [union's] ultimate objectives may be, the certain effect of its action is to impose a heavy burden, as well as widening of industrial strife, that the secondary boycott provisions were designed to prevent'.[93] Declining to accept the union's request to carve out a 'political boycott' exception to the applicable labour statute, the court remarked, '[t]here are many ways in which a union and its individual members may express their opposition to Russian foreign policy without infringing upon the rights of others'.[94]

iii. Export Controls

Even when implemented for politically ambiguous reasons, sudden restrictions on cargo exports have given rise to contract disputes. In *ONE Shipping Ltd v Hercules Inc*, the parties had agreed to a voyage charter to move gum turpentine from

[88] *International Longshoremen's Association v Allied International Inc*, 456 US 212 (USSC 1982) (Powell J).
[89] ibid.
[90] *International Longshoremen's Association v Allied International Inc*, 492 F Supp 334 (D Mass 1980) (Skinner J).
[91] *International Longshoremen's Association v Allied International Inc*, 640 F2d 1368, 1378 (1st Cir 1981) (Campbell J).
[92] *International Longshoremen's Association v Allied International Inc*, 456 US 212, 221 (1982).
[93] ibid, 223.
[94] ibid, 227.

Nicaragua to the US.[95] As the charterparty was being negotiated in 1979, unrest in Nicaragua was occurring between Somoza and Sandinista political factions. The charterer became concerned that its turpentine product would be damaged because it was being stored near where fighting was taking place, so it contracted to export the product out of the country on the *M/T Onesky*. The charterer applied for an export permit with the Somoza-led Nicaraguan authorities, but while the permit was still pending the Sandinistas overthrew the government. After assuming power, the new Sandinista government issued a decree prohibiting certain exports under the threat of criminal prosecution. Citing the decree, the customs authorities in Nicaragua refused to issue an export permit to the charterer. On this basis, the charterer cancelled the charterparty. The shipowner then sought damages in SMA arbitration. In the proceedings, the charterer alleged that it was entitled to cancel the contract on the basis of the doctrine of frustration and a general exceptions clause, which referenced 'restraint of princes'.[96] The shipowner alleged this was wrongful termination because the charterer was aware of the situation in Nicaragua at the time of contracting and also failed to disclose to the shipowner the seriousness of the political unrest in the exporting country. It also argued that the real reason for the inability to export the cargo was not an export embargo by the Nicaraguan authorities but rather a failure to obtain an export permit which could have been acquired if the charterer's local affiliate had acted more quickly. The panel held for the charterer. It found that the political situation in Nicaragua leading to the emergency decree prohibiting exports fell within the language of the 'restraint of princes' provision. The panel interpreted the Nicaraguan decree to mean that 'shipment of turpentine was prohibited' and that shipping it without a permit 'would expose' the contracting parties to criminal liability.[97] The panel explained that not only the charterer but also the shipowner was 'well aware of the political climate' in Nicaragua at the time of contracting.[98] Since the shipowner did not even attempt to make changes or modifications to the exceptions clause referencing 'restraint of princes', it was bound by the liability limitation 'incorporated in the charter party in its usual form'.[99]

SMA arbitrators addressed a similar question involving unexpected export restrictions imposed by Venezuelan authorities in *Pioneer Navigation Ltd v Chemical Equipment Labs Inc.*[100] The parties had contracted under a voyage charter to move industrial grade highway rock salt from Venezuela to the US on the bulk carrier *MN Genco Ocean*. During the loading process, Venezuelan officials demanded the loading to be stopped and the cargo discharged due to

[95] *ONE Shipping Ltd v Hercules Inc (The M/T Onesky)*, SMA 1828 (NY Arb 1983) (Jack Berg, J Bond Smith, and Donald L Caldera).

[96] ibid, 2.

[97] ibid, 3.

[98] ibid.

[99] ibid.

[100] *Pioneer Navigation Ltd v Chemical Equipment Labs Inc (The MN Genco Ocean)*, SMA 4357 (NY Arb 2019) (John F Ring Jr and David W Martowski) (Louis P Sheinbaum dissenting).

a lack of permits. The permits were apparently required under a Venezuelan decree that restricted the export of food products because economic turmoil and currency devaluation was creating a market for Venezuelan food products to be purchased in bulk to sell on at higher prices in foreign markets, including in the neighbouring countries of Colombia and Brazil. The decree identified specific products designated under the Venezuelan tariff codes. Although table salt was on the list, industrial grade highway salt was not. Nevertheless, despite the possible misapplication of the export permit rules, the vessel operators departed Venezuela without the cargo. The charterer terminated the charterparty, alleging that the events justified cancellation under its terms, which the shipowner contested. In SMA arbitration, the charterer argued that the governmental permitting obligations and orders to depart amounted to a *force majeure* event under the contract and that the refusal to allow the cargo export fell within the 'restraint of princes' exception, or, alternatively, principles of frustration and impracticability ended the contract by operation of law. The shipowner argued that the elements of *force majeure* were not met, because the provision at issue only referenced a 'withdrawal' of export permits, which the shipowner alleged had never been granted in the first place.[101] It further argued that the governmental orders should not be considered a 'restraint of princes' because the measures falling within that provision are 'national, embargo-type actions by governments that apply across the board'.[102] In addition, the shipowner argued the charterer's justifications for cancellation should fail because it was 'well aware of the risks inherent in Venezuelan trading'.[103] The panel majority agreed with the shipowner. It reasoned that the charterer's obligation to perform under the contract was not excused by the *force majeure* clause in part because the reasons for the Venezuelan government's refusal to authorise the salt export was that the vessel lacked proper export documentation, which is 'customary and commercially normal'.[104] Branding the charterer's export arrangement a 'rogue contract' the majority explained that there were serious risks of doing business in Venezuela because of 'political and economic crises for over a decade which has thrown its trade into turmoil'.[105] It found that the international shipping community was clearly on notice that 'trading with Venezuela is fraught with risk and uncertainty'.[106] Consequently, the events were foreseeable and 'self-inflicted' by the charterer, which precluded a determination the contract should be set aside on the basis of the 'restraint of princes' clause, frustration, or other parallel avoidance doctrines.[107] Thus, the majority refused to burden the shipowner with the loss, which was a 'blameless, innocent bystander to an illegitimate

[101] ibid, 12.
[102] ibid, 13.
[103] ibid.
[104] ibid, 15.
[105] ibid.
[106] ibid.
[107] ibid.

and prohibited rogue transaction that went awry'.[108] A dissenting arbitrator expressed a contrasting view that the Venezuelan authorities' actions amounted to both a *force majeure* event and 'restraint of princes'.[109] The dissent reasoned that as a 'matter of reality and commercial practicability', the disruption caused by the Venezuelan authorities was beyond the control of the charterer and that the contract clauses should have excused its performance even in the absence of a 'war or crisis'.[110]

iv. Tariffs

Although tariffs have long been an important tool of economic statecraft, they have given rise to surprisingly few published contract-related decisions in the shipping context. A nineteenth century American court tangentially addressed the maritime dimensions of the issue in *Coca v Morris*.[111] In that case, in the summer of 1894, a US-based exporter contracted with a carrier to move a shipment of lard from Chicago to its customer in Cuba. When the cargo was already on the vessel in transit to Cuba, the US government enacted tariff legislation – the Wilson Act – which levied higher duties on sugar and other products from Cuba.[112] Before the shipment arrived in Cuba, Spain passed retaliatory legislation, including tariffs on American lard. The buyers sued the sellers for the additional costs caused by the tariffs, but the lower court dismissed the claim by finding the defendant free from fault and instead placing responsibility on the steamship company, which had 'refused to receive the lard on board until the next sailing, which was a week later'.[113] The US Court of Appeals for the Seventh Circuit affirmed. It reasoned that since the Spanish tariffs were put in place when the goods were already en route to Cuba, this scenario could not have 'reasonably entered into the minds of the parties when the order for the shipment was made'.[114] Since the goods had been shipped nearly two weeks before the Spanish duty was imposed, '[n]o one could know then that the Wilson bill would become a law, much less could it be known or contemplated that, if it did become a law, in consequence of it the Spanish government would retaliate so quickly by imposing a higher duty upon lard imported from the United States'.[115] The court explained that '[w]hen the contract was made, the chance that any such result would follow as the effect of the passage of tariff laws in the two countries was highly remote, and, whatever it might have been, must be considered as taken by the persons ordering the

[108] ibid, 19.
[109] ibid, 21.
[110] ibid, 25.
[111] *Coca v Morris*, 107 F 688 (7th Cir 1901) (Bunn J).
[112] This tit-for-tat tariff exchange reflects a deterioration in relations between the US and Spain in the years leading up to the Spanish-American War.
[113] ibid, 692. The trial court's decision was unpublished.
[114] ibid, 691.
[115] ibid.

goods'.[116] Accordingly, the damages claimed by the buyer were 'highly speculative in character' and 'too remote'.[117] If there was any fault, the court determined, it was on the steamship company for a delay in loading that prevented the lard shipment from arriving in Cuba before the Spanish tariffs took effect.

Much more recently, an American court entertained the argument that a 'trade war' between the US and China was a basis for avoidance of a maritime contract. In *Shelter Forest International Acquisition Inc v COSCO Shipping (USA) Inc*, a US-based importer of lumber and building materials contracted with a Chinese carrier in 2018 under a service contract in which the carrier guaranteed a specified freight rate contingent on the importer meeting a minimum shipment quantity of 5,000 20 foot containers over the course of the contract.[118] After damage and delays relating to two shipments, the importer sued the carrier alleging breach of its terms. The carrier counterclaimed on grounds that the importer failed to meet the service contract's minimum quantity provision by shipping less than half of the required containers. In defending the counterclaim, the importer argued that its failure to perform was excused by an express *force majeure* clause and under the doctrine of supervening impossibility due to the US government's 'broad trade war against China', which included increased tariffs on imported wood products. The US District Court for the District of Oregon rejected the importer's argument.[119] The court reasoned that the *force majeure* provision, 'excused either parties' non-performance for 'acts of god, strikes, embargoes, or events similarly beyond the knowledge or control of either party' but not 'commercial contingencies, for example, changing markets, poor management decisions and business declines, etc'.[120] The court reasoned that 'courts have been particularly hesitant to find that market changes resulting from governmental policies constitute force majeure', especially in the context of fixed-price contracts designed to protect both parties from the risks of market fluctuations.[121] The importer also had acknowledged becoming aware of the 'impending tariffs' on wood products from China well before entering into the service contract with the carrier, which demonstrated the foreseeability of the disruption.[122] Even after the restrictive trade policies were put into place, the importer continued shipping Chinese lumber, which showed that it was 'not prevented from shipping with [the carrier] by unforeseen forces beyond their control'.[123] Neither did the tariffs impose a 'supervening impossibility' on the importer.[124] Instead, the court found the importer's

[116] ibid, 691–92.
[117] ibid, 691.
[118] *Shelter Forest International Acquisition Inc v COSCO Shipping (USA) Inc*, 475 FSupp 3d 1171 (D Oregon 2020) (Russo J).
[119] ibid, 1186.
[120] ibid.
[121] ibid.
[122] ibid, 1187.
[123] ibid.
[124] ibid, 1188.

conduct revealed it had affirmatively chosen to take its business elsewhere after a breakdown in the commercial relationship with the carrier. As a result, the importer 'forfeited its right to claim that the "trade war" excused its obligations' under the service contract.[125]

v. Import Bans

In *Select Commodities Ltd v Valdo SA (The Florida)*, the English Commercial Court addressed the charterparty implications of a Nigerian regulation banning the bulk import of vegetable oil.[126] The parties had agreed to a voyage charter to move vegetable oil from Indonesia to Nigeria on the *M/T Florida*. Prior to loading in 2003, the charterer learned that the Nigerian authorities had imposed the import ban. It then notified the shipowner of the situation and provided a letter from Nigerian authorities, which explained that the decision to ban vegetable oil was 'basically on health ground[s] and also to protect local producers of such item'.[127] The charterer took the position that due to the import ban, it was 'left with no alternative but to cancel the shipment' because the contract had become 'frustrated by this event'.[128] The shipowner countered that the charterparty 'must remain in full force'.[129] When the charterer refused to perform, the shipowner found substitute employment for the vessel, and it commenced arbitration to recover its losses. In the arbitration, the shipowner alleged that a liberties clause contained in the charterparty granted it explicit recourse in the event that performance of the contract would be affected by supervening illegality or frustration. Since the parties had contemplated the scenario, the shipowner contended, this foreclosed the charterer's non-contractual defence of frustration. The charterer countered that the clause did not expressly or impliedly address the doctrine of frustration and emphasised that the shipowner had been informed 'well in advance' that performance of the contract would be 'impossible'.[130] The arbitrator held in favour of the shipowner on the basis that the contract contained explicit language, which had the effect of precluding the application of the frustration doctrine. Yet the arbitrator acknowledged that 'but for' the application of the liberties clause, the charterparty would have been frustrated by the Nigerian import prohibition.[131] The charterer appealed to the English Commercial Court, which reversed on grounds that the liberties clause did not apply because the charterer alerted the shipowner of the Nigerian import ban before the cargo was ever brought forward to load in Indonesia.

[125] ibid. 1187.
[126] *Select Commodities Ltd v Valdo SA (The Florida)* [2007] 1 Lloyd's Rep 1 (Tomlinson J).
[127] ibid, 3.
[128] ibid.
[129] ibid.
[130] ibid, 4.
[131] ibid, 2.

The court determined that since the arbitrator had already made a finding that the contract would have been frustrated but for the application of the liberties clause, since the clause did not apply, the frustration doctrine did excuse the charterer's performance.

vi. Aid Cancellation

Another form of statecraft – manipulation of the levers of humanitarian aid – have also given rise to maritime contract disputes. In *Tradax Internacional SA v Government of Pakistan*, during the spring of 1971, the government of Pakistan chartered the bulk carrier *M/V Olga Maersk* to carry wheat from the US Gulf of Mexico to Chittagong, East Pakistan (now Bangladesh), under a transaction supported by the US Department of Agriculture implementing US legislation designed to assist developing nations by financing the shipment of food grains.[132] The charterer had obtained purchase authorisations from the US government and the vessel had been approved. The charterparty itself referenced the US statute establishing the financing arrangements.[133] Once the contract was agreed, the charterer nominated the port of Houston for loading, and the vessel arrived there on 4 April. As the vessel awaited permission to berth, on 10 April Indian troops crossed the border of East Pakistan in response to a separatist movement there. Two days later, the US government cancelled the purchase authorisations for the shipment 'because of the situation in East Pakistan and the resultant congestion in the ports of that country'.[134] The charterer notified the shipowner that without the US government financing it could not obtain the cargo for shipment, and, on those grounds, refused to perform. The shipowner took the position that the charterer was in breach of the charterparty, and, after obtaining substitute employment for the vessel, pursued a claim in SMA arbitration. In the proceedings, the shipowner alleged the contract was a 'straight commercial transaction' that was breached by the charterer's failure to provide a cargo in return for the agreed freight. The charterer countered that charterparty was terminated by the actions of the US government by preventing loading 'pursuant to its own policy decision and thus exercised force majeure or its equivalent which excused further performance'.[135] Characterising the actions by the US government as a 'de facto embargo which also frustrated the charter', the charterer emphasised that all such shipments to East Pakistan were cancelled by the US government's 'pursuance of its foreign policy and in the light of the chaotic physical conditions and politico-military situation following the outbreak of hostilities in East Pakistan'.[136] Moreover, the charterer

[132] *Tradax Internacional SA v Government of Pakistan*, SMA 779 (NY Arb 1973) (George T Stam and Eric A Skoglund) (John P Besman dissenting).
[133] ibid, 3.
[134] ibid, 2.
[135] ibid 4.
[136] ibid.

alleged that 'the war itself was sufficient reason for either party to the charter to declare the voyage frustrated'.[137]

The panel majority agreed with the charterer. It reasoned that the parties had predicated their agreement on the availability of cargo furnished under the US humanitarian assistance law. When the US government exercised its statutory right to modify the assistance programme, it 'frustrated the commercial object of the contract and its performance with the result that the contract itself was thereby dissolved'.[138] Although, theoretically, the charterer could have tried to convince the US government to finance the shipment of the same cargo to West Pakistan, 'this would have been in performance of a different Charter Party'.[139] A dissenting arbitrator expressed an alternative view that the withdrawal of US financial arrangement for the shipment was not the equivalent of an embargo because US law did not expressly exclude the application of alternative financing. Thus, according to the dissent, while a full embargo of US wheat to East Pakistan by Executive Order or otherwise may have justified the application of the doctrines of frustration or illegality, since the US regulatory action only addressed the financing component of the transaction, regardless of the Government of Pakistan's financial difficulties, it was in breach of its contractual obligations as charterer by failing to secure the cargo as agreed.

vii. Political Restrictions

Geopolitical dynamics have sometimes led to navigation limits and travel restrictions affecting crews of certain nationalities. These measures, too, have led to commercial disputes. Among the cases examining such scenarios is *Mana Maritime Ltd v Seanav International Ltd*.[140] In 1988, the parties had agreed to a five-year time charter for the vessel *Mana*, which contained a provision authorising worldwide trading subject to narrow limitations. Among these trading limits was a clause providing, 'if vessel calls any port in People's Republic of China then no direct calls between People's Republic of China and Taiwan'.[141] In February 1990, the vessel was sub-chartered to a third party. The sub-charterer ordered the vessel to perform a voyage from Brazil to Taiwan and then from Taiwan to the People's Republic of China. Invoking the trading limits clause, the shipowner refused the order on the basis that the vessel was not permitted to sail directly between Taiwan and the Chinese mainland because this would violate Taiwanese law and 'render the vessel liable to blacklist and proscription from ever calling at Taiwan again'.[142]

[137] ibid.
[138] ibid, 5.
[139] ibid, 4.
[140] *Mana Maritime Ltd v Seanav International Ltd (The Mana)*, SMA 2669 (NY Arb 1990) (Manfred W Arnold).
[141] ibid, 2.
[142] ibid.

A sole SMA arbitrator held for the charterer. The award noted that the clause limited direct sailings from the People's Republic of China to Taiwan while it did not totally bar 'either-direction trading'.[143] The arbitrator pointed out that it was surprising that the shipowner did not create a 'more specific and restrictive' clause due to its prior trading experience and awareness of 'potential problems of penalties and/or blacklisting' that could arise in the event of direct Taiwan to People's Republic of China voyages, which could have been accomplished by deleting the first part of the sentence of the trading limits clause contemplating a first calling to mainland China.[144] Taking into account the Taiwanese regulations and the economic consequences that might arise from their enforcement, the arbitrator reasoned that since the trading limits clause did not explicitly address the scenario, 'the responsibility of meeting the local or governmental regulations lies with the Owners'.[145]

A Canadian case, *Evergreen Marine Corp v Worldwide Carriers Ltd*, addressed a similar scenario involving the interpretation of a trading limits clause, which allowed trading within the Institute Warranty Limits, but excluded 'Communist and Communist Satellite ports'.[146] In 1969, the parties had agreed to a time charter for the vessel *Central Trust*, which was sub-time chartered and then sub-voyage chartered to move pulpwood from Canada to Yugoslavia. After seeing the bill of lading for the first time and realising the vessel was expected to go to Yugoslavia, the shipmaster refused to sail there on grounds it was a communist country. The shipowner then withdrew the vessel, invoking the trading limits clause, which the charterer disputed on grounds that the clause did not apply to Yugoslavia. The Exchequer Court of Canada, Nova Scotia Admiralty District, held for the shipowner. The court drew from expert witness testimony explaining that a communist state was 'one that is ruled or dominated by the communist party' such as the Soviet Union's ruling party, as well as the 'Communist Legue of Yugoslavia' that had been a 'satellite of the U.S.S.R' until 1947–1948 and 'remained steadfastly adherent to the communist ideology' even after subsequent diplomatic tensions with the Soviets.[147] The expert also referenced 'power centres' of the 'communist world' at the time, including the Soviet Union, the People's Republic of China, Cuba, and Yugoslavia, but also expressed the opinion that the contractual reference to 'Communist satellite ports' was essentially a 'meaningless' expression.[148] The expert further testified that Yugoslavia 'could not be described as a communist satellite', but explained that it was 'as

[143] ibid, 3.
[144] ibid.
[145] ibid. The arbitrator also noted that 'this is not, as argued a case of commercial frustration or Restraint of Princes either, but rather a case dealing with the allocation of possible additional voyage expenses and the loss of time'. ibid, 3.
[146] *Evergreen Marine Corp v Worldwide Carriers Ltd*, 1971 AMC 200 (Nova Scotia Admiralty District 1971) (Thurlow J).
[147] ibid, 202.
[148] ibid, 202–03.

communist as any other country'.[149] Another witness – a chartering agent for Yugoslavian companies in New York – described a different perspective, including the unique features of the Yugoslavian economy and society suggesting there was a particular 'Yugoslavian mentality' that could not be properly categorised as either communist or capitalist.[150] Other evidence was provided suggesting the governments of Taiwan and Panama both regarded Yugoslavia as a communist country. Taking these views into account, as well as the fact that the charterer had apparently taken deliberate steps to conceal the Yugoslavian destination, the court found that for the purposes of interpreting the contract, 'Yugoslavia was clearly a communist country during the time it was a soviet satellite' and that it has 'continued to be a communist country, in the popular sense of that expression' even though the country had 'long since ceased to be or to be regarded as a satellite of the U.S.S.R.'.[151]

Courts and arbitrators have also addressed commercial disruption caused by governmental authorities refusing to allow vessels to access ports due to the citizenship of crew members. In *Rudolph A Ootker v Hamlet Shipping Inc*, the parties had agreed to a time trip charter for a cargo of bagged flour from the US to Egypt on the *M/V Alcazar*.[152] When the vessel arrived off the coast of Florida, US officials refused to permit loading because they had received details regarding the Polish nationality of some of the crew members. The US Coast Guard notified the shipmaster that it would not allow the vessel to access the port until eight Polish officers that were serving on the crew were first disembarked and detained in a hotel while the vessel was loading because the port zone in Pensacola, Florida, was a 'sensitive naval defense area' and was restricted by an agreement between the US and USSR.[153] The parties consented to the restrictions and facilitated the disembarkation arrangement, but this caused a relatively minor delay of less than two days. Nevertheless, the charterer deducted hire for the lost time and refused to pay for bunkers consumed during the delay. The shipowner commenced SMA arbitration to collect. In arbitration, the shipowner argued that the US Coast Guard's refusal to allow the vessel to access the port for reasons of naval defence was a 'restraint of princes' under the charterparty's exceptions clause. The charterer argued that the 'restraint of princes' clause should not apply because the shipowner could have discovered the details that eventually caused the delay through 'reasonable due diligence' such as obtaining the necessary crew list, clearances, and visas before the vessel arrived. The charterer also contended that the loss of the Polish officers during the loading period amounted to a 'constructive deficiency of men' that triggered the off-hire clause. The arbitral panel agreed with the charterer.

[149] ibid.
[150] ibid, 204.
[151] ibid, 205.
[152] *Rudolph A Ootker v Hamlet Shipping Inc (The M/V Alcazar)*, SMA 1512 (NY Arb 1980) (Frank L Crocker, Manfred W Arnold, and Joseph Simms).
[153] ibid, 2.

It reasoned that the shipowner's decision to employ the eight Polish officers amounted to a 'deficiency of men' because the crew members were 'statutorily prohibited because of their nationality from entering the port of Pensacola'.[154] In addition, due to its 'experienced' position in the trade, the shipowner 'should have known' under the diplomatic agreement between the US and USSR that 'Polish and other Communist flag vessels and [crews] are forbidden entry into certain U.S. ports and should have made arrangements for the immediate relief of the restricted officers upon the vessel's arrival'.[155] Since the shipowner did not do so, this caused a delay, which justified the charterer in placing the vessel off-hire and refusing to pay for bunkers.

A similar form of political restriction was at issue in *Transnational Maritime Inc v East Europe Import Export Inc.* There, the parties had agreed to move a cargo of cement from Romania to the Middle East on the *M/S Eurymachus*.[156] At the time of the charter, in 1976, Romania was a communist country. Before loading, the shipowner notified the charterer that it would not be able to perform the contract as agreed because even though the vessel was registered in Panama it was beneficially owned by Taiwanese nationals and had a Taiwanese crew. Under Taiwanese law, its nationals were prohibited from travelling to communist countries, including Romania. The charterer commenced SMA arbitration to pursue recovery of lost profits for the unfulfilled contract. During the proceedings, the shipowner argued that it had previously contacted Taiwanese authorities regarding the travel restrictions before agreeing to the charter, and that it genuinely believed performance was authorised. Only later did it learn that the Taiwanese crew was not allowed to go to Romania under Taiwanese law. The shipowner also argued that the travel restrictions amounted to an unforeseeable 'restraint of princes'.[157] The charterer countered that the shipowner should have been more familiar with the regulations before entering into the contract and that its failure to deliver the vessel at the port in Romania was a clear breach of the charterparty. The panel agreed with the charterer that the shipowner's failure to present the vessel in Romania was a wrongful breach. However, it found that the charterer had not demonstrated actual damages and had taken no steps to mitigate perceived losses through affirmative action, such as contracting with another shipowner to move the cargo.[158]

For different reasons, the citizenship status of individuals aboard a vessel played a significant role in a delay imposed by Taiwanese port authorities in *CA Venezolana de Navegacion v Bank Line (The Roachbank)*.[159] In the spring of 1979, the *Roachbank* was under time charter when the charterer gave orders for the vessel

[154] ibid, 3.
[155] ibid.
[156] *Transnational Maritime Inc v East Europe Import Export Inc (The M/S Eurymachus)*, SMA 1274 (NY Arb 1978) (Manfred W Arnold, Hendrik H VanBiema, and Miachel J O'Riordan).
[157] ibid.
[158] The panel did not directly address the shipowner's 'restraint of princes' argument.
[159] *CA Venezolana de Navegacion v Bank Line (The Roachbank)* [1987] 2 Lloyd's Rep 498 (Comm) (Webster J).

to load at Singapore with plans to stop in Taiwan before continuing on to ports in South America. In the South China Sea, the *Roachbank* encountered a small boat carrying nearly 300 Vietnamese migrants (apparently war refugees) who were 'in a pitiful condition'.[160] Since the migrants appeared to be in distress, responding to the 'centuries-old tradition of seafarers' to rescue others in danger, the *Roachbank* crew embarked the migrants on board and carried them to the next port of call in Kaohsiung, Taiwan.[161] When the vessel arrived, the Taiwanese authorities refused to allow the migrants to disembark and required the vessel to remain outside the port. Negotiations ensued, where the shipowner ultimately agreed not to let any of the rescued migrants off the vessel and to provide a bank guarantee to cover any breaches of the agreement. Following this agreement, the Taiwanese authorities granted permission for the vessel to enter the harbour, where cargo work was finally performed with the migrants staying on board throughout. But the delay lasted more than a week, which led to a dispute between the shipowner and charterer as to whether the vessel was off-hire during the lost time. In arbitration, the majority found that the vessel remained on hire because the *Roachbank* was still technically capable of having its cargo discharged by stevedores while the rescued persons were 'marshalled away from the immediate working area'.[162] It reasoned the Taiwanese authorities' 'attitude' regarding the vessel was an 'extraneous' cause, and that the migrants on board did not become part of the vessel's history and characteristics that might have placed the vessel within the language of the off-hire clause.[163] On appeal, the English Commercial Court affirmed, finding that the vessel 'was not prevented from full working'.[164] Instead, the vessel itself remained 'fully efficient' which, under the terms of the charterparty, meant that neither the presence of the rescued persons on the vessel nor the position of the Taiwanese port authorities in denying entry were sufficient causes to place the vessel off-hire.[165]

viii. Law Enforcement

Some charterparty disputes arising out of law enforcement initiatives have also carried geopolitical intimations. In *Sucden Middle-East v Yagci Denizcilik Ve Ticaret Ltd Sirketi (The Muammer Yagci)*, the parties had agreed to a voyage charter to move a cargo of sugar for discharge in Algeria.[166] Due to the alleged use of false

[160] ibid, 499.
[161] ibid.
[162] ibid, 501.
[163] ibid. To demonstrate the potential relevance of a vessel's history, the arbitrators referenced a hypothetical example of another delay caused by a geopolitical controversy: that of a vessel that is refused access to a port in an Arab nation because it had previously called to an Israeli port, even if there is 'no tangible relic of that port call'. ibid.
[164] ibid, 508.
[165] Leave for appeal was denied. See *CA Venezolana de Navegacion v Bank Line (The Roachbank)* [1988] 2 Lloyd's Rep 337 (CA).
[166] *Sucden Middle-East v Yagci Denizcilik Ve Ticaret Ltd Sirketi (The Muammer Yagci)* [2020] 1 Lloyd's Rep 107 (Comm) (Robin Knowles J).

import documents presented during the discharge process, purportedly to evade the payment of customs duties on the cargo, Algerian customs authorities seized the cargo, which caused a delay to the voyage for more than four months. The charterparty contained a *force majeure* clause that provided that if an enumerated event occurred, 'time so lost shall not count as laytime or time on demurrage or detention'.[167] Among the listed *force majeure* events was 'government interferences'.[168] The shipowner sought to collect demurrage for the delays, but the charterer refused, citing the *force majeure* clause. In arbitration, the tribunal held for the shipowner on grounds that the seizure was not interference because it was an ordinary reaction to the use of what the authorities believed to be fraudulent documents. The charterer appealed to the English Commercial Court, which reversed the award. Focusing on the meaning of the word 'interferences' used in the *force majeure* clause, the court found that the seizure fell within its terms because it could not be considered 'routine'.[169] The court explained that '[i]n the usual course of things cargo is not seized and property rights are not invaded in that way, and that remains the case even if seizure is experienced frequently, perhaps in one part of the world or another'.[170] Although the seizure by Algerian authorities may have been expected or justified given the allegation of falsified import documents, the court found the seizure was a *force majeure* event, which released the charterer from its demurrage obligations.

Another case addressing disruption by purported law enforcement action is the SMA arbitration award *SA Marine Corp SA v Canfornav Ltd*.[171] In that case, the parties had agreed to a time charter for the *M/V Energy Ranger*. As directed by the charterer, the vessel was loading a cargo of concentrates for a voyage from Chile to Canada when the vessel was served an order of detention by Chilean authorities on the basis that the US Drug Enforcement Agency (DEA) alleged illicit drugs were hidden in the cargo. A large force of Chilean police and DEA officials boarded the vessel, interrogated and confined the shipmaster and crew, and performed a search lasting more than six days. As part of the search, the authorities cut an access hole into the ship's side shell in an effort to inspect a section of the hold that was otherwise inaccessible because the vessel had already been loaded with cargo. The search produced no evidence of drugs and the detention order was eventually lifted. The hole in the side of the ship was patched temporarily and the vessel sailed to Montreal via the Panama Canal and St Lawrence Seaway. On arrival, the vessel suffered additional delays to repair the vessel. The charterer put the shipowner on notice that it intended to place the vessel off-hire for the delay and sought additional discounts for bunkers consumed. The shipowners disputed

[167] ibid, 108.
[168] ibid.
[169] ibid, 109.
[170] ibid.
[171] *SA Marine Corp SA v Canfornav Ltd (The M/V Energy Ranger)* SMA 3817 (NY Arb 2003) (Austin L Dooley and A J Siciliano) (Miachel A Van Gelder dissenting).

these claims and demanded arbitration. In the SMA proceedings, the charterer alleged that the off-hire clause contemplated the actions of the Chilean and US authorities under its language referencing loss of time caused by 'restriction'. The charterer argued that this language was a 'specially negotiated (or "dickered") amendment' to the standard off-hire clause, which warranted attention.[172] The shipowner countered that the although the term was added to the off-hire clause, it was not separately negotiated and was instead a carry-over provision from a 'pro-forma' contract provided by the charterer.[173] The shipowner further argued that the detention in Chile was 'not akin' to the other circumstances contemplated by the off-hire clause and therefore should not be read to include governmental interference.[174] Instead, the shipowner alleged the delay fell within the 'restraint of princes' clause, which absolved it of liability.[175] The panel majority agreed with the shipowner. It found that the addition of the word 'restriction' to the off-hire clause did not have a 'stand-alone' meaning to capture the detention at issue and instead must be read alongside other causes within the provision that are similar in character, such as fire and breakdown that prevent 'full working of the vessel'.[176] Although the panel majority acknowledged both parties were apparently blameless for the botched law enforcement action, the majority emphasised that 'off-hire clauses serve to allocate specified risks and are not necessarily fault based'.[177] For this reason, the vessel remained on hire during the search-induced delay in Chile as well as during the later repairs in Canada that 'were the unavoidable consequence of the drug search'.[178] One arbitrator dissented to express the position that the erroneous actions of the Chilean and US authorities was a 'restriction' that was entirely distinct from the other explicitly mentioned causes making the term a 'new and independent off-hire event'.[179]

B. Marine Insurance

i. Customs Infringement

Insurance coverage disputes addressing war risk language can arise due to seizures occurring in peacetime. Among the leading American cases addressing this point is *Blaine Richards & Co Inc v Marine Indemnity Insurance Co of America*.[180] In that

[172] ibid, 4.
[173] ibid.
[174] ibid.
[175] ibid.
[176] ibid.
[177] ibid, 5.
[178] ibid.
[179] ibid, 9.
[180] *Blaine Richards & Co Inc v Marine Indemnity Insurance Co of America*, 635 F2d 1051 (2nd Cir 1980) (Lumbard J).

case, a US-based buyer purchased more than 10,000 bags of beans harvested in Ethiopia and Chile from a supplier based in France. Under the sales contract, there was an obligation for the supplier to fumigate the beans before ocean carriage. The supplier hired a fumigation company which used a pesticide called Phostoxin to fumigate the beans before departure. At the time, Phostoxin was used for fumigation in Europe, but it was not approved by the US Food and Drug Administration (FDA). When the vessel carrying the beans arrived at the port of Baltimore, Maryland, an FDA inspection team discovered an empty can of Phostoxin and powdery residue on the bean bags, which was deemed evidence of contamination. The FDA then detained the beans on grounds that they were 'adulterated'.[181] This caused a delay of six weeks until the cargo owner agreed with the FDA on a plan to recondition the beans. This gave rise to reconditioning costs, diminished value, and led to the cancellation of the cargo owner's sell-on contracts. The cargo owner made a claim against its marine insurer to recover under either an all risk policy or an accompanying war risk policy, but the insurer denied the claim. The cargo owner filed suit in the US District Court for the Eastern District of New York. In its motion for summary judgment, the insurer argued that there was no liability under the all risk policy because it contained an FC&S clause excluding coverage for losses due to 'seizure' and 'detention' occurring 'whether in time of peace or war and whether lawful or otherwise', and that it had no liability under the war risk policy because the FC&S clause contained an explicit carve-out for losses caused by 'seizure or destruction under quarantine or customs regulations' as well as 'delay, deterioration and/ or loss of market'.[182] The trial court agreed with the insurer and granted its motion.[183] On appeal, the cargo owner argued that the FC&S clause was 'not intended to exclude risk of detention by civil authorities in peaceful circumstances'.[184] But the United States Court of Appeals for the Second Circuit rejected this view and affirmed the trial court's decision in favour of the insurer. It reasoned that despite the original purpose of the FC&S clause to 'protect against risks of war', its application to detention by civil authorities was 'consistent with the general purposes of the Clause, which is to exclude from coverage losses arising from unforeseeable actions of sovereign states'.[185] In addition, it explained that 'the language of the Clause itself declares that such seizures or detentions in time of peace as well as in time of war are to come within the exception'.[186] Although the court acknowledged that FDA rules are not technically customs regulations, it found the war risk policy excluded the FDA detention because 'the

[181] ibid.

[182] ibid, 1052.

[183] *Blaine Richards & Co Inc v Marine Indemnity Insurance Co of America*, 1980 AMC 1919 (EDNY 1980) (Nickerson J).

[184] *Blaine Richards & Co Inc v Marine Indemnity Insurance Co of America*, 635 F2d 1051, 1053 (2nd Cir 1980).

[185] ibid.

[186] ibid.

phrase "customs regulations" in the war risks policy should be construed in a reasonable manner which would give proper effect to the intentions and expectations of the parties'.[187]

Other decisions have addressed the customs dimensions of war risk policy language, including *Commodities Reserve Co v St Paul Fire & Marine Insurance Co.*[188] In that case, a cargo owner sub-chartered space on a vessel called the *West Lion* to move a cargo of chickpeas and cumin seeds from Turkey to sell in Venezuela. After loading in Turkey, apparently without the consent or knowledge of the cargo owner the vessel operators temporarily painted a new name on the vessel and docked in Israel, where the vessel loaded a cargo of munitions to be carried along with the chickpeas and cumin seeds. The vessel operators departed Israel, repainted the name *West Lion* on the vessel, and continued on the voyage. As the vessel moved through Greek waters, Greek authorities arrested it for violating domestic regulations concerning the carriage of munitions. This caused a delay in which the chickpeas and cumin had to be transhipped onto another vessel to avoid spoilage or infestation and the cargo owner had to obtain an order from a court in Crete to authorise its release because the shipmaster refused to voluntarily release it without the cargo owner agreeing to a waiver of liability. Throughout this ordeal, the cargo was not damaged, but the cargo owner sought reimbursement from its insurer for associated expenses, including freight costs for the substitute vessel, cargo surveys, and legal action necessary to secure the court order to release the cargo. It cited language in the policy that expressly allowed recovery for infestation, but the insurer resisted liability, alleging that an FC&S clause in the policy excluded cover for losses arising from 'seizure' or 'detention'. The US District Court for the Northern District of California agreed and held for the insurer on summary judgment. The US Court of Appeals for the Ninth Circuit affirmed, but only in part. Regarding the transshipment costs, the court held that the 'dominant cause' of the potential loss of the cargo from infestation was the detention of the vessel in Crete.[189] The court explained, '[a]lthough transshipment may have been a prudent move because of the potential for infestation, the need to transship only existed because the ship had been detained'.[190] Thus, the trial court was correct that recovery for the transshipment costs driven by the detention was barred by the FC&S clause, despite infestation being a covered peril. As for the litigation expenses in Crete, however, the court found that the proximate cause was not actually the detention by the Greek authorities, but rather the shipmaster who refused to release the cargo. The court explained that '[w]hen the Greek authorities detained the ship they did not claim jurisdiction' over the cargo of chickpeas and

[187] ibid, 1054. The Second Circuit nevertheless remanded the case back to the lower court on the separate issue of whether the loss was proximately caused by the FDA detention or the contamination by Phostoxin on the vessel before departing Europe. There is no published decision on remand.
[188] *Commodities Reserve Co v St Paul Fire & Marine Insurance Co*, 879 F2d 640 (9th Cir 1989) (Farris J).
[189] ibid, 644.
[190] ibid.

cumin.[191] Instead, due to the shipmaster's conduct, the cargo owner was forced to secure a court order in Crete to compel the release of the cargo for transshipment. This part of loss was not excluded by the FC&S clause and therefore the cargo owner was entitled to recover from the insurer for those separate costs.

An English court recently addressed the war risk insurance consequences of a seizure performed by the Indonesian Navy in peacetime to enforce unlawful anchoring laws in *Delos Shipholding SA & Others v Allianz Global Corporate and Specialty SE & Others (The Win Win)*.[192] In February 2019, after it had discharged cargo in China and moved to Singapore for bunkering, the vessel anchored just outside the Singapore port limits in Indonesian territorial waters. On 17 February, the Indonesian Navy boarded the *Win Win* and detained the vessel and the shipmaster for entering Indonesian waters without permission. After weeks of negotiations, it became apparent that the authorities would not release the vessel without the payment of a bribe, which the shipowner refused to pay. Although this area had been used by internationally trading vessels for many years as an anchoring location without reprimand or detention by Indonesian authorities, anchoring there was technically in violation of Indonesian domestic law and Indonesia's enforcement was consistent with its sovereign rights under international law. The vessel remained in detention for more than six months and the shipmaster was prosecuted and convicted in criminal proceedings in Indonesia. The assured shipowner filed a claim with its war risk insurers. The policy at issue covered 'capture, seizure, arrest, restraint or detainment, or any attempt thereat', but also excluded losses when caused by actions 'under customs or quarantine regulations and similar arrests, restraints or detainments not arising from actual or impending hostilities'.[193] Invoking the exclusion, the war risk insurer denied the claim. In the English Commercial Court, the insurer argued that that the detention was a foreseeable result of the shipowner's voluntary conduct of anchoring in Indonesian waters unlawfully. The court rejected this view and held for the assured, finding that the detention was not an inevitable consequence of the shipmaster's actions, and that the war risk policy exceptions referencing customs, quarantine, or other 'similar' regulations did not apply.[194] The English Court of Appeal affirmed.[195] Interpreting the scope of the exceptions, the court reasoned that '[w]hat matters is not whether the regulation in question is characterised as a customs regulation under the domestic law of the state in which the vessel is arrested, but whether it regulates matters which commercial people would regard as typically governed by

[191] ibid, 645.

[192] *Delos Shipholding SA & Ors v Allianz Global Corporate and Specialty SE & Ors (The Win Win)* [2025] EWCA Civ 1019 (CA) (Males LJ).

[193] These were the American Institute War Risk Clauses.

[194] *Delos Shipholding SA & Ors v Allianz Global Corporate and Specialty SE & Ors (The Win Win)* [2024] 1 Lloyd's Rep 489 (Comm) (Dias J).

[195] *Delos Shipholding SA & Ors v Allianz Global Corporate and Specialty SE & Ors (The Win Win)* [2025] EWCA Civ 1019.

customs regulations'.[196] The court found the actions of the Indonesian authorities had nothing to do with regulating the import of goods ('customs') or of protecting health ('quarantine'), and were instead based on the Indonesian Navy's decision to 'assert its sovereignty over its territorial waters by arresting and detaining vessels which had anchored without permission'.[197] Since this action was not 'similar' to the customs or quarantine regulations referenced in the coverage exclusions, the war risk insurers were therefore liable for the claim.

ii. Political Acts

When addressing insurance issues involving governmental action, courts may be confronted with the awkward question of weighing the legitimacy of decisions made by other sovereign states. In *Panamanian Oriental Steamship Corp v Wright (The Anita)*, the English Court of Appeal was tasked with analysing whether a seizure of a vessel by Vietnamese officials as part of an anti-smuggling operation was a governmental act that warranted cover under an insurance policy.[198] In the Spring of 1966, the *Anita*, which was owned by a Panamanian corporation, was in the river near Saigon, Vietnam, when it was boarded by Vietnamese customs officials who conducted a search and found unmanifested cargo, including transistor radio sets that could be used as war materials, hidden behind the rudder. The officials escorted the *Anita* to the port where the shipmaster and some of the crew members were arrested. The *Anita* was then confiscated by order of a 'Special Court' that had been established by Vietnamese decree less than a month before the vessel's arrival in an apparent attempt to enhance anti-smuggling and anti-contraband efforts during the civil war in Vietnam. The vessel was covered by a marine insurance policy written on the SG form but without the usual FC&S clause. Instead of excluding war risks, the policy incorporated the 1959 Institute War and Strike Clauses, which expressly provided cover for 'capture, seizure, arrest, restraint or detainment', but also excluded losses arising from certain restraints 'by reason of infringement of any customs regulations'.[199] Following the seizure, the shipowner filed a notice of abandonment with its insurer, but the insurer denied the claim, contending that the loss was within the customs infringement exclusion, which led to litigation.

Holding for the shipowner, the English Commercial Court first explained that the term 'restraint' is intended to refer to 'political or executive acts, and does not include a loss caused by riot or by ordinary judicial process'.[200] After weighing

[196] ibid, para [49].
[197] ibid, para [58].
[198] *Panamanian Oriental Steamship Corp v Wright (The Anita)* [1970] 2 Lloyd's Rep 365 (Comm) (Mocatta J).
[199] ibid, 371.
[200] ibid, 372.

evidence regarding the nature of the Vietnamese proceedings and whether they were administered through legitimate legal process, the court held that the Special Court 'had no jurisdiction to order confiscation of the [vessel]' as there was no proof that the shipowner of the *Anita* had been involved in any attempt to import smuggled goods.[201] Moreover, the court found that although the initial restraint on the vessel during the arrest of the crew could be considered an enforcement of customs regulations, the vessel seizure could not be properly characterised as 'ordinary judicial process' and instead the Special Court acted as 'an extraordinary military tribunal outside the ordinary system of Vietnam'.[202] This was evidenced by the fact that the Special Court had apparently been directed by other military and political actors in the Vietnamese government, which showed its decision was not 'bona fide and impartial'.[203] But the English Court of Appeal reversed, reasoning that the trial court improperly placed the burden of proof on the insurer to show that the Special Court had acted without 'political direction', when this should have shifted to the shipowner after the insurer showed that there was smuggling on the vessel that had led to the confiscation.[204] At the same time, however, the court acknowledged, 'if there were no goods smuggled and the seizure was a put-up job, it would be quite different'.[205] Clarifying this notion of a 'put-up job', the court further explained that if there had been 'direct intervention by politicians commanding the [Special Court] to confiscate the vessel without any foundation for it', the result would have been different since the vessel seizure 'would not be by reason of customs regulations, but by reason of the political interference'.[206] Since there was no real evidence of this political intervention, the insurer properly denied cover by relying on the exclusion.

Another English court second-guessed the legitimacy of a vessel arrest in *Melinda Holdings SA v Hellenic Mutual War Risk Association (Bermuda) Ltd (The Silva)*.[207] In December 2008, Egyptian authorities arrested an oil tanker called the *Silva* and detained it for more than two years. The Egyptian authorities claimed the arrest was justified by an earlier Port Said court order involving the grounding of a different vessel off of Egypt in 1989, which, allegedly, led to environmental pollution and other damages that were never paid. The *Silva* was insured under a war risk policy, which provided cover for 'capture, seizure, arrest, restraint or detainment, and the consequences thereof' but contained an exclusion for claims arising out of 'ordinary judicial process'.[208] The shipowner

[201] ibid, 377.

[202] ibid, 378. The court noted that members of the Special Court who decided the case were actually wearing military uniforms under their judicial robes.

[203] ibid, 385.

[204] *Panamanian Oriental Steamship Corp v Wright (The Anita)* [1971] 1 Lloyd's Rep 487, 492 (CA) (Lord Denning MR).

[205] ibid.

[206] ibid, 493.

[207] *Melinda Holdings SA v Hellenic Mutual War Risk Association (Bermuda) Ltd (The Silva)* [2011] 2 Lloyd's Rep 141 (Comm) (Burton J).

[208] ibid, 143.

claimed war risk cover but the insurer denied the claim on the grounds that the arrest was subject to the exclusion. The English Commercial Court held for the shipowner. The court explained that for the arrest to be legitimate under Egyptian law, it must have been based on an 'arguable case' that the *Silva* was owned by the judgment debtors in the earlier controversy.[209] After weighing the evidence, the court found the insurer could not demonstrate an arguable case because there was actually 'no connection' between the *Silva* or its owners and the 1989 casualty.[210] Instead, the court found that the Egyptian arrest of the *Silva* 'was not an ordinary judicial process, but was an exercise of extortion from owners of an innocent and unconnected seagoing vessel'.[211] Holding that the war risk insurer was liable to provide cover, the court explained that '[t]here was effectively extortion by the State under a veneer of court process.' The Egyptian court, 'through its judicial and quasi-judicial powers, was acting piratically: just the risk that is intended to be covered by this insurance'.[212]

A similar argument was raised but rejected by an American court in *Swift Spindrift Ltd v Alvada Insurance Inc.*[213] In that case, the *M/V Swift Spindrift* was carrying a cargo of corn from Argentina to Libya when the time charterer ordered the vessel to first discharge some of the cargo in Belgium. The shipowner discovered that the real reason for this diversion request was due to a dispute between the Libyan state-owned cargo importer and another company attempting to arrest the vessel or its cargo in Belgium. The *Swift Spindrift* turned back to Libya, but once it arrived, the Libyan authorities arrested the vessel to enforce a civil claim filed by the Libyan importer. Complications related to the arrest and judicial proceedings in Libya caused a delay of more than 18 months. The shipowner eventually sold the vessel and brought claims against both its marine and war risk insurers, alleging that the arrest was covered either as a marine or a war peril. It argued that the policies covered 'commercial' arrests, not just restraints of princes, and, alternatively, even if the policies only covered 'non-commercial' arrests, the arrest that took place in Libya was 'not a standard commercial arrest' and instead was an exercise of sovereign power by the Mohamar Qadhafi regime.[214] The US District Court for the Southern District of New York rejected these arguments. First, it found that commercial arrests were not covered by the terms of either policy. Second, the court found that based on the evidence brought by the shipowner, the actions by the Libyan importer and the Libyan court were normal commercial actions and not exercises of sovereign power. With respect to the Libyan importer, the court explained that even if it was affiliated with the Libyan government, not every action of a state-owned entity is an exercise of sovereign authority. Addressing the actions of the Libyan court, the court acknowledged that its orders may have been

[209] ibid, 148.
[210] ibid, 145.
[211] ibid, 152.
[212] ibid. The court explained 'this was not ordinary judicial process. It was neither ordinary nor judicial.' ibid, 153.
[213] *Swift Spindrift Ltd v Alvada Insurance Inc*, 175 F Supp 3d 169 (SDNY 2016) (Alison J Nathan J).
[214] ibid, 174.

inconsistent or contradictory, but it found the shipowner failed to 'connect the specific actions of the Libyan Court in this case to an act of the Qadhafi regime'.[215] Since the shipowner only provided 'conclusory allegations to bridge the gap', it did not meet its burden to show the Libyan court's actions were more than that of a 'civil court resolving – perhaps incorrectly – a private commercial matter'.[216]

Even when there are allegations of political interference, courts in insurance cases may find the actions of foreign governments to be entirely valid, which may have coverage implications. In *Atlasnavios-Navegacao LDA v Navigators Insurance Co Ltd (The B Atlantic)*, a bulk carrier called the *B Atlantic* was preparing to load coal to export from Venezuela to Italy when divers performing an underwater pre-departure inspection on behalf of the Venezuelan authorities discovered three large bags of cocaine that had been strapped to the vessel's hull below the waterline near the rudder.[217] This smuggling attempt was apparently performed by third parties who were presumably associated with drug cartels aiming to transport the drugs from Latin America to Europe without the knowledge of the vessel operators. Although there was no evidence that the shipowner or the crew was involved or had knowledge of the drug smuggling scheme, the Venezuelan authorities detained the vessel and arrested the crew for violations of its anti-drug laws. The shipmaster and second officer were convicted in a jury trial and sentenced to nine years' imprisonment. The *B Atlantic* was also detained and confiscated by the Venezuelan government. The shipowner later served a notice of abandonment with its war risk insurer, but the insurer denied the claim. In the English Commercial Court, the claimant alleged that the loss was caused by the insured peril of 'any person acting maliciously or from political motive' and that the criminal conviction of the master and crew were 'politically motivated' since they played no role in the drug smuggling.[218] The insurer countered that the loss was caused by an excluded risk, namely 'arrest restraint detainment confiscation or expropriation … by reason of infringement of any customs or trading regulations'.[219] The court found that the shipowner was entitled to recover because the reason why the vessel was detained was due to the malicious acts of some unknown third parties. Addressing the separate argument that the vessel detention may have been politically motivated or that perhaps the Venezuelan authorities even planted the drugs on the vessel as a 'put-up job' as pretext to seize the vessel, the court found that the claimant did not meet its burden of proof.[220] According to the court, the

[215] ibid, 190.

[216] ibid, 190–91.

[217] *Atlasnavios-Navegacao LDA v Navigators Insurance Co Ltd (The B Atlantic)* [2018] 2 Lloyd's Rep 1, 8 (Lord Mance).

[218] *Atlasnavios-Navegacao LDA v Navigators Insurance Co Ltd (The B Atlantic)* [2015] 1 Lloyd's Rep 117, 124 (Flaux J).

[219] ibid, 127.

[220] ibid, 166. This notion of a 'put-up job' derives from the hypothetical raised in the *Anita* case discussed above. The court described this concept as making a distinction 'between what might be described as justified or "connected" political interference on the one hand and unjustified or unconnected interference on the other'. ibid, 127.

testimony of one key witness failed to provide 'any sensible explanation as to why the Venezuelan authorities would want to steal a twenty four year old bulk carrier, let alone a perfectly standard and unexceptionable cargo of coal'.[221] If there was any 'political interference', the court reasoned, it was to demonstrate a hardline stance on enforcing the anti-smuggling laws.[222]

The English Court of Appeal later reversed on the grounds that the loss could be attributed to both the malicious acts of third parties as well as to the infringement of a customs regulations, although the latter was the proximate cause of the detention.[223] The court reasoned that, viewing the two clauses together, it was consistent with the 'spirit of the policy' to find that the infringement clause manifested the aim to exclude cover for 'any detainment attributable to breach of customs laws'.[224] The UK Supreme Court affirmed this decision to the benefit of the war risk insurer, albeit on slightly different reasoning. The court explained that the third-party attempt at drug smuggling was not a 'malicious act' under the terms of the war risk policy, in part because there was no 'ill-will' or obvious intent to cause harm to any person or property.[225] Instead, the smugglers were attempting to move their drugs undetected. But even if the loss were to fall within the meaning of malicious acts, the court reasoned, the policy exclusion incapsulated detention due to customs violations, which included breaking Venezuelan law through drug smuggling.[226]

III. Reflections

The politically motivated oil embargos of the 1970s reveal the substantial commercial disruption that may emanate from coercive economic measures deployed by smaller nations acting in concert – not just major powers armed with the perception of military superiority and economic clout. Tapping into the political power of the 'oil weapon', export restrictions imposed by Libya and other oil-exporting Arab states produced access limitations, shortages, market uncertainty, and targeted obstruction, which led to disputes and wide-ranging caselaw addressing the commercial fallout. Some of these cases assessed solutions under the doctrinal lens of frustration. In the *Sicula Oceanica* case, the arbitral panel refused to accept the position that the contract was frustrated since the Libyan nationalisation of the oil sector and the export restrictions targeting Israeli allies did not

[221] ibid, 124–25.

[222] ibid, 128.

[223] *Atlasnavios-Navegacao LDA v Navigators Insurance Co Ltd (The B Atlantic)* [2016] 2 Lloyd's Rep 351 (Christopher Clarke LJ).

[224] ibid, 359.

[225] *Atlasnavios-Navegacao LDA v Navigators Insurance Co Ltd (The B Atlantic)* [2018] 2 Lloyd's Rep 1, 8.

[226] Neither the English Court of Appeal nor the UK Supreme Court revisited the allegation that the Venezuelan authorities orchestrated the ordeal out of political motive.

indefinitely prohibit cargo loading and instead only delayed it.[227] The panel was persuaded in part by the communication from Libyan officials suggesting loading instructions would be forthcoming despite the embargo-induced delays, which served as evidence that the restrictions would not disrupt performance beyond a short period, especially given that the voyage destination (in that case, Italy) was not covered by the announced restrictive measures. However, the *Alma Shipping Corp* case shows that the frustration doctrine can indeed excuse contractual performance in the event that an embargo unequivocally applies with indefinite effect to prohibit loading for a voyage to a destination covered by blanket restrictions (in that case, the US).[228] As demonstrated by the *Academy Tankers* case, other factors such as the foreseeability of embargo restrictions and the specific charterparty wordings may also be critical elements in resolving questions of frustration.[229] Due to the scale of the regional conflict occurring at that time of contracting and the common knowledge that oil producing states might target Israel's allies with restrictions, the parties had the foresight to contractually reference the prospect of political barriers to loading, which gave the arbitral panel an explicit basis to sustain the performance obligation. But as illustrated by the *Mobil Shipping* case, in the absence of an express provision, a constructive awareness of such risks under general prudence standards may be enough to preclude the finding of frustration.[230] Likewise, as reflected in the *Zuiho Maru* decision, even in the midst of an oil export embargo and rationing system implementation by Saudi Arabia, the ability to substantially perform the contract may foreclose the viability of the frustration defence.[231]

Resolving performance questions in the embargo context has often involved an evidentiary investigation that depends on an assessment of fluid geopolitical conditions, market responses, and performance alternatives. The existence of cargo source loading alternatives to evade the reach of embargos have been found relevant to offset the application of the avoidance doctrines. In the *Furness Bridge* case, the court determined the charterer had not met its burden in showing that cargo from an alternative port within the trading limits was not available to perform the voyage obligation to the Bahamas, which precluded a finding of frustration or impracticability following the Libyan restrictions.[232] Such determinations may become muddled when embargos cascade into governmental intervention for reasons beyond the underlying political controversy. The oil export restrictions in the *Skibs A/S Suderoy* case illustrates this knock-on phenomenon, as the Turkish

[227] *Sicula Oceanica SPA v Corco Tankers Inc (The Auriga Primo)*, SMA 1096 (NY Arb 1977).
[228] *Alma Shipping Corp v Amerada Hess Shipping Corp*, SMA 1111 (NY Arb 1977).
[229] *Academy Tankers Inc v Philips Petroleum*, SMA 1342 (NY Arb 1978).
[230] *Mobil Shipping and Transportation Co v Michail A Karageorgis SA (M/T Corona)*, SMA 961 (NY Arb 1975).
[231] *Mobil Shipping and Transportation Co v Michail A Karageorgis SA (M/T Corona)* [1977] 2 Lloyd's Rep 552 (Comm).
[232] *Seabridge Shipping Ltd v Antco Shipping Ltd (The Furness Bridge Seabridge Shipping Ltd v Antco Shipping Ltd (The Furness Bridge)* [1977] 2 Lloyd's Rep 367 (Comm).

government did not prevent cargo loading in order to align with the concerted oil embargos of the Arab states but rather to protect its domestic supplies following energy market turmoil driven by these external political decisions.[233] This caused the majority and dissenting arbitrators to disagree on whether the contract should be avoided: on one hand, the Turkish ban had been imposed unexpectedly to disrupt the expected performance, but at the same time there was still the potential to perform the contract by securing an alternative cargo from other exporting locations within the contract's trading limits. As evidenced by the *Amax Mineral Sales* case, oil embargo-based difficulties may also tumble into the bunkering context. The holding for the charterer represents a warning that the rumbling threats of market turmoil may equate to constructive notice for shipowners to secure fuel for voyage commitments even as a crisis begins to loom.[234]

Solutions for disruption caused by other forms of trade controls have resulted in similar reasoning. The *ONE Shipping* case reveals how such scenarios may trigger the application of mutual exceptions provisions in charterparties, as the arbitral panel found the sudden export restrictions on turpentine by the incoming Sandinista government of Nicaragua justified the charterer's reference to the standard 'restraint of princes' provision, while it also emphasised that the shipowner was aware of the political situation at the time of contracting but chose not to modify the agreement to address export control risk.[235] In contrast, the sudden salt export restrictions imposed by Venezuela in the *Pioneer Navigation* case was determined by the panel majority not to excuse the charterer, in part because the charterer knew the risks of doing business in that country.[236] Counterintuitively, positive economic statecraft in the form of aid and assistance has proved to generate similar contractual controversy. When such assistance is expected and relied upon but then suddenly revoked, it may take on the character of a prohibition. The *Tradax International* case offers a clear illustration, as the charterer had agreed to perform the contract to transport US origin agricultural products under development financing provided by the US government.[237] When the US government cancelled the assistance following a contentious border dispute involving India and East Pakistan, the charterer invoked frustration and *force majeure* defences, claiming that the revocation of assistance was a 'de facto embargo'.[238] Although the arbitral panel majority did not explicitly agree with this characterisation, it nevertheless found the charterer was excused from performance.

In the context of politically motivated boycotts, the *Universe Tankships* case shows how even minor offences like taking on supplies off a boycotted state

[233] *Skibs A/S Suderoy v JOC International BV (M/T Tore Knudsen)*, SMA 1108 (NY Arb 1977).
[234] *Amax Mineral Sales Corp v Interocean Shipping Co (The SS Nagano)*, SMA 1233 (NY Arb 1978).
[235] *ONE Shipping Ltd v Hercules Inc (The M/T Onesky)*, SMA 1828 (NY Arb 1983).
[236] *Pioneer Navigation Ltd v Chemical Equipment Labs Inc (The MN Genco Ocean)*, SMA 4357 (NY Arb 2019).
[237] *Tradax Internacional SA v Government of Pakistan*, SMA 779 (NY Arb 1973).
[238] ibid.

(in that case, South Africa) can lead to significant delays during subsequent calls.[239] In holding for the shipowner, a lesson gleaned from this scenario is the practical need for contracting parties in the vessel chartering context to exchange commercial intelligence regarding trading conditions around the world, so that counterparties have a genuine opportunity to make an informed risk assessment as to whether to approach boycott-enforcing ports, which may be critical in evaluating the application of standard clauses such as safe port warranties, which may simultaneously depend on compliance with both public and contractual obligations. The US Supreme Court decision in the *International Longshormen's Association* case shows how even 'secondary boycotts' imposed by non-state actors can result in substantial commercial disruption, as the labour union in that case reacted to the Soviet invasion of Afghanistan with politically-motivated obstruction.[240] Although the court found the union had acted improperly by refusing to work Soviet-connected vessels and cargo, the situation unveils the vitality by which powerful non-state institutions may unexpectedly react to geopolitical developments to impose their own forms of performance barriers.

Restrictions on port access based on politically motivated trading limits or the national affiliations and identities of crews and passengers on board vessels have caused a surprising number of commercial disputes. In the context of contractual geographic restrictions, courts and arbitrators have weighed both the language of trading limits along with the political realities necessary to enforce their terms. In the *Mana Maritime* case, the arbitral panel gave a strict reading to the trading limits clause that did not explicitly bar 'either direction trading' between the People's Republic of China and Taiwan, even though the long-simmering political enmity between the two governments may have warranted such contract drafting.[241] The trading limits clause in the *Evergreen Marine* case required the court to engage in a more comprehensive geopolitical analysis, as it could not apply the trading limits clause banning access to 'communist' ports without first probing the knowledge of expert witnesses on 1960s Yugoslavian society to determine the nature the country's political identity.[242] As for nationality restrictions, in the *Rudolph A Ootker* case, the arbitral panel addressed the costs of delays linked to the presence of Polish crewman by placing the compliance burden on the shipowner, rationalising that the restrictions triggered the standard 'deficiency of men' language in the off-hire clause, despite its silence regarding the means by which such a deficiency must arise.[243] Applying a similar rationale, the statutory and contractual communist port prohibition at issue in the *Transnational Maritime* case was found by the arbitral panel to impose a compliance burden on the shipowner, rather than the charterer, which

[239] *Universe Tankships Inc v Burmah Oil Tankers Ltd (The Universe Explorer)*, SMA 2016 (NY Arb 1984).
[240] *International Longshoremen's Association v Allied International Inc*, 456 US 212 (USSC 1982).
[241] *Mana Maritime Ltd v Seanav International Ltd (The Mana)*, SMA 2669 (NY Arb 1990).
[242] *Evergreen Marine Corp v Worldwide Carriers Ltd*, AMC 200 (Nova Scotia Admiralty 1971).
[243] *Rudolph A Ootker v Hamlet Shipping Inc (The M/V Alcazar)*, SMA 1512 (NY Arb 1980).

the shipowner breached by failing to investigate the consequences of employing a Taiwanese crew for a voyage to Romania in the midst of the Cold War.[244] The sudden and *ad hoc* port access restrictions imposed by Taiwanese officials in the *Roachbank* case made for a more difficult decision as neither the shipowner nor the charterer appeared to know how the port authority would react to the presence of Vietnamese migrants until the vessel arrived carrying hundreds of people in desperate need of help. Since the contract did not contemplate this scenario, this led to a rather surprising result, as the court found that despite the many rescued migrants crammed onto the deck of the vessel following a harrowing rescue operation in the South China Sea, the vessel itself was still capable of cargo work and therefore 'fully efficient', keeping it on hire to the shipowner's benefit.[245]

The task of assessing the legitimacy of such restrictions may put courts and arbitrators in the awkward position of determining whether actions of a sovereign state are genuine or some untoward form of politically motivated pretext. This has sparked queries as to whether judicial determinations of this kind infringe on international comity principles or on the domestic foreign relations responsibilities of governmental officers serving in political or diplomatic (rather than judicial) capacities. At least in American law, there is a long-standing discretionary practice of deferring to the executive – the President and the administrative agencies – on foreign relations matters in order to prevent diplomatic fallout from judicial review of foreign government decisions.[246] The theory is that this abstention may avoid embarrassing the government by characterising 'political questions' as more properly made by officials presumed to have expertise in foreign affairs. As illustrated by the *Swift Spindrift* case involving allegations of a politically motivated vessel arrest by Libyan authorities, American courts may seek to avoid the doctrine by distinguishing between sovereign and commercial acts.[247] English courts appear less concerned with infringing on comity concerns or separation of powers issues when assessing governmental acts in commercial cases. In the *Sucden Middle-East* case, the court found that the seizure of sugar by Algerian customs authorities was not a 'routine' governmental action, which allowed for its classification as governmental interference and a *force majeure* event.[248] The court in the *Melinda Holdings* case was far less diplomatic, reasoning that the vessel arrest authorised by an Egyptian court was not only unjustified and beyond ordinary judicial process but was actually more akin to an act of piracy.[249] The *Anita* case reveals a more deferential approach, as the appeals court accepted the legitimacy of

[244] *Transnational Maritime Inc v East Europe Import Export Inc (The M/S Eurymachus)*, SMA 1274 (NY Arb 1978).

[245] *CA Venezolana de Navegacion v Bank Line (The Roachbank)* [1987] 2 Lloyd's Rep 498.

[246] See eg Restatement (Third) of the Foreign Relations Law of the United States, § 1 and § 433.

[247] *Swift Spindrift Ltd v Alvada Insurance Inc*, 175 F Supp 3d 169 (SDNY 2016).

[248] *Sucden Middle-East v Yagci Denizcilik Ve Ticaret Ltd Sirketi (The Muammer Yagci)* [2020] 1 Lloyd's Rep 107, 109.

[249] *Melinda Holdings SA v Hellenic Mutual War Risk Association (Bermuda) Ltd (The Silva)* [2011] 2 Lloyd's Rep 141.

the Vietnamese 'Special Court' even though the trial judge had emphasised that it seemed to be more like a military tribunal than an impartial legal proceeding. As illustrated by the drug-smuggling seizure by Venezuelan authorities in the *B Atlantic* case, however, allegations of politically-motivated restraint – a 'put up job' – must be matched with sufficient evidence to gain traction in argument over the contractual implications.[250]

Even when the legitimacy of a governmental restraint is not a central point of contention, such scenarios may still lead to disputes over how to contractually classify such actions. When the transnational drug seizure operation in the *SA Marine Corp* case caused delays in which both the shipowner and charterer were found to be blameless, the arbitral panel could not reach a unanimous result on whether the events should be classified as a 'restriction' under the off-hire clause.[251] Such classification questions were also germane in the *Commodities Reserve* case, as the court grappled with how to characterise the insurance claim for transshipment costs arising out of the Greek detention of chickpeas and cumin comingled with Israeli munitions, which it ultimately found not to be subject to the FC&S exclusion under principles of proximate cause.[252] The *Blaine Richards* case dealing with whether an FC&S clause could be properly applied to fumigation-related restrictions raised similar questions of how to interpret war risk language under a class of customs seizures, ultimately holding that it could be applied in peacetime to react to 'unforeseeable actions of sovereign states'.[253] But as the recent *Win Win* decision starkly reveals, peacetime governmental restraint can be just as disruptive as war and piracy. And, accordingly, disruptive action performed by state naval assets, whether belligerent or not, may trigger insurer liability described in war risk terms. Each of these cases illustrate a more tenuous connection to statecraft motivations, but collectively they demonstrate the continued complexity of classifying governmental action when there are multiple options embedded in clauses drafted with geopolitical dynamics in mind. Such challenges resonate in the contemporary era as state authorities continue blocking, inspecting and detaining commercial vessels on the basis of varied justifications ranging from potentially legitimate regulatory enforcement to questionable political retribution.

As tariffs and non-tariff barriers take the geopolitical limelight, the *Coca v Morris* case remains evocative after well over 100 years buried in the archives apparently without judicial or academic citation. The case demonstrates how the sudden imposition of tariffs and countermeasures have long carried the propensity to throw up practical performance barriers leading to contract disputes.[254] The *Shelter Forest* case examines the modern context as the court assessed whether the cargo owner was excused for cancelling a long-term liner carriage

[250] *Atlasnavios-Navegacao LDA v Navigators Insurance Co Ltd (The B Atlantic)* [2018] 2 Lloyd's Rep 1 (UKSC).

[251] *SA Marine Corp SA v Canfornav Ltd (The M/V Energy Ranger)*, SMA 3817 (NY Arb 2003).

[252] *Commodities Reserve Co v St Paul Fire & Marine Insurance Co*, 879 F2d 640 (9th Cir 1989).

[253] *Blaine Richards & Co Inc v Marine Indemnity Insurance Co of America*, 635 F2d 1051 (2nd Cir 1980).

[254] *Coca v Morris*, 107 F 688 (7th Cir 1901).

contract when the US–China trade war suddenly limited the demand for lumber shipments. Although the court refused to accept the position that the tariffs or the compounding trade volatility excused performance under the doctrine of impossibility or by operation of an express *force majeure* provision, the implications of the decision are narrowed by the court's alternative finding that the true reason for the contract cancellation was the breakdown of commercial relations between the contracting parties. While the notion of a fixed price contract is sometimes construed as a mutually beneficial form of risk hedging that should generally preclude the application of avoidance doctrines, fully fledged import restrictions raise more serious obstacles than the wavering market conditions commercial contracts are expected to absorb. Recognising this distinction, in *Select Commodities* the court found the full-scale Nigerian vegetable oil ban justified contract avoidance under the doctrine of frustration.[255] As sweeping tariffs and other non-tariff barriers appear poised to shake the global economy under a new wave of protectionism, it is conceivable that such doctrinal arguments may resonate to excuse or modify performance obligations in instances where tariff rates rise to the level of a de facto import ban. Even so, explicit contract wordings remain the more prudent route to address these emerging risks, especially given the availability of freshly drafted model provisions designed to react to new and re-packaged forms of disruption.[256]

[255] *Select Commodities Ltd v Valdo SA (The Florida)* [2007] 1 Lloyd's Rep 1 (Comm).
[256] See eg BIMCO Force Majeure Clause 2022.

7

Conclusion

The cases examined in this book create both a patchwork and a touchstone to aid the resolution of commercial disputes caused by geopolitical volatility. Although they present a remarkable breadth of factual scenarios, they also reveal commonalities in industry adaptation, argumentation, and legal analysis. In wartime scenarios, charterparty and bill of lading cases have examined the liberty to avoid danger zones, the allocation of war cancellation rights, and the contractual implications of trading limits provisions, with parallel marine insurance cases addressing the delineation between marine and war perils, the consequences of governmental restraint, and the impact of geographically significant trading disclosures. Courts and arbitrators addressing the varied forms of unrest in chartering and carriage cases have surveyed the contractual implications of re-routing, obligations to assess the political safety of destination ports, and the reasonableness of voyage diversions, while the marine insurance cases have examined the untidy lines between war and terrorism, insurrection, barratry, and civil commotion. The piracy cases have addressed charterparty disputes weighing the discretion to avoid high risk zones, payment obligations during prolonged seizures, and the nebulous line between piratical and governmental interventions, while the marine insurance cases have covered the intersection between piracy and politically motivated commandeering, the contractual implications of rhetoric ascribing piracy terms to wartime acts, and the interplay between insurance policy provisions and principles of public international law. In sanctions cases, courts and arbitrators in the vessel chartering context have analysed the impact of licensing obligations, liability for enforcement penalties, implications for blacklisted parties, counterparty recourse for deceptive trading behaviour, and the practical complications of legal and reputation-based compliance processes. Marine insurance cases addressing sanctions issues have grappled with the scope of regulatory prohibitions, the measure of enforcement exposure, and difficulties caused by scrupulously compliant third-party financial institutions. Chartering and carriage cases covering other forms of statecraft have addressed disputes over export embargos, import restrictions, and crew nationality bans, while the corresponding marine insurance cases have analysed the intersection between governmental restraint and legitimate customs enforcement, including the troublesome prospect of political interference disguised under regulatory pretext. In these and many other contexts, courts and arbitrators have engaged in both doctrinal and contractual reasoning to address commercial disputes springing out of controversies ranging from the total world wars of the past to the nuanced trade wars of the present.

The frustration defence has been referenced in a variety of these cases. The doctrine has justified ending contracts due to British vessel requisition during the World Wars and vessel-trapping incidents following the outbreak of the Iran–Iraq War.[1] But the frustration doctrine has been invoked and rejected when voyage routes have been adjusted due to Suez Canal closures because the Cape of Good Hope option remained a viable alternative despite the higher costs.[2] The doctrine has also appeared in cases addressing pirate seizures and governmental commandeering. It was used as part of the solution when a vessel was hijacked, diverted, and ultimately stolen by Vietnamese soldiers after the fall of Saigon, but it was rejected when pirates seized a vessel off Singapore, in part because Chinese authorities quickly recovered it.[3] In sanctions cases, the frustration defence has been raised but rejected in several scenarios because the underlying obligations were found not to have been radically transformed, including when UK and EU sanctions on Iran only partially restricted insurance cover, when financial restrictions made vessel purchasing payments more complicated but still feasible, and when UN sanctions prohibited loading Iraqi oil but allowed for alternative performance.[4] Its relevance for interpreting a *force majeure* clause was rejected when US sanctions prevented the payment of freight in the contractual currency of US dollars.[5] In addition, the frustration doctrine was raised and rejected in several of the Libyan embargo cases but accepted in at least one.[6] It was also referenced as part of the basis for setting aside contracts when US humanitarian aid to East Pakistan was suddenly cut off and when Nigeria imposed sweeping bans on the import of foreign vegetable oil.[7]

While raised less frequently than the largely equivalent frustration formulation, wartime scenarios have occasionally justified references to the impracticability defence, including when Japanese submarines seriously damaged both ship and cargo off the coasts of California and where a combination of Greek governmental

[1] *Bank Line Ltd v Arthur Capel & Co* [1919] AC 435 (KB); *Earn Line Steamship Co Ltd v Sutherland Steamship Co Ltd (The Claveresk)*, 264 F 276 (2nd Cir); *Kodros Shipping Corp v Empresa Cubana di Fletes (The Evia)* [1982] 2 Lloyd's Rep 307 (HL).

[2] *Glidden Co v Hellenic Lines Ltd*, 275 F2d 253 (2nd Cir 1960); *Ocean Tramp Tankers Corp v V/O Sovfracht (The Eugenia)* [1963] 2 Lloyd's Rep 381 (CA); *Palmco Shipping Inc v Continental Ore Corp (The Captain George K)* [1970] 2 Lloyd's Rep 21 (Comm).

[3] *Wong Wing Fai Co v United States of America*, 840 F2d 1462 (9th Cir 1988); *Petroships Pte Ltd v Petec Trading and Investment Corp* [2001] 2 Lloyd's Rep 248 (Comm).

[4] *Islamic Republic of Iran Shipping Line (IRISL) v Steamship Mutual Underwriting Association (Bermuda) Ltd* [2011] 1 Lloyd's Rep 195 (Comm); *DVB Bank SE v Shere Shipping Co Ltd* [2013] EWHC 2321 (Comm); *Great Beluga Shipping Inc v Bayoil Inc (The Energy Explorer)*, SMA 3033 (NY Arb 1993).

[5] *RTI Ltd v Mur Shipping BV* [2024] 1 Lloyd's Rep 621 (UKSC).

[6] *Seabridge Shipping Ltd v Antco Shipping Ltd (The Furness Bridge)* [1977] 2 Lloyd's Rep 367 (Comm); *Sicula Oceanica SPA v Corco Tankers Inc*, SMA 1096 (NY Arb 1978); *Alma Shipping Corp v Amerada Hess Shipping Corp*, SMA 1111 (NY Arb 1977).

[7] *Tradax Internacional SA v Government of Pakistan*, SMA 779 (NY Arb 1973); *Select Commodities Ltd v Valdo SA (The Florida)* [2007] 1 Lloyd's Rep 1 (Comm).

requisition and mandatory re-routing to avoid Italian attack in the Mediterranean Sea led to cargo spoilage.[8] Impracticability reasoning has been referenced more sparingly in other contexts. The doctrine was raised and rejected in at least one of the Suez Canal closure cases, as the increased cost of the alternative route was found to be an inadequate basis to meet the doctrine's high standards.[9] However, impracticability was deemed the appropriate solution for setting aside a contract due to sanctions-based disruption when Turkish officials enforcing UN sanctions on Iraq shut down crude exports via the pipeline running through its territory.[10] Likewise, the notion of 'reasonable practicability' was referenced as part of the court's analysis in allowing a charterer to avoid performance after US sanctions on Iran led to complications with payment and permitting for Iranian importers to continue receiving scheduled banana cargoes from the Philippines.[11] However, the concept of impracticability was considered and rejected in the context of Libyan oil embargos because alternative cargos were available elsewhere, and it was dismissed as a defence following a Venezuelan permitting requirement on salt exports because the charterer was found to have assumed the risk of trading restrictions due to the volatile political conditions in the exporting country.[12]

The illegality doctrine has had a much more prevalent place in the case law, but, like the other doctrines, its relevance in resolving disputes has been varied. It has been found relevant in wartime contraband control cases, including those involving Spanish restrictions on the movement of Sicilian sulphur to the US during the Spanish–American War, British controls on metals to German allies during the Second World War, and at least tangentially in vessel trapping scenarios that occurred in the Shatt-al-Arab at the start of the Iran–Iraq War.[13] In each of these scenarios, although it was uncertain whether the contraband controls and navigation limitations would be enforced by the regulating states, it was determined that the consequences of violating governmental orders amounted to risks that justified the shipmasters' decisions to modify or delay performance. In addition, a version of an illegality argument was raised and rejected in at least one piracy case as the court found payment of ransom did not violate principles of public policy or morality, which carried implications for the insurance cover because it meant that the vessel was not irretrievably lost.[14] Illegality arguments also have been raised

[8] *Pope & Talbot Inc v Blanchard Lumber Co of Seattle*, 159 F2d 134 (9th Cir 1947); *Lekas & Drivas Inc v Basil Goulandris*, 306 F2d 426 (2nd Cir 1962).

[9] *American Trading & Production Corp v Shell International Marine Ltd*, 343 F Supp 91 (SDNY 1971), 453 F2d 939 (2nd Cir 1971).

[10] *Repsol Petroleo SA v Sun International Ltd (M/T Orduna)*, SMA 2967 (NY Arb 1990).

[11] *Laysun Service Co Ltd v Del Monte International GmbH* [2023] Lloyd's Rep Plus 15 (Comm).

[12] *Seabridge Shipping Ltd v Antco Shipping Ltd (The Furness Bridge)* [1977] 2 Lloyd's Rep 367 (Comm); *Pioneer Navigation Ltd v Chemical Equipment Labs Inc (The MN Genco Ocean)*, SMA 4357 (NY Arb 2019).

[13] *Steamship Styria v James L Morgan*, 186 US 1 (USSC 1902); *Amtorg Trading Corp v The Wildwood*, 133 F2d 765 (9th Cir 1943); *The Bamburi* [1982] 1 Lloyd's Rep 312 (London Arb).

[14] *Masefield AG v Amlin Corporate Member Ltd (The Bunga Melati Dua)* [2011] 1 Lloyd's Rep 630 (CA).

frequently in sanctions cases. The doctrine played a role in justifying suspension or modification of performance in the context of US trade restrictions on Iraq, Cuba, and Venezuela.[15] However, the illegality doctrine was rejected as grounds for avoidance in the context of UN sanctions on Southern Rhodesia and EU sanctions on Iran.[16] It was also found inapplicable when sanctions-based disruption created only a temporary or partial barrier to performance during the brief disagreement between Iraq and the UN over the renewal of the Oil-for-Food Programme, when the UK authorised temporary insurance cover for Iran's state-controlled vessels, and when the alleged unlawfulness of an insurance contract was based on foreign rather than domestic sanctions.[17] In the context of other forms of trade controls, illegality has been raised and rejected as a basis to avoid performance when Saudi Arabia instituted an export rationing scheme during a phase of regional oil embargos, and when a shipowner refused a charterer's orders to navigate to communist Romania due to restrictions imposed by Taiwanese law.[18]

The impossibility doctrine was repeatedly raised and rejected in the Suez Canal closure cases, given that the Cape of Good Hope alternative made the voyages technically possible even if economically unpalatable.[19] However, the defence was part of the court's solution in the Vietnamese soldier commandeering case, as the court found the events prevented the performance of the contract's objective.[20] Sanctions-based impossibility arguments have been found applicable to release a party from performance when UN sanctions caused Turkish officials to ban cargo loading and when US authorities suddenly delayed the discharge of sanctioned Iraqi crude, but the doctrine has been found to be an inadequate basis to avoid performance when UN sanctions only caused temporary barriers or when there were alternative ports capable of fulfilling the contract's aims.[21] On the thorny issue of whether payment processing through third party banks equates to impossibility, courts and arbitrators have expressed diverging opinions. The doctrine has been rejected when a counterparty affiliate was named on a US sanctions blacklist

[15] *Belship Navigation Inc v Sealift Inc (The M/V Huntsville)*, SMA 3429 (NY Arb 1998); *Nordic American Shipping A/S v Bayoil (USA) Inc*, SMA 2972 (NY Arb 1993); *Brujo Finance Co v Sea Energy Co (The MT Alkimos)*, SMA 4388 (NY Arb 2020).

[16] *Dundas Shipping & Trading Co Ltd v Stravelakis Brothers Ltd*, SMA 1174 (NY Arb 1977); *DVB Bank SE v Shere Shipping Co Ltd* [2013] EWHC 2321 (Comm).

[17] *Tankers International LLC v Bayoil Supply and Trading Ltd (The M/T Raphael)*, SMA 3739 (NY Arb 2002); *Islamic Republic of Iran Shipping Line (IRISL) v Steamship Mutual Underwriting Association (Bermuda) Ltd* [2011] 1 Lloyd's Rep 195 (Comm); *Sea Glory Maritime Co v Al Sagr National Insurance Co (The M/V Nancy)* [2014] 2 Lloyd's Rep 14 (Comm).

[18] *Kawasaki Steel Corp v Sardoil SPA (The Zuiho Maru)* [1977] 2 Lloyd's Rep 552 (Comm); *Transnational Maritime Inc v East Europe Import Export Inc (The M/S Eurymachus)*, SMA 1274 (NY Arb 1978).

[19] *Glidden Co v Hellenic Lines Ltd*, 275 F2d 253 (2nd Cir 1960); *Palmco Shipping Inc v Continental Ore Corp (The Captain George K)* [1970] 2 Lloyd's Rep 21 (CA); *Transatlantic Financing Corp v United States of America*, 363 F2d 312 (DC Cir 1966).

[20] *Wong Wing Fai Co v United States of America*, 840 F2d 1462 (9th Cir 1988).

[21] *Repsol Petroleo SA v Sun International Ltd (M/T Orduna)*, SMA 2967 (NY Arb 1933); *Nordic American Shipping A/S v Bayoil (USA) Inc*, SMA 2972 (NY Arb 1993); *Tankers International LLC v Bayoil Supply and Trading Ltd (The M/T Raphael)*, SMA 3739 (NY Arb 2002); *Great Beluga Shipping Inc v Bayoil Inc (The Energy Explorer)*, SMA 3033 (NY Arb 1993).

targeting Russia-connected entities and when EU-level sanctions on Iran restricted (but did not fully prohibit) contractual payments.[22] But the doctrine has been accepted to excuse performance when US sanctions on Iran not only led to payment disruption but also triggered an Iranian import permit moratorium to prevent the outflow of foreign currency reserves.[23] In other statecraft contexts, however, courts and arbitrators have been less receptive to the impossibility defence, including when Libyan officials implemented oil embargos, when Turkish officials established export restrictions to protect domestic energy supplies, and when US–China tariff policy reduced the economic benefits of a long-term carriage contract.[24] In each of these scenarios, it was determined that performance was indeed possible – it was just more difficult or expensive than originally contemplated.

Often in conjunction with doctrinal reasoning, courts and arbitrators have frequently resolved commercial disputes flowing from geopolitical disruption by referencing standard exceptions or risk-shifting clauses. Among them is the 'restraint of princes' clause, which has been successfully invoked in a variety of scenarios to excuse, modify, or shift performance obligations, including in a range of wartime cases, such as those involving British governmental requisitions, diversions to avoid the increased risks of seizures during the World Wars, and the Iraqi government's refusal to authorise vessels to depart from the Shatt-al-Arab.[25] But arguments hinging on restraint clauses have also been rejected in similar contexts, such as when the Brazilian government transshipped cargo through US ports in the Gulf of Mexico to avoid German U-boat attacks and when Greece recommended vessels flying its flag to refrain from entering Turkish waters following the short-lived confrontation over Cyprus.[26] Restraint clauses have been frequently raised in sanctions and statecraft cases, but they have usually been rejected as dispositive, including in cases affected by UN sanctions on Iraq, Libyan oil embargos, Turkish export restrictions, Nigerian boycotts, and politically-motivated Cold War era travel restrictions.[27]

[22] *Gravelor Shipping Ltd v GTLK Asia M5 Ltd* [2023] 2 Lloyd's Rep 239 (Comm); *DVB Bank SE v Shere Shipping Co Ltd* [2013] EWHC 2321 (Comm).

[23] *Laysun Service Co Ltd v Del Monte International GmbH* [2023] Lloyd's Rep Plus 15 (Comm).

[24] *Academy Tankers Inc v Philips Petroleum*, SMA 1342 (NY Arb 1978); *Seabridge Shipping Ltd v Antco Shipping Ltd (The Furness Bridge)* [1977] 2 Lloyd's Rep 367 (Comm); *Skibs A/S Suderoy v JOC International BV (M/T Tore Knudsen)*, SMA 1108 (NY Arb 1977); *Shelter Forest International Acquisition Inc v COSCO Shipping (USA) Inc*, 475 FSupp 3d 1171 (D Oregon 2020).

[25] *Earn Line Steamship Co Ltd v Sutherland Steamship Co Ltd (The Claveresk)*, 264 F 276 (2nd Cir 1920); *North German Lloyd v Guaranty Trust Co of New York (The Steamship Kronprinzessin Cecilie)*, 37 S Ct 490 (USSC 1997); *Lekas & Drivas Inc v Basil Goulandris*, 306 F2d 426 (2nd Cir 1962); *The Bamburi* [1982] 1 Lloyd's Rep 312 (London Arb).

[26] *Baker Castor Oil Co v Insurance Co of North America*, 157 F2d 3 (2nd Cir 1946); *Andros Compania Maritime SA v Mineral Importexport (The MV Andros Island)*, SMA 1548 (NY Arb 1980).

[27] *Nordic American Shipping A/S v Bayoil (USA) Inc*, SMA 2972 (NY Arb 1993); *Tankers International LLC v Bayoil Supply and Trading Ltd (The M/T Raphael)*, SMA 3739 (NY Arb 2002); *Sicula Oceanica SPA v Corco Tankers Inc (The Auriga Primo)*, SMA 1096 (NY Arb 1977); *Academy Tankers Inc v Philips Petroleum*, SMA 1342 (NY Arb 1978); *Seabridge Shipping Ltd v Antco Shipping Ltd (The Furness Bridge)* [1977] 2 Lloyd's Rep 367 (Comm); *Skibs A/S Suderoy v JOC International BV (M/T Tore Knudsen)*, SMA 1108 (NY Arb 1977); *Pioneer Navigation Ltd v Chemical Equipment Labs Inc (The MN Genco Ocean)*, SMA 4357 (NY Arb 2019); *Universe Tankships Inc v Burmah Oil Tankers Ltd (The Universe Explorer)*, SMA 2016 (NY Arb 1984); *Rudolph A Ootker v Hamlet Shipping Inc (The M/V Alcazar)*, SMA 1512 (NY Arb 1980).

However, restraint clauses have been identified as a basis to avoid performance in the context of Nicaraguan export controls following the Sandinista takeover and delays caused by a botched drug search operation in Chile.[28] The various insurance cover cases arising out of statecraft scenarios have also been addressed by entertaining the meaning of restraint clauses and their interplay with exclusions for other overlapping categories such as infringement of customs regulations, including in cases addressing extortion by Indonesian and Egyptian officials, and Vietnamese and Venezuelan seizures purportedly performed to combat contraband and drug smuggling.[29] These varied restraint decisions hinging on the source of the loss were naturally informed by the many war, unrest, and piracy cases addressing the cause of casualties as marine or war risks, which often depended on fact-specific inquiries into motivative factors and proximate cause.[30]

Additional standard provisions, such as off-hire and demurrage clauses, have been routinely referenced to allocate delay costs flowing out of geopolitical events, including in the aftermath of Iraq's invasion of Kuwait, Somali piracy hijackings, and the Taiwanese refusal to allow the disembarkation of rescued migrants.[31] Courts and arbitrators have also analysed similar problems by interpreting standard safe port warranties. In many of these cases, orders to destination ports were found not to violate these provisions, including when the parties contracted with the purpose of trading in high risk zones during the Persian Gulf Tanker War, when conflict suddenly re-ignited between Egypt and Israel in the Suez Roads, and when attacks on vessels by guerrilla fighters off Ethiopia had been a rare occurrence and therefore did not make unsafety a normal characteristic of the port.[32] At the same time, destination ports have been found unsafe when, for instance, a charterer ordered the vessel to Libya after terrorism threats in the Mediterranean Sea, and

[28] *ONE Shipping Ltd v Hercules Inc (The M/T Onesky)*, SMA 1828 (NY Arb 1979); *SA Marine Corp SA v Canfornav Ltd (The M/V Energy Ranger)*, SMA 3817 (NY Arb 2003).

[29] *Delos Shipholding SA & Ors v Allianz Global Corporate and Specialty SE & Ors (The Win Win)* [2025] EWCA Civ 1019 (CA); *Melinda Holdings SA v Hellenic Mutual War Risk Association (Bermuda) Ltd (The Silva)* [2011] 2 Lloyd's Rep 141 (Comm); *Panamanian Oriental Steamship Corp v Wright (The Anita)* [1971] 1 Lloyd's Rep 487 (CA); *Atlasnavios-Navegacao LDA v Navigators Insurance Co Ltd (The B Atlantic)* [2018] 2 Lloyd's Rep 1 (Comm).

[30] *Britain Steamship Co Ltd v The King* (1920) Lloyd's List Rep 245 (HL); *Standard Oil Co of New Jersey v United States*, 340 US 45 (USSC 1950); *Calmar SS Corp v Scott*, 345 US 427 (USSC 1953); *National Union Fire Insurance Co of Pittsburgh v The Republic of China*, 254 F2d 177 (4th Cir 1958).

[31] *Kuwait Petroleum Corp v I & D Oil Carriers Ltd (The Houda)* [1994] 2 Lloyd's Rep 541 (CA); *Tankers International LLC v Bayoil Supply and Trading Ltd (The M/T Raphael)*, SMA 3739 (NY Arb 2002); *Osmium Shipping Corp v Cargill International SA (The Captain Stefanos)* [2012] 2 Lloyd's Rep 46 (Comm); *CA Venezolana de Navegacion v Bank Line (The Roachbank)* [1987] 2 Lloyd's Rep 498 (Comm).

[32] *Motor Oil Hellas (Corinth) Refineries SA v Shipping Corp of India (The Kanchenjunga)* [1990] 1 Lloyd's Rep 391 (HL); *Vardinoyannis v The Egyptian General Petroleum Corp (The Evaggelos Th)* [1971] 2 Lloyd's Rep 200 (Comm); *K/S Penta Shipping A/S v Ethiopian Shipping Lines Corp (The Saga Cob)* [1992] 2 Lloyd's Rep 545 (CA).

when a charterer ordered a vessel carrying Iraqi crude to store off the coast of the UAE when it was committed to enforcing UN-mandated sanctions.[33]

Looking beyond these standard clauses, outcomes in many cases have depended on more explicit wordings developed for the purpose of addressing external disruption, including *force majeure* clauses. These contractual tools have been successfully referenced as a basis to avoid performance when, for instance, Turkish officials complied with UN sanctions by restricting pipeline access to Iraqi oil, when US sanctions on Iran prevented contractual payment in US dollars, when the US termination of a humanitarian aid programme disrupted the financing of pending food shipments, and when Algerian customs authorities seized a vessel's cargo without a legitimate justification.[34] But *force majeure* clauses have also been rejected in other scenarios, including when voyages have been diverted by Suez Canal closures and when the US–China trade war spiralled into the imposition of high lumber tariffs.[35] Other provisions designed to address disruptive contingencies styled as war cancellation and war risk clauses have led to similarly varied results. They have been found relevant to excuse performance when conflict between China and Japan escalated into war and when Egypt implicitly declared war on Britain and France.[36] Yet war cancellation clauses have been found inapplicable to excuse performance following a NATO operation in Kosovo, and led to directly contradictory arbitral outcomes in categorising the nature of the Korean War.[37] Although contextually distinct, similar reasoning has been adopted in cases attempting to categorise events for insurance purposes as either marine or war risks, which, depending on the precise language of the policies at issue, has led to fact-specific inquiries into geopolitical conditions. These include holdings that defections of crew members when the Chinese Communists pushed the Nationalists to Taiwan were simultaneously classified as barratry and seizure; that vessel captures by Nicaraguan Sandinistas were caused by both barratry and civil war; that damage and delays caused by political unrest in Mozambique and Venezuela were both riots and insurrections; and that prizes taken by Confederate

[33] *Arietta Compania Naviera SA v World Wide Transport Inc (The S/T Arietta Venizelos)*, SMA 733 (NY Arb 1972); *Ullises Shipping Corp v Fal Shipping Co Ltd (The Greek Fighter)* [2006] 1 Lloyd's Rep Plus 99 (Comm).

[34] *Repsol Petroleo SA v Sun International Ltd (M/T Orduna)* SMA 2967 (1993); *RTI Ltd v Mur Shipping BV* [2024] 1 Lloyd's Rep 621 (UKSC); *Tradax Internacional SA v Government of Pakistan*, SMA 779 (NY Arb 1973); *Sucden Middle-East v Yagci Denizcilik Ve Ticaret Ltd Sirketi (The Muammer Yagci)* [2020] 1 Lloyd's Rep 107 (Comm).

[35] *Glidden Co v Hellenic Lines Ltd*, 275 F2d 253 (2nd Cir 1960); *Shelter Forest International Acquisition Inc v COSCO Shipping (USA) Inc*, 475 F Supp 3d 1171 (D Oregon 2020).

[36] *Kawasaki Kisen Kabushiki Kaisha v Bantham Steamship Co Ltd* (1939) 63 Lloyd's List Rep 155; *Navios Corp v The Ulysses II*, 260 F 959 (4th Cir 1958).

[37] *CMA CGM SA v Beteiligung (The Northern Pioneer)* [2003] 1 Lloyd's Rep 212 (Comm); *Seven Seas Steamship Corp of New York v Prudential Steamship Corp of New York (The Simon Benson)* 1951 AMC 585 (NY Arb 1951); *Manning Brothers Inc of Delaware, Owners of Steamship Yankee Fighter v Albatross Steamship Co Inc*, 1951 AMC 579 (NY Arb 1951).

sympathisers during the US Civil War were either seizure, piracy, theft, or an overlapping combination of these contractual categories.[38]

Other specialised provisions, including multiple iterations of the BIMCO CONWARTIME clauses, have been dispositive in some cases, including Somali piracy disputes. However, their relevance has also been dismissed when viewed alongside inconsistent rider clauses.[39] Similarly, explicit provisions addressing the insurance consequences for exceeding trading limits or failing to pay an additional war risk premium were critical to resolving disputes involving trading in the Persian Gulf during the Iran–Iraq War.[40] More tailored clauses, including those designed to address the Suez Canal closures, piracy, and economic sanctions have aimed to address ambiguities in all-encompassing war and *force majeure* clauses. Although contractual references to Suez were not found particularly well suited to address closure scenarios, more recent cases interpreting language designed to allocate the risk of pirate seizures demonstrate the possible impact of such tailoring.[41] Sanctions cases in particular reveal how important these tools can be in directing equitable outcomes, as courts and arbitrators have repeatedly referenced them to justify performance avoidance, including where a charterer attempted to engage in a sanctions-busting STS transaction off Venezuela and when EU sanctions exposed an insurer to enforcement penalties if it continued covering Iran-connected vessels.[42] But despite their widespread adoption, sanctions clauses have also been found to be inapplicable where the shipowner did not provide sufficient proof of cargo owner blacklisting, where sanctions did not entirely prohibit insurance cover, and where the sanctions clause itself cast doubt on the contractual guarantees of payment to third parties.[43] These mixed results show that even with carefully drafted clauses aimed to address the prospect of geopolitical disruption, competing policy interests may cause courts and

[38] *National Union Fire Insurance Co of Pittsburgh v The Republic of China*, 254 F2d 177 (4th Cir 1958); *Ope Shipping Ltd v Allstate Insurance Co*, 687 F2d 639 (2nd Cir 1982); *National Oil Co of Zimbabwe (Private) Ltd v Nicholas Collwyn Sturge* [1981] 2 Lloyd's Rep 281; *Citgo Petroleum Corp v Starstone Insurance SE*, WL 2525651 (SDNY 2023); *Mauran v Alliance Insurance Co*, 73 US 1 (USSC 1867); *Babbit, Goode & Co v The Sun Mutual Insurance Co*, 23 La Ann 314 (SC Louisiana 1871).

[39] *Taokas Navigation SA v Komrowski Bulk Shipping KG (GMBH & Co) (The Paiwan Wisdom)* [2012] 2 Lloyd's Rep 416 (Comm); *Pacific Basin IHX Ltd v Bulkhandling Handymax AS (The Triton Lark II)* [2012] 1 Lloyd's Rep 457 (Comm); *Osmium Shipping Corp v Cargill International SA (The Captain Stefanos)* [2012] 2 Lloyd's Rep 46 (Comm); *Eleni Shipping Ltd v Transgrain Shipping BV (The Eleni P)* [2019] 2 Lloyd's Rep 265 (Comm).

[40] *Black King Shipping Corp and Wayang (Panama) SA v Mark Ranald Massie (The Litsion Pride)* [1985] 1 Lloyd's Rep 437 (Comm); *Bank of Nova Scotia v Hellenic Mutual War Risks Association (Bermuda) Ltd (The Good Luck)* [1991] 2 Lloyd's Rep 191 (HL).

[41] *Achille Lauro Fu Giaocchino & C v Total Societa Italiana Per Azioni* [1969] 2 Lloyd's Rep 65 (CA); *Eleni Shipping Ltd v Transgrain Shipping BV (The Eleni P)* [2019] 2 Lloyd's Rep 265 (Comm).

[42] *Brujo Finance Co v Sea Energy Co (The MT Alkimos)*, SMA 4388 (NY Arb 2020); *Melinda Holdings SA v Hellenic Mutual War Risk Association (Bermuda) Ltd (The Silva)* [2011] 2 Lloyd's Rep 607 (CA).

[43] *O v C* [2024] EWHC 2838 (Comm); *Tonzip Maritime Ltd v 2Rivers Pte Ltd* [2025] EWHC 2036 (Comm); *Mamancochet Mining Ltd v Aegis Managing Agency Ltd* [2018] 2 Lloyd's Rep 441 (Comm); *Oghiaanous Khoroushan Shipping Lines Co of Kish v Owner of the Vessel 'Tina I'* [2024] SGHC 12 (Singapore HC).

arbitrators to second-guess whether contractual performance should be avoided. Despite these limitations, as newly drafted clauses continue to come to market, they are now informed by the instructive insight of judicial and arbitral reactions to earlier iterations.

The geopolitical landscape is constantly changing, creating commercial consequences that mirror its mercurial character. In addressing such disruption, contracting parties, courts, and arbitrators must evaluate the practical implications of events falling along a sliding scale of physical and economic confrontation. These categories inevitably intersect and their boundaries often blur. As a result, disruption scenarios may not fit neatly into contractually defined classifications, particularly as hybrid war and statecraft tactics increasingly characterise conflicts in the modern world. But recognising that these techniques are rooted in the same grand strategies of global power competition, a key solution to resolving the resulting commercial disputes is to embrace cross-referencing by analogy beyond the limitations of political designations, contractual taxonomies, and traditional case law sources. As geopolitical turbulence is poised to continue unsettling international trade in the near term, decades of political and commercial controversy provide a vast body of guiding principles and illustrations, affording an invaluable opportunity to gather up lessons from the past as regenerated forms of disruption take shape on the horizon.

BIBLIOGRAPHY

Books

Ambrose, C, et al, *London Maritime Arbitration* (4th edn, Informa, 2017).

Baker, A, et al, *Time Charters* (7th edn, Informa, 2015).

Baldwin, DA, *Economic Statecraft* (Princeton University Press, 2020).

Beale, H (ed), *Chitty on Contracts* (35th edn, Sweet & Maxwell, 2023).

Bennett, H, et al, *Carver on Charterparties* (3rd edn, Sweet & Maxwell, 2024).

Biddle, S, *Nonstate Warfare: The Military Methods of Guerillas, Warlords, and Militias* (Princeton University Press, 2021).

Blackwill, RD and Harris, JM, *War by Other Means: Geoeconomics and Statecraft* (Belknap / Harvard University Press, 2016).

Blanchard, C, et al, *Arnould: Law of Marine Insurance and Average* (21st edn, Sweet & Maxwell, 2024).

Bowley, R, *Preventing Terrorist Attacks at Sea: Maritime Terrorism Risk and International Law* (Routledge, 2022).

Braw, E, *Goodbye Globalization: The Return of a Divided World* (Yale University Press, 2024).

Buglass, LJ, *Marine Insurance and General Average in the United States* (3rd edn, Cornell Maritime Press, 1991).

Copeland, DC, *A World Safe for Commerce: American Foreign Policy from the Revolution to the Rise of China* (Princeton University Press, 2024).

Cortright, D and Lopez, GA, *The Sanctions Decade: Assessing UN Strategies in the 1990s* (Lynne Rienner Publishers, 2000).

Davey, M, Davey, J, and Caplin, O, *Miller's Marine War Risks* (4th edn, Informa, 2020).

Davis, LE and Engerman, SL, *Naval Blockades in Peace and War: An Economic History Since 1750* (CUP, 2009).

Farnsworth, EA, *Contracts* (8th edn, Foundation Press, 2013).

Fishman, E, *Chokepoints: American Power in the Age of Economic Warfare* (Portfolio/Penguin, 2025).

Gaddis, JL, *The Cold War: A New History* (Penguin, 2007).

Gilman, J, et al, *Arnould: Law of Marine Insurance and Average* (20th edn, Sweet & Maxwell, 2020).

Girvin, S, *Carriage of Goods by Sea* (3rd edn, OUP, 2022).

Huang, Y, *Capitalism with Chinese Characteristics: Entrepreneurship and the State* (CUP, 2010).

Hazelwood, S, and Semark, D, *P&I Clubs: Law and Practice* (4th edn, Informa, 2010).

Irwin, DA, *Clashing over Commerce: A History of U.S. Trade Policy* (University of Chicago Press, 2017).

Jowitt, C (ed), *Pirates? The Politics of Plunder 1550–1650* (Palgrave, 2007).

Kraska, J, *Contemporary Maritime Piracy: International Law, Strategy, and Diplomacy at Sea* (Bloomsbury, 2011).

Kraska, J, and Pedrozo, R, *International Maritime Security Law* (Martinus Nijhoff, 2013).

Krepinevich, AF, *The Origins of Victory: How Disruptive Military Innovation Determines the Fates of Great Powers* (Yale University Press, 2024).

Lamb, CJ, *The Mayaguez Crisis, Mission Command, and Civil-military Relations* (US Joint Chiefs of Staff, 2018).

Levinson, M, *The Box: How the Shipping Container Made the World Smaller and the World Economy Bigger* (Princeton University Press, 2008).

Lowenfeld, AF, *International Economic Law* (2nd edn, OUP, 2008).

Mastanduno, M, *Economic Containment: CoCom and the Politics of East-West Trade* (Cornell University Press, 1992).

Michel, K, *War, Terror and Carriage by Sea* (Informa, 2004).
Merkin, R, *Marine Insurance: A Legal History* (Edward Elgar, 2021).
Meijer, H, *Trading with the Enemy: The Making of US Export Control Policy toward the People's Republic of China* (OUP, 2016).
Mulder, N, *The Economic Weapon: The Rise of Sanctions as a Tool of Modern War* (Yale University Press, 2022).
Murray, JE, *Murray on Contracts* (Lexis Nexis, 2011).
Navias, MS, and Hooton, ER, *Tanker Wars: The Assault on Merchant Shipping During the Iran-Iraq Crisis* (Bloomsbury, 1996).
Oermann, NO, and Wolff, HJ, *Trade Wars: Past and Present* (OUP, 2022).
Peel, E, *Frustration and Force Majeure* (4th edn, Sweet & Maxwell, 2021).
Perillo, JM, *Contracts* (7th edn, West, 2014).
Reilly, J, *Orchestration: China's Economic Statecraft Across Asia and Europe* (OUP, 2021).
Ricks, TE, *Fiasco: The American Military Adventure in Iraq* (Penguin, 2007).
Rose, FD, *Marine Insurance: Law and Practice* (2nd edn, Informa, 2012).
Ross, D, *Statecraft 2.0: What America Needs to Lead in a Multipolar World* (OUP, 2025).
Rubin, AP, *The Law of Piracy* (2nd edn, Transnational Publishers, 1998).
Soyer, B, and Tettenborn, A (eds), *Charterparties: Law, Practice and Emerging Legal Issues* (Informa, 2018).
Stavridis, J, *Sea Power: The History and Geopolitics of the World's Oceans* (Penguin, 2018).
Todd, P, *Maritime Fraud and Piracy* (2nd edn, Informa, 2010).
Weissmann, M, et al (eds), *Hybrid Warfare: Security and Asymmetric Conflict in International Relations* (Bloomsbury, 2021).
Winter, WD, *Marine Insurance: Its Principles and Practice* (McGraw-Hill, 1919).
Young, T, et al, *Voyage Charters* (5th edn, Informa, 2022).
Zarate, J, *Treasury's War: The Unleashing of a New Era of Financial Warfare* (PublicAffairs, 2015).
Zatarain, LA, *America's First Clash with Iran: The Tanker War, 1987–88* (Casemate, 2010).

Articles

Allison, G, 'Putin's Doomsday Threat: How to Prevent a Repeat of the Cuban Missile Crisis in Ukraine' *Foreign Affairs* (5 April 2022).
Berman, N, Ferragamo, M, and S Baumgartner, S, '*How Ukraine Overcame Russia's Grain Blockade*' *Council on Foreign Relations* (22 August 2023).
Bilal, A, 'Russia's Hybrid War Against the West' *NATO Review* (26 April 2024).
Blanchard, CM, 'Houthi Attacks in the Red Sea: Issues for Congress' *Congressional Research Service* (6 September 2024).
Bush, D, 'Ships Hit by Missiles as Ukraine Forces Defend Odessa and Mariupol' *Lloyd's List* (25 February 2022).
Byman, DL, 'Proxy Power: Understanding Iran's Use of Terrorism' *Brookings* (26 July 2006).
Churchill, F, 'Marsh McLennan Launces Ukraine Black Sea Port Facility' *Insurance Day* (15 November 2023).
Crump, L and Godard, S, 'Reassessing Communist International Organisations: A Comparative Analysis of COMECON and the Warsaw Pact in Relation to their Cold War Competitors' (2017) 27 *Contemporary European History* 85.
Diakun, B, 'Reward Outweighs Risk for Owners Trading into Ukraine's Danube River Ports' *Lloyd's List* (3 November 2023).
Diakun, B, 'Black Sea Risk Unchanged Despite Back-to-Back Incidents' *Lloyd's List* (23 September 2024).
Diakun, B, 'Piracy Exposure Increases in Somali Basin Because of Red Sea Diversions' *Lloyd's List* (28 November 2024).

Diakun, B and Bockmann, MW, 'Falls in Red Sea Ship Traffic Stabilise as Suez Transits Hit Fresh Low' *Lloyd's List* (21 February 2024).
Dickinson, ED, 'Is the Crime of Piracy Obsolete?' (1925) 38 *Harvard Law Review* 334.
Dixon, G, 'Iran Releases Chevron-Chartered Tanker After 15-Month Ordeal' *Tradewinds* (12 July 2024).
Farrell, H, and Newman, A, 'The Weaponized World Economy: Surviving the New Age of Economic Coercion' *Foreign Affairs* (19 August 2025).
Feyrer, J, 'Distance, Trade, and Income – The 1967 to 1975 Closing of the Suez Canal as a Natural Experiment' *National Bureau of Economic Research* (2009).
Flores, M, and Morales, NJ, 'Philippines Tells Beijing Words Must Match Actions in South China Sea' *Reuters* (19 June 2024).
Garon, S, 'Operation STARVATION, 1945: A Transnational History of Blockades and the Defeat of Japan' (2024) 46 *The International History Review* 535.
Goksedef, E, 'Houthis Offer Reassurance to "Compliant" Vessels with Red Sea FAQs' *Lloyd's List* (13 August 2025).
Goksedef, E, and Minchin, J, 'Türkiye to Refuse Entry to Israeli-linked Vessels' *Lloyd's List* (22 August 2025).
Gordon, J, 'Smart Sanctions Revisited' (2011) 25 *Ethics & International Affairs* 315.
Halberstam, M, 'Terrorism on the High Seas: The Achille Lauro, Piracy and the IMO Convention on Maritime Safety' (1988) 82 *American Journal of International Law* 269.
Harithas, B, et al, '"Liberation Day" Tariffs Explained' *Center for Strategic and International Studies* (3 April 2025).
Heath, JB, 'The New National Security Challenge to the Economic Order' (2020) 129 *Yale Law Journal* 1020.
Insurance Journal, 'Malacca Straits Removed from War Risk List' (9 August 2006).
Karlin, M, 'The Return of Total War: Understanding – and Preparing for – a New Era of Comprehensive Conflict' *Foreign Affairs* (22 October 2024).
Kilpatrick, RL, 'Maritime Sanctions Clauses' (2020) *Lloyd's Maritime and Commercial Law Quarterly* 565.
Kilpatrick, RL, 'Revisiting the Five Powers War Risk Exclusion' (2024) 73 *International & Comparative Law Quarterly* 551.
Kilpatrick, RL, 'Sanctions-based Impossibility' (2024) *Lloyd's Maritime and Commercial Law Quarterly* 221.
Kraska, J, and Wilson, B, 'Maritime Piracy in East Africa' (2009) 26(2) *Journal of International Affairs* 55.
Lane, A, 'Iran's Islamist Proxies in the Middle East' *Wilson Center* (12 September 2023).
Lewins, K, and Merkin, R, 'Piracy, Ransom and Marine Insurance' (2011) 35 *Melbourne University Law Review* 718.
Lloyd's List, 'Ukraine Strikes Cargoship it Claims was Laden with Iranian Weapons' (15 August 2025).
Lloyd's List, 'Reported Houthi Attacks in the Red Sea and Gulf of Aden: Maps and List of Attacks' (8 September 2025).
Marks, S, 'Houthi Threat Triggers Surge in Pirate Attacks Off Somalia Coast' *Insurance Journal* (5 July 2024).
Masters, J, and Merrow, W, 'Here's How Much Aid the United States Has Sent Ukraine' *Council on Foreign Relations* (15 July 2025).
Meade, R, 'Somali Piracy Is Back and a Show of Force from India May Not Be Enough to Stop It' *Lloyd's List* (25 March 2024).
Meade, R, 'Russia Lashes Out at NATO "Pirates" as UN Addresses Escalating Maritime Security Concerns' *Lloyd's List* (21 May 2025).
Meade, R, and Diakun, B, 'Over 300 Vessels and At Least 1,000 Seafarers are Stuck in Ukraine' *Lloyd's List* (24 March 2022).
Miller, G, 'How New Trump Tariffs on China, Mexico and Canada Could Impact Shipping' *Lloyd's List* (26 November 2024).
Miller, G, and Diakun, B, 'Ukrainian Grain Exports Rebound as Ship Arrivals Near Pre-War Levels' *Lloyd's List* (26 April 2024).

Minchin, J, 'IMB Report Shows Somali Piracy Spike' *Lloyd's List* (12 April 2024).
Minchin, J, 'Geopolitical Risk Shipping's Biggest Worry, Lloyd's List Poll Reveals' *Lloyd's List* (13 December 2024).
Minchin, J, 'Industry Updates Security Best Practice After "Unprecedented" Rise in Attacks' *Lloyd's List* (4 April 2025).
Mulder, N, 'The Trading with the Enemy Acts in the Age of Expropriation, 1914–1949' (2020) 15 *Journal of Global History* 81.
Murrill, BJ, 'The National Security Exception and the World Trade Organization' *Congressional Research Service* (28 November 2018).
Nightingale, L, 'Hormuz Disruption Could Unplug Gulf Ports from Global Trade' *Lloyd's List* (24 June 2025).
Osler, D, 'Somalia Piracy Resurgence Makes Kidnap & Ransom Cover Necessary' *Lloyd's List* (13 March 2024).
Osler, D, 'Red Sea Transits Now "Impossible" for Ships with US, UK or Israel Ties, Say Underwriters' *Lloyd's List* (5 September 2024).
Osler, D, 'Strait of Hormuz Closure May Trigger BIMCO Force Majeure Clause' *Lloyd's List* (30 July 2025).
Pedrozo, R, 'Protecting the Free Flow of Commerce from Houthi Attacks off the Arabian Peninsula' (2024) 103 *International Law Studies* 49.
Prasad, E, 'The Age of Tariffs: Trump is Launching a Turbulent New Era for the Global Economy' *Foreign Affairs* (3 April 2025).
Reuters, 'Iran Calls US Move to Seize Oil Shipment an "Act of Piracy"' (15 February 2021).
Renwick, N, and Abbot, J, 'Piratical Violence and Maritime Security in Southeast Asia' (1999) 30(2) *Security Dialogue* 183.
Robinson, K, and Merrow, W, 'The Arab Spring at Ten Years: What's the Legacy of the Uprisings' *Council on Foreign Relations* (3 December 2020).
Saul, J, 'Insurers Count the Cost of Ships Snagged in Ukraine Crisis' *Reuters* (24 February 2023).
Saul, J, and Rabinovitch, A, 'Israel's Ports Feel Strain as Shipping Traffic Slows After Attacks' *Reuters* (10 October 2023).
Scherner, J, 'Germany, Blockade and Strategic Raw Materials in the Era of the Two World Wars' (2024) 46 *The International History Review* 515.
Sutton, HI, 'Spate of Attacks on Ships in Middle East Points to Iran-Backed Group' *US Naval Institute News* (6 January 2021).
Tramazzo, JC, and Santicola, I, 'Russia's Interdiction of Neutral Merchant Vessels and the Law of the Sea' *Articles of War* (11 September 2023).
Verrastro, FA, and Caruso, G, 'The Arab Oil Embargo – 40 Years Later' *Center for Strategic & International Studies* (16 October 2013).
Wright, R, 'Pirates Targeting Ships Diverted from Red Sea, Warns UN Shipping Chief' *Financial Times* (21 February 2024).
Zagorodnyuk, A, 'Putin's Black Sea Blockade Leaves Millions Facing Global Famine' *Atlantic Council* (13 June 2022).
Zou, K, 'Piracy at Sea and China's Response' (2000) *Lloyd's Maritime and Commercial Law Quarterly* 364.

Other Materials

American Institute of Marine Insurers, 'Background Explanation for AIMU's 5 Powers War Exclusion Clause' (31 January 2023).
BIMCO, et al, 'BMP5: Best Management Practice to Deter Piracy and Enhance Maritime Security in the Red Sea, Gulf of Aden, Indian Ocean and Arabian Sea' (June 2018).
Bush GW, State of the Union Address (29 January 2002).
European Commission, Press Release: 'G7 Agrees Oil Price Cap: Reducing Russia's Revenues, While Keeping Global Energy Markets Stable' (2 December 2022).

European Parliamentary Research Service, 'EU Sanctions: A Key Foreign and Security Policy Instrument' (May 2018).
Joint War Committee, Circular JWLA-030 – Hull War, Piracy, Terrorism and Related Perils (4 April 2022).
Kennedy JF, Commencement Address at American University (10 June 1963).
Kennedy JF, Presidential Proclamation 3447, Embargo on All Trade with Cuba (3 February 1962).
Kennedy JF, Presidential Proclamation 3504, Interdiction of the Delivery of Offensive Weapons to Cuba (23 October 1962).
Khrushchev N, Statement on Cuban Crisis of 1962, (12 December 1962).
NATO, 'Collective Defense and Article 5' (4 July 2023).
NATO, 'Counter-piracy Operations (2008–2016)' (19 May 2022).
OFAC, Guidance on Implementation of the Price Cap Policy for Crude Oil and Petroleum Products of Russian Federation Origin (Revised) (20 December 2023).
Office of the US President, 'President Donald J Trump is Ending United States Participation in an Unacceptable Iran Deal' (8 May 2018).
Overall War-Marine Risk Settlement Agreement, 1945 AMC 1014.
Statement of the G7 and Australia on a Price Cap for Seaborne Russian-origin Crude Oil (2 December 2022).
Trump DJ, US Executive Order 14175 – Designation of Ansar Allah as a Foreign Terrorist Organization (22 January 2025)
UK HM Treasury Office of Financial Sanctions Implementation, 'Maritime Guidance: Financial Sanctions Guidance for Entities and Individuals Operating within the Maritime Shipping Sector' (December 2020).
United Nations, 'One Year of the Black Sea Initiative: Key Facts and Figures' (10 July 2023).
United Nations, 'At Security Council Meeting on Sabotage of Nord Stream Pipeline, Many Speakers Condemn Attacks on Critical Infrastructure, Stress Need for Accountability' (4 October 2024).
US Department of Justice, Press Release: 'Largest US Seizure of Iranian Fuel from Four Tankers' (14 August 2020).
US Department of State, Office of the Historian, 'Lend-Lease and Military Aid to the Allies in the Early Years of World War II'.
US Department of State, Office of the Historian, 'The 1967 Arab-Israeli War'.
US Department of State, Office of the Historian, 'The Suez Crisis 1956'.
US Department of State, 'Venezuela-Related Sanctions'.
US Department of Treasury, Department of State, Coast Guard, 'Sanctions Advisory for the Maritime Industry, Energy and Metals Sectors, and Related Communities' (14 May 2020).
US Department of Justice, 'Department of Justice Announces Forfeiture of North Korean Cargo Vessel' (21 October 2019).
US Trade Representative, 'Section 301 Investigation: Report on China's Targeting of the Maritime, Logistics, and Shipbuilding Sectors for Dominance' (16 January 2025).
US Trade Representative, 'Notice of Action and Proposed Action in Section 301 Investigation of China's Targeting the Maritime, Logistics, and Shipbuilding Sectors for Dominance' (2025) 90 Federal Register 17114.
US White House, 'Trump Administration's Actions Made Houthi Terrorists Pay' (25 March 2025).

INDEX

www.ingramcontent.com/pod-product-compliance
Ingram Content Group UK Ltd.
Pitfield, Milton Keynes, MK11 3LW, UK
UKHW020251290926
15470UKWH00002B/860